The Black Washingtonians

The Black Washingtonians

THE ANACOSTIA MUSEUM ILLUSTRATED CHRONOLOGY

**THE SMITHSONIAN ANACOSTIA MUSEUM AND CENTER
FOR AFRICAN AMERICAN HISTORY AND CULTURE**

WILEY

John Wiley & Sons, Inc.

Published by John Wiley & Sons, Inc., Hoboken, New Jersey
Published simultaneously in Canada

For general information about our other products and services, please contact our Customer Care Department within the United States at (800) 762-2974, outside the United States at (317) 572-3993 or fax (317) 572-4002.

Wiley also publishes its books in a variety of electronic formats. Some content that appears in print may not be available in electronic books. For more information about Wiley products, visit our web site at www.wiley.com.

ISBN 0-471-40258-3

Printed in the United States of America

10 9 8 7 6 5 4 3 2 1

CONTENTS

FOREWORD

SINCE I WAS A LITTLE GIRL, I HAVE BEEN A STUDENT OF HISTORY. I STILL have the biography of Booker T. Washington I won in a fifth-grade Negro History Week contest at (Bruce) Monroe Elementary School. Even then, I believed that history was about more important things than the past. Sitting in segregated schools in the nation's capital, I knew that the extraordinary history of black people lived on in our continuing battle for parity in citizenship. We could not wish for a stronger legacy than their tales of struggle against the odds. This book will help present and future generations not only admire this legacy with pride and appreciation but use it as a source of inspiration to go the full distance for citizenship, freedom, and respect in the modern world.

The history of black Washington is cherished by many families, like my own, who have lived here for generations. This volume traces the development of black Washington from 1791 to the present day.

Race and Democracy

African Americans have influenced the District of Columbia perhaps more than they have any other large American city. At Washington's founding in 1791, a quarter of its population was black. Formed from portions of two states, Maryland and Virginia, which together contained half of the blacks in the United States at the time, the city encompassed not only the slave trade but also blacks who purchased their freedom. Blacks often fled to the District, as my great grandfather Richard Holmes did. He walked off a plantation in Virginia, made his way to Washington, and worked building streets in the District before and after the Civil War.

Why the District? It was hardly a beacon of freedom. Not even whites had the self-government and the congressional representation that other Americans took for granted. Discriminatory laws and customs prevailed. Yet Washington was always a magnet for blacks. They were attracted by a unique mixture of advantages: a better life than was possible in the rest of the South, the willingness of other black people to challenge their condition, the city's climate of intellectual fertility, and the promise, still unrequited here, of equal citizenship. This book about black Washington offers a fascinating new way to understand what the District of Columbia was then and has now become, as African Americans helped build the city and left their signature on its cultural, political, and intellectual development.

Not unlike our country, two overarching issues have haunted the city—race and democracy. Throughout American history, as for most of the city's history, aspirations for equality and democracy warred with white fears of black domination. In Washington, D.C., most whites preferred their own disenfranchisement—no elected local city government and no congressional representation—to the risk of sharing power with the black minority.

Slavery and then segregation were cemented by the domineering power and will of Congress, the Supreme Court, and the Executive, all suffused with the ideology of racism. It took *Bolling v. Sharpe,* the District's equivalent of *Brown v. Board of Education,* to end segregation here when I was in high school.

Unique Cross-Currents

Before the end of slavery, the District was the most progressive city in the South for blacks. Slaves could sue in court to recover their freedom. Slaves, working on their own time, often could buy their freedom after several years. Even during the slavery era, free blacks outnumbered slaves in the city. Although blacks were denied public education when the city was being built, in 1807 three black men with little education themselves founded the first of many private schools for black children. African Americans worked in a wide spectrum of occupations. The black legacy of education and striving for self-realization and equal rights was embedded early in the District's African American culture.

Identity and Aspiration

Accustomed to the city's more enlightened racial climate during slavery times, blacks seized upon new opportunities that appeared after the Civil War. For a shimmering moment, radical Republicans promoted limited self-government and the elimination of segregation. Strong black institutions flourished, providing African American leaders for the city and the nation alike. Later, black residents gained earlier access than most African Americans to white-collar employment, even if they were limited to the lowest ranks of the federal government. Blacks in the District were also better educated than their counterparts elsewhere. The country's first public high school for blacks and my alma mater, Dunbar High School, and the African American flagship university, Howard, were in Washington. The university, the Freedmen's Bureau, Freedmen's Hospital, Freedmen's Bank, and the Association for the Study of Negro Life and History all helped to create a unique sense of identity and aspiration among Washington's blacks.

The city became a black intellectual and civil rights capital. Many African Americans who are remembered for their contributions to the capital or to the nation lived or worked in Washington, among them Benjamin Banneker, Frederick Douglass, Paul Laurence Dunbar, Carter G. Woodson, Duke Ellington, Mary McLeod Bethune, and Mary Church Terrell. During the twentieth century, forthright demands for racial equality and the prominence of Howard University made Washington the natural environment for a distinguished group of black intellectuals on the Howard University faculty—Ralph Bunche, E. Franklin Frazier, Alain Locke, Charles Houston, Dr. Charles Drew, and Kenneth Clark, among others.

Not surprisingly, the city's legacy of black protest, education, and striving made the District ripe territory not only for the civil rights movement of the 1960s but also for demands for local democracy and racial equality. Both self-government and congressional representation for the District were directly fed by the civil rights movement. Just as American blacks throughout the country won their rights only by methodically fighting each step of the way, District residents have engaged in a similarly organized and purposeful struggle to achieve full democracy, beginning with an elected school board (1968), congressional approval for a D.C. delegate (1971), and the Home Rule Act (1973). Considering that the District's struggle for equal citizenship has continued for more than two hundred years, its residents have shown remarkable resilience in fighting for each new right as long as it takes.

Triumphs and Setbacks

The District's fight for full democracy and congressional representation has been a history of triumphs and setbacks: congressional approval of the 1978 Voting Rights Amendment for two senators and a voting representative was undermined by the lack of ratification of the amendment by a sufficient number of states. The only debate and successful vote in 1993 on the New Columbia Admission Act for statehood, supported by House Democrats, was negated by Senate refusal to take up the bill. The approving vote in the House Committee of the Whole in 1993 was withdrawn when the Republicans took control of the House and changed the rules in 1995.

The remarkable history of black Washington is freighted with ironic meaning that underscores the city's own goals and grievances, because this history has occurred at the seat of our government, the major venue from which American notions of freedom have been proclaimed. Yet this is the capital where both slavery and segregation flourished, and where full democracy and congressional representation have always been denied. It was hard enough for the city's blacks to struggle against racial inequality for almost 150 years as part of a national struggle; it has been even more difficult for the city, without similar allies, to fight for rights denied to its residents alone.

The Path of Self-Liberation

However, the contradictions of the capital have encouraged, rather than deterred, protest. Washington has never been the exemplary capital the founders envisioned. At its creation, the capital was undeveloped, but it was not a tabula rasa. Washington was born with freedom denied. The city's liberation from official racism resulted from the struggles of its citizens. For Washingtonians to achieve congressional representation and full democracy, their path of self-liberation must be the same.

Eleanor Holmes Norton
House of Representatives, Washington, D.C.

FREE BLACKS AND SLAVES
1790–1861

The First Black Washingtonians

Before the District of Columbia was chartered, Congress wrangled over where to put it. Congressmen representing slaveholding states were determined that the capital be in a region favorable to slavery—somewhere under the influence of wealthy plantation owners and out of the hands of eastern industrial capitalists.

A ten-square-mile district—Virginia's Alexandria, Georgetown, and the rural countryside of Maryland—fit the bill. African Americans—some free, most enslaved—lived on the few settlements and plantations. To their numbers were added the first influx of black Washingtonians. They came as hackney coachmen, carpenters, bricklayers, painters, laborers, and other construction workers to build the city's new public structures and private buildings. Blacks helped to construct the Navy Yard, from 1800 to 1806, and then worked there. Free black women and hired-out slave women came to wash clothes and to sell produce, poultry, small game, fish, and whatever else they could to the workers. Blacks were also cooks, stewards, caterers, and porters for the boarding-houses, hotels, and restaurants that served the population. Some blacks also owned and operated such establishments.

As the capital grew, blacks dominated certain hospitality and service occupations, such as hauling and transporting, driving coaches, baking, cleaning and washing, and especially working as waiters. E. S. Abdy, traveling through the District in the early 1830s, observed that virtually all of the menial jobs—particularly in the hotels—were held by slaves, and that by the time of his visit, many free blacks eschewed these positions, having access to better ones. In Alexandria the fishing piers and the bakeries employed large numbers of black men. The Potomac River was also an important source of income. The historian Letitia Woods Brown writes in *Free Negroes in the District of Columbia, 1790–1846*: "The fishing landing in Alexandria continued to offer extensive job opportunities. In 1835 one booster for the District maintained that there were 150 fisheries on the Potomac requiring 6500 laborers. The 450 vessels used in the shad and herring fishing business used 1350 men to navigate them."

A Fluid Labor Market

Letitia Brown suggests that despite popular notions of a nineteenth-century black society rigidly divided along the lines of free and slave, black people in the District of Columbia experienced widely diverse work relationships and thus enjoyed very different levels of citizenship. Slaves for life, slaves for a specified term of service, indentured servants, hired-out slaves, and runaway slaves in hiding—all struggled toward freedom. In *Free Negroes* she writes,

> With the peculiar demands for building and service skills which grew with the capital, and the absence of a firm tradition that slavery was the only possible accommodation of black to white, a variety of work relations did occur. Many Negroes took advantage of the situation to work out arrangements that netted freedom. The same fluid labor market made it possible for free Negroes to survive. Humble as their jobs were, for the most part, they could find employment sufficient to sustain themselves.

Black men, both slave and free, were essential to the trade between eastern cities and the territory west of the District. They operated flatboats, sailing craft, and other vessels, and drove wagons loaded with merchandise and produce. Within the District, they provided public transportation between the boardinghouses and residences in Alexandria and Georgetown and the public buildings near Capitol Hill. Brown further notes, "Coachmen, draymen, waggoners, and hostlers were generally recruited from among the Negroes, slave and free."

Free blacks—African Americans who sold their own labor—were, however, at a distinct disadvantage. They had to compete with slaves in the District and those from Maryland and Virginia. After the 1820s a wave of Irish immigration drove many free blacks from jobs that they had traditionally held. In large-scale projects, such as the construction of the major canals in the late 1820s, managers hired mainly immigrants to fill the lowest levels of labor, instead of free blacks as they had previously done.

A Free Majority

After 1830 the absolute number of slaves and their percentage relative to free blacks began to decline. By 1840 the majority of the black population was free, as noted by Keith Melder in *City of Magnificent Intentions: A History of Washington, District of Columbia:* "Of all cities in the slave states, only in St. Louis, Baltimore, and Washington did free black people attain a majority in the African American community before the Civil War." Many free blacks immigrated to Washington from states such as Virginia and North Carolina, where existing laws were much more restrictive than in Washington. Other blacks in the District gained their freedom by being manumitted upon their owners' death (that is, by last will and testament), or they were deeded their freedom by their owners. Still others managed to buy their freedom—and often that of family and friends as well.

The growing community of free blacks formed a base of support for others' efforts to make their way out of slavery. Many free blacks made loans or contributed from their own savings to help friends meet their purchase price. Others donated in church or responded to petitions from strangers who needed to raise money to buy their freedom. Often such petitioners went door to door in the District, seeking contributions.

The Black Codes

The city was a hostile place for free blacks. By 1808 black codes regulated the movement and the activities of free blacks, and in 1812 the city council devised a pass system. Free blacks were kidnapped and sold into slavery in the city's teeming slave markets. Parents who were lax about keeping an eye on their children might find them chained to a slave coffle. Adults were waylaid, rendered unconscious, and sold south, where no one could verify that they had been free. Survival under such conditions depended on blacks' forming alliances with white people, preferably with men of wealth or power who would vouch for a black person's character in writing—as required by city statutes—and act as a safeguard for that individual's freedom. This dependence created a galling and insecure existence but was preferable to not having an endorser at all.

Black codes crippled the development of African American businesses and institutions: for example, certain ordinances in 1836 required large bonds of free blacks, restricted them to certain occupations, and placed them under permanent curfew. Sandra Fitzpatrick and Maria Goodwin write in *The Guide to Black Washington: Places and Events of Historical and Cultural Significance in the Nation's Capital:*

> The prohibition of "all secret or private meetings or assemblages whatsoever" beyond the hour of 10 o'clock p.m. was peculiarly oppressive and also inhuman, because directed against the various charitable and self-improving associations, including the Masonic, Odd-Fellow, and Sons of Temperance brotherhoods which the colored people had organized, and the meetings of which, to be dispersed before 10 o'clock, could be of but comparatively little benefit to the members. These societies in those years were more or less educational in character, and an important means of self-improvement. . . . These restrictions were, moreover, rigorously enforced, and it was but a few years before the war that a company of the most respectable colored men of the District, on their return from the Masonic lodge a few minutes of 10 o'clock, were seized by the scrupulous police, retained at the watch-house till morning, and fined.

The Center for Slave Trading

After 1830 Washington became the center of the interstate slave trade. According to Frederic Bancroft in *Slave Trading in the Old*

South, "Because the slave population in the District was small, trading depended on slaves brought from Maryland and Virginia, and fully nine-tenths were for distant markets. . . . What might be called the daily life of local trading was in or near the taverns or small hotels, at the public or the private jails, and about the country markets." Slave-owning farmers visiting open-air markets were often approached by traders seeking to buy the farmers' slave assistants. Most slave pens in the District were located downtown.

Local newspapers were filled with boldface ads for the sale and the auction of slaves. Some ads specified particular kinds of slaves that were wanted or were available. Until the market was thoroughly canvassed, newly purchased slaves were held in the city's public jails. Bancroft continues: "The largest gangs were likely to be from Baltimore, where the agents of District traders grouped selections from the best slaves received from the Eastern shore. The women with little children were carried in some vehicle. When more than a few, the men, handcuffed in pairs, fastened to a chain and followed by boys and girls, walked in double column, and the trader's mounted assistant brought up the rear."

After the slave trade was outlawed in 1850, local enforcers threw themselves into the Fugitive Slave Act, and the city's black codes were made even more stringent.

Free Black Academies

Washington's free black community went to heroic lengths to build educational institutions for black residents. The first black school was started in 1807 by Moses Liverpool, George Bell, and Nicholas Franklin. According to David L. Lewis's *District of Columbia: A Bicentennial History,* "A nominal tuition was required and, 'to avoid disagreeable occurrences,' an early announcement emphasized, 'no writings are to be done by the teachers for a slave, neither directly nor indirectly, to serve the purpose of a slave on any account whatsoever.' Great caution was essential; Mayor Robert Brent, sympathetic to their endeavor, had barely succeeded in quashing a council resolution to ban the instruction of free blacks." After the establishment of the Bell School, free black academies followed pell-mell. Mrs. Mary Billings of Georgetown opened her school on Dumbarton Street in 1810, moving to H Street in Washington City eleven years later. America's first black historian, George Washington Williams, wrote that "many of the better educated colored men and women now living . . . received the best portion of their education from her, and they all speak of her with a deep and tender sense of obligation."

The Great Influx of the 1860s

Before the great influx of ex-slaves during and immediately after the Civil War, the black population was concentrated north of the central city, southwest of the central core—in an area known as "the Island," because the Tiber River cut it off from the rest of the city—and in Foggy Bottom. Herring Hill, named for the main food staple that neighborhood families fished from Rock Creek, was a fifteen-block area that was home to east Georgetown's black community.

But after the 1860s, the District's black population was also "scattered throughout the southeast quarter of the city. The greatest concentration was along 4th Street, between the Navy Yard and East Capitol Street, with the blocks between 3rd and 5th Streets SE (east of the present Folger Library and the Library of Congress Annex) having the largest number of black homeowners. Black property owners resided elsewhere on Capitol Hill and along 9th and 10th Streets in the southwest section. The majority of blacks in the District lived in the northwest section, south of P Street and west of New Jersey Avenue." (Letitia Brown and Elsie Lewis, in *Washington from Banneker to Douglas, 1791–1870.*)

Many poor blacks lived in alleys, places with colorful names such as Slop Bucket, Temperance Hall, Willow Tree, Goat Alley, Pig Alley, and Tin Cup Alley. The living conditions in the alleys varied—some were dismal, squalid, and unhealthy; others were thriving communities of poor laborers and domestic servants.

A visitor to the District in the 1860s would have noticed the introduction of public streetcars. Although black coachmen protested the takeover of the city's lucrative transportation trade by these modern horse-drawn vehicles, the coachmen were unable to prevent the decline of their occupation. It was a troubling sign of the times.

1731

November 9. Benjamin Banneker is born in rural Baltimore County, Maryland. The son of Robert and Mary Banneker, an ex-slave and an English indentured servant woman, he teaches himself mathematics in his spare time. In 1753 he draws considerable attention from neighbors in the surrounding Maryland countryside when he constructs a working clock made entirely from wood. The wooden clock attracts many visitors, and Banneker becomes somewhat of a local celebrity. Borrowing books and a telescope from neighbors, including his friend and patron Andrew Ellicott, he teaches himself the fundamentals of astronomy.

1782

May. The Virginia Assembly passes legislation that spells out the legal requirements for manumission: slaveowners are allowed to free slaves by last will and testament or by written deed.

1784

March 23. Tom Molyneux is born to slave parents in Georgetown. His father, Zachary, considered the "founder of boxing in the United States," must have seen potential in Tom, who subsequently won local renown as a young boxer. When Tom was still a teenager, his master promised him freedom and $100 if he could defeat a local slave in the ring. Molyneux won the bout and, in doing so, won his freedom. He left for London, where he enjoyed success in the ring for a number of years.

1787

Holy Trinity Church is established in Georgetown. Its founding members include both white and black Catholics.

1788

Maryland cedes land for the capital. Some of the free black families living within the boundaries of the ceded territory include the Butlers, Days, Fletchers, Harmons, Hollands, Proctors, Rounds,

A tobacco wharf along the shores of the Chesapeake, c. 1750.

Savoys, Shorters, and Thomases. Prominent free black families in Prince George's County include the Allens, Grays, Nicholses, Plummers, and Turners.

1789

April 30. George Washington is inaugurated as the first president of the United States.

Virginia cedes land for the capital, including the town of Alexandria. Free black families in Alexandria at this time include the Coles, Fletchers, Jacksons, and Pisicoes.

Josiah Henson, the model for "Uncle Tom" in Harriet Beecher Stowe's *Uncle Tom's Cabin,* is born to slave parents in Charles County, Maryland. As a young man, Henson sells produce at the markets of Georgetown and in the District, where he meets abolitionists for the first time. Henson later moves to Kentucky, where he escapes with his family, and in the 1840s becomes a well-known abolitionist.

1790

July 16. Congress passes the Residence Bill, making way for the construction of the national capital on a site along the Potomac River, using land from both Maryland and Virginia. The laws of each state will govern the territory that each ceded to the District until Congress makes other provisions. The bill also gives the president the right to appoint three commissioners to oversee the development of the city.

Black laborers (slave and free) break ground, clear roads, and haul construction materials—including limestone from Aquia Creek quarry. Hired-out slaves provide much of the labor for buildings in the new capital.

1791

President Washington hires Major Andrew Ellicott to survey the boundaries of the ten-mile District of Columbia. Ellicott chooses Benjamin Banneker to assist him, despite Banneker's advancing age.

Secretary of State Thomas Jefferson appoints Pierre Charles L'Enfant to draft plans for the sites of major public buildings and primary streets of the federal city, which is to be called Washington City. Banneker occasionally joins Ellicott and L'Enfant at dinner in Suter's Tavern to discuss their progress. After working only three months, Banneker leaves Ellicott in Washington and returns home at the end of April 1791, due to poor health.

1792

The Pennsylvania Society for the Relief of Free Negroes Unlawfully Held in Bondage, an abolitionist group, helps Benjamin Banneker publish his first almanac, which is based on his own astronomical calculations. That same year Banneker writes to Thomas Jefferson, challenging Jefferson's belief in the racial inferiority of black people. Banneker publishes his almanacs yearly until 1797.

1794

George Bell and Sophia Browning Bell, a Maryland slave couple acquainted with Benjamin Banneker, earn a little money by preparing meals in their small cabin across the Eastern Branch for Major

The first census in the United States shows that the population of free blacks in the town of Alexandria is 52; there are 543 slaves.

Portrait of Benjamin Banneker on the frontispiece of his almanac, 1795.

Andrew Ellicott and his commissioners. Sophia, the mother of four, adds this to the other money she earns selling produce in the market stalls in Alexandria.

1796

Maryland legislation spells out the legal requirements for manumission: by final will and testament or by written deed, witnessed by two whites and submitted to a justice of the peace.

December 11. The School for Negroes opens in Alexandria with seventeen students under Archibald McLean.

1797

March 4. John Adams is inaugurated as president.

1799

Paul Jennings is born a slave on James Madison's plantation in Montpelier, Virginia. Madison will later become president of the United States and bring Jennings to Washington, D.C. Jennings's father is said to be Benjamin Jennings, an English trader at Montpelier; his mother is a slave on the Madison plantation. Jennings, as an adult, said this of his owner: "Mr. Madison, I think, was one of the best men that ever lived. I never saw him in a passion, and never knew him to strike a slave, although he had over one hundred; neither would he allow an overseer to do it."

October 2. The Navy Yard is established along the banks of the Anacostia River. It remains one of the most important sources of employment for black men until the 1870s, when it begins to refuse them employment.

1800

Sometime after the turn of the century, Alethia Browning Tanner, sister to Sophia Browning Bell, obtains the use of a small garden plot near the Capitol, where she starts to raise vegetables to sell in the market. She becomes a popular vendor and begins saving whatever money she can, with the goal of purchasing her and her family's freedom. Tradition claims that Thomas Jefferson was one of the customers for her market produce and that later Tanner

Alethia Browning Tanner. She purchases the freedom of her family in the 1820s.

Letter from Thomas Jefferson to Benjamin Banneker, August 1791.

I suppose it is a truth too well attested to you, to need a proof here, that we are a race of Beings who have long laboured under the abuse and censure of the world, that we have long been looked upon with an eye of contempt, and that we have long been considered rather as brutish than human, and Scarcely capable of mental endowments.

—Benjamin Banneker, letter to Thomas Jefferson, August 19, 1791

served as a housemaid for him during part of his residence in the capital.

August 30. The Gabriel Prosser slave rebellion in Richmond, Virginia, ignites fear and suspicion of slaves in Virginia and beyond—including in the District of Columbia. Prosser, a blacksmith inspired by the French and the Haitian revolutions, organized rural

The second census of the U.S. population takes place. The population of free blacks in the District of Columbia is 783; there are 3,244 slaves. Almost a quarter of Washington City's population is black; about 25 percent of them are free. The free black population continues to grow, the increase stemming from many sources. The District is a final or interim destination for many escaped slaves from Maryland and Virginia; they form a thriving underground part of the city's population.

Certificate of the October 23, 1796, marriage of two slaves at Holy Trinity Church in Georgetown.

Between Prosser's Tavern and the Brook Bridge, in the woods, was the rallying point, at which on the Saturday night of the storm . . . about 5 or 600 Negroes from Hanover and the adjacent country as far as Ground Squirrel Bridge were on that night to have assembled, armed in the best manner they could, with scythes, swords, and such guns as could be procured, and the work of death was to commence on Prosser the first victim; a few others were to share the same fate, and the party were then to march into town and massacre the male white inhabitants, FRENCHMEN alone excepted.

—The *Washington Federalist,* on Gabriel Prosser's slave revolt, September 25, 1800

A Negro Man

To be hired by the year, half yearly or quarterly A SOBER well disposed man about 26 years of age, cleanly, and has been many years employed as a coach driver, stable boy, and occasionally waiting at table, and working in the garden. His master wishes to hire him out in or about the city of Washington, he having a wife living near the District. He has never been accused or suspected of dishonesty. For further information apply to the printer.

—Advertisement in the *National Intelligencer and Washington Advertiser,* November 27, 1801

field laborers and other artisans like himself to free the slaves of Richmond.

1801

March 4. Thomas Jefferson is inaugurated as president.

December 4. In the pages of the *National Intelligencer and Washington Advertiser,* Toussaint L'Ouverture, "governour of St. Domingo," advertises a new department in St. Domingo, to be named L'Ouverture, whose capital city will be Gonaives. In the ad, he announces the availability of land lots and encourages readers to acquire them. He warns that new landowners must not allow their land to stand vacant without buildings, or their land will be confiscated: "The inhabitants of this new department in general and of the city of Gonaives in particular, ought to endeavor to show themselves worthy of this favor. They ought to redouble their zeal and emulation to render the capitol of this new department as flourishing as the principal towns of the city."

December. Mayor Robert Brent organizes a public market at 7th Street and Pennsylvania Avenue. It is called "Marsh Market" because of its low, swampy location. This is the precursor to the great Center Market, which rises on the same spot. Slave boatmen and wagoners bring vegetables and other produce from their masters' farms and plantations in Virginia and Maryland, to this and other markets in the District. Free blacks also fill the markets with their goods for sale.

Sophia Browning Bell, a slave belonging to Mrs. Rachel Bell Pratt (mother of Thomas G. Pratt, governor of Maryland), finally saves enough money to buy her husband his freedom from Anthony Addison, a prominent Maryland landowner. They have achieved this long-sought and hard-won goal by selling produce and dinners and taking advantage of any opportunity to earn a few coins. They had no bank account but secretly hoarded their money and entrusted it, bit by bit, to a black minister. George Bell, at forty years of age, is freed for the sum of $400. Sophia is one of three sisters owned by Rachel Bell Pratt. When Sophia falls deathly ill soon after this, George is able to buy her from her sickbed for £5. They later buy both of their surviving sons from Mrs. Pratt—both of them purchased "running" (as runaways)—but Mrs. Pratt refused to sell their daughter and held her as a slave until Mrs. Pratt's death.

1802

Congress grants a limited home rule charter to District residents. Some of its components change over the years, but it stands until 1871, when Congress revokes the city's home rule charter.

1804

March 13. James H. Fleet is purchased from slavery by his father, Henry Fleet. James establishes a popular school for free blacks in 1836.

1805

A resolution for the emancipation of all slaves in the District of Columbia is defeated in Congress.

1806

October 9. Benjamin Banneker dies in his Maryland home at age seventy-four. Shortly after his death, his small cabin burns down. Nearly everything in it is destroyed, including the wooden clock that first brought him to the attention of his neighbors.

1807

Three free black men, George Bell (Sophia Browning Bell's husband), Nicholas Franklin, and Moses Liverpool, build the first schoolhouse for black children in the District of Columbia. The men had all just recently been slaves and were themselves illiterate. Franklin and Liverpool—from the Chesapeake region of Virginia—worked as caulkers in the Navy Yard. George Bell was a carpenter. The school was a great step forward for the city's black community, but the building itself was a modest one-story wooden building. To prevent the school being shut down by hostile city authorities, Bell, Franklin, and Liverpool had to publicly ensure that no teacher would write anything for a slave. They could not risk being caught writing passes or forging manumissions and certificates of freedom

As two white persons were returning from the horse races, a few miles north of the city of Washington . . . they met on the road a free man of colour, who resided in the vicinity. They seized him, and bound him with ropes. His protestations that he was free, and his entreaties that they would accompany him to the house (but about half a mile distant), where his wife resided, and where he could satisfy them of his freedom, were in vain. Having fastened him by a rope to the tail of one of their horses, they were seen, by a citizen, who met them on the road dragging him in this manner, and beating him to make him keep pace with the horses. . . . On the following morning, this poor African was found by the side of the road, dreadfully bruised, and his eyes bloodshotten,—dead! . . . I was assured, that one of them had long been accustomed, in company with his own father, to the business of apprehending runaway slaves, and such free Africans as they could catch without certificates.

—Jesse Torrey,
American Slave Trade, 1822

for slaves. George Bell had been the primary proponent of the school, and in his honor it was called Bell School. A white man, Mr. Lowe, was the first instructor.

1808

January 1. The international trade in slaves is outlawed in the United States, causing the domestic slave trade to expand exponentially. Washington, D.C., becomes a major slave market, where traders congregate to purchase slaves from Virginia and Maryland for sale farther south. Most of the deals between buyer and seller take place in private taverns in the District. Coffles of slaves on their way to the slave markets are common sights in the nation's capital. Once in the District, they are incarcerated in one of the city's private jails and either shipped down the Potomac or organized into overland coffles.

Washington's first black codes are passed into law by the city council, providing for a 10 P.M. curfew for black people and a $5 fine on those found in violation.

1809

March 4. James Madison is inaugurated as president.

Henry Potter, an Englishman, establishes a school for blacks on F and 7th Streets, opposite the old Post Office Building. His school is quite successful and expands to a building on 13th Street.

October 3. Anthony Bowen is born in Prince George's County, Maryland, on the estate of William A. Bradley. Recognizing his outstanding intelligence and determination, Bradley's daughter-in-law teaches young Anthony to read and write. In 1830 Bowen buys his own freedom.

1810

Mary Billings (1776–1826), a widow who had arrived with her husband from England only ten years earlier, opens a school for blacks in Georgetown on Dumbarton Street. She begins by teaching white and black children, but when the opposition grows to integrated

If any slave shall be seen running any horses in any street or avenues of the city, within three hundred yards of any house or building, it shall be the duty of any constable to take such slave before a magistrate, and on his being convicted of such offence, he shall be publicly whipped, any number of lashes, not exceeding thirty-nine.

—*Ordinance of the District of Columbia*

The population of free blacks in the District grows to 2,549; there are 5,505 slaves.

RUNAWAY FOR SALE.

WILL be sold on Saturday the 26th of April next, for her jail fees and other expences, at the Jail in Washington County, District of Columbia, a yellow WOMAN, who calls herself Maria Prout. She is four feet ten inches high, says she is about 20 years of age.—— Sale to commence at 10 o'clock. Terms of sale, cash.

C. TIPPETT,
For W. Boyd, Marshal.

March 30—ts

Notice of a sale of a runaway slave at a jail in the District of Columbia in the Daily National Intelligencer, *April 2, 1814.*

classrooms, she decides to devote herself exclusively to educating black children. Children of the leading black families in the District attend the school. Billings continues teaching until 1822–1823; after her retirement, Henry Potter takes over her school. He is succeeded by another Englishman, Mr. Shay, who teaches at the school until his conviction and imprisonment in 1830 for assisting a slave to escape.

Anne Maria Hall becomes the first African American teacher in the District, when she opens a school on 1st Street on Capitol Hill. Despite having to secure several different sites for her school over the years, she teaches until 1835.

July 6. Alethia (Lethe) Browning Tanner, Sophia Browning Bell's sister, makes the final payment on her freedom and receives her manumission papers. She gives the last $275 of the $1,400 it cost to buy her freedom to Joseph Daugherty, who, at her request, had purchased her four days earlier from Rachel Bell Pratt.

The Washington Corporation Council passes an act that requires all free blacks residing in the city to register with city authorities.

Two white men kidnapping a black man outside Washington, D.C.

Thomas Tabbs' school was an institution peculiar to itself. Mr. Tabbs belonged to a prominent Maryland family, and was bred in affluence and received a thorough and polished education. He came to Washington before the war of 1812, and resided here until his death, which occurred ten years ago [1861]. He at once commenced teaching the colored people, and persistently continued to do so as long as he lived. He was called insane by some, but there was certainly a method in his madness. When he could find a school-room, he would gather a school, but when less fortunate he would go from house to house, stopping where he could find a group of poor colored children to instruct. At one period he had the shadow of a large tree near the Masonic Lodge at the Navy Yard for his school, and it was there that Alexander Hays, afterwards a teacher in Washington, but then a slave, learned his alphabet. Mr. Tabbs must have spent nearly fifty years in this mode of life.

—Moses Goodwin,
*History of Schools for the
Colored Population in the District
of Columbia,* 1871

1812

The city council requires all free blacks to register and to carry a pass proving that they are not slaves. It also increases fines for those involved in "nightly and disorderly meetings" to $20. Free blacks

The Colored Quarter of Washington, D.C.

unable to pay their fine will be held six months in the city jail; slaves are given forty lashes.

Christ Church in the Navy Yard establishes a Sabbath school for blacks, teaching the alphabet and the Bible.

June. The United States declares war on Great Britain, beginning the War of 1812. British troops, under the command of General Robert Ross, begin to make incursions along the Potomac.

1813

March 4. James Madison is inaugurated for his second term as president.

Summer. As the British plan to attack Washington, D.C., enslaved blacks in the city become restive.

Tobias Henson, a slave in Anacostia, purchases his freedom and begins making payments on twenty-four acres of farmland in Anacostia known as the "Ridge." By the 1830s he has saved enough money to purchase his children from their owner. Henson subdivides his land into lots for his family, which occupies the land until the 1940s. The Henson family land later becomes a part of the Stantontown community, centered on Stanton Road and Alabama Avenue SE.

I expect to patrole more frequently, and this is very necessary, for the blacks in some places refuse to work, and say they shall soon be free, and then the white people must look out. One Negro woman went so far as to steal her mistress's keys, and refused to return them, saying she soon pay her for old and new. This was in the city, and the Negro was confined. Should we be attacked, there will be great danger of the blacks rising, and to prevent this, patroles are very necessary, to keep them in awe. One other preventative at present is, the want of a leader.
—Vice President Elbridge Gerry, d. 1814, on the openly hostile attitude of some slaves, *The Diary of Elbridge Gerry, Jr.*

[I]n August, 1814, the enemy had got so near, there could be no doubt of their intentions. Great alarm existed, and some feeble preparations for defence [sic] were made. Com. Barney's flotilla was stripped of men, who were placed in battery, at Bladensburg, where they fought splendidly. A large part of his men were tall, strapping negroes, [sic] mixed with white sailors and marines. Mr. Madison reviewed them just before the fight, and asked Com. Barney if his "negroes would not run on the approach of the British?" "No sir," said Barney, "they don't know how to run; they will die by their guns first." They fought till a large part of them were killed or wounded and taken prisoner.

—Paul Jennings,
A Colored Man's Reminiscences of James Madison, 1865

1814

June 3. One hundred twenty-five black members of Montgomery Street Methodist Church—almost half of whose membership is African American—withdraw to form a separate church for themselves. It takes them two years to raise enough money for a new church, the Little Ark. This church remains under the jurisdiction of the Montgomery Street Church, which continues a policy of racial segregation within its congregation. Leaders in this effort to build a separate black church include Lucy Neal, Polly Hill, William Crusor, William Trumwell, Shadrack Nugent, Thomas Mason, and Tamar Green.

August. Over 4,000 British troops land thirty-five miles southeast of the city, preparing to march on the capital. Mayor James Black calls on the militia to take up positions east of the city. He also sets them to digging earthworks in Bladensburg, Maryland. Many free black men respond to his call. When British troops reach Bladensburg on August 24, they force the militia to retreat.

Engraving of slave coffle in front of the Capitol, showing the damage to the Capitol by British troops in 1814.

Well, on the 24th of August, sure enough, the British reached Bladensburg, and the fight began between 11 and 12. Even that very morning General Armstrong assured Mrs. Madison there was no danger. . . . Mrs. Madison ordered dinner to be ready at 3, as usual; I set the table myself, and brought up the ale, cider, and wine, and placed them in the coolers, as all the Cabinet and several military gentlemen and strangers were expected. While waiting, at just about 3, as Sukey, the house-servant, was lolling out of a chamber window, James Smith, a free colored man who had accompanied Mr. Madison to Bladensburg, gallopped [sic] up to the house, waving his hat, and cried out, "Clear out, clear out! General Armstrong has ordered a retreat!" All then was confusion.

—Paul Jennings,
A Colored Man's Reminiscences of James Madison, 1865

1815

The United States signs a peace treaty with Great Britain, ending the War of 1812.

December 19. About to be sold south, a black female slave leaps from the window of a three-story building in a desperate attempt to escape or commit suicide.

1816

Blacks from the Montgomery Street Methodist Church begin building the "Little Ark" on 27th and P Streets NW. This church becomes the Mt. Zion Methodist Episcopal Church in the mid-1840s.

Winter. Robert Finley arrives in the District of Columbia to advocate directly to Congress his ideas to remove free blacks from the United States and resettle them in some part of Africa. Finley writes a pamphlet, "Thoughts on the Colonization of Free Blacks," which he distributes in the city. He suggests that if Congress doesn't allocate funds to facilitate colonization, perhaps free blacks could be induced to pay their own fares to Africa.

December 21. The American Colonization Society is formed in Washington, D.C. Among the signatories of its constitution are Robert Finley, Bushrod Washington, John Randolph, Henry Clay, Daniel Webster, and William Thornton.

[D]uring the last session of congress (1815–1816) as several members were standing in the street, near the new capitol, a drove of manacled coloured people were passing by; and when just opposite, one of them elevating his manacles as high as he could reach, commenced singing the favorite national song, "Hail Columbia! Happy land," . . .

—Letter from Congressman
Adgate to Jesse Torrey

There shall be paid annually on the first day of January, the following tax on slaves, the property of residents of the City of Washington, by his or her owner, viz.: On male slaves between the ages of fifteen and forty-five, two dollars; and on female slaves between the age of fifteen and forty-five, the sum of one dollar.

—*Ordinance of the District of Columbia*

[A] black woman, destined for transportation to Georgia with a coffle, which was about to start, attempted to escape, by jumping out of the window of the garret of a three story brick tavern in F street [Miller's Tavern], about day-break in the morning. . . . In the fall she had her back and both arms broken! . . . Having found the house, I desired permission of the landlord to see the wounded woman; to which he assented. . . . On entering the room I observed her lying upon a bed on the floor, and covered with a white woollen blanket, on which were several spots of blood (from her wounds,). . . . Her countenance, though very pale from the shock she had received, and dejected with grief, appeared complacent and sympathetic. Both her arms were broken between the elbows and wrists, and had undoubtedly been well set and dressed; but from her restlessness she had displaced the bones again, so that they were perceptibly crooked. I have since been informed by the Mayor of the city, who is a physician, and resides not far distant from the place, that he was called to visit her immediately after her fall, and found, besides her arms being broken, that the lower part of the spine was badly shattered. . . . Asking her what was the cause of her doing such a frantic act as that, she replied, "They brought me away with two of my children, and wouldn't let me see my husband—they didn't sell my husband, and I didn't want to go;—I was so confused and distracted, that I didn't know hardly what I was about—but I didn't want to go, and I jumped out of the window;—but I am sorry now that I did it;—they have carried my children off with 'em to Carolina.' "

—Jesse Torrey,
American Slave Trade, 1822

To avoid being sold as a slave in Georgia, this woman jumps out of a window at Miller's Tavern, breaking several bones.

Free blacks kidnapped and sold into slavery.

1817

January. At the second meeting of the American Colonization Society, Bushrod Washington is elected president.

March 4. James Monroe is inaugurated as president.

March 19. Daniel Webster purchases Paul Jennings's freedom from former first lady Dolley Madison. Jennings agrees to serve Webster, in order to work off his debt at a rate of $8 a month.

Jesse Torrey, author of *American Slave Trade*, rescues three free blacks who were kidnapped and held, awaiting sale, in a private jail in the District of Columbia. Torrey sues for their freedom and is assisted in his suit by James Randolph and several notable Washingtonians, including General Van Ness and Francis Scott Key.

In response to the activities of the American Colonization Society, blacks begin organizing protest meetings in cities around the nation. Anticolonization activities increase over the years as the society's colonization efforts expand.

1818

George Bell, William Costin, and other blacks in the District organize the Resolute Beneficial Society to provide health and burial insurance for its members, as well as for indigent blacks. They also

In many cases, whole families of free coloured people have been attacked in the night, beaten nearly to death with clubs, gagged and bound, and dragged into distant and hopeless captivity and slavery, leaving no traces behind, except the blood from their wounds. . . . During the last winter. . . the house of a free black family was broken open, and its defenceless inhabitants treated in the manner just mentioned, except that the mother escaped. . . . The plunderers, of whom there were nearly half a dozen, conveyed their prey upon horses; and the woman being placed on one of the horses, behind, improved an opportunity, as they were passing a house, and sprang off; and not daring to pursue her, they proceeded on, leaving her youngest child a little farther along by the side of the road, in expectation, it is supposed, that its cries would attract the mother, but she prudently waited until morning, and recovered it again in safety.

—Jesse Torrey,
American Slave Trade, 1822

July 12, 1818, Georgetown

Know all men by these presents that I, John Eliason have for divers good causes thereunto moving have set free and have discharged from all service claimed by me or my heirs—my Black woman named Sarah Berry—and hope no person will molest her in traveling or attending to her regular duties, as I shall feel myself in duty bound to protect her again all violence.

—John Eliason
Manumission and Emancipation
Records, 1821–1862,
Records of U.S. District Courts, Circuit
Court of the District of Columbia

Mrs. Madison was a remarkable fine woman. She was beloved by every body in Washington, white and colored. Whenever soldiers marched by, during the war, she always sent out and invited them in to take wine and refreshments, giving them liberally of the best in the house. Madeira wine was better in those days than now, and more freely drank. In the last days of her life . . . she was in a state of absolute poverty, I think sometimes suffered for the necessaries of life. While I was a servant to Mr. Webster, he often sent me to her with a market-basket full of provisions, and told me whenever I saw anything in the house that I thought she was in need of, to take it to her. I often did this, and occasionally gave her small sums from my own pocket, though I had years before bought my freedom of her.

—Paul Jennings,
*A Colored Man's Reminiscences of
James Madison,* 1865

establish a free school for black children in the same building used by the old Bell School. The Beneficial Society School offers instruction until about 1822. Mr. Pierpont, the first instructor, teaches there for three years. John Adams, the second instructor, is the first male African American teacher in the District. Sixty to seventy-five students attend classes in the old Bell School building.

February. Frederick Douglass is born on Maryland's eastern shore.

1819

January 16. James Wormley is born. His father, Peter Leigh Wormley, owns a thriving livery business. James becomes a hack driver in this business and marries Anna Thompson, a free black woman, in 1841.

1820

Yarrow Mamout, a free black man and a practicing Muslim, owns several properties in Georgetown. He had been a slave and obtained his freedom, purchasing it himself. He later amasses considerable savings through his work as a drayman. He loses most of it when the bank fails but regains his financial standing by the early 1800s.

Several black members of Ebenezer Church's mixed congregation withdraw to form their own church. Moses Goodwin recalls in *History of Schools for the Colored Population in the District of Columbia* (1871) that

> some of the leading members among them, George Bell and George Hicks, became dissatisfied with their treatment, withdrew, and organized a church in connection with the African Methodist Episcopal church. At first, they worshipped in Basil Sim's Rope-walk, First Street east, near Pennsylvania Avenue, but subsequently in Rev. Mr. Wheat's school-house on Capitol Hill, near Virginia Avenue. They finally purchased the old First Presbyterian Church at the foot of Capitol Hill, later known as the Israel Bethel Colored Methodist Episcopal Church. Some years thereafter other members of the old Ebenezer Church, not liking their confined quarters in the gallery, and otherwise discontented, purchased a lot on the corner of C Street south

and Fifth Street east, built a house of worship, and organized the "Little Ebenezer" Methodist Episcopal Church.

At age fifteen, Maria Becraft opens a school for girls on Dumbarton Street. Maria is the daughter of William Becraft, a well-known free black man who worked as chief steward at a leading hotel in the District. Maria was known for her precocious intellectual ability, her beauty, and her religious piety. She attended Henry Potter's school and later Mrs. Billings's.

By the early 1800s the state of Maryland makes standardized forms available to slaveholders wishing to free their slaves. One commonly used example:

> Be it known that I _____ of _____ for divers good causes and considerations me thereunto moving as also in further consideration of the sum of _____ current money to me in hand paid have released from slavery, liberated, manumitted and set free My negro _____ being of the age of _____ and able to work and gain sufficient livelihood and maintenance I do declare _____ to be henceforth free, manumitted and discharged from all manner of servitude or services to me, My Executors, Administrators, Assigns, forever.

> Today personally appeared _____ party to the within instrument of writing before me the subscriber a Justice of the Peace of the County and district aforesaid and acknowledges the same to be her [or his] and to be free and manumitted, according to the act of assembly in such cases made and provided.

May 15. Congress passes an act that allows Washington City to hold biannual mayoral elections, as well as elections for an eight-member board of aldermen. The act also calls for the annual election of a twelve-member common council.

Araminta Ross is born in Dorchester County, Maryland. The exact year of her birth is unknown, but it is either 1820 or 1821. She becomes the famous Underground Railroad conductor Harriet Tubman.

The population of free blacks in the District of Columbia reaches 4,048; there are 6,277 slaves.

The city council petitions Congress to end the slave trade in the District of Columbia; Congress refuses.

The Corporation of Washington shall have power and authority, to restrain and prohibit the nightly and other disorderly meetings of slaves, free negroes and mulattoes, and to punish such slaves by whipping, not exceeding forty stripes, or by imprisonment, not exceeding six months for any one offence, and to punish such free negroes and mulattoes by penalties, not exceeding twenty dollars for any one offence, and in case of the inability of any free negro or mulatto to pay any such penalty and cost thereon, to cause him or her to be confined to labor, for any time not exceeding six calendar months.

—*Ordinance of the District of Columbia*

1821

Mary Billings moves her school from Dumbarton Street to a private home on H Street.

The city enacts additional restraints on free blacks. They must now present themselves in person before the mayor, show him documents proving their freedom and stating their occupations, and provide certificates signed by three white residents, vouching for the character of the family. Each free black person must also pay a "peace bond" of $20, with a white man as guarantor. If any black person is unable to comply with the law, that individual can be jailed and sold into slavery. Blacks are forbidden to hold meetings without prior permission from the mayor, and a 10 P.M. curfew is imposed on them.

William Costin (1780–1842), a free black man living in the District, challenges the 1821 law in court. Costin is a member of Washington's elite free black community, having arrived in the city around 1802. He bought the freedom of his wife, Philadelphia Judge (1780–1831), from Eliza Custis Law—to whom she had been given as a wedding present by Martha Washington, a common occurrence among wealthy slaveowning whites. Costin is also connected to some of the District's elite white families—allegedly through birth. His grandfather is said to be the father of Martha Washington, and Ann Dandridge, his mother, grew up on the same plantation as Martha Washington. He refuses to present himself before the mayor or to post bond. When brought before the justice of the peace, he is found in violation of the 1821 law and fined. Costin, however, will not give up; he appeals to the U.S. Circuit Court. The case is tried before Judge William Cranch, who reverses the decision of the justice of the peace and revokes the fine imposed on Costin, based on the fact that the law was retrogressively applied to him. Judge Cranch rules that the law cannot impose restrictions upon free blacks who resided in the city before 1821, but that it can be upheld against free blacks who migrated to the city after 1820, when the charter that granted law-making power to city officials became effective.

David Smith, an evangelical African Methodist Episcopal leader from Baltimore, is sent as a missionary to the District of Columbia

Several free persons of colour, of both sexes, and all a little shaded with a yellowish tint, being employed as servants in the house in which I lodge, I inquired of two of the females, a few days ago, whether they would like to go to Africa, as it was the country of their forefathers. One of them expressed great repugnance at going there, and the other said her fathers did not come from Africa, "and (said she) if they (the Americans) did not want us, they had no need to have brought us away: after they've brought us here, and made us work so hard, and disfigured the colour, I don't think it would be fair to send us back again."

—Jesse Torrey,
American Slave Trade, 1822

to preach to black Methodists. At first, Smith is challenged by local blacks, but he persists and goes on to establish the Israel Bethel A.M.E. (later C.M.E.) Church. Biographer and historian S. L. Nichols notes that initially meetings were held in Smith's mother's house and that the Israel Bethel Church was considered "a hotbed of free Negro leadership."

When members of St. John's Episcopal Church in Georgetown decide to make some improvements on its structure, they erect a separate staircase—on the outside of the building—for African American members. Black members had used the front door until then. The stairway leads directly to an upstairs window that has been enlarged to serve as an entryway.

1822

The first city directory is published.

Members of Israel Bethel Church join the African Methodist Episcopal denomination. Reverend David Smith (1784–188?) is its first A.M.E. pastor.

John Adams, former instructor at the Resolute Beneficial Society School, establishes his own school for blacks.

Henry Smothers, an alumnus of Mary Billings's school, opens a school for blacks in Georgetown, where he offers instruction at no cost. He later builds a schoolhouse behind his home at 14th and H Streets NW, and moves his students there. Enrollment reaches 150 students. The modest building that Smothers erects becomes an important site for blacks of that era—the later location not only of John Prout's Columbian Institute but also of John F. Cook's Union Seminary and the birthplace of the Fifteenth Street Presbyterian Church.

At age nineteen, Louisa Parke Costin, William Costin's daughter, establishes a school for black children in her father's home on A Street on Capitol Hill. She continues teaching there until her premature death in 1831. Her sister, Martha, reopens the school in 1839.

The presence of a Negro preacher was objectionable to many Negroes themselves. As early as 1821 Mr. Smith was assigned to Washington but his coming was the signal for personal attack, and he was mobbed by members of his own race, communicants of the Methodist Episcopal Church, who were opposed to the African Methodists. He persisted, however, and having secured an old school house for $300, entered upon his work with such zeal and energy that he commanded success. Among the men and women active in the first efforts were Scipio Beans, George Simms, Peter Schureman, George Hicks, Dora Bowen, William Costin, William Datcher, William Warren, and George Bell, one of the three colored men who fifteen years before had erected a building for a Negro school.

—John W. Cromwell, "The First Negro Churches in the District of Columbia," *Journal of Negro History,* 1922

Advertisement for the purchase of slaves in the Alexandria Gazette & Daily Advertiser, *February 5, 1822.*

December 23, 1823, Washington, District of Columbia

Whereas the undersigned Benjamin L. Lear . . . purchased Of William W. Ramsay of the United States Navy a certain mulatto man slave named Henry otherwise called Henry Orr for the sum of five hundred dollars; and whereas the said purchase was made by the said Lear with the sole intent to enable the said Henry to procure his freedom upon the repayment of the said sum of money to the said Lear; and whereas the said Henry hath repaid the same: Now therefore know all men . . . that I the said Benjamin Lear . . . do hearby discharge from slavery manumit, and set free, the said mulatto man Henry otherwise called Henry Orr.

—Benjamin L. Lear

July 1, 1825, Washington City

Having a desire to do to others as I would that they should do unto me, I do hereby manumit and set free . . . my faithful & valuable Negro woman Sylvia, now about twenty years of age. Sylvia was the property of Ann Hutchinson to which my agreement was with . . . for Sylvia to be set free at thirty-five years of age, but thanks be to God for putting in my hart to shorten her servitude.

—Jonathan Criddle

Both from Manumission and Emancipation Records, 1821–1862, Records of U.S. District Courts, Circuit Court of the District of Columbia

1823

Mt. Zion Methodist Church establishes a school for blacks.

December 23. Henry Orr, a personable and resourceful man owned by William and Catharine Ramsay, convinces Benjamin Lear to purchase him from the Ramsays, so that he can buy his freedom.

1825

March 4. John Quincy Adams is inaugurated as president.

John Prout succeeds Henry Smothers at the Smothers School and renames it the Columbian Institute. Ten years later he changes the name to the Columbian Academy. Struggling to keep the institution afloat, Prout is forced to begin charging twelve cents per month for each student. The fees enable him to greatly improve the level of instruction at the school.

The Grand Masonic Lodge of the District of Columbia is established by ten free black men.

1826

July 22. Gilbert Horton, a free black man visiting Washington from Peekskill, New York, is arrested when he is unable to produce a document that proves he is free. He is held in jail for almost a month while he tries to contact New York acquaintances who can vouch for his free status. Horton is eventually advertised for sale at a slave auction, in order to cover the costs of his jail stay. After the governor of New York intervenes and Horton's case is reported in local newspapers, he finally is able to produce evidence of his free status and is released on August 28. An outraged Congressman Ward from New York demands a congressional investigation, but little ultimately comes of it.

The Benevolent Society of Alexandria is established to liberate those illegally held in slavery, to provide relief and assistance to the free black community, and to educate people about slavery.

Alethia Browning Tanner purchases her oldest sister, Laurena [Laurana] Cook, and five of Laurena's children, including John Francis

Cook, from slaveowner Rachel Bell Pratt. Finally, all three sisters—Sophia, Alethia, and Laurena—are free.

Mrs. Tanner was alive to every wise scheme for the education and elevation of her race. It was through her efforts, combined with those of her brother-in-law, George Bell, that the First Bethel Church on Capitol Hill was saved for that society. When the house was put up at auction by the bank which held the notes of the society, these two individuals came forward, bid in the property, paid for it and waited for their pay till the society was able to raise the money. . . . She was also the housemaid of Mr. [Thomas] Jefferson during his residence at the capital, and [Senator] Richard M. Johnson, who was her friend, appears as the witness to the manumission papers of Laurena Cook, her sister, and of John F. Cook, the son of Laurena.

—Moses Goodwin,
History of Schools for the Colored Population in the District of Columbia, 1871

They are called slave traders, and their occupation is to kidnap every colored stranger they can lay their hands on. No matter whether he be free or not, his papers, if he chance to have any they can get at, are taken from him; and he is hurried to gaol, from whence, under pretence, [sic] that the documents he has in his possession are not satisfactory, or that he is unable to pay the expenses of his arrest and detention, he is sent off to the southern market.

—E. S. Abdy,
Journal of a Residence and Tour of the United States of North America From April, 1833, to October, 1834

1827

The Washington Corporation Council passes an act imposing a bond of $500 on free blacks, in addition to requiring two white people to vouch for their behavior in writing.

The prohibition forbidding a colored person to be abroad after 10 o'clock at night without a pass, under a penalty of "a fine," "confinement to hard labor," or "stripes upon the bare back," "well laid on," must at a glance impress every candid mind with surprise, and yet it is only upon considerate reflection that its atrociousness is revealed. A poor colored man finds a member of his family in a dying condition at midnight, and on his way for a doctor is seized by a wretch in the garb of a policeman, carried to a watch-house, and, without friends or money, is sent next day to the work-house. A colored man has a store containing a heavy stock of goods; it takes fire in the night, and his sons start for the rescue of their property, are seized by a relentless officer, and held, as in the other case, till morning at police headquarters. These are not imaginary cases.

—Moses Goodwin,
History of Schools for the Colored Population in the District of Columbia, 1871

Within thirty days after the first of October next, it shall be the duty of all free black and mulatto persons, males of the age of sixteen, and females of the age of fourteen years and upwards, who may then reside in the City of Washington, to exhibit satisfactory evidence of their title to freedom, to the Register of this corporation. . . . Every negro and mulatto found residing in the City of Washington, after the passage of this act, who shall not be able to establish his or her title to freedom . . ., shall be committed to the jail of the County of Washington, as absconding slaves.

—*Ordinance of the District of Columbia*

The Benevolent Society of Alexandria stated ... that [after nine to ten months of existence, it had] wrested twelve people of color from the grasp of the slave-traders; and that they had reason to believe there were several others, entitled to their freedom, who had been sold: "If it were not," they added, "for this detestable traffic, those who have a large number of slaves upon poor land," (such is most of the soil near Washington,) "would not long be enabled to hold them; as it generally takes the whole produce of their labor to clothe and support them; and the only profit of the owner is derived from the sale of the young ones."

—E. S. Abdy,
Journal of a Residence and Tour of the United States of North America From April, 1833, to October, 1834

Congress passes a law forbidding blacks to be on the Capitol grounds other than for reasons of business, under penalty of $20 or thirty days' confinement. They are no longer allowed to attend summer concerts on the terrace.

Benjamin Lundy. He organizes a petition against slavery in 1828.

Maria Becraft establishes a Catholic seminary school for black girls. It is sponsored by Father John Van Lommel, of the Holy Trinity Church in Georgetown—who also taught black boys three days each week. Becraft's school accommodates thirty to thirty-five boarding and day students from the best colored families of Alexandria, Georgetown, Washington, and the surrounding country.

1828

Lindsay Muse, a free black man, becomes a messenger for the secretary of the Navy. He holds this position until 1883. Muse becomes one of the most prominent blacks in the city, accumulating over $1,000 in real estate and serving as a leader in the Nineteenth Street Baptist Church.

Benjamin Lundy organizes a petition drive and collects over 1,000 signatures from District of Columbia residents requesting the end of the slave trade in the city.

Alethia Browning Tanner purchases her sister's remaining five children and five grandchildren from Rachel Pratt. She pays an average of $300 for each child. After freeing family members, she begins to purchase the freedom of family friends and their children.

1829

February 14. Solomon Brown is born to poor parents in Washington, D.C., near Boundary (Florida Avenue) and 14th Streets NW. After his father's death, the family becomes homeless.

March 4. Andrew Jackson is inaugurated as president.

Representative Charles Miner, from Pennsylvania, decries the continuing sale of slaves in the streets of the capital. He notes the recent sale of three black people in front of Lloyd's Tavern on the corner of 7th Street and Pennsylvania Avenue NW. They included a fourteen-year-old girl, Margaret, who was sold because her master fell behind in his rent.

Some of the most popular taverns for slave-trading activities are Lafayette Tavern on F Street between 13th and 14th Streets NW; Lloyd's Tavern; Beer's Tavern or Robey's Tavern on 7th Street, off

President's Levee, or all Creation going to the White House (1829) by Robert Cruikshank from 1841 parodies Andrew Jackson's 1829 inaugural.

Maryland Avenue; McCandless's Tavern, Georgetown; and Smith's Southern Hotel, Alexandria.

Alethia Browning Tanner buys the freedom of Alfred Cook, age twenty-two, for $350.

June 5. The St. Frances Academy for Colored Girls is formed in Baltimore by the Oblate Sisters of Providence. The Sisters of Providence also establish a separate school for boys. Until the establishment of the Miner School for colored girls in 1851, it is the only school in the region that offers education beyond the primary level to blacks.

They renounce the world, to consecrate themselves to God, and the Christian education of Colored Girls. . . . In fact these girls will either become mothers of families or household servants. In the first case, the solid virtues, the religious and moral principles which they have acquired when in this school, will be carefully transferred as a legacy to their children. . . . As to such as are to be employed as servants, they will be intrusted [sic] with domestic concerns and the care of young children. How important then will it not be, that these girls should have imbibed religious principles, and have been trained up in habits of modesty, honesty, and integrity.

–Advertisement for the St. Francis Academy for Colored Girls, *National Intelligencer,* October 25, 1831

1830

William Butler, who pays property taxes of $3,310 this year, is the largest of seventy-five African American landholders in the District.

Black men under the leadership of Richard Allen, William Whipper, Robert Purvis, and others develop an organization to sponsor "Annual Conventions of People of Color."

October 20. William A. Bradley, in consideration of $425, manumits Anthony Borren (Anthony Bowen). Bowen comes to the

The population of free blacks in the city is 6,152, which just about equals the number of slaves—6,119. Ten years later the absolute number of slaves decreases to 4,694, while the population of free blacks increases to 8,361. The centers of black population are in Foggy Bottom, north of the old downtown, and in southwest D.C., known as "the Island."

District, where he purchases a house in southwest D.C. ("the Island") with the help of Bradley. He marries Catherine Miles on May 26, 1828; after her death he marries Mary Collins on September 19, 1839.

William Wormley and his sister Mary establish a school for free blacks on the corner of Vermont and I Streets. Mary serves as instructor there until ill health forces her retirement a few years later. The school remains open under other instructors until it is destroyed by mobs during the Snow race riot.

1831

January 1. William Lloyd Garrison begins publishing the *Liberator.*

May. The *National Intelligencer* reports on a meeting of colored citizens who gathered to debate the merit of black emigration to Liberia. John Prout argues persuasively against the colonization plan: "Resolved, That this meeting view with distrust the efforts made by the Colonization Society to cause the free people of color of these United States to emigrate to Liberia on the coast of Africa, or elsewhere. Resolved, That it is the declared opinion of the members of this meeting, that the soil which gave them birth is their only true and veritable home, and that it would be impolitic, unwise, and improper, for them to leave their home without the benefits of education."

John F. Cook, Alethia Tanner's nephew, begins employment as assistant messenger for the U.S. government. Because he is now working full time, he can no longer attend classes at the Columbian Institute. He is barely literate but is still determined to pursue his studies and begins a course of self-education, reading and writing in his spare time. He soon develops such professional handwriting that he gets a job as a clerk.

August. Maria Becraft leaves her school in the charge of Ellen Simonds, one of her advanced students, and joins the Oblate Sisters of Providence convent in Baltimore, where she is known as Sister Aloyons. She teaches until her death in December 1833.

[I]t appears from the best information, that a number of negroes, chiefly runaways, combined on Sunday, for the purpose of plunder. . . . At Jerusalem the blacks made three desperate attempts to cross the bridge, but were repulsed with some loss. No whites have been lost in any of the skirmishes which have taken place. Those fellows commenced by murdering a family, taking their arms and horses, and pushing on to the next house with all possible speed, where they massacre every white, even to the infant in the cradle. They continue in this manner until they are interrupted, when they disperse and skulk about the woods, until another favorable opportunity occurs of collecting together and repeating their horrible massacres. Between 25 and 30 families have already been entirely destroyed.

—Early newspaper account of the Nat Turner slave rebellion, *National Intelligencer,* August 29, 1831

August 21. On a Sunday night in Southampton County, Nat Turner, Henry Porter, Samuel Francis, Nelson Williams, Will Francis, Jack Reese, and Hark Travis meet near a stream in a secret wooded spot and launch their plan to spread rebellion among Virginia slaves. The next morning the seven men begin killing slaveowners and their families in the immediate vicinity, starting with Nat Turner's owner, Joseph Travis. By the end of the next day, 60 to 80 slaves and 4 free blacks have joined Turner, and almost 60 whites have been killed. The band bypasses poor white families and white farmers who have no slaves. The seven men are soon ambushed and defeated in a skirmish with pursuing whites, but Nat Turner escapes, despite a massive manhunt. A reign of terror follows for African Americans in Virginia; in the areas around Southampton County, there are massacres by armed militias and companies of vigilantes. Mobs roam rural areas, seizing blacks and submitting them to questioning under torture. By one account, more than 120 blacks are killed in Southampton in one day.

October. The American Colonization Society publishes the following report from Liberia: "Despatches from this Colony, bearing date up to the 2d of September, have been received at the Office of the Colonization Society. The affairs of the Colony are highly prosperous, and the rumor (so industriously circulated some months ago by the enemies of the Society) of a great mortality among the emigrants by the *Volador,* which sailed in December last, wholly unfounded."

October 28. The Washington Corporation Council passes "An Act Providing Revenues for the Corporation," providing in part that "It shall not be lawful for the mayor to grant a license, for any purpose whatever to any free negro or mulatto except licenses to drive carts, drays, hackney-carriages, or wagons."

October 30. Nat Turner is captured in a field by a white farmer, Benjamin Phipps.

November 11. Nat Turner is hanged in Jerusalem, Virginia. After his death, surgeons dissect his body, and, according to contemporary accounts, his cadaver is skinned and souvenirs made from his

[I]mmediately upon that terrible occurrence [the Nat Turner insurrection], the colored children, who had in very large numbers been received into Sabbath schools in the white churches, were all turned out of those schools. This event, though seeming to be a fiery affliction, proved a blessing in disguise. It aroused the energies of the colored people, taught them self-reliance, and they organized forthwith Sabbath schools of their own. It was in the Smothers' school-house that they formed their first Sunday school, about the year 1832, and here they continued their very large school for several years, the Fifteenth street Presbyterian Church ultimately springing from the school organization.

—Moses Goodwin,
History of Schools for the Colored Population in the District of Columbia,
1871

One day I went to see the "slaves' pen"–
a wretched hovel, "right against"
the Capitol, from which it is distant
about half a mile, with no house
intervening. . . . It is surrounded by a
wooden paling fourteen or fifteen feet in
height, with the posts outside to prevent
escape, and separated from the building
by a space too narrow to admit of a free
circulation of air. At a small window
above, which was unglazed and exposed
alike to the heat of summer and the cold
of winter, so trying to the constitution,
two or three sable faces appeared,
looking out wistfully to while away the
time and catch a refreshing breeze; the
weather being extremely hot. . . . While I
was in the city, Robey had got possession
of a woman, whose term of slavery was
limited to six years. It was expected that
she would be sold before the expiration
of that period, and sent away to a
distance, where the assertion of her
claim would subject her to ill-usage.
Cases of this kind are very common.

–E. S. Abdy, on the slave pens attached
to Robey's Tavern in the District,
*Journal of a Residence and
Tour of the United States of North
America, From April, 1833,
to October, 1834*

skin. As a direct result of the Turner Rebellion, the colonization of free blacks and even the emancipation and the removal of black slaves in Virginia are publicly debated by the governor, state officials, and prominent slaveholders and in the House of Delegates.

1832

After working as a shoemaker to save money, at age twenty-two John F. Cook pays off his debt to his aunt Alethia Tanner.

April 10. Tobias Henson purchases his wife, Elizabeth, and his daughter, Matilda (or Matlinda), from their owner, Henry Evans.

1833

March 4. Andrew Jackson is inaugurated for his second term as president.

The American Anti-Slavery Society is organized.

April. James Enoch Ambush establishes a school for black children in the basement of the Israel Bethel Church that averages about seventy-five students each year. In 1843 Ambush builds a schoolhouse on "the Island," in the southwest part of the District of Columbia. The Ambush School, or Wesleyan Seminary, as it was also called, closes in 1865.

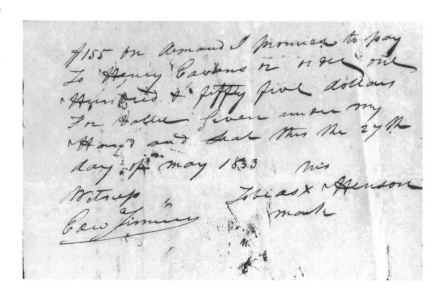

Promissory note between Tobias Henson and Henry Evans, 1833.

May 27. Tobias Henson makes arrangements with his family's former owner, Henry Evans, to purchase the freedom of his daughter Mary Addison. Evans is evidently sympathetic to Henson's desire for freedom, for he lends Henson $155 to pay for Mary's freedom, using Mary herself as collateral for the loan. Henson agrees for her to serve in Evans's household four days each week until the loan is paid off. If Henson defaults on the loan, Mary will be returned to slavery. Henson pays off the loan on November 1, 1839.

Benjamin McCoy, an African American, establishes a school for black children on L Street, between 3rd and 4th Streets. It accepts about seventy-five students each school year until 1849, when it closes.

Dear Sir:

Permit us to take the liberty of representing to you a burden that oppresses us most heavily, and of requesting your kind endeavors so to represent the case before the mayor and council that we may obtain all the relief that it is in their power to grant.

You must be aware that we pay nightly to the city a tax of $6 for permission to perform in the theatre. . . .

There is at present a law in force which authorizes the constables of the city to arrest the colored people if on the street after 9 o'clock without a pass. A great proportion of our audience consists of persons of this caste, and they are consequently deterred from giving us that support that they would otherwise do.

Can there be any modification of that law suggested, or will the mayor and council authorize us to give passes to those colored persons who leave the theatre for the purpose of proceeding directly to their homes? . . .

In a pecuniary point of view, we look upon this law as a detriment to us of $10 nightly; and we have great reason to hope that a law that rests so heavily upon us alone may meet with the kind consideration of the mayor and council, and be so modified as to relieve us from the heavy loss that it causes us at present to incur.

We have the honor to be, dear sir, your obedient servants.

—Jefferson & Mackenzie,
Managers of the Washington Theatre, 1833

October 17. John F. Cook organizes a benefit program to help a man buy his freedom from slavery.

For the Benefit of a Young Man about to disenthrall himself from Slavery

Doors open at 6 P.M. Program begins at 7 P.M. Admission: 12½ cents

John Francis Cook, Manager
Introductory Remarks by John Francis Cook

No. 1 Edwin Freeman	On Slavery and Freedom
No. 2 George Warren	On the Vanity of Wealth
No. 3 James Wright	Plato on Immortality of the Soul
No. 4 William Jasper	Brutus—On the Death of Caesar
No. 5 Alfred Jones	Campbell's Poem on Lord Ullin's Daughter
	Indignant sentiments on National prejudices, Hatred and slavery
No. 6 James Shorter	On the Battle of Linden, African Chief
No. 7 Charles Hawkins	An Address to Deity on the Wonders of Nature
No. 8 Eli E. Nugent	Epilogue to Addison's Cato
	Love of the World Detected on the Death of Christ
No. 9 John Freeman, Jr.	General Disruption of America
	Extract of an Oration on Slavery
No. 10 John F. Johnson	American Sages, An Address on Eloquence
A Dialogue on Self Interest	James Shorter
Serapewill	John Freeman
Timothy	John F. Johnson

Concluding Remarks by Benjamin C. Freeman, Assistant Manager

Program from a benefit organized by John F. Cook to assist a man in buying his freedom from slavery.

Reverend John F. Cook.

December. Thirty-seven blacks from the District of Columbia emigrate to Liberia aboard the *Argus*.

1834

At the age of about twenty-four, John F. Cook becomes director of the Columbian Institute, taking over from the venerable John Prout. Cook renames the school "Union Seminary" and develops a rigorous course of classical and practical studies.

The American Colonization Society reports its failure to convince Page C. Dunlop, James H. Fleet, and Washington Davis to honor their commitment to relocate to Liberia after the society has invested $3,911.26 to provide them with a medical education. Indeed, Fleet, who attended the Georgetown Lancasterian School, becomes an active and well-known teacher, political activist, and musician in the District of Columbia, and Dunlop, a local barber. Fleet also becomes active in the Negro Convention Movement.

Churches of the African Methodist Episcopal denomination hold their first conference in the District of Columbia, under the auspices of the Israel Bethel A.M.E. Church.

The fact of a colored conference being held in Washington City attracted considerable attention and was the occasion of much comment. White and colored people crowded the church during the session, and this was especially true of the sessions on Sunday, when the church was crowded all day to hear the ministers of the conference preach. The conference visited President Andrew Jackson in a body, and the President expressed his high appreciation of the work being done by the colored ministers for the salvation of their own people.

—Bishop James A. Handy,
Scraps of African Methodist Episcopal History, 1902

City of Washington From Beyond the Navy Yard, *1834, by William James Bennett.*

1835

The current cost of slaves being sold out of Robey's Tavern:

Babies 1 year to 18 months = $100	Children 7 to 8 years = $400
Young men = $750	Adolescent girls = $650
Men with field experience = $900–$1,000	Mechanics = $1,200

September. When a slave attacks Mrs. William Thornton, a prominent white Washingtonian, local whites launch a race riot known as the Snow riot, or "Snow storm," that lasts nearly a week. They accost a suspected abolitionist, Reuben Crandall, and march on the Epicurean Eating House, a popular restaurant owned by Benjamin Snow, an African American. After the rioters destroy the restaurant, located on 6th Street and Pennsylvania Avenue, they burn the homes and businesses of other blacks. During this conflagration, nearly all the schools for blacks are vandalized or destroyed. The mobs seek John F. Cook and, failing to find him, loot the Union Seminary and almost tear it down, brick by brick. Cook is saved by his employer, who gives him a horse to escape from the city. The rioters also put on a manhunt for William Wormley, a prominent black businessman. He and William Thomas Lee, a black schoolteacher, flee the city. After the riot, the Epicurean Eating House is reopened by another free black man, Absalom Shadd, who runs it for twenty years. The indomitable Cook finds refuge in Columbia, Pennsylvania, and opens a school there while he waits until it is safe to return to Washington. He does not return until August 1836.

John F. Cook becomes secretary of the Convention of the Free People of Color in Washington, D.C. Meeting James H. Fleet and Augustus Price at the Fifth Annual Conference in Philadelphia, he joins with other black men to make a stirring declaration for freedom.

1836

Because of the ongoing agitation from abolitionist groups around the country that began in the early 1830s, Congress enacts a gag rule that disallows petitions concerning the slave trade in the capital. Former president John Quincy Adams begins a campaign to repeal the gag rule.

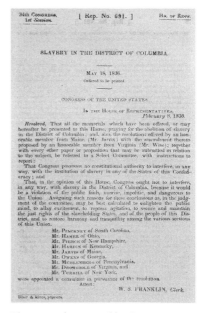

The gag rule enacted by Congress, published in The Anti-Slavery Examiner: The Power of Congress over the District of Columbia.

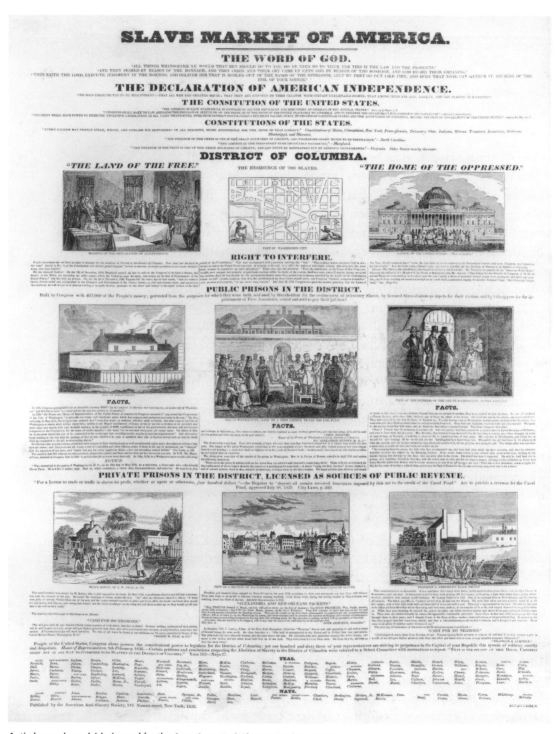

Anti-slavery broadside issued by the American Anti-Slavery Society, 1836.

At the height of their business, Isaac Franklin and John Armfield trade more slaves than any other traders in the area, perhaps in the whole country—as many as 1,000 to 1,200 slaves a year, to slave-holders in Mississippi, Alabama, and Louisiana. Franklin and Armfield conduct business out of a three-story house on Duke Street, where Armfield maintains his residence. (Armfield is in charge of purchasing slaves; Franklin tends to stay in New Orleans and Natchez, where he oversees the sale of slaves in those cities' high-bidding markets.) The slave pen (a place where slaves are held prior to sale) is in the back of the house. Men and women are generally held separately. Here, they are often "fattened" for a period and then given a new outfit before their sale. In 1836 Franklin and Armfield sell their business in D.C. A trader named George Kephart buys it, and his notorious slave-trading activities soon surpass his predecessors'. Kephart becomes somewhat of a local bogeyman to blacks; District slaves and those in Maryland and Virginia fear him.

May. The Washington Corporation Council passes another act limiting the occupations of free blacks. Licenses can be issued only in transportation—for driving carriages, carts, drays, hacks, and wagons. The act also prohibits blacks from operating eating establishments or taverns and raises their bond to $1,000. Free blacks must now obtain five white people to vouch for their behavior in writing. The act also bans blacks from swimming in the river, carrying guns, and entering gambling dens.

November 22. Isaac Carey is arrested and fined $50 for violating the prohibition against African Americans laboring at anything other than the designated occupations without a license. Carey, a perfumer, had continued to sell perfume. Carey argues that as a free man, he has the right to pursue any lawful occupation. The case is appealed to the Circuit Court, where Chief Judge William Cranch rules for Carey.

James H. Fleet establishes a school for free blacks on New York Avenue and 14th Street. The school is burned down by an arsonist in 1843. He opens another in 1846 on N and 23rd Streets NW, where he remains until he retires from teaching in 1851. He then devotes himself to performing and teaching music.

> Every free negro or mulatto, whether male or female, and every colored person who may be manumitted or made free in any manner, shall forthwith exhibit to the mayor satisfactory evidence of his or her title to freedom, and shall enter into bond, with five good and sufficient freehold sureties, in the penalty of one thousand dollars, conditioned for his or her good and orderly conduct....
>
> It shall not be lawful for the mayor to grant a license for any purpose whatever to any free negro or mulatto, or to any person or persons acting as agents, or in behalf of any free negro or mulatto, except licenses to drive carts, drays, hackney carriages or wagons, and huckstering licenses.... Nor shall any free negro or mulatto, nor any person acting for any free negro or mulatto, keep any tavern, ordinary, shop, porter-cellar, refectory, or eating-house of any kind, for profit or gain.
>
> —*Ordinance of the District of Columbia*

Black parishioners leave the Foundry Methodist Church to establish the Asbury Methodist Church. At first, they rent the old Smothers school building on H and 14th Streets.

1837

March 4. Martin Van Buren is inaugurated as president.

Fanny Muriel Jackson is born to a slave mother in the District of Columbia. When she gets her degree from Oberlin in 1865, she becomes one of the first black women to graduate from a university. Jackson leads the development of the Institute for Colored Youth in Philadelphia from that time until 1902. In 1881 she marries Reverend Levi J. Coppin; in 1902 she travels with her husband to South Africa to do religious work.

1838

Some members of Israel Bethel A.M.E. Church, led by John F. Cook and Charles Stewart, decide to build a church closer to their residences. They buy a lot and begin to raise money to erect the Union Bethel Church.

May. An alleged slave insurrection is discovered in the District of Columbia. It was planned by both whites and blacks, and several conspirators are arrested.

Fearing that some scenes in the play *The Gladiator* might be incendiary, managers of the National Theatre notify the public that black patrons will not be allowed in the main seating gallery. But even after the run of this particular play ends, blacks remain confined to segregated seats in the balcony.

1839

William Williams's private jail to hold slaves destined to be sold operates on the block between 7th and 8th Streets SW. It opens sometime in the late 1830s and quickly assumes most of the city's slaveholding business. In 1839 the fee is 25 cents per day per slave. It is here that two years later, trader James H. Birch holds Solomon

Northup, a free black man visiting from New York who was drugged and kidnapped from Gadsby's Hotel.

[William Williams's] "Slavepen" of Washington is situated near to the Capitol of Washington, and may be seen from it, although that gray house, the prison-house of the innocent, hides itself behind leafy trees. . . . At the little grated door . . . we were met by the slave-keeper, a good-tempered, talkative, but evidently a coarse man, who seemed pleased to show us his power and authority. Miss J. wished to have a negro boy as a servant, and inquired if she could have such a one from this place. "No! Children were not allowed to go out from here. They were kept here for a short time to fatten, and after that were sent to the slavemarket down South, to be sold; no slave was allowed to be sold here for the present. There were now some very splendid articles for sale, which were to be sent down South. Among these there was a young girl who had been brought up in all respects 'like a lady'; she could embroider and play on the piano, and dress like a lady, and read, and write, and dance, and all this she had learned in the family which had brought her up, and who had treated her in her childhood as if she had been their own. But, however, her mind had grown too high for her; she had become proud, and now, to humble her, they had brought her here to be sold."

All this the talkative slave-keeper told us.

—Frederika Bremer,
The Homes of the New World: Impressions of America, 1853

Black members of the First Baptist Church formally establish the First Colored Baptist Church (the Nineteenth Street Baptist Church). Its first pastor is Reverend Sampson H. White. Founding members include William Bush, Eliza Bush, Lavinia Perry, and Emily and William Coke.

1840

July 21. Christian Abraham Fleetwood is born in Baltimore to free black parents, Charles W. Fleetwood and Ann Maria Jones. Fleetwood, who will one day win a congressional medal for bravery, becomes an extremely influential black man in the District of Columbia. He is first tutored through the generosity of a white couple and later receives his education (as did free Washingtonian

Brick churches were out of the question in those days. The frame meeting house of the Zion Wesley . . . on D Street between Second and Third southwest, was the pioneer of an advancing civilization. Brick yards, vegetable gardens, and old fields were its sole companions. There were not a half dozen houses between it and the Arsenal, a mile and a quarter to the south. . . . Ox carts were more numerous than horses.

—John W. Cromwell,
"The First Negro Churches in the District of Columbia," *Journal of Negro History,* 1922

Reverend Sampson White, a founder of the First Colored Baptist Church.

James H. Fleet) through the auspices of the Maryland Colonization Society. Fleetwood travels to Liberia and Sierra Leone but returns to the United States to attend the Ashmun Institute in Pennsylvania. He graduates in 1860 and never returns to Africa.

Henry Orr manumits his thirty-year-old daughter, Sarah.

1841

March 4. William Henry Harrison is inaugurated as president. When Harrison dies in office on April 4, a month after his inauguration, Vice President John Tyler becomes president.

April. Solomon Northup, a free black man from Saratoga Springs, New York, is drugged and kidnapped from Gadsby's Hotel. He is taken by steamer to New Orleans, where he is first bought by William Ford, a rural minister and plantation owner.

Solomon Northup in a Washington slave pen.

One morning, towards the latter part of the month of March, 1841, having at that time no particular business to engage my attention, I was walking about the village of Saratoga Springs, . . . two gentlemen of respectable appearance, both of whom were entirely unknown to me . . . proposed to engage my services for a short period. . . .

We . . . proceeded to Washington, at which place we arrived just at nightfall, the evening previous to the funeral of General Harrison, and stopped at Gadsby's Hotel, on Pennsylvania Avenue. . . .

The next day there was a great pageant in Washington. The roar of cannon and the tolling of bells filled the air, while many houses were shrouded with crepe, and the streets were black with people.

Towards evening, I began to experience most unpleasant sensations. I felt extremely ill. . . . About dark the same servant conducted me to the room I had occupied the previous night. . . . when consciousness returned I found myself alone, in utter darkness, and in chains. . . .

I was sitting upon a low bench, made of rough boards, and without coat or hat. I was hand cuffed. Around my ankles also were a pair of heavy fetters. One end of a chain was fastened to a large ring in the floor, the other to the fetters on my ankles. I tried in vain to stand upon my feet. . . .

A key rattled in the lock—a strong door swung back upon its hinges, admitting a flood of light, and two men entered and stood before me. One of them was a large, powerful man, forty years of age, perhaps, with dark, chestnut-colored hair, slightly interspersed with gray. His face was full, his complexion flush, his features grossly coarse, expressive of nothing but cruelty and cunning. He was about five feet ten inches high, of full habit, and, without prejudice, I must be allowed to say, was a man whose whole appearance was sinister and repugnant. His name was James H. Burch, as I learned afterwards—a well-known slave-dealer in Washington. . . .

The door, through which Burch and Radburn entered, led through a small passage, up a flight of steps into a yard, surrounded by a brick wall ten or twelve feet high, immediately in [the] rear of a building of the same width as itself. The yard extended rearward from the house about thirty feet. The building to which the yard was attached, was two stories high, fronting on one of the public streets of Washington [7th Street NW]. Its outside presented only the appearance of a quiet private residence.

—Solomon Northup,
Twelve Years a Slave: Narrative of Solomon Northup, 1859

November. Black Presbyterians form the Colored Presbyterian Church. Organized under Reverend John C. Smith, the members

Died, very suddenly, at the Bank of Washington, during the night of the 30th, or early on the morning of the 31st May William Costin, free colored man, aged 62 years. The deceased filled the situation of Porter to the bank during the long period of twenty-four years, and his service therein was characterized by the most unflinching integrity and remarkable punctuality in the performance of his various duties. Possessing the unlimited confidence of the president, directors, and officers of the bank, millions of money were allowed to pass through the hands of the deceased; . . . It is due to the deceased to say that his colored skin covered a benevolent heart. . . . "Honor and shame from no condition rise. Act well your part, there all the honor lies."

—Notice in the *National Intelligencer,*
June 1, 1842

hold service in John F. Cook's Union Seminary—the old Henry Smothers school building. A year later the church is formally organized as the Fifteenth Street Presbyterian Church. In 1843 Cook is elected as its first pastor and continues in that role until his death in 1855. Located at 15th Street between I and K Streets NW, the church attracts many members of the black elite, including Cook's aunt Alethia Tanner. Cook also opens a school in the basement of the Fifteenth Street Presbyterian Church.

1842

Winter. Solomon Northup is sold to John M. Tibeats. Northup writes: "I was now compelled to labor very hard. From earliest dawn until late at night, I was not allowed to be a moment idle. Notwithstanding which, Tibeats was never satisfied. He was continually cursing and complaining. He never spoke to me a kind word. I was his faithful slave, and earned him large wages every day, and yet I went to my cabin nightly, loaded with abuse and stinging epithets."

Solomon Northup in his plantation suit.

1843

John F. Cook is ordained as the first black Presbyterian minister in the District of Columbia.

Reverend Daniel Alexander Payne arrives to minister at Israel Bethel A.M.E. Church. He remains until 1845, when he is called to Baltimore. Reverend Payne begins traveling around the country as a missionary and also begins to write the history of the A.M.E. church. Payne returns to the District of Columbia many times.

Solomon Northup is once again sold—this time to Edwin Epps.

Master Epps was a roystering, blustering, noisy fellow, whose chief delight was in dancing with his "niggers," or lashing them about the yard with his long whip, just for the pleasure of hearing them screech and scream, as the great welts were planted on their backs. When sober, he was silent, reserved and cunning, not beating us indiscriminately, as in his drunken moments, but sending the end of his rawhide to some tender spot of a lagging slave, with a sly dexterity peculiar to himself. . . .

During the two years Epps remained on the plantation at Bayou Huff Power, he was in the habit, as often as once in a fortnight at least, of coming home intoxicated from Holmesville. . . . Then it behooved the slaves to be watchful and exceeding wary. The first one who came within reach felt the smart of his lash. Sometimes for hours he would keep them running in all directions, dodging around the corners of the cabins. Occasionally he would come upon one unawares, and if he succeeded in inflicting a fair, round blow, it was a feat that much delighted him. The younger children, and the aged, who had become inactive, suffered then. In the midst of, [sic] the confusion he would slily [sic] take his stand behind a cabin, waiting with raised whip, to dash it into the first black face that peeped cautiously around the corner.

At other times he would come home in a less brutal humor. Then there must be a merry-making. Then all must move to the measure of a tune. Then Master Epps must needs regale his melodious ears with the music of a fiddle. Then did he become buoyant, elastic, gaily "tripping the light fantastic toe" around the piazza and all thorough [sic] the house.

—Solomon Northup,
Twelve Years a Slave: Narrative of Solomon Northup, 1859

1844

Congress repeals the gag rule; petitions to abolish slavery in the District are again heard in the halls of Congress.

At age fifteen, Solomon G. Brown is hired to provide technical assistance to Samuel B. Morse in testing the viability of Morse's electromagnetic telegraph system. Morse had received $30,000 from Congress to run telegraph poles and wires from Baltimore to Washington, D.C. Brown helps to coordinate the erection of the poles, and on May 24, a message is successfully transmitted. Brown later takes a job with the Morse Telegraph Company, the company that Morse established to develop the telegraph system.

1845

March 4. James K. Polk is inaugurated as president.

1846

Alexandria and Alexandria County are retroceded to the state of Virginia, reducing the ten-mile District by more than one-third. Part of the reason for the return of the area is Alexandria's economic dependence on slave trading. Some residents are afraid that abolitionists might prevail upon Congress to end or restrict trading activities if they remain part of the nation's capital.

1847

January 7. The *National Era*, a weekly antislavery newspaper, begins under editor Dr. Gamaliel Bailey. The paper enjoys particularly good literary columns and poetry—John Greenleaf Whittier serves as associate editor. Harriet Beecher Stowe's *Uncle Tom's Cabin* first appears to the public as serialized fiction in the *Era*.

December 3. Frederick Douglass joins with William C. Nell and Martin Delaney to publish the first issue of the *North Star*.

1848

April. Paul Jennings, the slave of Daniel Webster, meets with Daniel Drayton in March to discuss his escape from slavery aboard the *Pearl*, a ship that Drayton had the authority to load with cargo.

July 24, 1844, District of Columbia, Washington County

On this 24th July before the subscriber a Justice of the Peace in and for said county and District aforesaid personally appears John S. Chauncey and made oath according to law that he knows Thomas Proctor a bright mulatto man Twenty six years old to be free and born of free parents in Charles County Maryland.

May 2, 1846, District of Columbia, Alexandria County

To all whom it may concern be it known that I Mary Eliason of Alexandria County in the District of Columbia for divers good causes and considerations . . . have released from slavery liberated manumitted and set free . . . my negro man named Jacob Dodson being of the age of twenty eight years.

—Both from Manumission and Emancipation Records, 1821–1862, Records of U.S. District Courts, Circuit Court of the District of Columbia

The first issue of the North Star, *December 3, 1847.*

They agree on the date of April 15 for his escape, and seventy-seven black people, most of them slaves but some free, accompanying their relatives, leave on the *Pearl* in a desperate bid for freedom. Many of the fugitives were slaves of prominent and wealthy Washingtonians. Among those stealing away are members of the Edmonson family, an enslaved family well known among blacks and whites in the city for its accomplishments and proud bearing. Jennings himself decided not to go.

The ship casts off in the middle of the night but soon makes for shore because of a dangerous storm. Whites in the city, enraged by the number of slaves involved, launch a massive manhunt and begin grilling members of the black community. Judson Diggs, a free black hack driver, reveals the escape plan, and a posse soon recaptures the entire group. There are competing stories about Diggs's motive for betrayal. One story holds that he was spurned by one of the Edmonson sisters; another says that he transported one of the escaping slaves to the *Pearl* and was not adequately paid for his services. There are threats of mob violence in the city, and almost all of the black people involved are jailed and subsequently sold south. Edmund Sayres, the captain of the *Pearl,* and Daniel Drayton are sent to jail until they receive a pardon from President Fillmore.

The story of the Edmonsons was recounted from family stories in the *Journal of Negro History* by John Paynter, a great-grandchild of one of the Edmonson children: "There were altogether fourteen sons and daughters of Paul and Amelia who passed as devoutly pious and respectable old folks. Paul was a free man who hired his time in the city. Amelia was a slave. Their little cabin, a few miles out of the city of Washington proper, was so neat and orderly that it was regarded as a model for masters and slaves alike for many

Mary and Emily Edmonson. The story
of their family is told in the Journal of
Negro History.

miles around. They were thus permitted to live together by the
owners of Amelia, who realized how much more valuable the children would be as a marketable group after some years of such care
and attention as the mother would be sure to bestow."

Paynter notes in the *Journal of Negro History* that the adventure
of the *Pearl* was initiated on the occasion of celebrating the 1848
French Revolution:

In Washington especially, the event was joyously acclaimed. Public meetings were held at which representatives of the people in both houses of Congress spoke encouragingly of the recent advance toward universal liberty. The city was regally adorned with flags and bunting and illumination and music everywhere. The White House was elaborately decorated in honor of the event and its general observance, scheduled for April 13. A procession of national dignitaries, local organizations, and the civic authorities, accompanied by several bands of music and throngs of citizens, made its way to the open square (now Lafayette Park) opposite the White House. . . . Here and there huddled unobtrusively in groups on the fringe of the crowd were numbers of slaves . . . who whispered among themselves. . . . Coincident with this celebration there had arrived at Washington the schooner *Pearl* with Daniel Drayton as super-cargo, Captain Sayres, owner, and a young man, Chester English, as sailor and cook. . . .

The Edmonson boys actively promoted the scheme. . . . The news was passed to . . . 77 persons, all of whom faithfully appeared and were safely stowed away between decks before midnight. The *Pearl* cast free from her moorings shortly after midnight Saturday and silently, with no sign of life aboard, save running lights fore and aft, crept out to mid-stream and made a course towards the lower Potomac. The condition that obtained on Sunday morning after the discovery of the absence of so many slaves from their usual duties may be accurately described as approaching a panic. . . . Judson Diggs, one of their own people, a man who in all reason might have been expected to sympathize with their effort, took upon himself the role of Judas. Judson was a drayman and had hauled some packages to the wharf for one of the slaves, who was without funds to pay the charge, and although he was solemnly promised that the money should be sent him, he proceeded at once to wreak vengeance through a betrayal of the entire party.

Once recaptured, the entire party of slaves was marched back to the city amid taunting crowds: "The wharves were alive with an eager and excited throng all intent upon a view of the miserable folks who had been guilty of so ungrateful an effort. So disorderly was the mob that the debarkation was for some time delayed. This was finally accomplished through the strenuous efforts of the entire constabulary of the city." After arrest, most of the captives, including the Edmonson children, were bought by slave dealers to be sold south. The Edmonson children were purchased for $4,500 by Bruin and Hill slave dealers and sent to the New Orleans markets.

> In due course they arrived at New Orleans and were immediately initiated into the horrors of a Georgia pen. The girls were required to spend much time in the show room, where purchasers came to examine them carefully with a view to buying them. . . . Here also the boys had their hair closely cropped and their clothes, which were of good material, exchanged for suits of blue-jeans. Appearing thus, they were daily exhibited on the porch for sale.

After their father campaigned extensively for help throughout Washington, D.C., he was unable to raise sufficient money to purchase his children and went to New York to seek funds from antislavery groups. No one would help him, save for Reverend Henry Ward Beecher, who found the father weeping in despair on his front doorstep. Beecher was able to raise all of the money necessary to purchase the children from their slave pen in New Orleans.

> A day or two later, while looking from their window, they caught sight of their father and ran into his arms shouting and crying. . . . their free papers [were] signed and the money paid over. [The slave dealer] Bruin too, . . . was pleased with the joy and happiness in evidence on every hand and upon bidding the girls good-bye gave each a five dollar piece. . . .
>
> Upon their arrival at Washington they were taken in a carriage to their sister's home, whence the news of their deliverance seemed to have penetrated to every corner of the neighborhood with the result that it was far into the night before the last greetings and congratulations had been received and they were per-

mitted, in the seclusion of the family circle, to kneel with their parents in prayer and thanksgiving.

Former members of the Nineteenth Street Baptist Church establish the Second Baptist Church; Reverend H. H. Butler is the founding minister.

Union Wesley A.M.E. Zion Church is established by Bishop J. J. Clinton. The church, built despite much hardship by its founding members, is burned down by arsonists. John W. Cromwell, in his article "The First Negro Churches in the District of Columbia," published in the *Journal of Negro History* (1922), recalls:

> [T]hey bought the lot where this church now stands and built thereon a frame chapel which was contemptuously called the Horseshoe Church. After they had been there but a short time, there was a funeral at the chapel one day. Across from the chapel the Hibernian fire company was stationed. While the funeral services were being held in the chapel, two of these firemen came across the street and while one of them got inside of the hearse the other got up on the driver's seat and drove all around the streets, while the people were out looking for the hearse. When they came back, the one who was inside got out and said that he was Lazarus risen from the dead. This act so inflamed some of the white gentlemen that they had the firemen arrested and prosecuted. These two impious gentlemen became so indignant because of their arrest that they set fire to the chapel and burned it to the ground. These communicants, being homeless again, went back to the house of William Beckett on L Street and commenced to rebuild. This time they succeeded in erecting a brick building.

1849

March 4. Zachary Taylor is inaugurated as president. After Taylor's death on July 9, 1850, Vice President Millard Fillmore becomes president.

Two members of the Asbury Methodist Episcopal Church, John Brent and John Ingram, and seven other blacks establish John Wesley A.M.E. Zion Church. At first, the "Little Society of Nine" meets in John Brent's house at 1800 L Street NW. Founding members later purchase a lot on Connecticut Avenue and erect a frame church building in 1851.

1850

The Compromise of 1850 allows Congress to divide the new territories in the southwest into slaveholding and nonslaveholding territories. As part of the deal, the slave trade is finally outlawed in the District of Columbia.

The Fugitive Slave Act is passed. This law allows slaveowners to pursue escaping slaves into states that had outlawed slavery and effectively forces legal authorities in those states to hand over black persons accused of being escaping slaves to their pursuers. The law provides no opportunity for blacks who were falsely accused to defend themselves upon their arrest but instead mandates their return to the South. Former slaves who escaped years ago and settled in northern cities are suddenly vulnerable to former masters who can appear at any time with a court order for their arrest and can compel their return to slavery. From this date onward, escaped slaves who come to Washington—people like Richard John Holmes, great-grandfather of Congresswoman Eleanor Holmes Norton, who escaped from Virginia in the 1850s—will have to depend on a network of free blacks and sympathetic whites to avoid the slavecatchers.

New black codes are enacted for the District. The bond for free blacks is reduced to $50, and free blacks immigrating to the city have just five days to register or face arrest and fines. Blacks are prohibited from holding meetings without prior permission.

Solomon Northup continues to plot his escape from a plantation in the swamplands of Louisiana. He even tries to get a letter to his family in New York but is betrayed by the white man whom he entrusts to mail it.

July 21, 1850
I have been today to a Methodist church of free negroes. . . . The theme of the preacher was a common one—conversion and amendment, or death and damnation. But when he spoke of different failings and sins, his descriptions were as graphic as his gestures. When he spoke about the sins of the tongue, he dragged this "unruly member" out of his mouth, and shook it between his fingers very energetically. On his admonishing his audience to bid farewell to the devil, and turn away from him (after he had vehemently proclaimed the damnation which the Evil One would drag them into), his expressions took such a strong and powerful hold of his hearers, that the whole assembly was like a tempestuous sea. One heard only the cry, "Yes, yes!" "Farewell! Forever!" "Yes, Amen!" "Nevermind!" "Go along!" "Oh God!" "Farewell!" "Amen, amen!" &c.

After that . . . the preacher announced that a slave, a member of the congregation, was about to be sold "down South," and thus to be far separated from his wife and child, if sufficient money could not be raised in Washington to furnish the sum which the master of the slave demanded for him. . . . A pewter plate was set upon a stool in the church, and one silver piece after another rang joyfully upon it.
—Frederika Bremer,
The Homes of the New World: Impressions of America, 1853

My great object always was to invent means of getting a letter secretly into the post-office, directed to some of my friends or family at the North. The difficulty of such an achievement cannot be comprehended by one unacquainted with the severe restrictions imposed upon me. In the first place, I was deprived of pen, ink, and paper. In the second place, a slave cannot leave his plantation without a pass, nor will a post-master mail a letter for one without written instructions from his owner. I was in slavery nine years, and always watchful and on the alert, before I met with the good fortune of obtaining a sheet of paper.

While [his master] Epps was in New-Orleans, one winter, disposing of his cotton, the mistress sent me to Holmesville, with an order for several articles, and among the rest a quantity of foolscap [writing paper]. I appropriated a sheet, concealing it in the cabin, under the board on which I slept.

After various experiments I succeeded in making ink, by boiling white maple bark, and with a feather plucked from the wing of a duck, manufactured a pen. When all were asleep in the cabin, by the light of the coals, lying upon my plank couch, I managed to complete a somewhat lengthy epistle. . . .

That night, while broiling my bacon, Epps entered the cabin with his rawhide in his hand.

"Well, boy," said he, "I understand I've got a larned nigger, that writes letters, and tries to get white fellows to mail 'em.

Wonder if you know who he is?"

–Solomon Northup,
Twelve Years a Slave: Narrative of Solomon Northup, 1859

Allen A.M.E. Chapel is founded in the community of Good Hope in Washington, D.C. It becomes the center of a group of black small landholders in the area.

December 3. Myrtilla Miner (1815–1866), a white teacher from Brookfield, New York, who recently taught in Mississippi, begins offering instruction at her Colored Girls School, also known as the Miner School. Miner's first classes are held in a rented room on 11th Street near New York Avenue, in the house of a black man, Edward C. Younger. Miner later recalls that "The school opened with 6 pupils in December 1851, but in two months increased to 40." By that time, Miner has moved to a building on F Street between 18th and 19th Streets, in the house of another black family. One month later, she is forced to move again, due to threats of arson. Although many whites, such as future District mayor Sayles J. Bowen and

Myrtilla Miner, founder of the Colored Girls School.

Parents often come saying, "will you take my daughter into your school? I cannot read even the Bible, but I want her taught, so that she can read it to me."

It has often been necessary to reply "there is no more room. I cannot find space for another scholar at present, and you must wait awhile." "But," they urge, "my daughter is just now the age to be in school, and soon she must be at work to earn her living, and help her parents educate the other children." One father came, bringing a fine looking child, about nine years old; fairer than many who claim pure Anglo-Saxon origin, and presented her to me, saying, "will you educate my daughter? I have so many children I can hardly feed and clothe them, much less give them learning, but I want this one taught; and if you will educate her you may have her." The answer was, "yes, I will teach her, if you will not prevent her being a teacher or a missionary. . . ."

From the fact that the school was visited during the first four months of 1853 by more than one hundred persons, from various parts of the country, and by some many times, we hope a healthful influence may be widely disseminated and prove beneficial to other locations beside Washington.

—Letter from Myrtilla Miner, 1854

writer Harriet Beecher Stowe, support her efforts and contribute funds for the school's upkeep, Miner is the victim of ongoing harassment for the next few years, and arson remains a constant threat. As a result, the Miner School is forced to relocate several times.

1852

February. Solomon G. Brown begins working at the Smithsonian Institution in the Transportation Department. He becomes an all-around museum assistant and an essential part of behind-the-scenes operations. By 1869 he is the institution's first black registrar. He also does scientific and educational illustrations for the Smithsonian. In the District, Brown is an active and well-known supporter of social uplift groups and relief efforts, as well as a popular public speaker at African American gatherings, lecturing on various subjects at churches, schools, and other organizations.

June. Solomon Northup again makes plans to escape.

In the month of June, 1852, . . . Mr. Avery, a carpenter of Bayou Rouge, commenced the erection of a house for Master Epps. . . . Having had some experience under Tibeats as a carpenter, I was taken from the field altogether, on the arrival of Avery and his hands.

Among them was one to whom I owe an immeasurable debt of gratitude. Only for him, in all probability I should have ended my days in slavery. He was my deliverer a man whose true heart overflowed with noble and generous emotions. To the last moment of my existence I shall remember him with feelings of thankfulness. His name was Bass, and at that time he resided in Marksville. . . .

At the appointed hour we met on the bayou bank, and creeping among the high weeds, I lighted the candle, while he drew forth pencil and paper and prepared for business. I gave him the names of William Perry, Cephas Parker and Judge Marvin, all of Saratoga Springs, Saratoga county, New-York. I had been employed by the latter in the United States Hotel, and had transacted business with the former to a considerable extent, and trusted that at least one of them would be still living at that place.

—Solomon Northup, on another attempt to escape,
Twelve Years a Slave: Narrative of Solomon Northup, 1859

In a commemorative pamphlet published on her school's second anniversary, Myrtilla Miner makes this promise: "We can give no pledge for the future, but the present promise is, that when these girls are mature, many of them will become teachers, and by their refinement and good morals exert such an influence upon their associates, as shall relieve the world of much degradation and consequent misery.

"Having been a teacher of white children for twenty years, I may be allowed an opinion respecting the capacity of these colored children, and I do unequivocally assert, that I find no difference of native talent, where similar advantages are enjoyed, between Anglo-Saxons and Africo-Americans."

1853

January. Solomon Northup finally wins his freedom. He arrives back in Washington on January 17, 1853, twelve years after he was kidnapped and sold into slavery. James H. Birch, the slave trader, is arrested for kidnapping.

Monday morning, the third of January, 1853, we were in the field betimes. It was a raw, cold morning, such as is unusual in that region. I was in advance, Uncle Abram next to me, behind him Bob, Patsey and Wiley, with our cotton-bags about our necks. Epps happened (a rare thing, indeed,) to come out that morning without his whip. He swore, in a manner that would shame a pirate, that we were doing nothing. Bob ventured to say that his fingers were so numb with cold he couldn't pick fast.

Epps cursed himself for not having brought his rawhide, and declared that when he came out again he would warm us well; yes, he would make us all hotter than that fiery realm in which I am sometimes compelled to believe he will himself eventually reside.

With these fervent expressions, he left us. When out of hearing, we commenced talking to each other, saying how hard it was to be compelled to keep up our tasks with numb fingers; how unreasonable master was, and speaking of him generally in no flattering terms. Our conversation was interrupted by a carriage passing rapidly towards the house. Looking up, we saw two men approaching us through the cotton-field. . . .

I seized my old acquaintance by both hands. I could not speak. I could not refrain from tears.

"Sol," he said at length, "I'm glad to see you."

I essayed to make some answer, but emotion choked all utterance, and I was silent.

—Solomon Northup, on the day he wins his freedom,
Twelve Years a Slave: Narrative of Solomon Northup, 1853

Lectures upon scientific and literary subjects were given by professional and literary gentlemen [at the Miner School], who were friends to the cause. The spacious grounds afforded to each pupil an ample space for a flower bed, which she [Miner] was enjoined to cultivate with her own hands and to thoroughly study. And an excellent library, a collection of paintings and engravings, the leading magazines and choice newspapers, were gathered and secured for the humble home of learning. . . . It was her custom to gather in her vacations and journeys not only money, but everything else that would be of use in her school, and in this way she not only collected books, but maps, globes, philosophical and chemical and mathematical apparatus, and a great variety of things to aid in her instruction in illustrating all branches of knowledge.

—Moses Goodwin,
History of Schools for the Colored Population in the District of Columbia,
1871

March 4. Franklin Pierce is inaugurated as president.

March. Myrtilla Miner opens an expanded high school near N Street and New Hampshire Avenue NW, charging $15 per school year. The school is housed in a small wooden building (two stories, 25-by-35 feet) on a large lot of three acres, beautifully landscaped with flower beds and fruit trees. The dormitory is in the attic of the building, and Miss Miner lives there along with her students. As many as sixty students are in residence, even though the school is

---

If I do not entirely mistake the opinion which the citizens of this District will entertain of the character and fatal consequences of this enterprise, they will almost universally, without distinction of party or class emphatically protest against it, and will confidently expect that the advocates of this measure will promptly abandon it, as an unjust and dangerous interference with the interests and feelings of a separate and independent community.

. . . The standard of education which is proposed is far beyond the primary branches, and will doubtless from time to time be advanced. Is it, then, just to ourselves, or humane to the colored population, for us to permit a degree of instruction so far beyond their political and social condition, and which must continue to exist in this as in every other slaveholding community? With this superior education there will come no removal of the present disabilities, no new sources of employment equal to their mental culture; and hence there will be a restless population, less disposed than ever to fill that position in society which is allotted to them.

. . . [I]n considering this view of the subject, we cannot forget the events which disturbed the peace of our country some few years since, consequent upon the act of Drayton and Sayres; . . .

And still further, we cannot tolerate an influence in our midst which will not only constantly disturb the repose and prosperity of our own community and of the country, but may even rend asunder the "Union itself." Such a protest it is the duty of our corporate authorities to make. Its beneficent effect may be to persuade the supporters of this scheme to abandon its further prosecution; but, if otherwise, the responsibility will be with those who by their own wanton acts of aggression make resistance a necessity and submission an impossibility.

—Former mayor Walter Lenox, in the *National Intelligencer,*
opposing the Myrtilla Miner school for free blacks

at full capacity with forty students. By 1858 the library contains about 1,500 books, 12 newspapers, and 26 magazines. Instruction includes history, drawing, philosophy, geography, literature, penmanship, arithmetic, and astronomy. Among the supporters of the school are S. J. Bowen, who will later be elected mayor of the District of Columbia, and Johns Hopkins of Baltimore.

Anthony Bowen establishes the YMCA for colored men. In 1912 it is relocated to 1816 12th Street NW, then moved to the True Reformer's Hall, a building designed by black architect William Sidney Pittman. The 12th St. Branch is the first YMCA established for blacks in the country. In 1972 the 12th Street YMCA is renamed the Anthony Bowen YMCA, in honor of its founder.

Reverend Anthony Bowen. He establishes the first YMCA for black men.

1854

William Calvin Chase is born to free black parents in Washington. He attends school at the Fifteenth Street Presbyterian Church.

1855

March 21. John F. Cook dies. His sons, John F. Cook Jr. and George F. T. Cook, leave their studies at Oberlin University to return to Washington, D.C., and run their father's school until 1867, when it finally closes.

1856

May. Senator Charles Sumner is assaulted with a cane as a result of his verbal attacks upon pro-slavery forces in Kansas and slavery supporters in the U.S. Congress. Sumner saves some particularly acerbic criticism for Senator Andrew Butler. While Sumner is sitting in the Senate chamber a short time later, Preston Brooks, Butler's nephew, begins to beat him with a cane.

Anthony Bowen, along with several other blacks, establishes the E Street Mission, a small church on E Street between 9th and 10th Streets in southwest Washington, D.C., in a house owned by Bowen. After moving to 8th Street SW, the church changes its name to St. Paul and joins the A.M.E. conference. The church is known as a safe haven for escaped slaves. Bowen also continues to serve as a conductor on the Underground Railroad, secretly meeting boats at the 6th Street Wharf and arranging refuge for escaping

While most of the District's Negroes earned their living as unskilled laborers or servants, others sought their livelihood by producing and selling a variety of commodities such as crabs, oysters, strawberries, garden products, nets, baskets, and firewood. They marketed their wares either at one of the District's public markets or peddled them in carts about the street.

—Dorothy Provine,
"The Economic Position of Free Blacks in the District of Columbia, 1800–1860,"
Journal of Negro History

Black woman selling oysters near the Navy Yard, 1870–1880s, by J. H. Cocks.

slaves. The District of Columbia is a favorite destination for blacks escaping from slavery in Virginia. From here, they are often sent to Pennsylvania and north to Canada, but some escaped slaves seek to remain in Washington, trusting abolitionists and members of the city's black community to shield them from slavecatchers.

1857

March 4. James Buchanan is inaugurated as president.

March 5. The U.S. Supreme Court's Dred Scott v. Sanford *decision denies full citizenship to African Americans. The legal case involves Dred Scott, a slave who with his master had resided in Illinois and in Missouri. He argued that his residence in a free state and in the free territory of Missouri made him a free man.*

1858

Free blacks establish St. Augustine's Catholic Church on 15th Street NW, near M Street. They remain at this site until 1961, when the church moves to the corner of 15th and V Streets NW.

1859

January. Frederick Douglass puts out the first issue of *Douglass' Monthly*.

October 17. John Brown and a small band of men stage a raid at Harpers Ferry.

ARRIVAL AT WASHINGTON.

Black coachmen meeting white arrivals, from Harper's Weekly, *April 18, 1858.*

For pro-slavery southerners, Harpers Ferry is a warning, a fore-shadowing of the Civil War and the coming struggle over slavery.

The *Richmond Enquirer* voices its concern in an editorial shortly after the incident: "The Southern people have heretofore disregarded the ravings of Northern fanatics, because they believed such madness to be merely a pecuniary speculation; but the amount of money with which these wretches at Harpers Ferry were supplied shows that the Northern fanatics mean more than words, and are determined to wage with men and money the 'irrepressible conflict' to the bitter end. . . . Large purchases of percussion caps, with orders for more from New York, were made last week in that city. Whence came this money?"

October 19. John Brown and almost all of his men are overcome by armed soldiers and captured. Brown is sentenced to death and is executed by hanging on December 2.

1860

Two of the best-known and most well-to-do African American businessmen in the city are feed dealers: Alfred Lee and Alfred Jones. Alfred Lee owns more than $12,000 worth of real estate, including a stylish home on H Street NW; by the time of his death in 1893, he has amassed over $250,000. Alfred Jones owns $6,000 in real estate and $10,000 in personal property.

Elizabeth Keckley arrives in Washington after purchasing her freedom in St. Louis. She begins working as a seamstress for Senator Jefferson Davis's wife and other congressmen's wives. Eventually, her customers also include Mary Todd Lincoln.

James Wormley, home from his travels in Mississippi and in the California gold mines, opens a catering business on I Street and 15th Street NW in the mid-1860s. His wife, Anna, opens a candy shop next door. At this time, catering in the District of Columbia involves the preparation and the home delivery of meals for customers, often congressmen or businessmen who are temporary residents. Usually, two hot meals a day are provided by the caterer.

Spring. The Miner school for colored girls is set afire. Moses Goodwin, in *History of Schools for the Colored Population in the District of Columbia*, remembers it this way: "Miss Miner was asleep in the

At the Gallows

Brown descended the cart and mounted the platform with the same imperturbable, wooden composure which had distinguished him at every step of his progress. He was dressed in a well worn suit of black cassimere. . . . The sheriff and jailor mounted the platform with Brown, and quickly adjusted the white cap over his head and the rope round his neck, and had tied his feet securely. Then occurred another remarkable exhibition of nerve by Brown. He was requested to take his place on the drop (trap door), "I cannot find it blindfold; guide me to it," he answered in the same tone of voice as if asking for a chair. He was placed in position, and then there was an unpleasant pause of some eighteen minutes while some companies at a distance were brought up. The sheriff made some explanation to the prisoner about the delay. "I don't care," he replied, "only don't keep me waiting unnecessarily."

—The *Evening Star*,
December 3, 1859

The population of free blacks in the District of Columbia is 11,131; there are 3,185 slaves. Free blacks outnumber slaves by almost four to one.

The top ten occupations for African Americans in the District of Columbia are washerwoman (1,154), domestic servant (1,517), laborer (887), waiter (286), cook (225), seamstress (204), wagoner (118), hack or coach driver (113), nurse (68), and brickmaker (64).

St. Augustine Catholic Church,
c. 1900.

Many of the poorer blacks . . . lived along Washington's alleys bearing such names as Temperance Hall, Willow Tree, Goat Alley, and Tin Cup Alley. Their dwellings were either flimsy frame shacks or converted carriage houses and horse stables behind the more respectable homes of the whites. The rooms were tiny, with the first floor built level with the ground. Blacks were packed indiscriminately in these slums with poor whites, mainly Irish immigrants.

—Dorothy Provine,
"The Economic Position of the Free Blacks in the District of Columbia, 1800–1860," *Journal of Negro History*

second story alone, in the night time, but the smell of the smoke awakened her in time to save the building and herself from the flames, which were extinguished. The school girls, also, were constantly at the mercy of coarse and insulting boys along the streets, who would often gather in gangs before the gate to pursue and terrify these inoffensive children, who were striving to gather wisdom and understanding in their little sanctuary."

The American Colonization Society establishes its headquarters in an impressive new building erected on Pennsylvania Avenue, off 4th Street.

December 20. South Carolina secedes from the Union.

1861
February. The Confederate States of America are formed. Six more southern states—Mississippi, Florida, Alabama, Georgia, Louisiana, and Texas—declare their secession from the Union.

March 4. Abraham Lincoln is inaugurated as president. Vice President Hannibal Hamlin is accused of being part black by political opponents during the election campaign because of his dark coloring and his stance as an abolitionist.

March 16. Abraham Lincoln tries to obtain employment for William Johnson, a black man who accompanied him from his home in Springfield, Illinois, to the District of Columbia. Lincoln had originally intended for Johnson to work in a domestic capacity in the White House, but the other servants would not accept the newcomer. Lincoln writes to several acquaintances in Washington on behalf of Johnson:

> Executive Mansion, March 16, 1861
> Hon. Gideon Welles:
> Dear Sir:
> The bearer, (William) is a servant who has been with me for some time and in whom I have confidence as to his integrity and faithfulness. He wishes to enter your service. The difference of color between him and the other servants is the cause of our separation. If you can give him employment you will confer a favour on
>
> > Yours truly,
> > A. Lincoln

Nine-year-old Daniel A. Murray arrives in Washington, D.C. Ten years later he will get his first job with the Library of Congress. Murray becomes one of the most influential bibliographers of African American literature in the country.

April 12. Confederates fire on Fort Sumter in the harbor of Charleston, South Carolina.

April 17. Virginia joins the Confederacy. Virginia's secession from the Union leaves the District vulnerable. Northern states respond to the call for volunteers, but the border states refuse. Mobs in Baltimore throw stones and shoot at trains carrying troops from Massachusetts to the capital. Four soldiers are killed in the melee, and thirty are injured. In Maryland, railroad tracks are vandalized, and there is serious threat of the state seceding, thus surrounding the capital with enemy forces. For six days the capital is unable to receive reinforcements while telegraph lines are vandalized, disrupting communications with the outside world. At last, the 7th New York Regiment arrives.

April 23. Jacob Dodson, a free black Washingtonian who went on exploratory and mapping expeditions with John C. Frémont, sends the following letter to the secretary of war:

> Sir:
>
> I desire to inform you that I know of some three hundred of reliable colored free citizens of this City, who desire to enter the service for the defence of the City.
>
> I have been three times across the Rocky Mountains in the service of the Country with Fremont and others.
>
> I can be found about the Senate Chambers, as I have been employed about the premises for some years.

April 29. Jacob Dodson receives a reply from Secretary of War Simon Cameron, refusing the help of black men in the District.

Union Army troops are billeted on the grounds of the Capitol, where black vendors find them a lucrative source of customers for produce, prepared foods, and other goods. By the end of spring, over 50,000 troops are encamped around the city and outside its limits.

Even after most of the troops are deployed, the wartime economy drives up the cost of living in the city, hurting most blacks, who are mainly domestic workers, service workers, and laborers.

May 23. Three Virginia men held in slavery in that state escape and make their way to Fort Monroe, where they request asylum. This creates a legal dilemma for commanding officer General Ben Butler.

June. General Ben Butler, on his own initiative, declares slaves escaping into the ranks of the Union Army to be contraband and refuses to return them to slavery. Word of freedom so close by gets out to surrounding communities of slaves, and they pour into Fort Monroe, Virginia, creating another dilemma for the Union Army, for Lincoln and his Cabinet, and for Congress.

July. Large numbers of ex-slaves from Virginia and Maryland come to the District to escape bondage. Congress and military officials soon clash with local government officials over how to handle the situation. District marshal Ward H. Lamon pursues a policy of returning escaped slaves to their owners, and soon the city jail is full. Abolitionists and black leaders are outraged, and Lincoln is forced to intervene. He orders the marshal to stop arresting newly arriving blacks.

August 6. Congress passes a Confiscation Act that provides for the seizure of all goods and assets—including slaves—that were used to promote the Confederate rebellion.

August 30. John C. Frémont, commander of Union forces in the West, imposes martial law in Missouri and declares all slaves free. Northern black communities and abolitionist leaders celebrate Fremont's order, and sympathetic newspapers spread the word that freedom seems at hand. President Lincoln, however, tells Fremont to rescind his order.

FROM FREEDOM TO JIM CROW

1862–1917

Overleaf:

Blacks celebrate the abolition of slavery in the District of Columbia, 1866.

Portraits: left, *Nannie Helen Burroughs;* right, *Alain Locke.*

ACKNOWLEDGING THAT SLAVERY WAS THE UNDERLYING CAUSE OF THE Civil War, African Americans quickly seized opportunities that the war provided. Black leaders like Frederick Douglass hoped that by proving their loyalty and value to the Union as fighting men, blacks could gain support in ending slavery and the harsher aspects of racial subjugation. Black abolitionists rallied to support the Union and were among the most vocal advocates for recruitment of black men into the military.

Rallying the Union

In the District of Columbia, the redoubtable John F. Cook, Reverend Henry McNeal Turner, and Anthony Bowen recruited the U.S. Colored Forces. Over 3,500 black men from Washington, D.C., ended up serving, including Christian A. Fleetwood, who received a Congressional Medal of Honor for his heroism in battle.

As soon as hostilities began, masses of escaped slaves—labeled contraband—crossed to Union lines. Escaping from slaveholders in the upper South, most migrated to the District of Columbia by way of Virginia and Maryland. Until Congress stepped in, many were captured and forced back into slavery.

In her memoir, *Behind the Scenes, or, Thirty Years a Slave, and Four Years in the White House*, Elizabeth Keckley, who operated a successful dressmaking business that served prominent Washington women (including, ironically, the wives of both Abraham Lincoln and Jefferson Davis), writes that "In the summer of 1862, freedmen began to flock into Washington from Maryland and Virginia. They came with a great hope in their heart and with all their worldly goods on their backs. Fresh from the bonds of slavery, fresh from the benighted regions of the plantation, they came to the Capitol looking for liberty, and many of them not knowing it when they found it." Keckley and other local blacks worked tirelessly to provide shelter, food, and clothing. Most of the blacks arriving in the District were poorly prepared to survive without some kind of assistance, and means of livelihood for the migrants—who were still considered contraband—were hard to come by.

The Triumph Over Slavery

On April 16, 1862, President Lincoln signed into law a bill outlawing slavery in the District of Columbia. The bill also provided funds to compensate slaveowners being deprived of their property. For black Washingtonians, it was a glorious moment, representing the triumph of a long and hard-fought battle against overwhelming odds to end slavery in the nation's capital. It also, they believed, foretold the future, one in which—perhaps—the last political and economic restraints could be removed from the city's black residents. Not only in the District of Columbia, but all around the country, the day seemed to herald the possibilities of a new era.

Community Life

The 1860s also saw the beginning of the some of the District's earliest black neighborhoods: Murder Bay (the present site of Federal Triangle); Southern Anacostia; Barry's Farm; Duff Green's Row (1st Street SE, between East Capitol and A Street). While black communities east of the river and some areas in southeast and northwest D.C. were beautiful, with well-appointed homes, conditions in other sites were horrible, often swampy and malarial, with no sewage systems. Sometimes there were outbreaks of dysentery due to the contaminated water supply. Alleys and private land behind residences were broken up, and cheap housing—hovels, really— was erected to rent to the freedmen and their families. The federal government also provided housing for the ex-slaves in tents and wooden barracks in settlements like Camp Barker, 11th Street near the Navy Yard, and on Analostan Island.

John Washington, a historian who chronicled black Washington community life in the 1800s and early 1900s, notes in *They Knew Lincoln* that "The contrabands often lived in the old wooden barracks constructed for the soldiers. When the soldiers would change from these places, or the army would move away, the colored people would move in."

Day by day, as the ex-slaves poured into the city, their housing and sanitary conditions became more desperate. Still the contrabands kept coming. They could be seen on foot, in buggies, and in farm wagons traveling toward Washington. By April 1863 there were about 10,000 contrabands in the city. Black and white churches held benefits, and black relief societies, such as the Contraband Relief Society—organized by Elizabeth Keckley—were formed to help this new population. The Israel A.M.E. and Union Bethel Churches were especially notable in their efforts to help the ex-slaves arriving in the city.

Increased Opportunities

On a national level, Reconstruction seemed to imply that the goals blacks had fought for were within reach: an end to racial violence; an opening of economic opportunities that had hitherto been closed to blacks; an absolute freedom of movement and control over one's own labor; the ability to elect black men to political office and to have effective political representation; and the ability to build schools and provide education for black children and adults. In the District of Columbia, organizing the black community to provide resources for masses of arriving ex-slaves spurred the development of a strong infrastructure for existing black institutions.

As the number of black people in the city grew, hostility increased on the part of certain white Washingtonians. Congressmen, residents, and local officials who were opposed to black political power devised several plans in an unsuccessful effort to thwart black suffrage. But in December 1866, Congress mustered enough votes to override a presidential veto and to approve black male suffrage in the District of Columbia, and in June 1868 blacks were elected to citywide positions for the first time.

In 1869 seven blacks were elected to the City Council; the following year six were elected. In 1871 Congress established a territorial government with a governor, an eleven-member Governor's Council appointed by the president, an elected Board of Education, and an elected twenty-two-member House of Delegates. President Grant appointed Frederick Douglass, along with two other black men, to the Council, and two black men were elected to the House of Delegates. But by 1874 the experiment with suffrage was over. Congress abolished the territorial government and replaced it with three commissioners appointed by the president.

According to custom, certain appointed positions traditionally went to black men: marshall of the District, District recorder of deeds, and register of the treasury were all held by prominent African Americans. Later these positions included assistant district attorney for the District, auditor of the Navy, collector of Customs, and assistant U.S. attorney general. The federal government became a prized source of employment.

The Elite Society

Seven years after the Emancipation Proclamation, and for the first time in U.S. history, African Americans occupied seats in Congress. In 1870 Hiram Revels was elected to the U.S. Senate by the Mississippi legislature, the first African American to sit in Congress. During the Reconstruction era, twenty black men were elected to the House of Representatives, and one black man was elected to the Senate. They and their wives added to the vibrant black social life in the nation's capital.

The marriage of Senator Blanche K. Bruce and Josephine Wilson, the daughter of a socially prominent family from Cleveland, Ohio, created new excitement in elite black society in the District. Williard Gatewood, who has written extensively on the black elite, noted their impact in *Aristocrats of Color: The Black Elite, 1880–1920*: "The Bruces returned to Washington in time for the reconvening of Congress late in 1878. The senator had leased a large house at 909 M Street, but because it was undergoing extensive renovation they temporarily took up residence near Howard University in the home of

Virginia-born John Mercer Langston, who was in Haiti serving as United States minister. The Langston home, a fourteen-room house on 4th and Bryant Streets NW, was known as Hillside Cottage. It had for some years been the center of social life for Washington's black elite. Here Caroline Wall Langston had presided over receptions, teas, musicales, and literary gatherings as the grand lady of black society. The new mistress of Hillside Cottage, who was no less skilled in the art of entertaining, continued that tradition."

In the District, public funding was available for the freedmen's schools and for a new public high school that was the apex of black secondary education for the entire nation. Howard University and Freedmen's Hospital also attracted the nation's brightest and most creative black intellectuals and professionals. Charles Douglass, one of Frederick Douglass's sons, bought a parcel of beachfront land along Chesapeake Bay and developed a thriving vacation community in Highland Beach, Maryland. The future seemed auspicious for the black middle class and elite in the District of Columbia.

The elite in Washington's black community were professionals—doctors such as Charles B. Purvis; professors of higher education like Richard Greener; dentists; businessmen like James Wormley, proprietor of one of the best hotels in the city; lawyers and statesmen like John Mercer Langston; men who held federal appointments, such as Frederick Douglass or Judge Robert Herberton Terrell; and ministers like Reverend J. Sella Martin and Daniel Payne. The *Washington Bee* labeled the members of this aristocratic group the black "Four Hundred." Some elite black women also worked in professional fields—Sara Fleetwood was a nurse at Freedmen's Hospital; Mary Church Terrell taught, and later she served on the Board of Education. Many occupied their time with work in their churches, contraband relief during the Civil War, and social work among the city's indigent black communities and in institutions such as the Home for Destitute Colored Women and Children.

The Black Middle Class

There was also an active and highly educated middle class—clerks in federal agencies, teachers, business men and women. This group formed the backbone of black self-help efforts.

In the late nineteenth and early twentieth centuries, black middle-class communities developed in places like Strivers' Row—the area along U Street—Shaw, Georgetown, and Hillsdale. Many black leaders lived in the row houses on Swann Street. In *The Secret City: A History of Race Relations in the Nation's Capital,* the historian Constance Green writes about the difficulties that black families had in finding decent housing: "Rising rentals hastened the exodus of Negro householders who in the seventies had lived along 16th Street a few blocks above Lafayette Square and out beyond Scott Circle. As the real estate boom in northwest Washington gained momentum, colored people moved farther from the center of the city. Whether sheer economics or, as rumor had it, combinations of real estate agents kept respectable Negroes from moving into desirable localities, the result was the same. It did not mean that clear-cut solid black belts arose outside of which Negroes could not find housing; some intermixing of white and Negro dwellings continued down into the 1930s. But by 1900 the barrier of caste, seemingly collapsed in the late 1860s, had become stronger than ever." The tight-knit, pre–Civil War African American population, centered largely in Capitol Hill, in Washington City's downtown neighborhoods, and on "the Island" in southwest Washington, D.C., gave way to more dispersed black communities in the pastoral southeastern part of the city, across the Eastern Branch, and in the cosmopolitan urban neighborhoods of the northwest quadrant.

Backlash

The post-Reconstruction backlash against black political power in the District of Columbia revealed itself in the growing segregation of public dining places, hotels, and theaters. More important, sources of local employment for African Americans began to disappear. After the 1870s the Navy Yard, which had been one of the main providers of employment for black men, refused to hire them. Federal offices began to create segregated working environments—as early as 1904 in some offices of the Bureau of Engraving and Printing. But it was the advent of the Wilson presidency that put a seal on the political and social aspirations of black Washingtonians in the new century's first quarter.

Among local residents, rumors of President Wilson's predilection for racial segregation preceded his inauguration. Soon after his arrival, black employees in federal offices were screened off from their compatriots and restricted to newly designated Jim Crow restrooms and lunchrooms. Civil service applicants were required to submit photographs, and the few federal appointments that blacks had been allowed to receive in the past were now reserved for whites. The combined impact of reintroducing stringent segregation in public facilities, withholding federal employment opportunities, and the lack of citywide elections and the leadership opportunities lost therein all chipped away at the political and economic infrastructure of black communities in Washington, D.C.

The resistance to segregation in the federal workplace was led by black Washingtonians but was taken up in all parts of the country. Kathleen Wolgemuth writes in a 1959 issue of the *Journal of Negro History* that "from Autumn 1913 on, after Wilson's approval of federal segregation had been made public and evidence on the size and extent of the official policy mounted, Negro opposition was united, hitting hard at what was felt to be the most serious blow at Negro rights since the days of slavery. . . . Wilson himself received letters of protest from every state in the Union, from blacks and whites. . . . Petitions were another method of protest. Circulated in cities throughout the country and sent to the President, they varied in size from a few hundred signatures to one brought by William Monroe Trotter which was purported to contain over 21,000 names."

World War I: The War to Preserve Freedom

World War I marked a period of massive migration for African Americans. The labor demands of wartime industries brought thousands of black workers from rural areas of the South to northern and midwestern cities. The war also caused some dissension among black political leaders. W. E. B. DuBois and most officials in the NAACP called for black men to join the military and to support the war effort. Others, like William Monroe Trotter and A. Philip Randolph, urged blacks to withhold their support, pointing out the irony of fighting for a country that denied them the rights of full citizenship. Emmett Scott came to Washington to serve as a special adviser to the secretary of war on Negro affairs; other black wartime appointments followed.

Washington blacks for the most part supported the war, despite their dissatisfaction with the Wilson administration. Some Howard University students volunteered and served in French regiments, and black Washingtonians successfully led the struggle for a black officers training camp at Fort Des Moines. Many District blacks—like Archibald Grimké—were torn. Grimké first opposed the segregated Officers' Training Camp, then accepted its inevitability as the only way that blacks would be allowed to participate in the war effort. In his book *The Negro in the Making of America,* the historian Benjamin Quarles observes of the period immediately after war was declared: "Negroes of military service age quickly rushed to the colors after the declaration of war, the lure of the uniform exercising its customary potency. Negro college students left their classrooms to answer the call, and the American Negro Loyal Legion sent word to Washington that it could raise 10,000 volunteers on short notice. Army officials were not quite prepared for such a Negro eagerness to enlist, and, after a few weeks of uncertainty, the War Department issued an order to halt the recruitment of colored volunteers. As barbershop proprietor George Myers wryly told Vice President Thomas R. Marshall, 'It looked as if the Negro like a burglar would have to break into this war as he did the others.' "

1862

January 1. At the outbreak of the Civil War, Christian A. Fleetwood is completing a brief stint as founding editor of the *Lyceum Observer,* a newspaper that is ultimately unsuccessful.

Elizabeth Keckley organizes members of her church to collect funds for the relief of newly arriving freedmen. Frederick Douglass donates over $200, and President and Mary Todd Lincoln are regular contributors, but the bulk of the funds comes from blacks in Washington, D.C.; Boston; and New York. This is the beginning of the Contraband Relief Association.

The National Freedmen's Relief Association begins its operations in the District of Columbia. Josephine Griffing is the representative for Washington, D.C.

Weather clear and Spring like. To Hallie at half past 7 p.m. Saw the New Year in at Bethel. Home with H afterwards. Wrote to Mr. Geo for the first time since he left. Called on Gussie. Saw Mrs. M. M. B. Went to Hallie's & thence to Fair with K.C. Home with Big H.

—The first entry of 1862 in Christian A. Fleetwood's diary

Company E, 4th U.S. Colored Troops, at Fort Lincoln.

Elizabeth Hobbs Keckley, dressmaker to Mary Todd Lincoln.

After a severe flogging, Mary Dines came across an old newspaper clipping describing a trip to Washington, where she had once visited with her mistress and the children on a shopping trip. . . . By the light of the following moon she made her getaway, and traveling for many nights with the aid of friendly slaves, she arrived on the Maryland side of the Eastern Branch near the old Navy Yard Bridge. Here she met a hay-wagon going to town and she was hidden in the straw and carried to an old stable in an alley on Capitol Hill. . . . Here she remained for a few days, then went to live on the "Island" [southwest Washington, D.C.] with some colored people and worked for them for a little pay and keep. When the war broke out she went to live in a Contraband Camp off 7th Street, near where Howard University now stands.

—John E. Washington,
They Knew Lincoln, 1942

The Freedmen's Hospital is established to care for the medical needs of the large population of ex-slaves migrating to the District of Columbia from Virginia, Maryland, and other states of the upper South. In 1862 several houses in East Washington are converted into a hospital for ex-slaves, under the care of Dr. Daniel Breed. By autumn of this year, the massive numbers of arriving men and women cause a housing and medical-care crisis for the city. In response, military officials establish Camp Barker, where ex-slaves are housed in army barracks. The hospital at Camp Barker, under the supervision of Dr. Amos Pettigrew, is labeled "Freedman's Hospital" (and later, "Freedmen's Hospital"). The camp consists of one-story frame buildings around a square of ground between R and S Streets and between 12th and 13th Streets. Much of the money that pays for services to the freedmen comes from a special tax on the wages of black teamsters and laborers working in Washington, D.C., and Virginia. Camp Barker serves as a makeshift hospital until 1865, when the residents are relocated to the grounds of the old Campbell Hospital.

March. The American Tract Society starts a school for ex-slaves, the 15th Street Presbyterian Church sets up a Colored Mission Sabbath School for newly arriving ex-slaves, and the National Freedmen's Relief Association starts three schools for freedmen.

April 16. Abraham Lincoln signs into law a bill outlawing slavery in the District of Columbia, freeing approximately 3,000 blacks. The law also provides for monetary compensation (not to exceed $300) for each slaveowner in the District, with each slave's value to be determined by three appointed commissioners. One million dollars in federal funds are to be set aside for the compensation of slaveowners—and $100,000 are designated to support colonization of the freed slaves.

In the District, churches, literary and social societies, and abolitionist groups hold celebratory meetings and begin the daunting task of preparing the freedmen and -women—many of whom came directly from rural areas—to survive and prosper in the city.

This indeed has been a happy day to me sights have I witnessed that I never anticipated one of which I will relate The Chambermaid at Smith's . . . is a slave so this morning I went there to inform her of the passage of the Bill when I entered The cook her and another Slave woman who has a slave son were talking relative to the Bill expressing doubts of its passage & when I entered they perceived that something was ahead and immediately asked me "What's the news?" "The Districts free" says I pulling out the "National Republican" and reading its editorial when I had finished the chambermaid had left the room sobbing for joy. The slave woman clapped her hands and shouted, left the house saying "let me go and tell my husband that Jesus has done all things well."

—A friend writes to the Fleetwood family

A few weeks after the bill ending slavery in the District is signed, the city's black codes are repealed, resulting in new economic and business opportunities for blacks. Curfew restrictions, which had hampered blacks' entrepreneurial efforts, are lifted. An increasing number of blacks are hired for federal jobs.

Reverend Sandy Alexander establishes the First Baptist Church in Georgetown; parishioners call it the Ark.

May. Congress passes a bill requiring Washington, Georgetown, and the county part of the District of Columbia to develop separate public schools for blacks. Ten percent of black property taxes are to be set aside to support black education, and a separate board of trustees is appointed by the secretary of the interior to oversee the schools. Although congressional supporters anticipate about $3,000 for colored school revenues from taxes levied on the black community, in actuality, only $265 of the taxes collected from black residents are awarded to Washington colored schools the following year, and in Georgetown no funds are given to these schools.

May 22. The rapidly increasing population of ex-slaves in the District exacerbates tensions between military officials and local government authorities over their treatment. District and local authorities tend to follow a strict reading of the August 6, 1861, act

We are gathered to celebrate the emancipation, yea, rather, the Redemption of the enslaved people of the District of Columbia, the exact number of whom we have no means of ascertaining, because, since the benevolent intention of Congress became manifest, many have been removed by their owners beyond the reach of this beneficent act.

Our pleasing task then, is to welcome to the Churches, the homesteads, and circles of free colored Americans, those who remain to enjoy the boon of holy Freedom.

—Reverend Daniel A. Payne, "Welcome to the Ransomed, or Duties of the Colored Inhabitants of the District of Columbia"

A district jail in use as a slave pen.

that allows slaves of rebel supporters to be freed. Their efforts to maintain their old policy of arresting migrant blacks and holding them until they can be returned to their owners soon result in a city jail filled beyond capacity. Most federal and military officials, however, refuse to return slaves even if their owners are Union supporters. In a test of will, District marshal Ward Lamon's deputies arrest several ex-slaves and put them in jail. Unfortunately, one of the arrested ex-slaves is Althea Lynch, recently employed as cook for General James S. Wadsworth, commanding officer of the Military District of Washington. Wadsworth, enraged at Lynch's arrest, orders Lamon to release her immediately. When he refuses, Wadsworth sends a military contingent to storm the city jail and secure her and, for good measure, to release the other blacks as well. Secretary of State Seward is forced to step in to prevent the conflict from escalating.

June. Congress authorizes the exchange of diplomats with Haiti and Liberia, the first black-governed nations to be recognized by the U.S. government.

July 16. In an attempt to solve the growing "problem" of the freedmen, Congress provides an additional $500,000 to colonize emancipated slaves. This brings the total amount of funds for colonizing freed blacks to $600,000. Lincoln, an enthusiastic supporter of this effort, begins to look for a suitable place to settle the freedmen.

July 17. In response to tremendous pressure from black leaders and white abolitionists—and to events on the battlefield—Congress

Ex-slaves, labeled contraband by the federal government, in Camp Brightwood.

Friends, don't you see de han' of God in dis? Haven't we a right to rejoice? You all know you couldn't have such a meetin' as dis down in Dixie! Dat you all knows. I have a right to rejoice; an' so have you; for we shall be free in jus' about five minutes. Dat's a fact. I shall rejoice that God has placed Mr. Lincum in de president's chair, and dat he wouldn't let de rebels make peace until after dis new year. De lord has heard de groans of de people, and has come down to deliver! You all knows dat in Dixie you worked de day long, an' never got no satisfacshun. But here, what you make is yourn. I've worked six months; and what I've made is mine! Let me tall you, though, don't be too free! De lazy man can't go to heaven. You must be honest, an' work, an' show dat you is fit to be free; and de Lord will bless you an' Abrum Lincum. Amen.

—George Payne, an ex-slave from Virginia, speaks at a midnight watch service at a local contraband camp, celebrating the arrival of freedom with the New Year

passes a Militia Act that repeals the 1792 law prohibiting the recruitment of African American soldiers. The Militia Act permits the enrollment of freed blacks in the war effort for "any labor of any war service." Black soldiers are paid at a lower rate than white recruits, however, and this soon becomes not only a source of contention within the ranks of black soldiers but also a political issue for black leaders and their supporters in Congress.

September 22. Lincoln announces the Emancipation Proclamation, to take effect on January 1, 1863. From that date, all slaves held in Confederate states will be forever free.

Seeing such a multitude of people in and around my church, I hurriedly went up to the office of the first paper in which the Proclamation of freedom could be printed, known as the *Evening Star,* and squeezed myself through the dense crowd that was waiting for the paper. The first sheet run off with the proclamation in it was grabbed for by three of us, but some active young man got possession of it and fled. The next sheet was grabbed for by several, and was torn into tatters. The third sheet from the press was grabbed for by several, but I succeeded in procuring so much of it as contained the proclamation, and off I went for life and death. Down Pennsylvania I ran as for my life, and when the people saw me coming with the paper in my hand they raised a shouting cheer that was almost deafening. As many as could get around me lifted me to a great platform, and I started to read the proclamation. I had run the best end of a mile, I was out of breath, and could not read. Mr. Hinton, to whom I handed the paper, read it with great force and clearness. While he was reading every kind of demonstration and gesticulation was going on. Men squealed, women fainted, dogs barked, white and colored people shook hands, songs were sung, and by this time cannons began to fire at the navy-yard, and follow in the wake of the roar that had for some time been going on at the White House. . . . Great processions of colored and white men marched to and fro and passed in front of the White House and congratulated President Lincoln on his proclamation. The President came to the window and made responsive bows. . . . It was indeed a time of times, and a half time, nothing like it will ever be seen again in this life.

—Reverend Henry McNeal Turner, pastor of Israel Bethel A.M.E. Church, *The Negro in Slavery, War and Peace*

September. As part of his colonization scheme for ex-slaves, Lincoln authorizes a plan to establish a colony of African American ex-slaves in the Chiriqui province of Central America. The Chiriqui plan is later quashed by Secretary of State Seward.

September 27. Acting as liaison and agent for the Chiriqui colonization project, Senator Samuel C. Pomeroy speaks at a rally for ex-slaves organized at the McClellan Barracks, urging them to sign up for the expedition.

1863

January 1. The Emancipation Proclamation goes into effect, granting freedom to slaves in the Confederacy. Slaves in Maryland, Delaware, Missouri, Kentucky, and Tennessee are not included. Nor are the slaves freed in Union-held areas of Virginia and Louisiana. In cities all over the North blacks and abolitionists hold meetings, church services, parades, and social gatherings in celebration.

February. Colonel Ernest Roumain arrives in Washington to represent the nation of Haiti. He is the first black diplomat ever to serve in Washington.

March 3. Myrtilla Miner's Institution for the Education of Colored Youth is incorporated by congressional act. As part of its mission statement, it aims to "educate and improve the moral and intellectual condition . . . of the colored youth of the nation."

March 25. Adjutant General Lorenzo Thomas of the Union Army is ordered into southern states to recruit freed black men to serve in the war effort. By the end of June, he has recruited twenty brigades of black troops from the Mississippi Valley.

April. Ex-slave families begin to settle in the area east of the Eastern Branch (the Anacostia River). By the spring of 1863, 10,000 blacks have migrated to the city, most from Maryland and Virginia. By 1865 the number will grow to 40,000.

April 4. Alexander Augusta is appointed surgeon in the Union Army and receives the rank of major, becoming the highest-ranking black man in military service. He had only recently volunteered for the army's medical service, in October 1862. His gift for medicine

When the city bells rang in the New Year—the year of their freedom—men and women jumped to their feet, yelled for joy, hugged and kissed each other and cried for joy. Many could not stand the excitement and fell into trances all over the house while the crowd yelled "Praise God," and kept yelling "Freed at last." . . . One old brother who was blind as a bat yelled out aloud that he was thankful to God that he had lived to see the day of freedom come.

—Mary Diners,
in John E. Washington's
They Knew Lincoln, 1942

The Navy Yard Bridge in the 1860s, viewed from the Maryland side of the Eastern Branch. Many black families settled here, and the area became known as Anacostia.

and medical administration must have been obvious, for by the end of the year he is put in charge of Freedmen's Hospital, where he remains until the spring of 1864. Augusta becomes the first African American to head a hospital in the United States.

April 16. Blacks celebrate the first anniversary of the end of slavery in the District of Columbia.

April 17. Christian A. Fleetwood enlists in the 4th U.S. Colored Troops, Company G.

May 8. During a recruitment rally at Israel Bethel A.M.E. Church, Reverend Henry McNeal Turner signs up 800 black men to volunteer for service. They form the 1st U.S. Colored Troops, and the District of Columbia gets its first black troop regiment. (The Union's first black regiment was the 54th Massachusetts Volunteers.) Other local blacks, including John F. Cook Jr., Anthony Bowen, and Frederick Douglass, join the recruiting effort. They successfully raise enough black men to form two companies of black troops. After they are examined (presumably by black army surgeon Major Alexander Augusta), black recruits spend the night in Israel Bethel A.M.E. Church. The next day they are marched to the Soldier's Retreat, and

Lieutenant Webster of the Union Army.

the day after that finds them bivouacked on Analostan Island (now Theodore Roosevelt Island). By the end of the Civil War, almost 3,500 black men have volunteered.

President Lincoln appoints Reverend Henry McNeal Turner as chaplain to the 1st U.S. Colored Troops.

May. The Army begins settling ex-slaves in the former estate of General Robert E. Lee. "Freedmen's Village" becomes a temporary home to more than 3,000 black people.

May 22. The Bureau of Colored Troops is established by the U.S. War Department.

May 27. Black Louisiana regiments distinguish themselves in battle when making a successful assault over difficult ground on Confederates entrenched at Port Hudson. The black 1st and 3rd Louisiana Native Guards, along with the 1st Engineers, suffer tremendous casualties and lose the dashing Captain André Cailloux, who had been prominent in the free colored community in New Orleans. Cailloux is given a state funeral with full pomp and circumstance, and his actions and heroic death are reported in northern newspapers. Such accounts are the source of great pride to northern blacks. But there are troubling reports that Confederates are killing black soldiers who are taken prisoner.

It was during the Civil War, however, that the influence of Israel was at its maximum. Then it was that the intellectual genius, the fiery pulpit orator, the daring and unique Henry McNeal Turner, was not only a conspicuous preacher but preeminent as a national character. These were stirring times. All eyes were on Washington. Israel Church played a leading part in the drama. Here the members of Congress, prominent among whom at the time were Benjamin F. Wade, Thaddeus Stevens and Henry Wilson, addressed the Negro citizens on the dominant issues of the day, buoying them up in the midst of their darkness and gloom. At this time the Israel Lyceum was an institution not unlike the Bethel Literary Association of thirty years later, that drew the most intellectual men to listen to lectures, participate in discussions, and read dissertations on timely topics.

—John W. Cromwell, "The First Negro Churches in the District of Columbia," *Journal of Negro History,* 1922

Freedman's Village, Arlington, Virginia.

July 18. The Massachusetts 54th, an all-black regiment headed by Colonel Robert Gould Shaw, leads Union troops on an attack on Fort Wagner. Colonel Shaw and three other officers are killed in action and the regiment suffers heavy casualties, but the heroism and steadfastness of the 54th squelch many of the reservations expressed in the press about black men's willingness and ability to fight.

July 30. Faced with growing public resentment over Confederates' treatment of captured black troops, President Lincoln issues General Order 100, which orders that "for every soldier of the United States killed in violation of the laws of war a rebel soldier shall be executed, and for every one enslaved by the enemy or sold into slavery a rebel soldier shall be placed at hard labor . . . until the other shall be released." The order is never enforced.

August 18–19. Christian A. Fleetwood embarks for Camp Belger, where he is mustered in as a sergeant.

Frederick Douglass visits the White House and has his first audience with President Lincoln. Douglass thanks Lincoln for issuing General Order 100, offers his opinions about the war effort, and urges Lincoln to press ahead. He also complains about the disparity in pay between black and white soldiers and argues that black men should be allowed to become officers.

December. The bronze statue *Freedom* is raised to the top of the cupola on the dome of the Capitol building. Philip Reed, enslaved master mechanic, assisted in the casting process.

The District's first horse-drawn streetcar line is the Washington and Georgetown Railroad. The company maintains strictly segregated seating, however, with blacks—even women and the elderly—being forced to ride up front with the driver. This situation not only is humiliating but exposes the black passenger to inclement weather. A movement begins to end discrimination on the street cars. Senator Charles Sumner, a leader in this effort, works tirelessly in Congress from 1863 until 1865 to defeat this practice.

Man shot and brought in by pickets last night. . . . Broke camp at Burnt Ordinary. Marched to Williamsburg. Cavalryman shot in woods. Camped at old place— Ft Macgruder. Weather clear and quite cold.

—Major Christian A. Fleetwood's diary entry, November 10, 1863

A most abominable day and rainy no end. . . . This year has brought about many changes that at the beginning were or would have been thought impossible. The close of the year finds me a soldier for the cause of my race. May God bless this cause, and enable me in the coming year.

—Major Christian A. Fleetwood's diary entry, December 31, 1863

A nineteenth-century streetcar in the District of Columbia.

1864

Despite Congress's attempt to fund public schools for black children by ordering that black property taxes be diverted to support them, Georgetown provides only $70 for the 1864 school year, and the City of Washington provides $410. Black political leaders argue that this represents only a small portion of black property taxes.

February 1. On a cold, rainy day Major Alexander Augusta boards streetcar No. 32. Upon entering, he is informed by the conductor that colored people must ride up front with the driver. When Augusta protests that he would become drenched and he refuses, he is thrown off the streetcar. He writes a letter of complaint to the assistant secretary of war on February 8:

> [I] had been summoned to attend a Court Martial as a witness in the case of Private Geo. Taylor who was charged with causing the death of a colored man last August the said colored man having died in the hospital of which I was at the time in charge. I started from my lodgings at the corner of 14th and I Streets on the morn-

Enlistment record for a James L. Adams in the U.S. Colored Troops, 1863.

ing of Feb. 1st for the purpose of proceeding to the hospital in order to obtain some notes relative to the case. As my time was short and it was raining very hard at the time, I hailed the car which was passing just as I came out of the door, and it was stopped for me, but as I was in the act of entering, the conductor informed me that I would have to ride on the front with the driver. I told him I would not, and asked him why I could not ride inside. He stated that it was against the rules for colored persons to ride inside. I attempted to enter the car, and he pulled me out and ejected me from the platform. The consequence was I had to walk the whole distance through rain and mud, and was considerably detained past the hour for my attendance at Court. On my arrival, I reported the case to the Court, and the President, Col J. H. Willetts informed me that I must make my statement in writing. . . . There are persons living in the neighborhood who saw the transaction and who can corroborate my assertions.

Trusting that something may speedily be done to remedy such evils as those we are now forced to submit to.

Black Washingtonians establish St. Martin's Church (named after St. Martin de Porres) at 15th and L Streets NW. St. Martin's is the first black Catholic church in the city. The church is renamed St. Augustine's, and a new building next to the original church is dedicated in 1876.

Reverend Henry Bailey and other black worshipers establish the Fourth Baptist Church in a wooden frame building lit by oil lamps. The church, which is later rededicated as Metropolitan Baptist Church, also has a strong and energetic second pastor—Reverend Robert Johnson, who serves from 1870 to 1903.

March. Reverend Henry Highland Garnet is appointed pastor at the Fifteenth Street Presbyterian Church, where he serves until October 1866.

April 16. The celebration of emancipation in the District features a parade of 10,000 black people marching to the White House, where President Lincoln speaks to the gathered crowd.

April 16. Flora Batson, known for her broad vocal range, is born in the District of Columbia. In 1867 she leaves with her family for Rhode Island and starts singing professionally at Storer College in Harpers Ferry, West Virginia, and in People's Church of Boston. By 1885 she is touring Europe and performing in New York City concert halls. Batson achieves international fame as a concert vocalist, singing ballads and opera until her death on December 6, 1906.

April. Black troops of the 9th Corps, under Major General Ambrose E. Burnside, march down Pennsylvania Avenue on their way to Brandy Station, Virginia. The black troops whoop and shout in recognition of President Lincoln as they pass the presidential reviewing stand.

The corps formed up at about 11:00 A.M. to begin a slow march down New York Avenue towards the heart of the city. The dense columns pressed on until they reached Fourteenth Street, where a halt was called to allow the long procession to close up. Then the men made the turn south to march past Willard's Hotel. Waiting on a second-floor balcony to review the troops was a small crowd of notables, including the sideburned Burnside and President Abraham Lincoln. . . . These were the first black troops that Lincoln had ever formally reviewed.

—Noah Andre Trudeau,
Like Men of War: Black Troops in the Civil War, 1862–1865, 1998

June. A delegation of Washington black men from Israel Lyceum presents a petition to Congress with 2,500 signatures requesting suffrage for black men in the District of Columbia.

June. Congress passes a bill mandating that Washington and Georgetown fund colored public schools according to their proportion of the total school population. District federal courts are also to contribute funds, resulting from court-imposed fines and forfeitures. But colored schools never receive this money. By the

Arrived at Fortress Monroe. Disembarked and to Camp Hamilton. Met several acquaintances. Visited 6th and dined then slept. Awoke and to Camp with Chaplain to Hampton. Visited Dress parade of 5th and 6th. Busy till taps. Slept on stretcher. Weather fine.

—Major Christian A. Fleetwood's diary entry, April 26, 1864

Up and breakfasted early. Lay still all of the cool of the day. Started in the heat. Marched toward Petersburg. Formed line of battle, saw fight between gunboats and battery. . . . Arrived at City Point 11 eve. Weather clear and hot.

—Major Christian A. Fleetwood's diary entry, May 9, 1864

Up at break of dawn and under way. Our division and white troops of Gen Smith went into action early charges out of woods. Cut up badly. Regiment broke and retreated. Fired into by 5th Mass Last regiment Charged with 22nd Took the battery. Advanced Upon works [undecipherable] I lay under their fire for all balance of the day advancing by degrees in line. About 7 p.m. final charge made. Seen guns taken by our regiment. Our loss pretty heavy. Slept. . . . Weather fine and warm.

—Major Christian A. Fleetwood's diary entry, June 15–16, 1864

Waked early and sent to get Regiment up. Returned and lay down till the mine was exploded on Reservoir Hill. Got up and saw the columns of attack pitching in. Fearful cannonading . . . Col Div of [9th? 7th?] Corps charged or attempted broke and run! Devil blame 'em. Weather fine.

—Major Christian A. Fleetwood's
diary entry, July 30, 1864

end of the school year, they have received only $628 out of a public school budget of $25,000.

July. The Fugitive Slave Act is repealed by Congress.

July 17. Congress passes the Enlistment Act, which provides that white privates will receive $13 per month, whereas blacks will receive $10 each month. In addition, whites will receive a clothing allowance of $3.50. After protest from black and white civil rights supporters, the difference in pay is eliminated.

August 19. Frederick Douglass is invited to the White House to discuss President Lincoln's plan for helping southern blacks escape from bondage.

Woke today with chills and fever. Turned in again after reports. Lay by taking physic all day. No letters. No news. Weather overcast.

—Major Christian A. Fleetwood's
diary entry, September 4, 1864

It was about 8 o'clock A.M., when I called on the president. Upon entering his reception room we found about a dozen persons in waiting, among them two colored women. I had quite a pleasant time waiting until he was disengaged. . . .

The president was seated at his desk. Mrs. C. said to him, "This is Sojourner Truth, who has come all the way from Michigan to see you." He then arose, gave me his hand, made a bow, and said, "I am pleased to see you."

I said to him, "Mr. President, when you first took your seat I feared you would be torn to pieces, for I likened you unto Daniel, who was thrown into the lion's den; and if the lions did not tear you into pieces, I knew that it would be God that had saved you; and I said if he spared me I would see you before the four years expired, and he has done so, and now I am here to see you for myself." . . .

He then showed me the Bible presented to him by the colored people of Baltimore. . . . I have seen it for myself and it is beautiful beyond description. After I had looked it over, I said to him, "This is beautiful indeed; the colored people have given this to the head of the government, and that government once sanctioned laws that would not permit its people to learn enough to enable them to read this book. And for what? Let them answer who can."

—Sojourner Truth,
Narrative of Sojourner Truth

September. General William Tecumseh Sherman marches through Georgia, sacking Atlanta.

September 29. Christian A. Fleetwood's actions on September 29 will lead to his receiving the Congressional Medal of Honor. In a letter written years later Fleetwood described his actions in this way: "Seized the colors after two color bearers had been shot down, and bore them nobly through the fight."

October 29. President Lincoln signs his name in Sojourner Truth's *Book of Life*, the autograph scrapbook that she carries on her visit to the White House.

December. Sojourner Truth is hired by the National Freedman's Relief Association "to be a counselor to the freed people at Arlington Heights, Va." Truth serves as teacher, nurse, and counselor at the contraband camp until 1866.

1865

January 31. The Thirteenth Amendment is passed, abolishing slavery in the United States.

February 1. Senator Charles Sumner sponsors Boston attorney and physician John Rock as a candidate to practice before the Supreme Court; Chief Justice Salmon P. Chase swears him in.

February 12. Reverend Henry Highland Garnet delivers a sermon to the House of Representatives. The choir of the Fifteenth Street Presbyterian Church accompanies him.

March 3. The act creating the Bureau of Freedmen, Refugees and Abandoned Lands is signed into law, and General Oliver Otis Howard assumes command. Freedmen's Hospital is placed under the Bureau. From 1865 to 1872, the Freedmen's Bureau establishes 56 hospitals around the country, treating over 430,000 people and employing more than 135 medical doctors to attend to health needs of the ex-slaves.

Got out the regiment and after much tribulation and several unsuccessful attempts to catch a nap, we embarked on board a gunboat and debarked at Jones Landing. Marched up to works. Bivouaced at Deep Bottom. Dined and slept with 5 U.S. C. [R?]. Stirred up regiment. . . . coffee boiled and line formed. Moved out and [indecipherable] charged with the 6th at daylight and got used up, saved colors. Remnants of the two gathered. . . . Marching in line and flank all day long saw Gen Grant and staff, both Birneys and other "stars." Retired at night and stacked arms and moved three times ending at a captured stronghold where we spent the remainder of the darkness. . . . Drilled a squad in morning. Rebels charged our lines three times repulsed. Lying in ravine one man killed. Moved in eve. Threw up embankments to protect flanks of position. First night sleep since 27th. Weather changed to the bad.
—Major Christian A. Fleetwood's diary entry, September 28–30, 1864

In a storm all day Night very rough . . . Amused at the sudden conversion of the boys by the storm A night of prayer for once. Quite an agreeable change from the usual swearing. Will it outlast the storm
—Major Christian A. Fleetwood's diary entry, December 21, 1864

On Tuesday, January 31, 1865, the final vote was taken in the House. That afternoon the chamber was packed as never before; among the spectators were numerous senators, five Supreme Court justices, and a host of well-dressed women who took over the reporters' gallery, doubtless preferring to see history made than to read about it. The Negro, too, was on hand, his presence chronicled by spectator Henry Highland Garnet. . . .

White and colored grew still and tense as the clerk called the roll. When he had run down the alphabet, the clerk handed a piece of paper to the Speaker, Schuyler Colfax. With every eye upon him, Colfax announced the fateful vote: yeas, 119; nays, 56. The measure had been carried: Congress by a two-thirds majority in both houses had voted to send to the states a constitutional amendment abolishing slavery throughout the United States.

Schuyler's announcement of the yeas and nays was greeted by deafening cheers. The ladies waved their handkerchiefs; the men clapped and shook hands in turn. Some danced for joy, pulling others around with them. For ten minutes the demonstrations went on, with the chair making no effort to restore order.

—Benjamin Quarles,
Lincoln and the Negro, 1962

March 4. Abraham Lincoln is inaugurated for his ill-fated second term. Black troops march in the inaugural parade for the first time.

In another first for the federal capital, African Americans receive invitations to the inaugural reception to meet the president and the first lady. Frederick Douglass is among the many distinguished black guests who attend.

For the first time in my life, and I suppose the first time in any colored man's life, I attended the reception of President Lincoln on the evening of the inauguration. As I approached the door, I was seized by two policemen and forbidden to enter. I said to them that they were mistaken entirely in what they were doing, that if Mr. Lincoln knew that I was at the door he would order my admission, and I bolted in by them. On the inside I was taken charge of by two other policemen, to be conducted as I supposed to the President, but instead of that they were conducting me out the window on a plank.

"Oh," I said, "this will not do, gentlemen," and as a gentleman was passing in I said to him, "Just say to Mr. Lincoln that Fred Douglass is at the door."

He rushed in to President Lincoln, and almost in less than a half a minute I was invited into the East Room of the White House. . . . Mr. Lincoln saw me; his countenance lighted up, and he said in a voice which was heard all around: "Here comes my friend Douglass."

—Frederick Douglass in Allen Thorndike Rice's
Reminiscences of Abraham Lincoln by Distinguished Men of His Time, 1888

The Freedmen's Bureau sets up schools for blacks in old army barracks around the city.

March. Led by Senator Charles Sumner, Congress passes a law prohibiting racial segregation on streetcars in the District.

April 3. Richmond falls.

April 9. Under General Robert E. Lee, the Confederacy surrenders at Appomattox Court House.

April 14. Lincoln is assassinated. Some whites thought to be sympathetic to the Confederacy are visited by gangs that threaten them

Admission to the U.S. Supreme Court of the first colored lawyer, John Rock, 1865.

with violence and arrest if their houses aren't draped with mourning. When Lincoln's body is taken to the White House to be prepared for burial, Washingtonians line the streets, expressing their sorrow.

April 15. Andrew Johnson is sworn in as president.

With help from northern Baptists, Wayland Seminary is established to train black men for the ministry.

July 4. The Colored People's Educational Monument Association, led by John F. Cook and William Syphax, holds a memorial service for Abraham Lincoln on the grounds of the White House.

August. Freedmen's Hospital is relocated to the grounds of the Campbell Hospital on 7th and Florida Avenues (Boundary Street). The hospital consists of one-story frame buildings previously used as cavalry barracks and has a 600-bed capacity. Along with health care, the hospital seeks to minister to the broader needs of the newly freed, largely migrant population. An industrial school that teaches sewing

At noon on March 4, Lincoln was to be sworn in for his second term. In the line that marched from the White House to the Capitol were four companies of the Fifty-fourth Regiment of the United States Colored Troops, forming part of the military escort. The Negro soldiers were cheered all along the route. Keeping step close behind them were three lodges of Negro Odd Fellows—Union, J. R. Brooks, and Friendship—dressed in full regalia and bearing a gold-laced silk and satin banner with a portrait "of some colored celebrity."

—Benjamin Quarles,
Lincoln and the Negro, 1962

Old "Sis" Thomas lived . . . [on the corner of 10th Street] . . . with her daughter and little son George. She came into the neighborhood just before Lincoln was assassinated, and said she could see ghosts all of the time, but she said she wasn't afraid of them and knew how to talk to them. She said that dogs howled and chickens were crowing for days before Lincoln's death, and when a large picture of Lincoln fell off the wall and a bird flew into the room, she just knew someone was going to die in the neighborhood.

—John E. Washington,
They Knew Lincoln, 1942

The [streetcar] conductor grabbed me by the shoulder and jerking me around, ordered me to get out. I told him I would not. . . . When we arrived at the hospital, the surgeons were called in to examine my shoulder and found that a bone was misplaced.

—Sojourner Truth,
Book of Life

and common household duties is also part of the facility. Several buildings on the property of the old Campbell Hospital are later renovated and provided as homes to middle-class black families.

September. Sojourner Truth is appointed to a nursing position at Freedmen's Hospital, to promote "order, cleanliness, industry, and virtue among the patients." Truth is opposed to the segregated streetcar system and has attacked it from the time of her arrival in Washington until its demise. She is an effective opponent.

Sojourner, having occasion to ride [upon the city streetcars], signaled the car, but neither conductor nor driver noticed her. Soon another followed, and she raised her hand again, but they also turned away. She then gave three tremendous yelps, "I want to ride! I want to ride!! I WANT TO RIDE!!!" Consternation seized the passing crowd—people, carriages, go-carts of every description stood still. The car was effectually blocked up, and before it could move on, Sojourner had jumped aboard. Then there arose a great shout from the crowd, "Ha! ha! ha!! She has beaten him," &c. The angry conductor told her to go forward where the horses were, or he would put her out. Quietly seating herself, she informed him that she was a passenger. "Go forward where the horses are, or I will throw you out," said he in a menacing voice. She told him that she was neither a Marylander nor a Virginian to fear his threats; but was from the Empire State of New York, and knew the laws as well as he did.

—Sojourner Truth,
Book of Life

December. In a referendum, white male residents in Georgetown and Washington decide whether the vote should be extended to black men. The returns in both places show the overwhelming majority opposing black suffrage, but only a small percentage of residents voted.

December. A bill is introduced in Congress that would extend the vote to black men in the District of Columbia.

1866

January. The Convention of Colored Men convenes at the Fifteenth Street Presbyterian Church under the leadership of Reverend Henry Highland Garnet. It petitions Congress for "equal rights before the law, including the right of impartial suffrage."

February 7. Representatives of the Convention of Colored Men visit President Andrew Johnson to urge him to support the vote for black men. Among those attending are George T. Downing, a businessman from Rhode Island; Frederick Douglass; John Jones, a Washingtonian; and William Whipper, a Pennsylvania businessman. They are unsuccessful in their efforts, however, and Johnson vetoes the bill that would grant suffrage to black men in the District.

April. Congress passes the Civil Rights Act of 1866, extending citizenship to blacks, and declares them "entitled to equality of treatment before the law, any statute to the contrary notwithstanding."

Congress passes a bill to expand education for the freedmen living around the District. The bill provides empty army barracks for schools and money to build additional schools; it also gives the trustees of the colored schools the authority to sue city officials for money due to them under the terms of the colored school law of 1864.

Matthew A. Henson is born in Charles County, Maryland. He is orphaned at an early age and sent to live with an uncle in Washington, D.C. Henson, along with Lieutenant Robert Peary, will later be one of the first men to reach the North Pole.

December. A bill passes in Congress that provides for universal male suffrage in the District. President Johnson vetoes it, and Congress musters the votes to override the presidential veto. The bill calls for one year's residency in the District and withholds the vote from paupers, minors, convicts, and men who have "given aid and comfort to the enemy." After the granting of male suffrage, black men become active in Republican clubs in all wards of the city and play an important role in the 1867 city elections.

1867

January 10. The National Equal Rights League of Colored Men holds its annual convention in the District.

Blacks voting for the first time in the District of Columbia, 1867.

March 2. President Johnson signs the act that grants Howard University a charter. General Oliver Otis Howard becomes its first president.

General Oliver Otis Howard buys the 375-acre farm of James Barry in Anacostia and divides it into lots, which he sells to freedmen at prices of about $200 to $300 an acre. The freedmen are allowed to pay in installments. The Freedmen's Bureau also helps the home-builders by donating most of the lumber used in constructing the houses. This is the origin of the Barry's Farm community, later renamed Hillside.

Memories of Barry's Farm

To one who has witnessed the transition of this community, stage by stage, from a condition of rustic and arcadian simplicity, into one that embodies every phase of the cosmopolitan life of a city, it almost seems as though he has witnessed the unfolding of a panorama. Gone are the many ill kept roads, the paths across open fields, the wells and springs that were the only water supply, the white washed houses, the yards with their pigs and chickens, the market gardens and orchards. It is hard to imagine the boys who collected cows from home to home in the morning and herded them over the roads to Fort Stanton to graze, returning them in the evening at milking time. The great bell that rang from the old yellow school house on Nichols Avenue, then called Asylum Road, this and the bell that rang every hour at St. Teresa's Catholic Church were to many the sole means of telling the time. The jingle of the bells on the sleigh horses in winter, the merry parties of youngsters who coasted on sleds from the Asylum gates, down Nichols Avenue to Morris Road. The delight of the boys in the long vacation days was to go fishing and swimming in the shallow waters of the Eastern Branch, which has long since been reclaimed to form the present site of the Naval Air Station and the recreation grounds of East Potomac Park.

Solemn and saddened hush prevailed at the news of a death in the community. On these occasions the sympathetic came to assist in washing and dressing the deceased; the body was then laid out on an ironing board, supported by two chairs to await the coming of the sad faced undertaker. . . . If a hearse could not be hired, some neighbor's wagon was used and the family followed in borrowed buggies and wagons, while sympathetic friends followed on foot to Jake Moore's Burying Ground, a place now called Rosemont Cemetery. . . .

In later years pleasure parks containing ample pavilions for dancing and refreshment stands were opened on Nichols Avenue, Sumner, and Stevens Roads. The two most prominent were Eureka Park and Green Willow Park. The most popular orchestras were the Genesta and the Capitol City.

–Charles Howard, longtime resident of the Barry's Farm neighborhood, taken from his manuscript (Ella Pearis collection, Anacostia Museum)

James Bland (1854–1911), musician and composer, arrives in Washington, D.C. His father, Allan Bland, brought his family to the city so that he could attend Howard University and work at

Composer James Bland.

the Patent Office. James is expected to follow his father's example and dutifully enrolls in Howard University. But his love of music and his talent lead him to abandon his studies for music. At age thirteen, Bland is performing in hotels and restaurants around Washington.

June. The first city election with universal suffrage is held. Richard Wallach is elected mayor.

1868

June. Blacks are elected to citywide positions for the first time. John F. Cook Jr., a clerk in the city tax collector's office and the older son of John F. Cook, is elected to the board of aldermen. Stewart Carter, a popular barber, is elected to the common council. Sayles J. Bowen is elected mayor with the help of black voters; he provides public works employment that lays sewer lines and paves and modernizes much of the city. Bowen is sympathetic to the plight of refugee blacks in the city, and much of the public works employment benefits these newcomers. Political opponents use the charge that the public works are really efforts to "buy" blacks' votes with jobs.

June 13. The Fourteenth Amendment is passed. It bars prominent supporters of the Confederacy from federal or state office unless Congress specifically removes the prohibition by a two-thirds vote, and it upholds the validity of the U.S. debt. Most important for African Americans, it confers citizenship on ex-slaves, in an effort to support their basic political rights and to undercut the black codes and antiblack laws being established in the southern states. The amendment also penalizes states for denying suffrage to black men.

Autumn. Howard University Medical College is established. Twenty-five student "tickets" are printed for classes at the Medical School, but only eight students attend the first class. Opening exercises are held at the First Congregational Church on the corner of 10th and G Streets NW on November 5, 1868. Since the Medical College Building is not yet completely renovated, classes are tem-

The new mayor [Sayles J. Bowen] was immediately confronted by two serious dilemmas—black poverty and a white groundswell to move the national capital from a southern-minded milieu to a more central and more cosmopolitan locus somewhere in the North or Midwest. Mayor Bowen rightly saw both problems as being cut from the same cloth: employ black laborers to rebuild the city and the two dilemmas would dissipate. During the two years of his administration, Bowen created work for hundreds of freedmen, but at the politically suicidal price of overwhelming the city with debt.

David Levering Lewis,
*District of Columbia:
A Bicentennial History*, 1977

Howard University Medical Department, 1869–1900.

porarily housed in a building improvised for that purpose. From the very beginning, efforts are made to provide the Medical Department with the finest faculty and equipment. But much of the Medical Department's success ultimately lies in its association with the Freedmen's Hospital. Silas L. Loomis serves as the first dean; Robert Reyburn serves as dean of faculty from 1870 to 1871. These two white men suffer the consequences of being connected with the first medical school for African American physicians: both Reyburn and Loomis are dismissed from the Medical Department of Georgetown College, and the private practices of the entire faculty are subjected to a boycott, greatly restricting these doctors' incomes.

Congress passes legislation closing down all Freedmen's Bureau activities, except those affecting Civil War veterans and education. The bureau is authorized to make gifts of buildings to private charitable associations that work with the freedmen and women. But by 1868 there still remain at Freedmen's Hospital about 350 patients who are deemed too ill or too old to be released or relocated to other parts of the country. In addition, large numbers of freedmen in need of medical care reside in the District of Columbia and surrounding areas, thus the hospital's facilities and staff are transferred to Howard University.

John Mercer Langston, the first dean of Howard University Law School.

George F. T. Cook, the younger son of John F. Cook Sr., is appointed superintendent of colored schools. Under his watch, education for black students greatly improves; they are offered a wide range of instruction and are taken on field trips to the Library of Congress, Congress, and other places of interest.

John Mercer Langston, attorney and abolitionist, arrives in Washington, D.C.

1869
January 13–16. The National Convention of Colored Men holds its convention in the District.

March 4. Ulysses S. Grant is inaugurated as president.

March. Congress removes "colored" and "white" from the text of District laws and regulations and allows black men to serve on juries. Blacks win election to the City Council in the city's seven wards and a black alderman is elected, but the election is one of the most violent in the city's history.

May. The City Council passes a civil rights bill imposing a $20 fine on public entertainment establishments that deny access to a person due to color or race.

Howard University Law School begins accepting students, immediately attracting candidates from all over the country. Educator and political leader John Mercer Langston is appointed the first dean. He serves until 1873, when he becomes vice president of the university until 1875.

Will Marion Cook is born in the District to John and Isabelle Cook. Recognized as a young musical prodigy, Cook attends Oberlin Preparatory School Conservatory of Music and also studies in Berlin.

November 18. Christian A. Fleetwood and Sara Iredell are married.

December 6. Two hundred fourteen men and women, representing workers from around the country, gather in Union League Hall to establish the National Colored Labor Union. Led by trade unionist Isaac Meyers, those in attendance include Washingtonian John M. Langston, J. Sella Martin, and George P. Downing from Rhode Island. Among the women attending is Mary Ann Shadd Cary (1823–1893), a former abolitionist newspaper publisher and lecturer from Windsor, Canada, who has recently moved to the District.

Wedding portrait of Christian A. Fleetwood and Sara Iredell, 1869.

1870

January. The first issues of the *New Era* are published. Frederick Douglass and Reverend J. Sella Martin, pastor of the Fifteenth Street Presbyterian Church, are its founding editors. Douglass moves his family to Washington, D.C., and settles in a rowhouse at 316 A Street NE.

January. The Mississippi legislature elects clergyman Hiram Revels to the U.S. Senate; he is the first African American elected to Congress. But when Revels is presented in Congress, his credentials are challenged by Senator Willard Saulsbury of Delaware, Garrett Davis of Kentucky, George Vickers of Maryland, and John Stockton of New Jersey. Three days of debate follow, but at the end, Revels's supporters prevail and he is seated. Revels serves until the end of this session of Congress.

January 15. The Howard medical faculty publishes a call to all "physicians in the District of Columbia in favor of extending equal rights and privileges to regular practitioners of medicine and surgery" to convene. The multiracial group meets in the same First

Blacks selling items at Central Market, 1870–1880s, by J. H. Cocks.

Congregational Church in which the Medical Department first met to form the National Medical Society.

February 3. The Fifteenth Amendment is ratified, giving African Americans additional federal clout in their fight for the right to vote. When the amendment is ratified on March 30, 1870, blacks hold celebrations throughout the country. Over 20,000 people march in Baltimore and then gather to hear Frederick Douglass speak.

Blacks continue migrating in large numbers to the District of Columbia from the South, especially from Virginia and Maryland. For example, in 1840 blacks made up one-third of the population; in 1860 the proportion of blacks fell to one-sixth; by 1870 blacks once again make up one-third of the city. For the most part, these newcomers occupy the worst areas of the city. Some of the dwellings are located on marshy, swampy land, exposing their tenants to dampness and fever.

March. The City Council adds bars, restaurants, hotels, and other places of amusement to the kinds of establishments prohibited from discriminating against black people. The fine is also increased to $50.

Opponents of Mayor Bowen organize and manage to elect Matthew Emery as mayor, along with six black city councilmen. Mayor Emery soon encounters the same trouble as Bowen—he runs up the city's debt by continuing city improvements.

November. The Miner Fund, an organization that commemorates the educational work of Myrtilla Miner, opens a small public high school in the basement of the Fifteenth Street Presbyterian Church. Emma J. Hutchins, a white teacher from New Hampshire, is the first principal. The Preparatory School quickly establishes a reputation for excellence. Although the first class is scheduled to graduate in 1875, most of its students are drafted as instructors in other schools before that time.

The First Colored Baptist Church is formally incorporated as the Nineteenth Street Baptist Church.

Mary Ann Shadd Cary, a student at Howard University Law School, attends the Woman Suffrage Convention in Washington, D.C., after which she petitions the Judiciary Committee of the House of Representatives for the right to vote. In her petition she notes the achievements of black women and argues that, as a taxpayer living in the District of Columbia, she should have the same rights as a male resident of the city.

Frederick Douglass is appointed secretary of the commission to investigate the feasibility of a U.S. annexation of Santo Domingo.

Frederick Douglass, second from right, en route to Santo Domingo, 1870.

Concluding its visit, the commission issues an official report favorable to annexation.

1871

February 21. Congress combines Washington City, Georgetown, and Washington County under one territorial government for the first time. The mayor and the board of aldermen are replaced by a governor and an eleven-member council, both appointed by the U.S. president for a period of four years. (Frederick Douglass is appointed a member of the governor's council, along with two other blacks: John Gray, a successful caterer, and Adolphus Hall, a local miller.) An elected House of Delegates with twenty-two members replaces the city council. Two African Americans, Solomon G. Brown, a Smithsonian Institution employee, and James A. Handy, an A.M.E. bishop, are elected to the House of Delegates. An elected board of education is created, and a nonvoting delegate in the U.S. House of Representatives is allowed. Congress also establishes two bodies: the Board of Health, to oversee the city's growing public health problems; and the Board of Public Works, to continue the city's improvements. Both boards are appointed by the president. John Mercer Langston, head of Howard University's law school, becomes legal adviser to the Board of Health. Alexander Shepard is appointed to the Board of Public Works. Shepard immediately begins an aggressive construction and renovation campaign, burdening taxpayers and bankrupting the city once again.

Solomon G. Brown, a member of the House of Delegates in 1871.

February. Senator Hiram Revels, serving on the Committee for the District of Columbia, along with Senator Charles Sumner, leads the fight to desegregate District schools, but the bill to integrate the schools is defeated.

After an extended period of working in Paris, James Wormley returns home to open the Wormley Hotel at 15th and H Streets. The Wormley Hotel becomes one of the most fashionable hotels and dining rooms in the city and a popular spot for political meetings and bargaining sessions during the 1877 presidential campaign.

James Wormley, owner of the Wormley Hotel.

Mary Ann Shadd Cary registers to vote, becoming one of the few female registered voters in the District of Columbia.

The National Colored Labor Union continues to decline. Though it holds its annual convention, by the end of the year it is defunct.

Joseph Douglass is born in the District of Columbia. He becomes one of the most talented black classical musicians of the 1890s, playing the violin in concerts throughout the United States. Douglass is the grandson of Frederick Douglass—also a violin player.

Mary J. Patterson becomes principal of the Preparatory High School. She remains until 1884, with the exception of the 1872 school year, in which Richard T. Greener, the first African American to graduate from Harvard, serves as interim principal.

Daniel Murray, a native of Baltimore, begins working at the Library of Congress. His career will last for more than fifty years, and he becomes one of the most recognized authorities on black literature.

1872

June. The District territorial government passes a civil rights law that bars racial discrimination in most public places. It imposes a $100 fine upon violators and suspension of their operating license for one year.

Thomas W. Chase is elected to the D.C. House of Delegates, serving two terms. Born into slavery near Annapolis, Maryland, in 1844, he drove a coal wagon in the District as a young man but was fired when his employer discovered that he could read and write. He attended Howard University and graduated from its law school. Chase practiced law until his election. At age eighteen, his wife, Anna Harrison, escaped with her parents from a plantation in Caroline County, Virginia, and arrived in Washington. Anna and Thomas Chase have thirteen children, including William T. Chase, who later becomes associate editor of the *Washington Eagle*.

Howard Law School graduate Charlotte Ray becomes one of the first women to graduate from a law school in the United States and the first African American woman attorney.

Thomas W. Chase, D.C. delegate.

1873

John Esputa founds the Colored American Opera Company. Its first performance, *The Doctor of Alcantara,* is at Lincoln Hall on February 3 and 4.

African Americans are refused seats in the balcony of the National Theatre, where they had been allowed to sit since being ejected from the main gallery in 1838.

March 4. Ulysses S. Grant is inaugurated for his second term as president.

Black congressmen and their wives attend President Grant's inaugural ball.

African American expatriate Alexander Crummell, a clergyman educated at Oneida Institute in the United States and at Queens College, Cambridge, in England, returns to the United States and settles in the District of Columbia, where he founds St. Luke's Episcopal Church.

1874

One of the last acts of the territorial government is to rename the Barry's Farm community. It is renamed Hillsdale, upon the initiative of black members Solomon Brown and Frederick Douglass.

March. Frederick Douglass becomes president of the Freedman's Savings and Trust Company, the savings institution created by the Freedmen's Bureau to assist ex-slaves in managing their wages. The bank has an impressive building at 1507 Pennsylvania Avenue NW and operates several branches around the country. Blacks support the bank and trust that the federal government will guarantee their small accounts. But by the time Douglass arrives, the bank is already on the verge of collapse. Speculative investments and unsecured loans have depleted funds and undermined depositors' confidence. Douglass finds the situation embarrassing, and he is forced to defend his role of providing a stable image for an insolvent financial institution.

"Say, John, I Heard the Other Day"

Say, John, I heard the other day
From sister Phoebe Perry
The Hillsdale folk across the way
Will go to Harper's Ferry.
When do they go and on what date?
I think I can remember,
Oh, yes, I heard our preacher say
The fifth day of September.
Of course you know I will be there
And bring my wife and daughter
If only I can raise the fare,
One dollar and a quarter.
—Verse written by Solomon Brown
to promote the Barry's Farm
community's annual excursion to
Harpers Ferry

June. Congress abolishes the three-year territorial government for the District, partly due to its financial difficulties, replacing it with three commissioners appointed by the president. This temporary arrangement was planned to decrease the city's debt, but the system becomes permanent in 1878 under the Organic Act. The experiment with black suffrage is over.

July 1. The Freedmen's Savings and Trust Company fails, taking with it the savings of thousands of black families. Corruption by bank shareholders, who were white, and bad loans close the bank. In 1879 Senator Blanche K. Bruce leads the investigation into the failure of the congressionally chartered institution. In the end, depositors receive only three-fifths of their money back.

July 31. Reverend Patrick F. Healy becomes president of Georgetown University. He is the first African American to hold this post. Until his resignation in 1882, Healy transforms the university, increasing its size and modernizing its academic programs.

The *New National Era* stops publication.

Autumn. White and colored school systems in the District are combined into one system.

Reverend Patrick F. Healy, the first African American president of Georgetown University.

1875

March. Congress passes the Civil Rights Act of 1875, providing for equal accommodations for blacks in public places and on public transport.

March. Blanche Kelso Bruce is seated in the U.S. Senate. Bruce serves a full term, representing Mississippi until 1881. A strapping, broad-shouldered man, he is also gracious and politically savvy and quickly becomes a dominant figure in Washington. His friends and associates include the Grimké family, the Frederick Douglass family, and other members of the political and social elite.

Senator Blanche K. Bruce.

December 19. Future historian Carter G. Woodson is born to ex-slaves James Henry and Anne Eliza Woodson in West Virginia.

1876

The Miner Normal School opens at 1613 P Street NW. The course of study lasts two years. Potential students must be at least sixteen years old, must be of good moral character, and must pass an entrance exam in reading, writing, arithmetic, geography, grammar,

Emancipation Monument *by Thomas Ball.*

I remember, just as clear as if it were yesterday, all the children put in for street-car fare and we went on a long trip to see a statue of Lincoln freeing a colored man. Gee, this man was looking so happy, as his chains had been broken, and he was on one knee trying to get up! It was called the Emancipation Statue. We also had Emancipation Day exercises in all the colored schools and a grand parade down Pennsylvania Avenue.

—John E. Washington,
They Knew Lincoln, 1942

and U.S. history. The tuition is free to all who promise to become teachers; those not entering the teaching profession have to pay $10 per year.

April 14. The *Emancipation Monument* is dedicated in Lincoln Park. Frederick Douglass and John Mercer Langston speak at the dedication ceremony; President Ulysses S. Grant and other officials of the federal government also attend.

John W. Cromwell establishes the *People's Advocate*, a black weekly newspaper that is published until 1884.

1877

February 26. The final elements of the "Hayes Compromise" or the "Wormley Hotel Agreement" are set in place during meetings at the Wormley Hotel. This political arrangement gives Rutherford B. Hayes victory in the presidential election, in exchange for withdrawing the remaining federal troops from the South and adopting a more conciliatory policy toward the South. Southern negotiators promise to protect the newly won political rights of ex-slaves.

March 4. Rutherford B. Hayes is inaugurated as president.

President Hayes appoints Frederick Douglass marshal of the District of Columbia. It is a four-year appointment, and Douglass is the first African American approved by the U.S. Senate to a presidential appointment. Yet black Washingtonians are annoyed to discover that certain ceremonial responsibilities have been deleted from Douglass's duties. For example, President Hayes does not allow Douglass to oversee the presentation of guests to the president at formal White House receptions.

Frederick Douglass and Richard T. Greener debate at a conference of the American Social Science Association at Saratoga Springs, New York. The issue: whether the mass migration of black people from the South to the Midwest and the plains states is good for black people. Greener argues that the exodus will expand black people's political and economic opportunities and will remove them from the harsh racial oppression of the South. Douglass argues that blacks should stay and fight for equality right where they are.

Frederick Douglass purchases a substantial property in Uniontown (later renamed Anacostia) and moves his family to a large farmhouse there, which he names Cedar Hill.

July 1. Benjamin O. Davis is born to Louis Patrick Henry Davis and Henrietta Stewart Davis at 1830 11th Street NW. Despite his father's objections, Davis joins the army. He embarks on a brilliant career—first with the 9th Cavalry and later as brigadier general of the 4th Cavalry Brigade.

The Preparatory High School holds its first commencement ceremonies. Eleven students graduate: Dora E Baker, May L. Beason, Fannie M. Costin, Julia C. Grant, Fannie E. McCoy, Cornelia A. Pinckney, Carrie E. Taylor, Mary E. M. Thomas, James D. C. Craig, John A. Parker, and James B. Wright.

Twenty-two blacks leave the Nineteenth Street Baptist Church to form the Berean Baptist Church. They hold church services in the Sumner School until 1901, when they erect a church at 2033 11th Street.

John Mercer Langston is appointed consul general to Haiti and chargé d'affaires to the Dominican Republic, where he remains until 1885.

1878

June 11. The Organic Act of 1878 eliminates home rule and reinstitutes the system of three city commissioners. The act also guarantees a federal subsidy equal to half the city's expenses and mandates that the U.S. president appoint the members of the District Supreme Court.

Artist William E. Braxton (1878–1932) is born in the District. He becomes one of the first black expressionist painters. He receives some recognition after his figural studies of black nineteenth-century actor Ira Aldridge and writer Alexander Pushkin are published. Braxton's work is exhibited at the Harmon Foundation in 1928 and later at the Smithsonian Institution and the National Gallery of Art.

June 24. Senator Blanche K. Bruce marries Josephine Wilson, schoolteacher and member of a prominent black family in Cleveland. After a European honeymoon, they return to an active political and social life in the District. Mrs. Bruce becomes known as a gracious and fashionable hostess of social events. The Bruces' first son, Roscoe Conkling Bruce, is named after the senator's great friend and ally Senator Roscoe Conkling of New York. Senator Conkling stepped up to escort freshman senator Bruce to take the oath of office, after the senior senator from Mississippi, James Alcorn, refused to do so.

Booker T. Washington spends an academic year studying at Wayland Seminary.

Francis Grimké moves to the District of Columbia to become pastor of the Fifteenth Street Presbyterian Church. Shortly thereafter, he marries Charlotte Forten, daughter of Philadelphia abolitionist John Forten.

Black southern families begin a mass exodus to Kansas and the midwestern states. Over 40,000 people, known as Exodusters, migrate from the South, encouraged by such leaders as Moses "Pap" Singleton of Tennessee and Henry Adams of Louisiana.

1879

January. Richard T. Greener becomes dean of the Howard University Law School. He serves in this capacity until July 1880. After that time, he practices law in the District.

The Preparatory High School relocates to the Sumner School building. Mary J. Patterson remains principal.

At age twenty-three, aspiring newspaper editor John Edward Bruce starts his own newspaper, a weekly called the *Argus*. After it fails, he launches the *Sunday Item* in 1880. Undaunted by its collapse, he starts the *Washington Grit* in 1884. He has been writing for black newspapers since he was a teenager, and in 1882, at age twenty-six, he becomes editor of a black Norfolk newspaper, the *Republican*. News is in his blood; he serves as correspondent for a number of papers and as editor and founder of several of his own. He becomes a household name when he begins writing a weekly column, "Bruce Grit," in 1884. Bruce moves to New York City, where he continues writing until his death in 1924.

Alexander Crummell and black parishioners establish St. Luke's Episcopal Church.

Mt. Zion Cemetery is established in Georgetown.

1880

June 12. The Washington Cadet Corps is organized under the leadership of Captain D. Graham.

John Edwin Washington is born in Annapolis, Maryland. As a child, he is sent to live with his grandmother Caroline Washington, who lives near Ford's Theatre, where Lincoln was assassinated. He grows up playing marbles and ball in the alleys behind Ford's Theatre and later chronicles the history of the old free black community that lived around E Street in downtown Washington, D.C. He develops a particular interest in Abraham Lincoln and in 1942 publishes *They Knew Lincoln,* a book about Lincoln and blacks.

1881

February 22. James Reese Europe, conductor and composer, is born in Mobile, Alabama. His family moves to Washington, D.C., where he learns to play the piano under the tutelage of Joseph Douglass. As director during World War I of the 15th Regiment Band, he introduces brass-band jazz to major European cities under the Allies.

March 4. James Garfield is inaugurated as president.

There was no dancing that was not a sin, except "shouting" and tapping on the floor with the feet; no swing, but the religious swaying to and fro, and no club but the church. Once in a great while, the different churches would give a big picnic to raise money, and even had excursions, but almost every week in some houses there was a parlor social gathering for the young people where they played such games as "in the well," "turning the bottle," "spinning the plate," and "swinging partners."

—John E. Washington,
They Knew Lincoln, 1942

Sheet music for Lieutenant James Reese Europe and his band.

President Garfield appoints Frederick Douglass recorder of deeds for the District of Columbia. Blanche K. Bruce is appointed register of the treasury. He serves in that position until 1885.

Howard University's Dental College is established, after it is recognized that graduates of the Medical College might end up practicing in remote areas of the South and should have basic dentistry skills. By the 1884–1885 school year, the catalog offers a substantial program of courses in dentistry.

July 2. President Garfield is shot in the Baltimore and Potomac railroad station in Washington, D.C. He succumbs to his wounds on September 19.

September 20. Chester A. Arthur is sworn in as president.

Bishop Daniel Alexander Payne establishes the Bethel Literary and Historical Association at the Metropolitan African Methodist Episcopal Church.

Bishop Daniel Alexander Payne lays the cornerstone for a grand new building for the Metropolitan A.M.E. Church.

In the early 1880s a group of black men and women interested in politics, literature, and the arts begins meeting each Saturday. Calling itself the Saturday Circle or the Saturday Nighters, the group continues to meet until the early 1900s. It eventually includes some of the most brilliant and creative minds in the city, such as Reverend Francis J. Grimké and Charlotte Forten Grimké, Fannie Shippen Smith, Anna J. Hayward Cooper, May Miller, Edward W. Blyden, and Georgia Douglas Johnson.

1882

William Calvin Chase begins publishing the *Washington Bee*, a weekly newspaper in the District of Columbia. It quickly becomes one of the most important black newspapers in the country and a touchstone for the local African American community.

Walter H. Brooks becomes pastor of the Nineteenth Street Baptist Church. Already politically active and a prolific poet, Brooks remains at the church until his death in 1945. Under his guidance, the Nineteenth Street Baptist Church sponsors many cultural and social events, and Brooks himself supports several important black organizations.

1883

Ford Thompson Dabney, musician and producer, is born in the District. A theater owner in Washington, D.C., he begins a talent bureau

William Calvin Chase, publisher of the Washington Bee.

Offices of the Washington Bee, *located at 1109 I Street NW, 1900s.*

for black entertainers in the 1920s, tours with James Reese Europe, and for eight years leads the orchestra for Florenz Ziegfeld's Midnight Frolics in New York City.

Reverend Alexander Crummell organizes the Conference of Church Workers Among Colored People to protest the lack of African American bishops in the Episcopal Church.

Nannie Helen Burroughs and her mother move to Washington, D.C., from Orange County, Virginia.

May 5. Josiah Henson dies in Dresden, Canada.

Mary Ann Shadd Cary receives her law degree from Howard University Law School.

October 15. In a series of decisions known as the Civil Rights Cases, the Supreme Court holds that requiring places of public accommodation to serve African Americans is a violation of the right of private property. These decisions end the federal government's efforts to ensure the rights guaranteed in the Fourteenth Amendment.

1884

January 24. Frederick Douglass marries his copyist, Helen Pitts, a white woman who is a former teacher at Hampton Institute and an activist in the women's rights movement. Reverend Francis Grimké performs the ceremony in the parsonage of the Fifteenth Street Presbyterian Church.

Former South Carolina secretary of state Francis L. Cardozo becomes principal of the Preparatory School. Presently, the school has an enrollment of 172 students. By 1886 the school will serve 247 students.

After the closure of the National Medical Society, members of the faculty meet in the offices of Dr. Reyburn to form the Medico-Chirurgical Society of the District of Columbia. The American Medical Association and the Medical Society of Washington continue to refuse admission to African American doctors.

October. James Wormley, owner of the Wormley Hotel, dies in Boston. His body is returned to the District, where it lies in state and is viewed by hundreds of mourners at the hotel.

1885

March 4. Grover Cleveland is inaugurated as president.

Photographer Daniel Freeman (1868–?) opens his first studio in Washington, D.C., claiming to be the first black photographer in

At the outset, as an old watchman on the walls of liberty, eagerly scanning the social and political horizon, you naturally ask me, What of the night? It is easy to break forth in joy and thanksgiving for Emancipation in the District of Columbia. It is easy to call up the noble sentiments and the starting events which made that measure possible. It is easy to trace the footsteps of the Negro in the past, marked as they are all the way along with blood. But the present occasion calls for something more. How stands the Negro to-day? What is the outlook, and what is his probable future?

—Frederick Douglass on the 21st anniversary of Emancipation in the District Congregational Church, April 1883

New Year's Day was a great day in the Clarks' and all of our homes. All who came just had to eat a plate of black-eyed peas and hog jowls. Aunt Eliza said this would give us good luck for all of the New Year, but if any woman came to our houses on New Year's morning, keep her out, because she would bring you bad luck for the year.

—John E. Washington, *They Knew Lincoln*, 1942

the city. In 1895 Freeman installs the exhibit of the District of Columbia in the Negro Building at the Cotton States Expositions in Atlanta, Georgia.

The Banneker Relief Association is established to provide funds for the Sojourner Truth Home in the District.

Francis J. Grimké leaves the Fifteenth Street Presbyterian Church to become pastor of the Laura Street Presbyterian Church in Jacksonville, Florida.

1886

Washingtonian Hugh Browne, recently returned from Liberia, becomes instructor of physics at the Preparatory High School. There, he introduces an innovative system of instruction that emphasizes student experimentation. Browne remains at the school until 1898. He later teaches at Hampton and becomes principal of a black school in Baltimore and of the Institute for Colored Youth in Philadelphia. Browne also receives several patents for his inventions.

The Metropolitan A.M.E. Church on M Street NW is completed.

1887

Black Civil War veterans who have formed and maintained themselves as battalions since the end of the war are incorporated into the National Guard as the 1st Separate Colored Battalion of the District National Guard under the command of Major Christian Fleetwood. They hold annual competitive drills that become popular social occasions for black Washingtonians.

Mary Church (1863–1954), daughter of Memphis millionaire Robert Church, arrives in Washington to teach at the Preparatory School. Shortly after her arrival, she meets Robert Herberton Terrell (1857–1925), a graduate of Harvard and Howard University School of Law, head of Latin instruction at the school, and one of the most eligible black bachelors in the city.

Anna Julia Cooper begins teaching math and Latin at the Preparatory School.

Mary Church Terrell, a teacher at the Preparatory School.

1888

July. Angry blacks tear down the wall separating the white residents of LeDroit Park from the adjoining black community. The wall is particularly egregious to those Howard University students and black neighborhood residents who are forced to walk around the walled-off LeDroit Park in order to get downtown. Although the walls are soon replaced, in 1901 they are finally removed permanently.

October 15. Captain Arthur Brooks is appointed military instructor of the Colored High School Cadet Corps, succeeding Major

I was fortunate in having as commander of the cadet corps Major Arthur Brooks, Commander of the First Separate Battalion of the D.C. National Guard. . . . Major Brooks taught us, among the other things . . . the vice of approximation. He was a stern disciplinarian. When we stood at attention, feet turned out, they had to be at the precise angle, thumbs along the seam of the trousers.

—Rayford Logan, recalling his cadet corps and its participation in President Wilson's inauguration in "Growing Up in Washington: A Lucky Generation," Columbia Historical Society Records

Christian Fleetwood, who founded the cadets. He commands the cadets until 1918.

The Capital Savings Bank, owned and operated by blacks, takes in more than $117,000 in deposits from District residents during its first year. Located at 609 F Street NW, it closes in 1902–1903.

In his account of growing up in the District, John Washington recalls some of the herbal medicines that blacks used to fend off illness. One elderly woman, Aunt Eliza, had a gift for healing. She used "pot likker" as a rub to cure lameness. For colds, she used goose fat; for aches and pains—even headaches—she would rub dried hog jowls over the affected part, and the pain would disappear.

1889

January 1. The first Catholic Afro-American Congress convenes in Washington, D.C. The Catholic Afro-American Congress Movement is established in the late nineteenth century, as a large number of black people join the Roman Catholic Church. Father Augustus Tolton (1854–1897), the first black priest to serve in America, celebrates the opening mass.

March 4. Benjamin Harrison is inaugurated as president.

Blanche K. Bruce is appointed recorder of deeds for the District of Columbia. This position puts Bruce in an advantageous economic and political position from which to launch his real estate and insurance ventures. He also adds considerably to landholdings that he has already amassed in Mississippi.

Ida B. Wells-Barnett becomes the first woman elected to the post of secretary in the National Afro-American Press Association, at its annual conference being held in the District.

Frederick Douglass is appointed minister and consul general to Haiti. He serves until July 30, 1891, when he resigns his post.

[E]very winter, my grandmother had to buy a big goose and let it hang out of the window to freeze for so many nights and days. Then she would put it in a big pan and roast it for old Aunt Eliza, who skimmed all of the grease off the pans and stored it away in bottles. When you had a cold and your nose just wouldn't stop running, old Aunt Eliza would have your parents rub your nose, temples, and hands and feet with goose grease and you would get well in a jiffy. In the spring of every year, she gave all the children in the neighborhood sassafras tea, to make our blood thin and get the old devil out.

—John E. Washington,
They Knew Lincoln, 1942

Francis J. Grimké returns to the Fifteenth Street Presbyterian Church. He retires in 1925 but remains active at the church until his death in 1937.

1890

Kelly Miller joins the faculty of Howard University, lecturing in math and later also in sociology.

Will Marion Cook becomes director of the American Orchestra Club, a musical club and performing group organized by Christian Fleetwood.

John Mercer Langston wins election to the House of Representatives from Virginia. He serves only one term.

1891

The Preparatory School for Colored Youth moves to a new building at M Street and New Jersey Avenue NW and is renamed the M Street High School. Francis L. Cardozo remains principal until 1896.

October 28. Schoolteacher Mary Church weds department head Robert Herberton Terrell.

Lillian Evans (1891–1967) is born to Dr. Wilson B. Evans and Anne Brooks. She begins performing as a child and, under the tutelage of her mother, who taught music in the public school system, becomes well known in the District of Columbia. She attends Miner Teachers College and Howard University, where she continues her musical studies under Lulu Vere Childers. Under the professional name of Madame Evanti, Evans becomes an acclaimed opera soprano, touring internationally until shortly before her death.

1892

June. Anna Julia Cooper and Helen Cook form the Colored Woman's League of Washington, D.C. The league organizes relief efforts for destitute black families and leads the struggle for improved sanitation in alley dwellings and better public schools for black children. The organization is also responsible for introducing kindergartens into the colored public school system.

The M Street High School opens in a new building. The curriculum includes the classics, Latin, and math; there is also a military cadet corps. The school quickly becomes the most highly rated secondary school for blacks in the country. Some affluent and striving blacks from the South even relocate their families or board their children with District friends and relatives so that the children might attend the school.

October 31. Anti-lynching crusader Ida B. Wells-Barnett lectures at Metropolitan A.M.E. Church. Wells is disappointed at the low turnout.

Joseph H. Douglass, Frederick Douglass's grandson, offers violin instruction in his office at 934 F Street NW.

Andrew Hilyer, an accountant in the U.S. Treasury Department, establishes the Union League of the District of Columbia. He publishes the Union League Directory, listing local black businesses, in 1892, 1894, and 1901.

Henry Lewis organizes the Amphion Glee Club. It becomes one of the most popular performing groups in the city.

1893

February 3. Anti-lynching activist Ida B. Wells-Barnett delivers a keynote lecture at the Metropolitan A.M.E. Church. Frederick Douglass, Lucy Moten, and Anna Julia Cooper, teacher at the M Street High School, host the event, and Mary Church Terrell introduces Wells. This time Wells-Barnett's lecture is a success; the church is filled to capacity and she receives almost $200 in donations from the audience. Wells-Barnett decides to use the money to hire a Pinkerton agent to investigate the lynching of Henry Smith, who was publicly tortured and burned to death by a mob of 10,000 people in Paris, Texas.

March 4. Grover Cleveland is inaugurated as president. The Colored High School Cadet Corps, under the leadership of Major Arthur Brooks, marches in the presidential inaugural parade for the first time.

Edward E. Cooper begins publishing the *Colored American*, an illustrated weekly magazine, out of offices at 459 C Street NW.

Economic depression sweeps the nation, and many in the District suffer from its effects. One casualty is the Wormley Hotel, which the family is forced to sell to Charles Gibbs. Gibbs retains the name of the hotel until 1897.

Offices of the Colored American.

Voluntary neighborhood organizations established by whites are called citizens' associations; those by blacks, civic associations. Some neighborhoods have both. One of the oldest of the latter is the Deanwood Civic Association.

P. B. S. Pinchback, former lieutenant governor of Louisiana, and his wife, Nina, move to Washington, D.C. Their grand home on Bacon Street near the Chinese embassy becomes a center of black elite social activities.

A group of black families, including the Hilyers and the Fleetwoods, donates funds to purchase and dispense coal, food, clothing, and other supplies in its neighborhood during the 1893 depression. Sara Iredell Fleetwood dispenses the goods from her own home at 2230 6th Street. Mrs. Evelyn D. Shaw begins visiting black families in alleys to improve their living conditions.

Elizabeth (Libba) Cotten is born in Chapel Hill, North Carolina. She teaches herself to play the guitar and writes "Freight Train," a blues song, at age twelve. She moves to Washington as a teenager and begins playing the blues guitar.

1894

Daniel Hale Williams is made surgeon-in-charge of Freedmen's Hospital. Before he moved to Washington, D.C., he had already come to the public's attention as the founder of Chicago's Provident Hospital. In 1893 he successfully performed heart surgery on a man who had been stabbed in the chest. In the course of the operation, Dr. Williams sewed up the membrane surrounding the heart. It was one of the first such operations to be performed in this country. His achievements at Freedmen's Hospital have an immediate impact upon medical education at the university, particularly in the area of surgical instruction. Williams also organizes the first program for interns at the hospital, making Freedmen's Hospital and Provident Hospital two of the few hospitals that provide such training to black medical graduates. Williams also establishes a Training School for Nurses at Freedmen's Hospital in 1894.

Informal self-help and racial uplift groups abound. Black men and women organize relief efforts and cultural groups, such as the Booklovers Club. Established in 1894 as a reading circle of a few women, it later expands its efforts to develop cultural programs and excursions for black schoolchildren.

December 9. Reverend Alexander Crummell, founder of St. Luke's Church, retires as its rector.

December 26. (Nathan) Jean Toomer is born in Washington, D.C. He grows up in the home of his grandfather, P. B. S. Pinchback.

1895

February 20. Frederick Douglass dies at his home, Cedar Hill, in Anacostia. His body is viewed by thousands of Washingtonians at the Metropolitan A.M.E. Church. He is buried in Rochester, New York, next to his first wife, Anna.

Will Marion Cook makes his solo debut performance at Carnegie Hall in New York City.

June 25. Albert Irvin Cassell is born in Towson, Maryland. Cassell later becomes one of the most prominent African American architects, launching a successful career from his position as instructor and later head of Howard University's Department of Architecture in the 1920s.

The Freedmen's Hospital ambulance system is set up by Dr. Daniel Hale Williams.

Mary Church Terrell is appointed to serve on the Board of Education for the District of Columbia; she holds the post until 1901.

Amanda Bowen establishes the Sojourner Truth Home.

September 18. Booker T. Washington gives his "Atlanta Compromise" speech at the Atlanta Cotton States and International Exposition. Washington urges political compromise on the part of black

And now you may ask me—What is the conception of life which my experiences have wrought within me?

My answer is, first of all, that no age, no Church, no people are ever left, by the Almighty, destitute of grand prophets, devoted priests, and glorious reformers.... "The age of chivalry is not gone!" Never in all the history of the world has the Almighty been wanting of the gallant spirits, ready, at any sacrifice, to vindicate the cause of the poor and needy, and to "wax valiant in fight" for the downtrodden and oppressed. "The glorious army of the Apostles," "the goodly fellowship of the Prophets," "the noble army of Martyrs," have never yet come short, in finality. Their ranks are unbroken, unceasing, and immortal! "When the enemy shall come in like a flood, the Spirit of the Lord shall lift up a standard against him."

—Reverend Alexander Crummell's farewell sermon, St. Luke's Church, December 9, 1894

The National League of Colored Women on the steps of Cedar Hill, Frederick Douglass's home.

leaders pressing for their rights and counsels them to "Cast down your bucket where you are—cast it down in making friends in every manly way of the people of all races by whom we are surrounded." He reassures southern whites that "In all things that are purely social we can be as separate as the fingers, yet one as the hand in all things essential to mutual progress." The speech immediately launches him into the national scene and makes him a celebrity spokesman for African Americans. But many blacks resent his message of conciliation.

Woodlawn Cemetery is established on Benning Road.

1896

May 18. The Supreme Court rules in *Plessy v. Ferguson* and establishes the "separate but equal" principle that undergirds segregation of the races in schools and other social structures across the South. It holds that such segregation is not a violation of the Fourteenth Amendment if the segregated population is provided with equal facilities. This decision legalizes segregation and leads to increased underfunding for black education.

July. The National League of Colored Women and the National Federation of Afro-American Women meet in Washington at the Nineteenth Street Baptist Church and merge to form the National Association of Colored Women. Mary Church Terrell is selected as the first president and serves until 1901. Some of the most powerful and politically influential black women in the country are in attendance, including Ida B. Wells-Barnett (with her four-month-old son), Margaret Murray Washington, Rosetta Sprague, Frances Ellen Harper, Josephine St. Pierre Ruffin, and—to the delight of the other delegates—Harriet Tubman!

James E. Walker, a Washington teacher, is commissioned as a first lieutenant in the 1st Separate Battalion in the District of Columbia National Guard. By 1909 he is made captain and in 1912 becomes major of the battalion, replacing Major Arthur Brooks.

Sara Fleetwood is in the first class of nurse graduates from the Training School for Nurses established by Daniel Hale Williams at Freedmen's Hospital.

1897

March 4. William McKinley is inaugurated as president.

March 7. Ex-slave and slave narrative author Harriet Jacobs dies in Washington, D.C.

May 9. Author Rudolph Fisher is born in the District of Columbia. Despite being trained in medicine at Howard University and working as a physician, Fisher will become famous for his Renaissance-era novels and short stories.

Major James E. Walker.

The Training School for Nurses class of 1896. Sara Fleetwood is in the back row, far left.

Blanche K. Bruce is appointed register of the Treasury.

The American Negro Academy is established in the District of Columbia by Reverend Alexander Crummell, former rector of St. Luke's Episcopal Church. The academy is founded to promote African American scholarship, create an archives for black research, and promote the publishing of scholarly work. Local historian and writer John Cromwell is the primary organizing force behind the organization; W. E. B. DuBois becomes its first president. Professor Kelly Miller writes the group's first published paper, criticizing white scholars for predicting the extinction of the African American population.

Major Arthur Brooks, head of the Colored High School Cadet Corps, is appointed commander of the 1st Separate Battalion of the D.C. National Guard, where he serves until 1912. Taking on many different jobs for the White House, including messenger in the War Department, doorkeeper for the White House, and custodian of the Executive Mansion, Brooks becomes a confidant of several presidents. He remains on the staff of the White House until his death on September 7, 1926.

November 15. John Mercer Langston dies in Washington, D.C.

1898

Will Marion Cook writes the musical score for *Clorindy, Or the Origin of the Cake Walk*. The musical, written in collaboration with Paul Laurence Dunbar, is a Broadway hit. Under the name Will Marion, he composes for the popular vaudeville team of Bert Williams and George Walker. *In Dahomey* is a popular favorite.

February. Dr. Daniel Hale Williams resigns from his position as chief surgeon at Freedmen's Hospital. He marries Alice Johnson, a Washington schoolteacher, one month later and returns to Chicago with his new bride. Dr. Austin M. Curtis takes over as chief surgeon.

Paul Laurence Dunbar arrives in Washington, D.C., on the heels of his successful tour of England. He begins working in the Library of Congress under the direction of Daniel Murray but soon leaves that position to live off his literary income. On March 6 he marries Alice Ruth Moore, a schoolteacher who is a talented writer herself. After Dunbar and his wife separate in 1902, he returns to Dayton, Ohio.

June. U.S. troops arrive in Cuba. Among them are members of four all-black regiments: the 24th Infantry, the 25th Infantry, and the 9th and 10th Cavalry.

1899

January 26. May Miller, daughter of Howard University scholar Kelly Miller and teacher Annie May (Butler) Miller, is born in Washington, D.C. May grows up in a house filled with the most creative and influential African American scholars and writers of the period.

April 29. Edward Kennedy (Duke) Ellington is born in Washington, D.C. He earns his nickname as a schoolboy because his mother keeps him so well dressed. Growing up next to the clubs and the performance halls of U Street, he is exposed at an early age to some of the country's most gifted musicians and entertainers. At nineteen he organizes his own band, and two years later he is playing professional engagements under the name of Duke's Washingtonians.

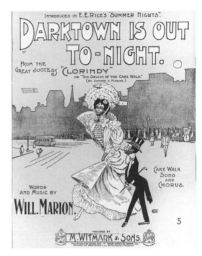

Sheet music for Darktown Is Out To-night, *by Will Marion Cook, 1898.*

Paul Laurence Dunbar, the first African American to gain national prominence as a poet.

Librarian Daniel Murray (1852–1925) is asked to prepare a display on Negro literature for the American Exhibit at the 1900 Paris Exposition.

The school board votes not to close colored schools for the annual Emancipation Day parade, signaling the displeasure of the city's upper-class blacks and heralding the end of the grand Emancipation celebrations in the District.

Black schoolchildren.

June 14. Benjamin O. Davis, son of Washingtonians Louis Patrick Henry Davis and Henrietta Stewart Davis, is sworn into the U.S. army and begins his long and successful career in the 9th Cavalry. He serves in the far west, in the Philippines, in the Southwest during the Mexican Revolution, and in Liberia.

Robert H. Terrell is appointed principal of the M Street High School.

1900

The White House's annual Easter egg hunt remains integrated. Black children take part in the festivities on the White House grounds.

Easter egg hunt on the White House grounds.

May 29. Booker T. Washington speaks at the Bethel Literary and Historical Association. He urges a moderate program of economic self-help and limited political agitation. Rayford Logan describes the literary society as "the most important lyceum of colored people at the turn of the century [where] some of the most noted colored men and women of the day spoke to large audiences."

July. The First Pan-African Conference is held in London, England. Among the attendees are W. E. B. DuBois, Trinidadian Henry Sylvester Williams, and delegates from the United States, the Caribbean, and Africa. M Street School teacher Anna Julia Cooper reads her paper on "The Negro Problem in America"; she becomes a member of the executive committee.

July 4. Lewis Alexander (1900–1945), actor, poet, essayist, and theater pioneer, is born in Washington, D.C. He attends Dunbar High School and Howard University, where he becomes involved in the Howard Players, the Playwrights' Circle, the Aldridge Players, and the Ethiopian Art Players. He later directs several theater groups in Washington, including the St. Vincent de Paul Players, the Ira Aldridge Players of Grover Cleveland School, and the Randall Community Center Players.

The graduating class of Howard University Law School, 1900.

Booker T. Washington founds the National Negro Business League to promote and support black businesses.

At age seventeen, Addison Scurlock moves to the District of Columbia from North Carolina to become an apprentice to photographer Moses P. Rice.

A civil rights suit is brought against the owners of the Washington Opera House for refusing to seat a black ticket holder, and it results in a victory—of sorts—for the plaintiff. He is awarded only one cent.

1901

January 29. Representative George H. White of North Carolina, the last of the Reconstruction-era black congressmen, delivers his farewell speech to the gathered members of the House of Representatives. He will be the last black person to serve in Congress for twenty-eight years.

March 4. William McKinley is inaugurated for his second term as president.

Representative George H. White's Farewell Speech, January 1901

Mr. Chairman: I want to enter a plea for the colored man, the colored woman, the colored boy, and the colored girl of this country.

I would like to advance the statement that the musty records of 1868, filed away in the archives of Southern capitols, as to what the Negro was thirty years ago, is not a proper standard by which the Negro living on the threshold of the twentieth century should be measured. Since that time we have reduced the illiteracy of the race at least 45 percent. We have written and published nearly five hundred books. We have nearly eight hundred newspapers, three of which are dailies. We have now in practice over two thousand lawyers, and a corresponding number of doctors. We have accumulated over $12,000,000 worth of school property and about $40,000,000 worth of church property. . . .

We are operating successfully several banks, commercial enterprises among our people in the Southland, including one silk mill and one cotton factory. We have 32,000 teachers in the schools of the country; we have built, with the aid of our friends, about 20,000 churches, and support seven colleges, seventeen academies, fifty high schools, five law schools, five medical schools and twenty-five theological seminaries. We have over 600,000 acres of land in the South alone. . . . All this was done under the most adverse circumstances. We have done it in the face of lynching, burning at the stake, with the humiliation of Jim Crow cars, the disfranchisement of our male citizens, slander and degradation of our women, with the factories closed against us, . . .

Now, Mr. Chairman, before concluding my remarks I want to submit a brief recipe for the solution of the so-called American Negro problem. He asks no special favors, but simply demands that he be given the same chance for existence, for earning a livelihood, for raising himself in the scales of manhood and womanhood, that are accorded to kindred nationalities. . . .

This, Mr. Chairman, is perhaps the Negro's temporary farewell to the American Congress; but let me say, phoenixlike he will rise up some day and come again. These parting words are in behalf of an outraged, heartbroken, bruised and bleeding, but God-fearing, people, faithful, industrious, loyal people, rising people, full of potential force.

Anna Julia Cooper becomes principal of M Street High School. She serves in this capacity until 1906.

When Congress codifies District laws, it does not incorporate the civil rights provisions into the new municipal code. Segregation is once again entirely legal in the District. However, a few public places, like the Library of Congress, the D.C. public library, the streetcar system, and the train stations, are not resegregated.

Highland Beach becomes a popular summer resort community for black Washingtonians, including the Douglasses, Anna Julia Cooper, the Wormleys, and the Terrells. Bowen's (later Flagg's) Cottage and Ware's Hotel serve black vacationers.

Andrew Hilyer publishes for the last time his *Twentieth Century Union League Directory: A Historical, Biographical and Statistical*

Andrew Hilyer, publisher.

Anna Julia Cooper at her desk at M Street High School.

Study of Colored Washington, at the Dawn of the Twentieth Century and After a Generation of Freedom.

Amanda Hilyer (wife of Andrew Hilyer) begins organizing the Samuel Coleridge-Taylor Choral Society to perform the work of the internationally famous black composer Samuel Coleridge-Taylor.

May 1. Sterling Brown, writer, poet, and critic, is born in Washington, D.C. (d. 1989). He attends Dunbar High School and graduates from Williams College. He attends Harvard University and begins teaching at Howard University in 1929.

September 6. President McKinley is shot in Buffalo, New York. He dies on September 14.

September 14. Vice President Theodore Roosevelt is sworn in as president.

October 10. Frederick D. Patterson, president of Tuskegee Institute from 1935 to 1953, is born in Anacostia, the youngest son of William and Mamie (Brooks) Ross. His parents have only recently moved to the District of Columbia from Texas with William's five older brothers and sisters.

Due to the influence of Booker T. Washington, Robert H. Terrell is appointed justice of the peace in the District of Columbia, the first such appointment for an African American in the city.

October 16. Booker T. Washington is invited to dine at the White House by President Theodore Roosevelt. As a result, Roosevelt is harshly criticized in the southern press.

Musician and composer James Bland returns to Washington, D.C., in hopes of resuscitating his flagging career. He writes the music and lyrics for a production called *The Sporting Girl* but makes very little from the sale of the work.

1902

February. Dr. Austin Curtis, former surgeon-in-chief at Freedmen's Hospital, enters private practice at 1535 14th Street NW in offices located at the A.M.E. Church.

Richard John Lewis Holmes is appointed one of the first African American firefighters in the city. He is the son of Richard John Holmes, one of many blacks who escaped slavery in Virginia in the 1850s.

The True Reformer Building is erected at 1200 U Street NW. The imposing five-story building is designed by black Washingtonian John A. Lankford. The United Order of True Reformers, a black fraternal organization established in Virginia, is housed in the building until 1911. A variety of businesses operates out of the building, making it the social and business hub of the neighborhood. It also houses a dance hall and the offices of the 1st Separate Battalion, which conducts drills in the basement.

Armstrong Technical High School opens. It is named for General Samuel Chapman Armstrong, founder of the Hampton Institute; the first principal is Dr. Wilson Bruce Evans, father of opera soprano Lillian Evanti.

The competitive drill between Armstrong and M Street High Schools becomes an annual event. In June 1902 the first interschool

If Christ Came to Washington—He Would Find

Henry P. Slaughter giving a dinner.

W. C. Payne getting up a new organization.

Negro ability in want of a profitable market.

John F. Cook steering clear of entangling alliances.

Negroes colonized in the obscure corners of our theaters.

Color discrimination in many branches of the public service.

Female school teachers who strangely prefer salary to matrimony.

Self-respecting Negroes boycotting the discriminating theaters by Staying away from them.

Robert Pelham, Jr., studying law, and decanting upon the palmy days of ye *Detroit Plaindealer.*

Five hundred teachers and department clerks who ought to have deposits in the Capital Savings Bank.

—The *Colored American,*
February 22, 1902

competition is held between Armstrong and M Street High School. By the 1920s over 900 boys are in training every year for the competition, and the crowd numbers more than 20,000.

1903

Harriet Gibbs Marshall (1868–1941), music director for colored schools, establishes the Washington Conservatory of Music and School of Expression for black students in Washington, D.C. The school is located at 9th and T Streets NW.

The Samuel Coleridge-Taylor Choral Society is chartered with a constitution and by-laws. The society brings Coleridge-Taylor to Washington, where he leads an acclaimed performance of his trilogy The Song of Hiawatha ("Hiawatha's Wedding Feast," "The Death of Minnehaha," and "Hiawatha's Departure") before an integrated audience.

Ionia Whipper, daughter of South Carolina activists, receives her medical degree from Howard University School of Medicine. She practices obstetrics until shortly before her death. Not content merely with practicing medicine, she organizes efforts, such as the Tuesday Evening Club, to help unwed mothers and delinquent girls and establishes several other institutions, as well as caring for many girls in her own home.

The Capital Savings Bank, the District's only black bank, closes.

The True Reformer's Building opens to the public; it is located in the heart of the U Street corridor.

July 22. Francis L. Cardozo Sr. dies.

December. Archibald Grimké is elected president of the American Negro Academy.

1904

June 3. Charles R. Drew is born in Washington, D.C., to Richard and Nora (Burrell) Drew. Drew later becomes renowned for his contributions to research on blood plasma.

Archibald Grimké, president of the American Negro Academy.

Mary Church Terrell attends the International Congress of Women in Berlin.

Jean Toomer and his mother move to New York City. Following her death in 1909, the family moves back to Washington, D.C.

The *Colored American* ceases publication, due to lack of financial support. Its publisher, Edward E. Cooper, dies in poverty four years later, a victim of his ambition to publish the first African American illustrated magazine.

Edwin B. Henderson is appointed to teach physical education at M Street High School and Armstrong High School. The first certified black male physical education teacher in a public school system in the country, Henderson later becomes head of the department of physical education for the two black high schools. Born on School Street in southwest D.C., he is well known for writing many letters to the editors of local newspapers, attacking racial segregation. Henderson retires from the school system in 1954.

1905

March 4. Theodore Roosevelt is inaugurated as president.

May 5. The Phyllis Wheatley YWCA, the oldest YWCA in D.C., is founded by black women, including Rosetta Coakley Lawson and Bettie Cox Francis.

June. W. E. B. DuBois organizes the Niagara Movement, a precursor of the National Association for the Advancement of Colored People (NAACP).

Lieutenant Benjamin O. Davis is appointed professor of military science at Wilberforce University.

Mary Burrill (1879–1946), one of the earliest known black women playwrights, begins teaching at M Street High School. She is an instructor there until 1944.

Lulu Vere Childers is appointed instructor of methods and music at Howard University. Under her guidance, the university establishes a department of music in 1906 and a music conservatory in 1912.

Richard Bruce Nugent is born in Washington, D.C. Bohemian, short story writer, poet, and playwright, Nugent becomes well known for his Harlem Renaissance–era literature. He transforms one of his short stories into a play—Sahdji, an African Ballet—which is produced by Howard University in 1925.

Archibald Grimké leaves Boston to relocate to Washington, D.C., to live with his daughter, Angelina.

Black professional men establish the Mu-So-Lit Club, an all-male literary and cultural organization that sponsors literature readings, musical performances, balls, and other events. Its Lincoln-Douglas Debate Dinner, an annual event, becomes an important cultural event in the city.

1906

Camp Pleasant is organized by the Associated Charities. It provides time away from the city during the hot summers for poor black children and their mothers.

May 6. Writer William Waring Cuney is born in Washington, D.C. Cuney attends Howard and Lincoln universities and later becomes the art and music columnist for *The Crisis: A Record of the Darker Race.* One of his most popular works is the poem "No Images," which wins first prize for poetry in a contest run by *Opportunity* magazine in 1926.

Jessie Redmon Fauset is hired as a Latin instructor at M Street High School, where she teaches until she resigns in 1919 to join W. E. B. DuBois in publishing *The Crisis.* Fauset later helps to edit the monthly *Brownies' Book* and publishes several novels.

Mary Church Terrell accepts another appointment to the District Board of Education; she serves until 1911.

1907

The U.S. Supreme Court upholds the right of railroads to segregate passengers traveling between states.

William Sidney Pittman (1875–1958), Tuskegee Institute faculty member and architect, designs the Negro Building for the Jamestown Exposition. Constructed entirely by blacks, the building contains exhibits featuring black achievements.

Ernest Everett Just joins the Howard University faculty as an instructor in English. By 1908 he has left English for biology, in which he received undergraduate training at Dartmouth University. The following year Just leaves for advanced graduate training in marine biology at Woods Hole, Massachusetts.

Addison Scurlock wins the Gold Medal for Photography at the Jamestown Exposition.

Jesse Lawson establishes the Inter-Denominational Bible College (later Frelinghuysen University), an institution for black adult education.

Kelly Miller (1863–1939) is appointed dean of Howard University's College of Arts and Sciences. One year later he publishes the first of his most significant works, *Race Adjustment*.

The second chapter of the Alpha Phi Alpha fraternity is founded at Howard University. The fraternity was established in 1906 at Cornell University.

Alain Locke, recent graduate of Harvard University, becomes the first African American selected as a Rhodes Scholar. He attends Hertford College in England and later the University of Berlin from 1910 to 1911.

Several black families purchase homes and property in the Brookland neighborhood. The home of Daniel and Marie Brandon at 1501 Hamlin Street NE was frequently used for community gatherings and social events such as card parties and sewing groups.

1908

January 15. The first black sorority, Alpha Kappa Alpha, is founded at Howard University by eight students, including Ethel Hedgeman and Lucy Diggs Slowe.

The Murray Brothers Printing Company, publishers of the *Washington Afro American* and the *Tribune,* opens at 922 U Street NW.

The building is designed by black architect Isaiah T. Hatton and is constructed by black workers.

Employees in front of the Murray Brothers Printing Company, 1900s.

1909

February 12. The National Association for the Advancement of Colored People (NAACP) is established in New York.

March 4. William H. Taft is inaugurated as president.

March. Maggie Rogers begins working as a maid in the White House under the stern supervision of Colonel Arthur Brooks. After decades of service, she begins a memoir of her days as first maid to the first ladies. Rogers dies without completing her book, but her daughter, Lillian Parks, who also works at the White House for many years, publishes her story. The African American White House domestic staff is a small, close-knit, hierarchical community. The jobs behind the scenes at the White House are considered prestigious positions by class-conscious black Washingtonians during the first part of the century.

October 19. Nannie Helen Burroughs establishes the National Training School for Women and Girls on 50th and Grant Streets in

The White House had quite an effect on Mama. She wanted everything in our house to be as elegant as possible, and as she saved enough money, she would buy additional pieces of furniture. These additions may have come from the second-hand store, but they were always in such good taste, that they looked as though they might have come from that wonderful White House—at least to my eyes.

—Lillian Rogers Parks,
*My Thirty Years Backstairs
at the White House*, 1961

A cooking class at the National Training School for Women and Girls.

Lincoln Heights, with the assistance of the National Baptist Convention. Her goal is for the school to instruct students in the "three B's: Bible, bath, and broom" (the school motto). In the 1920s Burroughs authored two church plays, The Slabtown District Convention, a comedy about Baptist conventions, and Where Is My Wandering Boy Tonight?—a play with a Mother's Day theme. Burroughs manages the school until her death in 1961.

Georgia Douglass Johnson moves to the District of Columbia at age twenty-four.

Carter G. Woodson arrives in Washington, D.C., to teach in the public school system. While teaching in various schools, including the prestigious M Street High School, Woodson earns his Ph.D. from Harvard University. He becomes principal of Armstrong High School in 1918 but resigns in 1919 to take a teaching position at Howard University.

1910

Robert H. Terrell is appointed judge in the Municipal Court of the District of Columbia. He serves in this position until shortly before his death in 1925. He also begins to teach at Howard University Law School and remains there until 1925.

Willis Richardson (1889–1977), playwright and drama anthologist, essayist, and poet, graduates from M Street High School. He is a founding member of the Washington Branch of the Krigwa Players and a member of the literary group The Saturday Nighters. His plays include *The Chip Woman's Fortune* (1922), *The Deacon's Awakening* (1920), and *The Broken Banjo* (1925).

The Crisis: A Record of the Darker Race, the official monthly publication of the National Association for the Advancement of Colored People, begins publication. W. E. B. DuBois is the editor.

Black neighborhood groups in Washington, D.C.—after being rejected by the Federation of Citizens' Associations—form their own umbrella group, the Federation of Civic Associations.

August 22. The Howard Theatre opens for business at 620 T Street NW. Owned and operated by blacks, it quickly becomes the pride and joy of the black community. The theater begins showcasing black bands and singers, black vaudeville, and traveling shows. The Howard Theatre introduces some of the most important black singers and musicians of the era during its Amateur Night performances and becomes one of the most important venues on the "Chitlin' Circuit," a tour of black theaters. Its heyday was perhaps the 1920s, when it was a hub of entertainment that drew nationally renowned artists to the city. Next door to the Howard Theatre was Frank Holliday's billiard parlor, one of the most popular gathering spots in town for young and "sporting" men.

1911

Howard University students Frank Coleman, Oscar J. Cooper, and Edgar A. Love (known on campus as the Three Musketeers) establish the first chapter of Omega Psi Phi. Ernest Just serves as faculty adviser. University officials refuse to recognize the fraternity until 1914.

The Washington chapter of Sigma Pi Phi, the first black Greek letter society (begun in 1904), is founded by Henry Minton. A number of elite African American men in the District join.

The Howard University Players in Shakespeare's The Merry Wives of Windsor, *c. 1911.*

William H. Lewis is appointed assistant attorney general of the United States by President Taft. He is the first African American to hold this post. As with other important appointments of African Americans, this one came about due to Booker T. Washington's influence.

Addison Scurlock opens his photo studio at 900 U Street NW.

Charles Houston, the only child of William Houston, a District attorney, and Mary Houston, a teacher, graduates from M Street High School. William Houston also taught law at Howard University Law School.

1912

The Washington branch of the NAACP is formed at Shiloh Baptist Church under the leadership of Reverend J. Milton Waldron. Waldron has a brief and stormy tenure as president, however, and a year later he is removed from office and replaced by Archibald Grimké. Waldron draws attention when he begins campaigning for President Wilson and later gives a speech endorsing racial disfranchisement as part of his effort to gain an appointment in the Wilson administration.

Reverend William H. Jernagin is appointed pastor of Mt. Carmel Baptist Church. He quickly becomes one of the most active and well-known churchmen in the city. A lifelong Republican, Jernagin takes leadership roles in many efforts to challenge racial segregation in the District of Columbia. He is also active in national church affairs, organizing the National Fraternal Council of Negro Churches. He and his wife, Cordelia Woolfolk Jernagin, arrived in the city earlier this year, and their house at 1728 Webster Street NW becomes a popular gathering place. Jernagin is a native of Machulaville, Mississippi.

Alain Locke is appointed to the faculty of Howard University, where he begins teaching English, and later philosophy.

Ernest Everett Just is selected to oversee the Department of Physiology at Howard University Medical School. Just also continues to teach zoology in the College of Arts and Sciences.

December 18. Benjamin O. Davis Jr. is born to Elnora Davis and Lieutenant Benjamin O. Davis Sr. at 1830 11th Street NW. At the time Davis Sr. is stationed at Fort Russell in Wyoming.

1913

Ida B. Wells-Barnett refuses to march in segregated formations in the National American Woman's Suffrage Association parade in Washington, D.C.

February 18. Twenty-two women leave the Alpha Kappa Alpha sorority to form the Delta Sigma Theta sorority.

[Bishop Alexander] Walters persuaded DuBois to support Wilson and to throw the weight of *The Crisis* against Roosevelt and Taft, if Wilson would make a statement in behalf of Negroes. Wilson, in October, 1912, sent Walters a categorical statement over his signature "of earnest wish to see justice done the colored people in every matter; and not mere grudging justice, but justice executed with liberality and cordial good feeling.... I want to assure them that should I become President of the United States they may count upon me...." This promise gave DuBois such satisfaction that he resigned from New York Local No. 1 of the Socialist party in order to escape discipline for not voting the Socialist ticket.... According to DuBois, [however], Wilson said in the course of a visit by the bishop to the White House in 1915: "By the way, what about that letter that I wrote to you during the campaign? I do not seem to remember it." When Walters handed the letter to Wilson, "the President forgot to return it."

—Rayford Logan,
The Negro in American Life and Thought: The Nadir, 1877–1901, 1954

My memories of life at 1830 11th Street are undoubtedly a mixture of things I can actually recall and other things people have told me. I remember the icehouse directly across the street, its small buildings in which blocks of ice were stored. . . . I remember the streetcars that passed our house going south to downtown Washington and north toward Walter Reed Hospital. I remember Katzman's Grocery on the corner of 11th and T Streets, only a few doors from our house. . . . I remember quite well the Lincoln and Republic theaters on U Street, and the hill on 13th Street where I took my sled when we had snow.

—Benjamin O. Davis Jr.,
*Benjamin O. Davis, Jr., American:
An Autobiography*, 1991

I was in my last year of high school in Washington when Wilson was elected. Negroes showed grave concern, especially when some newly elected Southerners publicly declared that they had come to Washington to "fight niggers and likker." For a time we wondered whether the colored high school cadets would march, as they had done for many years, in the inaugural procession. We did, and folklore to the contrary notwithstanding, Wilson did not turn his back on us. (I was captain of the front Negro cadet company.)

—Rayford Logan,
*The Negro in American Life and
Thought: The Nadir, 1877–1901*, 1954

March 4. Woodrow Wilson is inaugurated as president. Wilson ushers in a new era of segregation in federal agencies, leaving some blacks angry and disappointed because they risked ridicule in their communities for abandoning the Republican Party and voting for him.

May. The National Democratic Fair Play Association, an organization recently formed in Washington, D.C., to promote segregation in the federal workforce, holds its first mass meeting. The association launches an intensive letter-writing and lobbying campaign to remove blacks from federal jobs and to segregate the remaining black workers.

June. Archibald Grimké is elected president of the Washington, D.C., branch of the NAACP. He initiates a series of meetings and a press campaign against Wilson's new segregation policies. In October he stages a mass protest rally at the Metropolitan A.M.E. Church. The NAACP takes a leadership role in fighting segregationist initiatives in Congress; Grimké successfully organizes opposition to several segregationist measures in the House and the Senate, including a bill that would have prohibited interracial marriages in the District of Columbia. Under Grimké's direction, the D.C. branch of the NAACP becomes the most active in the country.

October 27. The NAACP organizes a huge mass meeting in Washington to protest segregation in the federal workforce. William McAdoo, secretary of the Treasury, reads a letter to the gathering, in which he denies that segregation is a problem in the Treasury Department. It is loudly booed by the crowd.

President Wilson orders segregated seating and has screens placed in government offices to separate black office workers from whites. He also begins removing blacks from some civil service positions. In the Post Office Department and the Bureau of Engraving the government puts up folding screens and hastily constructed partitions around black employees and bars them from lunchrooms and restrooms used by other workers. By the end of 1913 federal employees are effectively segregated. The following year the federal Civil Service begins to require photographs of all applicants.

Within a few months after his inauguration it had become evident that members of Wilson's cabinet were quietly but effectively establishing the color line in their departments. Particularly in the Post Office and the Treasury, in both of which Negroes were numerous, office spaces in these departments began to be segregated or screened off, as were lunchrooms and restrooms. Soon the few good jobs traditionally held by Negroes, such as Register of the Treasury and representatives to Haiti and Liberia, were assigned to whites. Moreover, in May, 1914, the Civil Service began to require photographs of persons taking examinations (the stated purpose being to prevent impersonation)–a practice which, added to the customary one of permitting an appointing officer to make his own choice among the three top applicants, tended to increase the incidence of racial discrimination.

–Benjamin Quarles,
The Negro in the Making of America, 1964

I have recently spent several days in Washington, and I have never seen the colored people so discouraged and so bitter as they are at the present time.

–Booker T. Washington, letter to President Wilson, August 1913

November 6. William Monroe Trotter and Ida B. Wells-Barnett head a delegation of blacks to the White House, bearing a petition with 20,000 signatures protesting increased segregation in the federal government.

The Black Industrial Savings Bank is founded by John Whitelaw Lewis. Opening at 2000 11th Street NW, the bank serves black patrons until it closes for two years in 1932. It reopens as the Industrial Bank of Washington under Jesse Mitchell, an African American businessman from Texas. Black architect Isaiah T. Hatton designed this building, as he has several other outstanding structures in the neighborhood.

1914

January 14. Dudley Randall, poet and founder of Broadside Press, is born in the District of Columbia. He writes his first poem at age four. In 1981 he will become the first poet laureate for the city of Detroit.

Jesse E. Moorland, Howard University alumnus and trustee, donates his collection of books on black America and Africa to Howard University. This collection becomes the nucleus of the current Moorland-Spingarn Research Center.

Jean Toomer graduates from M Street High School.

Phi Beta Sigma fraternity is established at Howard University by A. Langston Taylor, Leonard Morse, and Charles I. Brown.

November. Monroe Trotter again leads a delegation to visit President Wilson to discuss African American concerns about segregation. Wilson gets angry at the tone of Trotter's argument and throws them out.

September 28. Christian Fleetwood dies of heart failure.

1915

D. W. Griffith's film *Birth of a Nation* is released. This controversial film documents events from the Civil War to the rise of the KKK. Despite claims of the film being racist, it is a box-office hit.

Carter G. Woodson, pioneer historian of black Americans, establishes the Association for the Study of Negro Life and History.

Biologist Ernest Just is awarded the Spingarn Medal by the NAACP for pioneering work in his field.

Alain Locke lobbies Howard University's Board of Trustees to establish a series of classes on blacks and on race relations in the United States; on African history and culture; and on black people in other countries. His international approach is innovative and ahead of its time.

October. *The Star of Ethiopia,* a pageant about the history of the colored race from prehistoric times to today, is presented by the Horizon Guild to an audience of about 5,000 people at the American League Ball Park. The costume play was written by W. E. B. DuBois, partly to counteract the negative impact of *Birth of a Nation.*

Dr. N. T. Pannell and his wife, Mrs. R. L. Pannell, establish the Washington, D.C., branch of the International Liberty Union of the World. This fraternal organization quickly gains over 400 members in the city, partly because of the great influence that the Pannells have among District blacks. The Pannells have long been active in a number of social clubs, religious organizations, and mission work. The goals of the International Liberty Union of the World are to "tear down race prejudices and to promote union and fraternity in all men."

Richard Ware establishes Ware's Department Store, the first black-owned and operated department store in the city, at 1832 14th Street NW.

November 14. Booker T. Washington dies after a long illness in Tuskegee, Alabama.

1916

January. Professor James M. Gregory, the first graduate of Howard University, dies at his daughter's home in Baltimore. He began teaching at Howard University in 1868 and became a trustee of the D.C. public schools in 1886. He ends his career as president of the New Jersey Street Manual Training and Industrial School.

The M Street High School opens in a new building on 1st Street, between O and N Streets NW. Francis and Archibald Grimké would like the school to be named after Charlotte Forten Grimké. The *Washington Bee* suggests that the commissioners of the District, charged with selecting a name for the new colored high school, narrow their choices down to three: James M. Gregory, a notable educator and the first graduate of Howard University; John R. Francis, a District doctor and member of the board of education; or Paul Laurence Dunbar, "whose name is a household word in the home of every American Negro." The school is renamed the Paul Laurence Dunbar High School and continues to attract the country's best scholars as instructors, as well as the brightest African American students.

Black political activists in Washington testify in front of the House District Committee, protesting the increase of segregation in the District. Archibald Grimké, Whitfield McKinlay, and Assistant District Attorney James A. Cobb make statements.

June. Major James E. Walker, commanding officer of the 1st Separate Battalion of the District of Columbia National Guard, takes his battalion to Arizona to participate in the Mexican campaigns.

Carter G. Woodson begins publishing the *Journal of Negro History*.

Henry Grant, graduate of New York University and the Washington Conservatory of Music, begins teaching music at Dunbar High School. Grant becomes one of Washington's most important musicians, playing an important role as instructor and mentor to rising musicians, giving acclaimed performances and recitals, and organizing choirs and glee clubs.

Ware's Department Store, the only black-owned department store in the District, thrives after its well-publicized and much talked-about opening.

1917

The Central Committee of Negro College Men at Howard University, Washington, D.C., is organized to prove the willingness of blacks to fight in WWI.

March 25. Major James E. Walker and the 1st Separate Battalion of the District of Columbia National Guard are ordered to guard the White House and various strategic sites in Washington, D.C., in preparation for the oncoming war. The Washington African American community sees this assignment as a declaration of trust and recognition for its previous service in the military.

April. President Wilson declares war on Germany. The army rejects most of the black men who volunteer. On May 18th Congress passes the Selective Service Act, which calls for all able-bodied American citizens to enlist. Over 400,000 blacks will be accepted for service, and nearly 40,000 of them will serve in two all-black divisions, the 92nd and 93rd, formed in November and December of 1917.

May 19. The Colored Officers Training Camp for WWI is established at Fort Des Moines, Iowa. The first candidates arrive on June 15. In the middle of October, 639 black men are made officers.

Many are former members of the 1st Separate Battalion and the Colored High School Cadet Corps. College graduate Charles Houston is commissioned as a first lieutenant in the infantry but then requests a transfer to artillery, where he is made a second lieutenant in the 351st Field Artillery.

Spring. A. Philip Randolph and Chandler Owen begin publishing *The Messenger* in New York City.

Mary Church Terrell, Julia F. Coleman, and Jeanette Carter form the Women Wage-Earners Association to help black women workers organize for better wages and working conditions; for the most part they are not wanted in local trade unions.

NAACP branch meeting, Washington, D.C., 1917.

The disgraceful murdering of colored men and women, and the destruction of their homes in East St. Louis, Ill., places another blot on Christian (?) America. Can this be the confirmation and jolly celebration of the uniting of the blue and the gray?

—The *Washington Bee*, July 21, 1917

July. Antiblack race riots in East St. Louis result in the deaths of scores of men, women, and children.

Joel Spingarn and some black leaders demand that the War Department establish an officers training camp for blacks. Others argue that this would only reinforce racial segregation within the armed forces. The issue of separate camps divides many black leaders. Some are adamantly opposed to the idea, while others, such as W. E. B. DuBois and Robert Russa Moton, think that it provides the only opportunity for black men to participate in the war.

African American migration from rural to urban areas and from the South to the North increases due to labor shortages on the home front. Black people generally work in the hardest, dirtiest occupations.

Debate continues within the African American community over whether blacks should support the war effort or volunteer. W. E. B. DuBois and others argue that a visibly involved black community will help in the struggle against racism; others, like A. Philip Randolph and Hubert Harrison, argue that blacks should fight for democracy at home. In Washington, D.C., Reverend Francis Grimké refuses to buy Liberty Bonds, and his brother Archibald Grimké publicly questions whether blacks should fight for the country.

Charles S. Skinner opens the C. S. Skinner Company, a "Negro Automobile Agency, Repair Shop, Accessory Store, Driving School, Owned and Managed Entirely by Negroes," at 2009 Georgia Avenue NW.

Jesse and Rosetta Lawson establish Frelinghuysen University as an academic university. They first opened the school in 1907 as the Inter-Denominational Bible College, a bible study school, on 2011 Vermont Avenue NW. The couple name the university after U.S. senator Frederick Frelinghuysen of New Jersey, who supported black political efforts during Reconstruction. In 1921 the university is moved to a building at 1800 Vermont Avenue NW.

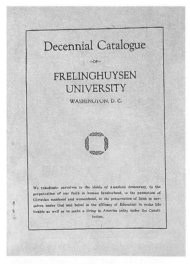

Frelinghuysen University catalogue.

December. Thirteen black soldiers are executed in Houston, Texas, in a military court martial. Sixty-three men were charged with murder when racial violence broke out between black soldiers of the 24th Infantry and the local police. Despite pleas and protests from black newspapers and black leaders around the country, the thirteen men are executed in a racially charged atmosphere. In response, Archibald Grimké writes the poem "Her Thirteen Black Soldiers." He requests that DuBois publish it in *The Crisis*, but DuBois—thinking it too inflammatory—refuses. The *Atlantic* also declines, but in October 1919 the *Messenger*, a radical black newspaper, publishes Grimké's poem.

Her Thirteen Black Soldiers

For her at her bidding they marched ready to die,
For her they gave their bodies to wind and rain and cold,
For her they marched without turning or tiring to face her enemies,
For her they charged them and their cannon, . . .
For her they laid their all at her feet, her thirteen black soldiers.
And she hanged them in anger and hate,
And buried them in nameless disgrace.

—Archibald Grimké, 1919

BUILDING A BLACK COMMUNITY

1918–1945

A T THE END OF WORLD WAR I, BLACK WASHINGTON VETERANS CAME
home to find the city significantly changed. Government
agencies and offices had expanded and brought in thousands of
wartime workers (primarily from the South) to fill temporary jobs.
The population had increased, and new housing and residential
projects sprang up to accommodate it. Black and white residents
were thrown into competition for jobs and housing. The resulting
friction often played out in the pages of the local media: the black
press highlighted instances of racial injustice and demanded an
end to exclusionary housing and employment practices, and mainstream media focused their coverage on criminal activity in the
black community.

The Segregated Federal Workplace

The black middle class was still reeling from the impact of President Wilson's segregation of the city's federal workforce. Washington was basically a company town: the federal government and
businesses and enterprises associated with it, such as printing,
provided most of the area's employment. The segregation of formerly integrated workplaces was traumatic to local blacks, not
only because it seemed to happen all at once, but because it was so
insidious. It was also handled clumsily, as if designed to humiliate
and rub raw the feelings of a community that had lionized its

federal white-collar and clerical workers, promoting them to solid standing in the local African American aristocracy.

Red Summer

The black press called the summer of 1919 the "Red Summer" because of racial violence that spread across the country. More than twenty-five cities suffered riots, in which over a hundred blacks were killed by white mobs. During riots in the nation's capital, most black citizens responded by staying inside their homes and waiting out the storm. But some black men organized into armed bands and patrolled their neighborhoods. Despite their horror and shock at being attacked in the very shadow of the Capitol, at the unexpectedly brutal nature of the attack, and at the reluctance of the police to protect them, black Washingtonians were proud that they had fought back. As John Lovell Jr. wrote in 1939 in *The Crisis*:

> Washington Negroes, in spite of their phenomenal culture, would have moved very slowly but for the so-called rowdy element. Let anyone who wishes to deny this read the records of the 1919 riot before he enlists on the negative side. The highfalutin' Negroes would have taken 50 years to get the self-respect the boys from the bucket-of-blood got in a few days. The boys had always questioned the method of soft blandishment. They still do. When the riot burst the capital city open, and the bigwigs started holding conferences to determine how best to ameliorate and pacify, "the boys" merely went to work and set a machine gun or two on top of the Howard Theatre.

The New Negro Renaissance

In the early 1920s Washington, D.C., was still a sleepy southern town; in fact, almost 200 small working farms still existed in the city. But for black Washingtonians the period served as a milestone of cultural achievement and consolidation. The black downtown in Shaw began to coalesce as a national capital of black performing arts with the openings of the Whitelaw Hotel, the Dunbar Theatre and the Lincoln Theatre, and Harrison's café; at the same time, the Mutual Housing real estate company began to steer large numbers of black families to Shaw area residences; the Armstrong High School versus Dunbar High School cadet drill competitions increased in importance; and (because Glen Echo Park did not admit blacks) the Suburban Gardens amusement park opened in Deanwood.

On the corner of 15th and S Streets NW, the poet Georgia Douglas Johnson held Saturday night salons that helped bring about a home-grown arts renaissance that not only fed upon but also influenced the arts renaissance in Harlem. The heyday of the Howard Theatre was also during the 1920s and 1930s.

In the 1920s Logan Circle, an affluent neighborhood previously called Iowa Circle, presented a showcase of middle- and upper-class black homes. David L. Lewis points out that Jack Johnson, Adam Clayton Powell Jr., and Charles M. "Sweet Daddy" Grace were among the blacks living there. The city's churches also flourished during this time. The national headquarters of the United House of Prayer for All People was established on 601 M Street NW in the 1920s, and in the 1930s and 1940s Bible Way Church, under the leadership of Bishop Smallwood E. Williams, became one of the area's most influential black churches.

Partly as a result of opportunities created by the Works Progress Administration (WPA) and the increasing importance of photographs to black local newspapers, African American photography also flourished in the years between the two world wars. Washingtonians Joseph Curtis, Addison Scurlock, and Robert McNeill were three rising stars in this field.

The Growing Struggle against Segregation

The anti-lynching movement monopolized black public attention in the 1930s. Led by people such as Walter White, James Weldon Johnson, and W. E. B. DuBois, blacks fought lynching on several fronts. In Washington the NAACP branch battled Congress to pass anti-lynching legislation. Locally, the New Negro Alliance kept pressure on retail shops, grocery stores, and other local businesses to hire blacks in other than menial positions. The alliance attracted the brightest and most ambitious of Washington's black political leaders. Mary Church Terrell, Walter E. Washington,

William Hastie, John Aubrey Davis, Belford V. Lawson Jr., Robert C. Weaver, and Mary McLeod Bethune were active supporters. The National Theatre was also at the center of the struggle against segregation. Sandra Fitzpatrick and Maria Goodwin recall that the arrival of *Green Pastures* and the pressure to allow blacks to see that production led to a Jim Crow performance staged exclusively for blacks. The National Theatre was one of the last holdouts in the city and did not allow blacks to attend its shows until the early 1950s.

In the 1940s and 1950s Freedmen's Hospital, on the campus of Howard University, had the only completely integrated staff and hospital wards in the nation's capital. Many middle-class and well-to-do black families patronized it because they could receive the best-quality medical care with no risk of embarrassment from racially discriminatory treatment.

The Howard University Community

Howard University attracted the best black scholars in the country to serve on its faculty. Despite their accomplishments, most renowned black intellectuals were still unable to find positions in mainstream universities during the period before desegregation. From the 1920s to the 1950s, Howard University was home to important scholars like Alain Locke, Kelly Miller, Ernest Just, E. Franklin Frazier, William Leo Hansberry, Rayford Logan, Carter G. Woodson, Lorenzo Dow Turner, Albert Cassell, Robert Todd Duncan, Abram Harris, and Sterling Brown. Under the close watch of Charles Hamilton Houston, Howard University Law School became the most important and influential institution training black lawyers, turning out the disciplined and well-schooled legal strategists of the civil rights movement. The Howard University faculty, staff members, and their families, along with those of Freedmen's Hospital, formed a distinct and closely bonded community, strengthened by ties of friendship, marriage, and residential closeness.

Across the Anacostia River

Blacks also continued to build and buy homes across the Anacostia River in the far southeast area of the city. The Henson family (descendants of the stalwart ex-slave Tobias Henson) owned much of the land in Stantontown, but as Louise Hutchinson notes in *The Anacostia Story, 1608–1930,*

> [In] the 1940s . . . condemnation proceedings were instituted under the Alley Dwelling Act and the authority of the National Capital Planning Commission (headed by Ulysses S. Grant III). The land was taken and their homes were razed. In a final effort to protect their homes and land, the Hansons [the family had changed its name from Henson] had sent a letter of appeal to Mrs. Eleanor Roosevelt with the hope that she could successfully intercede in their behalf. This, however, was to no avail. The family cemetery was included in the parcel of land condemned. . . . Another portion of the Henson tract was sold to the federal government during World War II, and Camp Simms, a civil defense facility that is still in the community, was built there. At one time members of the family lived on this land on a street named Smith Place (named for Richard Smith, Tobias Henson's grandson).

The Coming Battles for Black Neighborhoods

The unsuccessful struggle of the Henson family to hold onto its land is a preview of the battles between the advocates of urban renewal initiatives, such as the Alley Dwelling Act and the Redevelopment Land Agency, and the black residents who wanted to preserve their neighborhoods. Whole neighborhoods were uprooted and their residents dispersed and forced to relocate in other parts of the city. Blacks who had lost their homes due to urban renewal projects could not easily find suitable housing in the city because so many apartment buildings, housing projects, and neighborhoods did not allow black families to move in.

1918

January. The 1st Separate Battalion of the National Guard in the District of Columbia is merged with other black units to form the 372nd Infantry Regiment of the 93rd Division. The men of the 1st Separate Battalion are shipped to Camp Stuart in Newport News, Virginia; in March, they are ordered to Europe. The segregation there and the hostility of their southern commanders radicalize young Rayford Logan, who joined the battalion in July 1917. Sergeant-Major Logan begins to organize boycotts and protests against some of the worst aspects of his treatment in the military. He continues these antisegregation efforts long after his regiment is shipped to France for combat duty.

March 29. Singer and Broadway star Pearl Bailey is born in Newport News, Virginia.

July 2. Nineteen-year-old Duke Ellington marries Edna Thompson. The following year Edna gives birth to their only child, a son; they name him Mercer Kennedy Ellington.

After graduating from Howard University with a degree in musical studies the previous year, Lillian Evans marries Roy Tibbs, a professor of music at the university. She begins touring professionally shortly thereafter. Friend and author Jessie Fauset suggests the professional name Madame Evanti—a combination of Evans and Tibbs.

The Birth of a Race is released. The film is seen as an antidote to the racial propaganda in D. W. Griffith's *Birth of a Nation*.

October. An influenza epidemic hits the city. Schools and many public places are closed, courts recess, but more than 35,000 are stricken in the city, and more than 3,500 die. The flu plague lasts about one month—from September to October.

November 11. Armistice is declared. Black soldiers have increased expectations upon their return to the United States, due to wartime promises about democratic rights shared by U.S. citizens. Black and white Washingtonians pour into the streets to celebrate. Pennsylvania Avenue is the center of the festivities, as thousands of people parade up and down the street, cheering and banging pots and pans.

Georgia Douglas Johnson (1886–1966), poet, playwright, and one of the leading members of the Washington literati during the Harlem Renaissance, publishes her first book of poetry, *The Heart of a Woman and Other Poems*. She is married to Henry Lincoln Johnson, recorder of deeds, and their home, known as Halfway House and located on 1461 S Street NW, is a literary salon for black artists and intellectuals of the area who meet regularly on Saturday nights. Dubbed "the Saturday Nighters," the group first formed in the early 1880s. Johnson's other publications include *Bronze* in 1922. The poems, which focus on prejudice and racism, mark a change in her tone; by that time she has come under the influence of the New Negro movement. *An Autumn Love Cycle* is published in 1928 and *Share My World* in 1962. Her plays include *Blue-Eyed Black Boy* (1930), *Saturday Morning in the South* (1925), and *William and Ellen Craft* (1935).

Georgia Douglas Johnson, poet and playwright.

Behold! The living thrilling lines
That course the blood like madd'ning wines,
And leap with scintillating spray
Across the guards of ecstasy.
The flame that lights the lurid spell
Springs from the soul's artesian well,
Its fairy filaments of art
Entwines the fragments of the heart.
    —Georgia Douglas Johnson,
    The Heart of a Woman, 1918

1919

February. The First Pan-African Congress, a follow-up to the first Pan-African Conference held nineteen years prior, convenes in Paris, France. The U.S. government refuses to grant passports to African Americans who want to attend. Among those elected are W. E. B. DuBois as secretary, Blaise Diagne—a Franco-Senegalese activist—as president, and Rayford Logan. Also active are Jessie Fauset, W. H. Jernagin, and Ida Gibbs Hunt, former teacher at the M Street High School.

A scandal erupts when the black press reports that H. M. B. Moens, a professor of anthropology, has taken nude photographs of black female high school students. A formal investigation exonerates the assistant superintendent of schools, Roscoe Conkling Bruce, the son of Senator Blanche K. Bruce, but leads to the dismissal of a popular black schoolteacher.

Lucy Diggs Slowe becomes principal of Shaw Junior High School, the first black junior high in Washington, D.C.

Edward William Brooke III, later to become the first black senator since Reconstruction, is born in the neighborhood of LeDroit Park to Edward and Helen Brooke. The family soon moves to 1262 Hamlin Street in the Brookland area. They are active members of St. Luke's Episcopal Church, where Edward serves as lay reader. Edward attends Shaw Junior High School, joining its cadet corps. He later attends Dunbar High School.

Carter G. Woodson joins the history department at Howard University.

Yancey Peters, a government worker, served as a Navy Department messenger for thirty-three years.

For the first time since before the Civil War, the District of Columbia Fire Department is segregated. The first all-black firehouse, Engine No. 4, opens on the 400 block of Virginia Avenue SW. After this time, black men who pass the exam and are accepted into the department are confined to separate firehouses. The fire department has been integrated until now.

June. Archibald Grimké is awarded the Spingarn Medal by the NAACP.

During what is called "the Red Summer" by the black press, more than twenty-five race riots break out across the country.

Summer. Local newspapers publish a series of articles alleging a crime wave by Negroes. This adds fuel to a racially tense situation already made difficult by the presence of hundreds of white and black servicemen recently released from the military and now competing for jobs and housing. The news articles, focusing on alleged sexual assaults by black men upon white women, are in full throttle by July. Led by the *Washington Post,* local newspapers create a sham consensus for racial violence. A *Post* article notes approvingly the "scores" of blacks arrested for questioning and the growing vigilantism of white residents.

July 7. "Posses Hunt Assailant," reads the headline of the *Washington Post;* and in an inflammatory article headlined "Negro Again Attacks," the *Washington Post* reports on the attempted assault of a white woman by a black man near the suburban village of Somerset.

Newspaper headline regarding the racial riots in the nation's capital.

July 9. The NAACP sends a letter to the *Washington Post* and other dailies, "calling their attention to the fact that they were sowing the seeds of a race riot by their inflammatory headlines and sensational news articles."

July 19. Theodore Micajah Walker goes in search of his neighbor's children when they do not return home. During the search, he is spotted and pursued by a mob. Just as they are about to seize him, he turns and fires his weapon at the crowd. A nineteen-year-old marine is killed. William L. Houston, Charles Houston's father, serves as the defense lawyer, but an all-white jury later convicts Walker of murder.

July 20. Howard University history professor Carter G. Woodson is nearly caught up in the violence of another mob. As he is walking home, past Pennsylvania Avenue and 8th Street, he sees a crowd of soldiers chasing a black man. Woodson quickly ducks into a doorway until they pass and he continues toward 8th Street. But there, he runs into a crowd in the midst of lynching another black man. The vigilantes are too involved in their torment of their victim to notice him, and Woodson runs for his life.

July 21. The *Washington Post* provides details of the violence in a front-page article:

SCORES ARE INJURED IN MORE RACE RIOTS
Soldiers and Sailors Attack in Dozens of Melees
Pennsylvania Avenue the Scene of Most of Fighting

At an early hour this morning two more serious fights between whites and negroes broke out at Ninth and E and Eighth and E streets northwest.

. . . Along [Pennsylvania Avenue], from Seventh street to Fifteenth street northwest, groups of soldiers, sailors, marines, and white civilians opposed with fists and clubs other groups composed of negroes who with seeming willingness, threw themselves into a dozen of melees. Scores of negroes and their opponents were injured, some seriously.

Then, inexplicably, the *Post* adds fuel to the fire by reporting that local white servicemen were ordered to engage in a paramilitary "clean-up" operation:

It was learned that a mobilization of every available service man stationed in or near Washington or on leave here has been ordered for tomorrow evening near the Knights of Columbus hut on Pennsylvania avenue between Seventh and Eighth streets. The hour of assembly is 9 o'clock and the purpose is a "clean-up" that will cause the events of the last two evenings to pale into insignificance."

Post editors are later unable to account for the call-up described in the article. No military order of the kind had been issued.

July 22. James Weldon Johnson arrives to investigate the Washington riots for the NAACP.

July 26. The *Washington Bee* lambastes the police department's inaction in preventing or stopping attacks on blacks but takes pride in pointing out that blacks in the District, unlike black communities victimized in many other cities around the country this summer, fought off their attackers.

July 27. Marcus Garvey incorporates the Black Star Line.

September 17. President Wilson and General John Pershing lead a victory march of U.S. troops down Pennsylvania Avenue. As in most other cities in the country, black troops are excluded, and the 1st Separate Battalion is not included in the Washington parade. Only New York City allows black troops to participate in its victory parade.

Washingtonian Henry Grant organizes the National Association of Negro Musicians in Chicago. After graduating from the Washington Conservatory of Music and School of Expression, in 1916 Grant begins teaching music at Dunbar High School and performing. He is also an active choir director and composer. A popular but demanding music teacher, Grant is one of Duke Ellington's early instructors and mentors.

November. The National Equal Rights League, headed by William Monroe Trotter, holds its convention in Washington, D.C., where more than 250 people attend.

I reached Washington early in the evening of July 22. As the train neared the capital I could feel the tenseness of the situation grow. It showed itself in the air of the passengers as they read the newspapers, with their glaring headlines telling of the awful night before and intimating that the worst was yet to come. . . .

Although on the night before shots had blazed all through the night at the corners of Seventh and T Streets and Fourteenth and U, I could detect no signs of nervousness on the part of the colored people living in the section. They had reached the determination that they would defend and protect themselves and their homes at the cost of their lives, if necessary, and that determination rendered them calm.

Still, under the outward calm, there was a tautness that could be sensed. Wild rumors had been circulating all day foreboding terrible things; and these things, whatever they might be, the colored people had made up their minds to meet. But as darkness came on, the rain began to fall, and later it fell in torrents; so it may be that the rain had something to do with the things that did not happen.

—James Weldon Johnson,
reporting for the NAACP

A newspaper article praising blacks for fighting off their attackers during the riots in July 1919.

The Whitelaw Hotel opens. It is the first black-owned and developed hotel in Washington, D.C. John Whitelaw Lewis financed its construction by selling shares within the black community. He also exclusively used black tradesmen in the construction. Located in the area known as Black Broadway, the hotel attracts a large number of prominent blacks.

The New York Age *reporting on black troops being excluded from the Washington, D.C., parade that took place in February 1919.*

1920

April. Bob Harrison, a native Washingtonian, opens Harrison's Café at 455 Florida Avenue NW. It quickly becomes one of the most popular restaurants in the Shaw area, especially among the Howard University community. Ten years earlier, Harrison met with success by selling his homemade molasses candies, "Harrison's Old Fashioned Molasses Kisses," in local drugstores. He took his savings from that venture and opened this café. The motto of the café is

A middle-class family.

"Eat at Home or Eat at Harrison's." Harrison is married to Lottie Davis, the cousin of Lieutenant General Benjamin O. Davis.

May 25. Militant blacks, disenchanted with the NAACP's political program and the role of whites in the leadership, come together to form the Friends of Negro Freedom. The founding conference is held in Washington, D.C., in the spring. Led by socialists A. Philip Randolph and Chandler Owens, Washingtonian attendees include

Archibald Grimké; Neval H. Thomas, a teacher at Dunbar High School; E. B. Henderson, physical education instructor; Carl Murphy, editor of the *Baltimore Afro-American;* and Carter G. Woodson. "Economic, political, civil, social and intellectual freedom" was the program of the new organization, which was to be "international in scope, including the Haitians, West Indians, South Americans and Africans. . . . In speaking of the New Crowd Negro, we do not refer to age, but to point of view. There are young Negroes with the Old Crowd point of view, and older Negroes with the New Crowd point of view." The organizers added the following: "N.B. All measures, policies and methods will be strictly lawful."

Zeta Phi Beta Sorority is founded on the campus of Howard University, Washington, D.C.

Carter G. Woodson is fired from Howard University at the request of university president J. Stanley Durkee—partly due to Woodson's refusal to spy on his colleagues and keep Durkee informed about the activities of other university instructors.

Jean Toomer; Georgia Douglas Johnson; Clarissa Scott, Emmett Scott's daughter; playwright Mary P. Burrill; E. C. Williams, head of Howard University Library School; Mary Craft, daughter of abolitionists William and Ellen Craft; and other local blacks join to form a Washington writer's group. Although Toomer provides a spark of electric genius, Georgia Douglas Johnson becomes the group's nurturing and maternal central figure.

The Dunbar Theatre opens in the Southern Aid Society Building. Located at 7th and T Streets NW and designed by black architect Isaiah T. Hatton, the building becomes an early landmark of black Washington's social and cultural aspirations. The Southern Aid Society was the oldest black insurance company in the country.

The Mutual Housing real estate company opens an office on U Street NW and begins to purchase apartment buildings in the area and rent them to African Americans. As more blacks arrive, whites depart in even greater numbers.

Howard University is the nucleus of Washington's Negro athletics. Through its annual Thanksgiving football classic with Lincoln University, held every other year at home, it has given to the Negro life of Washington a prestige among other cities and a magnetic influence over vicinal districts which no other field of Negro life in the capital can approximate. Practically every village, town and city in the United States is affected by this great athletic event. It draws to Washington more than ten thousand people from other sections of the country, creating an occasion similar to the carnival season in New Orleans and other cities. Every day for approximately a week scores of important social affairs are held. These consist of breakfast, matinee, and evening dances, poker games, bridge parties, slumming, cabaret parties, and numerous other entertainments.

—William Jones,
*Recreation and Amusement Among Negroes in Washington, D.C.:
A Sociological Analysis of the Negro in an Urban Environment,* 1927

August. The Nineteenth Amendment is ratified, giving women the vote for the first time in the United States.

November. The annual Thanksgiving Day Howard-Lincoln football game at Griffith Stadium greatly increases in popularity after 1919, becoming one of the favorite social events of the year. As many as 25,000 people attend.

The competitive drill between Armstrong and Dunbar High Schools, another annual event, also becomes one of the most popular athletic and social occasions in the city.

An amusement park for blacks opens. Suburban Gardens, in Deanwood, is located on seven acres, with rides, booths and concession stands, a dancing pavilion, and a playground. Suburban Gardens remains open for almost ten years.

1921

March 4. Warren G. Harding is inaugurated as president.

July. Carter G. Woodson establishes Associated Publishers, a small firm that publishes books on African American history.

August. The Second Pan-African Congress is held, with sessions in London, England; Brussels; and Paris. Organizers include Blaise Diagne, W. E. B. DuBois, Jessie Fauset, Rayford Logan, and Ida Gibbs Hunt.

Jean Toomer begins working as temporary superintendant of a small school for black children in rural Georgia. This experience provides much of the material for his literary masterpiece Cane, published two years later.

William L. Houston begins teaching law at Howard University Law School. He remains at the university until 1936, when he retires as professor emeritus of law.

Jazz pianist and composer Billy Taylor is born in Greenville, North Carolina, but soon moves to the District of Columbia with his

On the day of the drill thousands of colored pedestrians pass through the streets of the city, carrying the colors of the school of their choice; hundreds of automobiles, elaborately decorated with school colors and loaded with a group of merrymakers race noisily through the streets, resounding the joy of their occupants. . . . The competitive drill not only accentuates the popularity of the winning school for the successive year by increasing attendance and strengthening the morale of the student body, but it enhances the status of the successful officers. This status which the individual wins in the competitive drill remains with him for many years. In all his future activities he is referred to as X, who won such and such a medal in the Dunbar-Armstrong Competitive Drill.

—William Jones,
*Recreation and Amusement Among Negroes in Washington, D.C.:
A Sociological Analysis of the Negro in an Urban Environment,* 1927

family, where he attends Dunbar High School. After taking piano lessons from Henry Grant, who also taught Duke Ellington, Taylor becomes a renowned jazz musician.

Thomas Montgomery Gregory, Alain Locke, and Marie Moore-Forrest establish the Howard University Players in the Department of Dramatic Arts.

After receiving his B.A. in architecture from Cornell in 1919, Albert I. Cassell becomes head of the Department of Architecture at Howard University in 1921.

1922
The Citizen's Golf Club, sited on grounds near the Naval Hospital, is organized by Dr. M. L. Grant.

February. The Lincoln Theatre opens on U Street. The Lincoln Colonnade, a ballroom and banquet hall located behind the theater, becomes one of the most popular sites for young people in the area.

May 30. At the dedication of the Lincoln Memorial, invited blacks are kept apart in a segregated section at the ceremony. Robert Russa Moton is the featured speaker, but most blacks leave the dedication in protest. This incident is discussed in nearly every black household in the city, with black newspapers questioning why federal officials subjected black leaders of such high esteem—and invited guests, at that—to such humiliation.

June. Carter G. Woodson returns to the District of Columbia after a two-year stint in West Virginia as president of the West Virginia Collegiate Institute. He purchases a three-story rowhouse at 1938 9th Street NW, which also serves as headquarters for the Association for the Study of Negro Life and History and as a workroom, warehouse, and shipping outlet for his publication activities. Woodson bequeaths the building to the association upon his death.

June 17. George Theophilus Walker is born in Washington, D.C. He becomes one of the best-known African American composers of his era.

Twenty-one distinguished guests of the nation at the dedication of the Lincoln memorial yesterday got up from their seats and left the exercises when they found they had been jimcrowed.

The guests had been given green colored tickets calling for "Platform Section Five." They found themselves shown to a small enclosure in front of the speakers' stand and roped in from the rest of the audience. Whitfield McKinlay, well-known local real estate dealer, when shown to a rough bench as a seat was told by the armed guard to sit down. "I'll think about it," Mr. McKinlay said. "Well think damned quick," replied the guard.

Immediately a near riot ensued and the crowd demanded the transfer of the marine elsewhere. When the officer in charge said that it was the only thing to do to keep colored people in their place, twenty-one persons arose as one and left the enclosure and the building.
—The *Baltimore Afro-American*, June 2, 1922

174

Dedication of the Lincoln Memorial, May 30, 1922.

Lucy Diggs Slowe is named dean of women at Howard University, Washington, D.C.

After graduating from Harvard University, William Leo Hansberry begins teaching at Howard University in the Department of History. A few years later Hansberry offers "Ancient African Civilizations," the first university course focusing on African civilizations in the country, and he enthusiastically begins to recruit new students to study African history and culture.

August 12. Frederick Douglass's home on 1411 W Street SE in the Anacostia section of Washington is established as a historic site.

When Pearl Bailey is four, she and her family move to 1300 Florida Avenue NW in Washington, D.C. Later her family moves to 1207 5th Street NW.

The Prince Hall Masonic Temple is completed on 1000 U Street NW.

1923

Jean Toomer's novel *Cane*, portraying life in Washington, D.C., and in the rural South, is published.

I can remember rolling Easter eggs at the zoo and playing in Lincoln Memorial Pool. . . . Papa always had some kind of old car. He never seemed to get a new one. And I remember we went around the reservoir in Papa's open-topped car on Sundays as a treat. The Lincoln and Republic theatres are located on U Street, and that's where our friends would be after Sunday school. . . . While the Lincoln and Republic theatres were on U Street, where all the fancy people strolled, the Dunbar, Broadway, and a few others were on Seventh Street. We were not allowed to go to the Midcity and the Elmo; they were a bit rough.

—Pearl Bailey,
The Raw Pearl, 1968

By the 1920s, as a direct result of the Howard and Lincoln Theatres, Washington had become the national headquarters of the black entertainment industry. [Sherman] H. Dudley's theatrical circuit had become part of the national circuit of black theatres, known as the Theatre Owners Booking Association. Washington soon became the principal staging area for black vaudeville. The shows were developed here and then dispatched to various areas of the country. During this period the Colored Actors Union was established in Washington with over 1,000 local members and its own newspaper.

—Henry Preston Whitehead, unpublished manuscript, Anacostia Museum

Black Washingtonian playwright and actor Lewis Alexander appears on Broadway in 1923 in the Ethiopian Art Players' productions of *Salome* and *The Comedy of Errors.*

August 2. President Harding dies in San Francisco, California. Calvin Coolidge assumes the presidency.

August 3. Calvin Coolidge is sworn in as president.

Duke Ellington leaves Washington, D.C., for New York City, to take his chances in the dinner clubs and nightclubs in Harlem.

1924

Albert I. Cassell completes the design for the gymnasium at Howard University. Cassell later designs the school's College of Medicine (1928), Frederick Douglass Hall (erected in 1936), the Chemistry Building (1936), and the Founders Library (1939). Cassell also designs the Masonic Temple (1930) and the Odd Fellows Temple (1932) in the District of Columbia.

Now an attorney with advanced graduate degrees, Charles Houston begins to practice in his father's law firm. Although other attorneys, including William Hastie, later join the firm, Charles Houston remains there until his retirement in 1950.

Alma Thomas receives the first degree in fine arts awarded by Howard University. After a career teaching art in Shaw Junior High School, she retires in 1960 to become one of the area's finest artists.

May 1. Alain Locke submits a detailed plan and a rationale for the development of an African Studies Department at Howard University to Howard University president J. Stanley Durkee, but university trustees reject the idea.

November. Langston Hughes arrives in Washington, D.C., to live with his mother and stepbrother. At first they stay with relatives in LeDroit Park. Then, wanting to live on their own, they rent a series of apartments: on 12th Street NW, then at 1917 3rd Street NW, and finally at 1749 S Street NW. Langston works in a laundry; his mother takes a job as a domestic. Despite his determination to attend Howard University, Hughes remains in Washington for little more than a year.

1925

March 4. Calvin Coolidge is inaugurated as president.

March. Alain Locke edits a special edition of the *Survey Graphic* magazine devoted to the "New Negro," which proclaims a "Negro Renaissance" and highlights emerging and established black writers and scholars. This seminal publication heralds the beginning of the Harlem Renaissance.

March. Langston Hughes becomes personal assistant to Carter G. Woodson; he also regularly sits in with the "Saturday Nighters," the weekend salons hosted by Georgia Douglas Johnson.

August 8. More than 30,000 Ku Klux Klansmen in full regalia march down Pennsylvania Avenue, from the Capitol to the Sylvan Theater at the foot of the Washington Monument. Local blacks observe the parade at the intersection of Pennsylvania and 7th Street.

The *"New Negro" issue of* Survey Graphic, *March 1925.*

After studying and lecturing in Africa, Alain Locke returns to Howard University but is fired as part of a university reorganization plan. A media campaign develops to pressure J. Stanley Durkee, president of Howard University. Members of Howard University's faculty form the Howard Welfare League, to remove J. Stanley Durkee from his position as president. Durkee has provoked animosity among many faculty members by dismissing or threatening to dismiss some of the university's most popular and accomplished scholars, including Kelly Miller, Carter G. Woodson, Alain Locke, and Ernest Everett Just.

Archibald Grimké resigns as president of the Washington branch of the NAACP, becoming president emeritus.

Rayford Logan returns from a period of living in France. After his discharge from the Army in 1919, he had not come back to the United States until now, when he accepts a position on the faculty of Virginia Union University in Richmond, Virginia.

*Klansmen marching down
Pennsylvania Avenue, 1925.*

At the end of the summer, Madame Evanti returns from a successful whirlwind tour of Europe and receives critical acclaim in local papers.

Edward Christopher Williams, librarian and head of the Romance Languages Department at Howard University, writes a series of stories for the *Messenger* on Washington, D.C.'s elite black society, "Letters of Davy Carr, a True Story of Colored Vanity Fair."

James Herring establishes the art department at Howard University and later the art gallery in 1930. The Howard University Art Gallery provides exhibiting opportunities for many of the most respected artists of the 1930s and 1940s.

Langston Hughes resigns from his position as personal assistant to Carter G. Woodson because the workload prevents him from writing. He takes a job as busboy at the Wardman Park Hotel (now the Marriott Wardman Park Hotel).

Lillian Evanti makes her professional debut singing with the Paris Opera in a performance of *Lakmé*.

Anna Julia Cooper receives her doctorate from the University of Paris. She purchases an expansive home at 201 T Street NW in LeDroit Park, where she hosts monthly meetings for French speakers and French language teachers called, "Les Amis de la Langue Francaise."

The National Capital Country Club is established for affluent blacks in the District of Columbia. It features a golf course and tennis courts and serves as venue for a number of social events.

Street life is transient. This explains why it appeals. It furnishes the new, the fine, and the sordid. . . . The shrieking of the sirens, the clanging of bells, the dense traffic, the flood of lights, the markets, the music stores with their outside amplifiers, accidents—all an ever-changing scene—this is what places street life among the foremost recreational forces in the city.

—William Jones,
Recreation and Amusement Among Negroes in Washington, D.C.: A Sociological Analysis of the Negro in an Urban Environment, 1927

Madame Lillian Evanti costumed as Lakmé, 1925.

Poet Vachel Lindsay gives a public poetry reading at the Wardman Park Hotel. Blacks are barred from attending, but ambitious hotel busboy Langston Hughes sees his opportunity. While he is waiting on Lindsay's table, he simply places three of his best poems at the side of Lindsay's dinner plate. During the reading, Lindsay stops and reads Hughes's poems aloud, applauding the work of the "busboy poet." He also writes an encouraging note to Hughes. The press picks up on the idea of the busboy poet and besieges the hotel in search of Hughes. The furor goes on for so long that Hughes is forced to quit his job.

December. Alain Locke publishes *The New Negro*.

December. Robert H. Terrell dies in his home at 1615 S Street NW.

1926

February. Langston Hughes leaves Washington, D.C., for Lincoln University in Pennsylvania.

Robert H. Terrell, D.C.'s first African American municipal court judge.

Negro History Week is introduced by Dr. Carter G. Woodson and the Association for the Study of Negro Life and History.

June. Carter G. Woodson is awarded the Spingarn Medal by the NAACP.

Howard University students go on strike to demand the replacement of President J. Stanley Durkee. The university has not yet had a black president, and Durkee has grown increasingly tyrannical in running the school. Despite the additional funds and the financial support that he brought to the university, Durkee is forced to resign and is replaced in 1926 by Mordecai Johnson, the university's first black president.

The Bohemian Tavern opens in the basement of 2001 11th Street NW. This fashionable nightclub is a popular gathering spot for black Washingtonians.

December. Kelly Miller challenges Harlem's growing reputation as the African American cultural capital. In an article in *Opportunity* entitled "Where Is the Negro's Heaven?" he argues that Washington is the cultural center of African Americans.

August 1, 1926, Washington Post *article on the appointment of the first black president of Howard University.*

In the mid-1920s when I worked for Dr. [Carter G.] Woodson, he set an example for industry and stick-to-it-tiveness for his entire staff since he himself worked very hard. He did everything from editing *The Journal of Negro History,* to banking the furnace, to writing books, to wrapping books.

. . . One time Dr. Woodson went away on a trip which those of us in his office thought would take about a week. Instead he came back on the third day and found us all in the shipping room playing cards. Nobody got fired.

Instead he requested our presence in his study where he gave us a long and very serious talk on our responsibilities to our work, to history, and to the race. . . .

My job was to open the office in the mornings, keep it clean, wrap and mail books, assist in answering the mail, read proofs, bank the furnace at night when Dr. Woodson was away, and do anything else that came to hand. . . .

My most responsible job covering a period of several months was the arranging in alphabetical order of all the names in Dr. Woodson's compilation of the "Thirty Thousand Free Negro Heads of Families." It was like alphabetizing the phone book.

—Langston Hughes,
"When I Worked for Dr. Woodson,"
Negro History Bulletin, March 1950

1927

Popular dances for teenagers and young Washingtonians include the "Black Bottom," the "Bump," and the "Prosperity Crawl." Social clubs are popular among their parents. Dozens of such clubs are organized around neighborhoods, mutual friendships, a love of dinner parties, or high school ties. Any number of mutual interests

A flyer advertising "The Prosperity Ball," sponsored by the Masonic Temple, located on 10th and U Streets, NW, 1933.

[W]hen I came to reside in Washington, less than three years ago . . . I went to dinner at the lovely home of a very prominent and able woman who occupies a high position in the educational world and is almost weekly feted and honored by some great college or university, and was altogether humbled at the simplicity of her reception and her constant and courteous attention. . . . It is in this exquisite company too, that I learned that more was to be gleaned in five minutes concerning the worth-while activities of the world, particularly literary pursuits, than could be heard in several hours in the New York that I know.

—Brenda Ray Moryck,
Opportunity magazine, August 1927

or shared histories are at the center of clubs like the Bluebirds, Bachelor-Benedict, the Back Biters, the Earls, What Good Are We, and the Buggy Riders. Boat rides are also popular outings. The *E. Madison Hall* excursion boat, owned and operated by a black man, Captain J. O. Holmes, is a steamer 160 feet long that seats 800 and has 20 staterooms. The excursion season begins about the first Sunday in May and lasts through September. Two or three trips down the Potomac to the River View resort are made each day.

April 14. Historian and scholar John W. Cromwell dies in Washington, D.C.

August. Poet Langston Hughes and writer Brenda Ray Moryck discuss Washington's black society in the pages of *Opportunity* magazine.

As long as I have been colored I have heard of Washington society. Even as a little boy in Kansas vague ideas of the grandeur of Negro life in the capital found their way into my head. A grand uncle, John [Mercer] Langston, had lived there during and after the time of colored congressmen and of him I heard much from my grandmother. Later when I went to Cleveland, some nice mulatto friends of ours spoke of the "wonderful society life" among Negroes in Washington. And some darker friends of ours hinted at "pink teas" and the color line that was drawn there. . . .

Washington is one of the most beautiful cities in the world. For that I remember it with pleasure. Georgia Douglas Johnson conversed with charm and poured tea on Saturday nights for young writers and artists and intellectuals. That too, I remember with pleasure. Seventh Street was always teemingly alive with dark working people who hadn't yet acquired "culture" and the manners of stage ambassadors, and pinks and blacks and yellows were still friends without apologies. That street I remember with pleasure.

—Langston Hughes,
"Our Wonderful Society: Washington," *Opportunity* magazine, August 1927

1928

Cardozo Business High School opens.

Oscar DePriest, from Illinois's Third Congressional District, becomes the first African American elected to the House of Representatives in the twentieth century. There is an uproar in some of the newspapers when his wife is invited to a White House event hosted by the first lady, Mrs. Herbert Hoover.

After years of growing national and international acclaim, Alain Locke returns to the faculty at Howard University, becoming an adviser to Mordecai W. Johnson. Locke reshapes the university's liberal arts courses and creates the Division of Social Sciences. He lobbies once again for the creation of an African Studies Department.

Ralph Bunche is appointed as an instructor at Howard University after receiving an M.A. in political science from Harvard University.

The Washington Negro has the only complete school system in the country practically under his own control. . . . The colored high and normal schools enroll over three thousand pupils above the eight [sic] grade level. This number of secondary students cannot be approximated in any other city—not even New York, Philadelphia and Chicago, with a much larger total Negro population. The faculties of these high and normal schools are recruited by graduates from Harvard, Yale, Columbia, . . .

The Negroes of Washington have reached the point of complete professional self sufficiency. Howard University has turned out an army of physicians, lawyers, teachers and clergymen, . . .

The capital city furnishes the best opportunity and facilities for the expression of the Negro's innate gayety of soul. Washington is still the Negro's Heaven, and it will be many a moon before Harlem will be able to take away her scepter.

—Kelly Miller,
Opportunity magazine, 1928

Ralph Bunche, Howard University instructor.

Sterling Brown, an instructor at
Howard University.

The program of the 1929 Frelinghuysen University baccalaureate service,
at which Anna Julia Cooper was inaugurated as the second president of the
university.

By the following year, he has organized the political science department at Howard. Bunche serves as the first head of that department.
He later returns to Harvard to finish his doctorate.

1929

March 4. Herbert Hoover is inaugurated as president.

White House maid Maggie Rogers's daughter, Lillian Rogers, begins
working at the White House to sew and do light maid's work. Due
to a childhood encounter with polio, Lillian walks with crutches,
but she rises in the ranks of the domestic staff by working hard.
Most of the White House maids and butlers have other part-time
jobs to make ends meet.

Though Mrs. Hoover was a kind and considerate woman, she was so busy
concentrating on making each party the finest, that she didn't see the worried
faces of the staff, who were losing their savings while the banks went under,
and had to take care of their unemployed relatives on the small salaries of the
White House. Mama was making $80 a month, and I was making $48.

—Lillian Rogers Parks,
It Was Fun Working at the White House, 1969

Numa Adams (1885–1940) becomes the first black dean of Howard
Medical School. He recruits new instructors, seeking out the most
outstanding men and women in their fields, and encourages physicians on the faculty to pursue doctorates and postdoctoral studies by
locating funding for advanced medical education.

Sterling Brown joins the faculty of Howard University, where his
literature classes become so popular that enrollment sometimes
exceeds a hundred students.

Charles H. Houston is appointed the vice dean of Howard University Law School. He sets out to create a cadre of black attorneys
dedicated to the legal pursuit of civil rights for African Americans.

Anna Julia Cooper is appointed the second president of Frelinghuysen University in Washington. She remains president until

1940, when she becomes the school's registrar. Frelinghuysen provides African American adults with affordable evening classes geared toward a college degree; classes are held at Cooper's LeDroit Park home.

Students attending class at Frelinghuysen University.

Elwood Street establishes the Community Chest; Frederic Delano serves as president and Kelly Miller as vice president. For the first time a major charitable organization distributes funds to both white and black charities in the city.

October. The stock market crashes, causing a serious economic depression. The Great Depression also brings an increase in social upheaval and political unrest. One of the first casualties is the Howard Theatre, which closes due to financial failure.

1930

February 25. Archibald Grimké dies in his home, attended by his brother Francis and his daughter, Angelina.

Educator and local political activist Neval Thomas dies in Washington, D.C.

The NAACP and other civil rights organizations criticize the U.S. War Department for racially segregating Gold Star mothers. When the War Department volunteers to pay for American Gold Star mothers to visit the graves of their sons in Europe, they require black mothers to travel in separate ships from white Gold Star mothers. Despite a media campaign by the NAACP, the policy is not rescinded. As a result, few African American mothers participate in the program.

William Hastie, childhood friend and protégé of Charles H. Houston, graduates from Harvard University Law School. He receives his doctorate in juridical science in 1933 and joins the Washington law firm of William and Charles Houston.

Dr. William Montague Cobb, a graduate of Howard University Medical School, begins his internship at Freedmen's Hospital. He joins the medical faculty in the early 1930s and is a popular professor of anatomy for more than forty years. Cobb becomes well known for his research and his publications in physical anthropology that challenge theories of racial inferiority. He also becomes an eminent historian and author, often writing articles on African American history for the Journal of Negro History.

Dorothy Porter is appointed head librarian of Howard University's special "Negro collection." Porter, a Howard graduate, begins to organize the massive holdings, most of which had been contributed to the university by Jesse E. Moorland. In 1946 Porter acquires the library of NAACP attorney Arthur B. Spingarn, adding over 5,000 books to the collection. Together, these two contributions make up the foundation of what will become the Moorland-Spingarn Research Center. Due to Porter's efforts, the collection grows from more than 6,000 holdings in 1933 to more than 180,000 in 1973. Born in Warrington, Virginia, in 1905 and raised in Montclair, New Jersey, Porter came to Washington in order to attend Miner Normal School; she also went to Howard University, graduating in 1928. One year later she married artist James Amos Porter. The couple was at the center of the city's black arts and intellectual activities. After James Porter's death, Dorothy Porter marries economist and historian Charles Wesley in 1979. She retires from the university in 1973.

1931

After Howard University Law School stops offering evening classes, attorney George A. Parker establishes the Robert H. Terrell Law School. The Terrell school offers classes five days a week and awards a law degree in four years. It remains open until 1950.

Ionia Whipper organizes the Lend-A-Hand club to raise funds for a building to house black unwed mothers.

Benjamin Brawley joins the faculty of Howard University. Brawley becomes one of the most well-known black scholars of his time, writing articles on literature, drama, music, and African American history. Brawley remains at Howard University until his death in 1939.

Duke Ellington presides over the grand reopening of the Howard Theatre. He performs to a full house for a week.

When the segregated National Theatre hosts the musical play *Porgy and Bess*, black Washingtonians, including Ralph Bunche, organize a protest that results in the theater allowing blacks to sit in the main gallery during the play's run. After it ends, however, the theater returns to its policy of segregation.

1932

May 29. Twenty thousand WWI veterans arrive in Washington, D.C., to beseech Congress to immediately distribute their veterans' bonuses. (They are not due to receive them until 1945.) The Bonus Marchers establish camps and shanties in Anacostia and other parts of the city. Many black veterans are among them.

June. President Hoover speaks at Howard University's commencement program. This is his first public appearance before a black audience.

June. Rayford Logan, pursuing his Ph.D. at Harvard University, arrives in Washington, D.C., to work for Carter G. Woodson and the Association for the Study of Negro Life and History. Logan stays with the association until September 1933, when he takes a position at Atlanta University.

July. Douglas MacArthur and Major Dwight Eisenhower lead troops to rout the men and destroy the encampments of the Bonus Marchers. But almost 10,000 of them remain behind in the city.

July. Benjamin O. Davis Jr. reports to West Point military academy. Four years later he becomes the fourth African American to graduate from West Point.

The *Journal of Negro Education* begins publication at Howard University.

October 1. President Hoover meets with over a hundred African American leaders. This event, when the president meets his visitors on the White House lawn, is the first time that he is photographed with blacks.

John Randolph Pinkett Sr. opens a real estate office at New Jersey Avenue and N Street NW. Born September 27, 1888, in Lincolnia, Virginia, he moved to the District at the turn of the century to attend M Street High School. Pinkett quickly becomes one of the leading black businessmen in the city, active in political and civic affairs.

Freelance photographer Robert McNeill, "Self-Portrait."

1933

March 4. Franklin D. Roosevelt is inaugurated as president.

Benjamin O. Davis Jr. in 1942. He would go on to have a distinguished military career.

August 28. The manager of the Hamburger Grill on U Street fires his all-black staff and replaces them with whites. Black customers, led by John Aubrey Davis, maintain a boycott and picket until the manager relents and brings the black workers back—with an increase in pay and a reduction in hours. The success of this action encourages the boycotters to create an ongoing organization—the New Negro Alliance.

Davis, a Dunbar High School graduate, just returned from Williams College, where he received a degree in literature. Born in 1913 in the District, he grew up in the antisegregation movement, participating in protest activities throughout his youth. The goal of

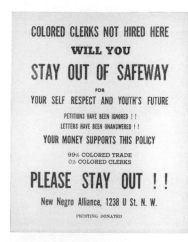

"Stay Out of Safeway," New Negro Alliance flyer.

the New Negro Alliance "is to improve the economic and civic status of the Negro through the securing of more and better jobs, increasing earning power, and the stimulation of Negro Business."

After the Hamburger Grill, the alliance targets the A&P grocery stores, High's Ice Cream stores, Peoples Drug Store, Kaufman's Department Store, and finally, the Sanitary Grocery Company (later Safeway Grocery Stores), which leads them all the way to the Supreme Court.

Mary Church Terrell, Mary McLeod Bethune, and many other prominent black Washingtonians join the picket lines. Walter E. Washington, later the first black mayor of the city, Eugene Davidson (later head of the D.C. NAACP), William Hastie (later governor of the U.S. Virgin Islands), Howard University professor N. Naylor Fitzhugh, John Aubrey Davis, attorney Belford V. Lawson Jr., M. Franklin Thorne (later manager of the Langston Terrace housing project), R. Grayson McGuire (owner of the McGuire family funeral homes), and Robert C. Weaver are among the leaders of the New Negro Alliance. Operating largely out of the offices of Belford V. Lawson at 1232 U Street NW, the alliance even puts out a weekly newspaper, the *New Negro Opinion,* for about five years. After a number of significant successes, alliance activities end around 1941.

"Don't Buy Where You Can't Work"– Slogan of the New Negro Alliance

The next target [of the New Negro Alliance] was the *Washington Star* which had no black newspaper boys. After three weeks of negotiations and the threat of a boycott, the *Star* changed its hiring policies. The Alliance picketed Kaufman's Department store on 7th Street during its busy Christmas season. From triumph to triumph the activists brought economic pressure on U Street businesses, including High's Ice Cream stores (Shaw Junior High School students gave up ice cream!) and the national A & P food chain.

—Sandra Fitzpatrick and Maria Goodwin,
The Guide to Black Washington: Places and Events of Historical and Cultural Significance in the Nation's Capital, 1990

Mary McLeod Bethune, civil rights leader.

September. Black organizations come together to create the Joint Committee on National Recovery, a lobbying group focused on ending racial discrimination within the National Recovery Administration (NRA). Robert C. Weaver, a young Harvard-educated economist, and John P. Davis, an attorney, run the organization. Blacks suffered from racial discrimination in all of the New Deal agencies, but they had high expectations of the NRA, whose purpose was to regulate workers' salaries and labor conditions.

September. In response to growing criticism of racial discrimination within relief agencies and in federal hiring, an advisory position on Negro affairs is created by Secretary Harold Ickes. The first such adviser appointed by Ickes, Clark Foreman, is a white man. African American newspapers protest that the position should have been awarded to a black man. Later, blacks are appointed as racial advisers in various agencies, including Eugene Kinckle Jones in the Department of Commerce, William H. Hastie in the Department of Interior, and Mary McLeod Bethune in the National Youth Administration. This group of early black appointees forms the nucleus of the Black Cabinet, a network of high-ranking blacks in the federal government. Led by Bethune and Robert C. Weaver, who serves in the Public Works Administration, the group meets informally to coordinate strategies for improving the condition of blacks.

Robert C. Weaver, a member of the Black Cabinet.

September. Leaders of the New Negro Alliance take on the local A&P. After negotiations with store management yield no results, members of the New Negro Alliance picket the A&P store on 9th and P Streets NW. Three days later, two alliance picketers are arrested: James Ward and Dutton Ferguson. Other A&P stores are added to the picket line at 7th and S Streets NW and on 11th Street NW. Although these stores operate in black neighborhoods, and their clientele is largely black, they have no black clerks, and their black employees are confined to the lowest-wage blue-collar work. "Don't Buy Where You Can't Work" is the slogan popularized by the campaign.

William Hastie, Belford Lawson, and Edward P. Lovett argue that the arrest of the picketers violates the constitutional rights of the defendants, and the court rules in their favor. By December the grocery store chain gives in and hires eighteen black store clerks. The New Negro Alliance next targets Kaufman's Department store at

1316 7th Street NW and High's Ice Cream store on 11th and Irving Streets NW, popular with Howard University students. After the local A&P chain agrees to hire over thirty black store clerks, the alliance urges blacks to patronize it, instead of the Sanitary Grocery Company.

Elder Lightfoot Solomon Michaux opens the Happy News Café, offering meals for 1 cent to impoverished Washingtonians. Michaux's Church of God on Georgia Avenue and V Streets NW is especially popular with many Washingtonians who have come to the city from Virginia, Michaux's home state, and from North and South Carolina. Michaux later purchases a building at 7th and T Streets NW to house homeless families.

December 15. After negotiations fail, the New Negro Alliance begins picketing Kaufman's Department Store. It hopes that the threat of picketers during the store's busy holiday season will motivate the managers to meet its demand to hire black clerks, but the store obtains an injunction against the alliance on January 5 of the following year, and the picket line is stopped. Peoples Drug Store, however, fights back. The chain managers refuse to hire black clerks, even after sixteen months of picket lines. The New Negro Alliance has to finally withdraw all pickets and give up trying to integrate the drugstore. Peoples also maintains its segregated lunch counters.

1934

Arthur Mitchell defeats Oscar DePriest in a bid for the Chicago congressman's seat.

Congress creates the Alley Dwelling Authority, which later changes its name to the National Capital Housing Authority (NCHA). It eliminates many of the alleys and razes the housing.

May 7. Indian activist Mohandas "Mahatma" Gandhi writes a letter to editor Carl Murphy that is printed in the *Washington Afro American*. Gandhi denies reports by a white author that he supports racial segregation and writes, "Prohibition against other people eating in public restaurants and hotels and prohibition of marriage between coloured people and white people I hold to be a negation of civilization."

Professor Kelly Miller retires from Howard University.

September 17. The High Ice Cream Company obtains an injunction against the New Negro Alliance, and its members are forced to abandon their picket line.

Mabel Keaton Staupers is named executive secretary of the National Association of Colored Graduate Nurses. Staupers, a graduate of Freedmen's Hospital School of Nursing (Howard University College of Nursing), leads a campaign to integrate the armed forces nursing corps during World War II.

1935

May. The Works Progress Administration (WPA) is created as a federal agency.

Mary McLeod Bethune establishes the National Council of Negro Women. Bethune, who lives at 316 I Street NW (she later moves to 1812 9th Street NW), also receives the Spingarn Medal in 1935.

May Miller publishes *Negro History in Thirteen Plays*. Miller, the daughter of Kelly Miller, is a poet, a teacher, a playwright, and an anthologist. Born in Washington, D.C., she studied at Howard University and is an active member of the New Negro literary movement in Washington. She is a member of Georgia Douglas Johnson's "Saturday Nighters," and she later serves as poetry coordinator for the Friends of Art in the District of Columbia Program for Public Schools. Miller is later appointed to the District of Columbia Commission on the Arts and Humanities. Her other works include the books of poetry *In the Clearing* (1959) and *Poems* (1962), as well as the stage plays *Pandora's Box* (1914), *Within the Shadow* (1920), and *The Cuss'd Thing* (1926).

Jazz musician Jelly Roll Morton leaves New York City for Washington, D.C., where he performs in nightclubs along the U Street corridor. Morton finally settles in a club located over a sandwich shop,

I have not lived as [a Negro], nor do I really know whether there is any colored blood in me or not.

—Jean Toomer,
The *Baltimore Afro-American*,
December 1, 1934

where he plays the piano and acts as floor manager and bouncer. The club, the Blue Moon Inn or the Jungle Inn, is one of the least expensive places along the strip and the crowd is often rowdy, but many Howard University professors and students spend their free time there. This club also gave Pearl Bailey her start.

Alain Locke establishes the Associates in Negro Folk Education, along with Lyman Bryson, a professor at Columbia University. The ANFE publishes nine "Bronze Booklets" between 1936 and 1942.

Dr. Charles Drew, one of the District's most celebrated figures, joins the faculty of the Howard Medical School. As part of a fellowship, Drew pursues postgraduate studies at Columbia University from 1938 to 1940. While there, he writes "Banked Blood," a dissertation on blood preservation that establishes him as the nation's leading expert. Drew returns to Howard as professor of surgery and later head of the Department of Surgery (1941–1950) at the Medical School. He also serves as chief surgeon (1944–1946), chief of staff (1944–1946), and medical director (1946–1948) at Freedmen's Hospital.

Attorney Charles H. Houston is appointed special counsel to the NAACP. Houston takes over the NAACP's legal strategy in the battle against segregation.

1936

February. Black leaders, including Ralph Bunche and John P. Davis, form the National Negro Congress, an umbrella organization of smaller protest groups. A. Philip Randolph becomes its first president, while Davis, its most ardent member, virtually runs the organization himself until the end of World War II. Howard University English professor Alphaeus Hunton Jr. helps to develop the organization in the District.

From 1936 to 1939, Sterling Brown serves as editor of Negro affairs for the Federal Writers' Project. While there, he argues that the interviews with former slaves have primarily been designed to elicit nostalgic endorsements of slavery. He successfully changes the focus of the interviews so that ex-slaves provide information about daily life, work, and living conditions.

Mary McLeod Bethune is appointed head of the Division of Negro Affairs in the National Youth Administration. She is the only black leader who is consistently able to gain direct access to the president, partly based upon her friendship with Eleanor Roosevelt.

While a teenager, Edward Brooke works selling hot dogs and ice cream at Griffith Stadium during the summers. He graduates from Dunbar High School in 1936 and enters Howard University, where he is a popular and socially active student.

D.C.'s first low-income public housing project for blacks opens at 12th and K Streets SE. Hopkins Place is named in honor of Mrs. Archibald Hopkins, a housing activist who lobbied local and national housing authorities to improve the conditions of alleys and low-income neighborhoods.

July. The Frederick Douglass Memorial and Historical Association and the National Association of Colored Women join together to preserve Frederick Douglass's home in Anacostia. They vow to raise $100,000 for the perpetual upkeep of the home and its grounds.

Langston Terrace, a federal housing complex of over 200 units, is constructed on Benning Road NE. Designed by black architect Hilyard Robinson, the buildings feature bas-reliefs created by artist Dan Olney. The bas-relief on the front building is called *The Progress of the Negro Race.*

August 7. Mary McLeod Bethune convenes the first meeting of the Black Cabinet, or the "Federal Council on Negro Affairs," as Bethune prefers to call the group. From this date, black appointees in the federal government begin meeting to discuss ways to increase federal services for blacks and to improve living standards for poor black communities.

Howard University School of Music hosts a musical concert featuring renowned contralto Marian Anderson at Dunbar High School. The school's auditorium is filled to capacity.

1937

January 20. Franklin D. Roosevelt is inaugurated as president. For the first time in history, a majority of blacks votes the Democratic ticket in the presidential election. Roosevelt's good standing with African American voters is partly due to the reputation that Eleanor Roosevelt enjoys in the black press as a supporter of civil rights and a friend of the downtrodden.

January. Mary McLeod Bethune presides over the first of two National Conferences on the Problems of the Negro and Negro Youth at the Department of Labor.

Sterling Brown publishes his best-known works: *Negro Poetry and Drama* and *The Negro in American Fiction*. Alain Locke serves as general editor.

March. William Hastie is appointed to the district court for the Virgin Islands by President Roosevelt. He serves until 1939, when he leaves to become dean of Howard University Law School.

Howard University School of Music hosts another musical concert featuring Marian Anderson at Dunbar High School. Again the acclaimed singer performs to a full house, and the sponsors plan to find a larger venue for next year's performance.

Carter G. Woodson begins publishing the *Negro History Bulletin*, a supplement to the *Journal of Negro History*. It is heavily illustrated and written for the general public and for schoolchildren.

June 13. Eleanor Katherine Holmes is born in Washington, D.C. She graduates from Dunbar High School in 1955.

July 26. The U.S. District Court for the District of Columbia decision supports the Sanitary Grocery Company and rejects the arguments of the New Negro Alliance that the organization should be allowed to maintain a picket line in front of stores that refuse to hire blacks. This decision upholding a lower court decision forces the alliance to appeal to the Supreme Court.

The Boys Club of the Metropolitan Police takes over the True Reformer's Hall on U Street. The building is renovated and made into a recreational facility.

The Homestead Grays, a baseball team with the Negro National League, begins playing in Washington, D.C. The city's black sports fans are also enthusiastic supporters of the Washington Pilots and the LeDroit Tigers, other local black baseball teams that play in Griffith Stadium. From the start, the Negro National League boasted some of the best players, black or white. Opening day of the Negro National League attracts international attention. There is even a black World Series and an All-Stars game. At the height of its popularity in the 1930s and the 1940s, the Negro League's games attract crowds of over 25,000 people. The integration of major league baseball led to the decline of the Negro leagues; by the end of the 1950s they were virtually defunct.

December 17. Black leaders in the District of Columbia declare this to be New Negro Alliance Day.

1938

March 28. The Supreme Court rules that the city cannot prohibit the New Negro Alliance from picketing the Sanitary Grocery Store. This decision removes the obstacles to the picket lines and paves the way for the alliance's success. Black Washingtonian Belford V. Lawson serves as its lead attorney.

May. Jazz musician Jelly Roll Morton visits musicologist Alan Lomax in the Library of Congress for the first time. Morton does a series of recordings for the library.

Howard University professor Kelly Miller begins a campaign to build a National Negro Museum at Howard University.

Howard University School of Music hosts its third annual musical concert featuring Marian Anderson. This time the university leases facilities at the Rialto Theatre.

Rayford Logan joins the faculty of Howard University.

December. Jelly Roll Morton is stabbed while performing at the Jungle Inn. The assailant first stabs him in the head from behind; when Morton turns, he is stabbed above the heart. Morton survives the attack but two days before Christmas leaves the District forever.

It is to be noticed that every Negro writer, author and scholar has a collection . . . in his private library. Every Negro University or College has a Negro Library containing books and documents bearing on the race question. White institutions which are now covering this field of social inquiry are accumulating material of this type. But none of these collections are able to cover the field adequately or competently as a Museum is calculated to do.

—Kelly Miller
The *New York Amsterdam News,* 1938

"The Black Cabinet," March 15, 1938. Mary McLeod Bethune is in the center of the first row.

1939

February. Howard University's School of Music begins to look for a suitable venue for its fourth Marian Anderson concert. The Rialto Theatre is unavailable, and the organizers search for an even larger concert hall for the Easter Sunday concert. At first they try to reserve Constitution Hall, but the Daughters of the American Revolution refuses to relax its policy of racial segregation and unconditionally turns down the request. The organizers then try to reserve the auditorium in Central High School, a large public school in the District, but the superintendant of schools and the board of education refuse to allow an event where either the performers are African Americans or the audience includes blacks. Marian Anderson, interviewed in the *New York Times,* expresses hurt and disappointment that she is the victim of racial discrimination in the nation's capital, "after having appeared in almost every other capital in the world."

The NAACP and religious and civil rights leaders establish the Marian Anderson Citizens Committee, an organization formed to protest the exclusion of Anderson and other blacks from facilities like Constitution Hall. Their campaign of letter writing and petitions forces the board of education to reconsider its earlier

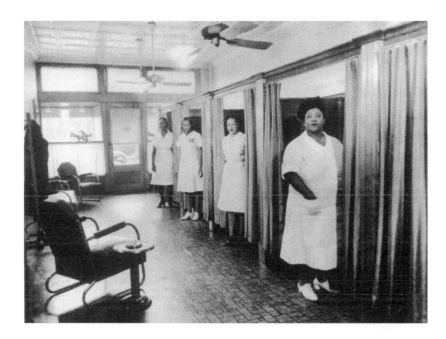

Hairdressers at the Lula B. Cooper French Beauty Salon, c. 1939.

decision; the board offers to allow the concert at Central High School if it is agreed by all parties not to set a precedent, and that the board will never again have to entertain such a petition. Such conditions prove too galling for the committee members, and the negotiations end without agreement. Anderson's manager, Sol Hurok, suggests an outdoor concert staged on the grounds of the Lincoln Memorial; the committee members and Secretary of the Interior Harold Ickes agree that the symbolism of such a venue is entirely appropriate. Over 75,000 people gather to hear Marian Anderson sing on Easter Sunday, and the concert is broadcast across the nation.

April 2. Marvin Pentz Gay II (later Marvin Gaye) is born to Marvin and Alberta Gay in Washington, D.C. The family first lived at 1617 1st Street SW. Young Marvin grows up worshiping and singing in the House of God Church, where his father, Elder M. P. Gay, is minister. As a child he enjoys the strong sense of community in the black neighborhoods of Southwest Washington. He attends William Syphax Elementary School on Half Street and later William Randall Junior High.

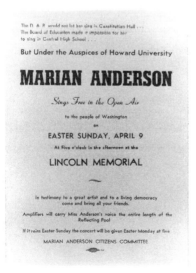

Flyer for "Marian Anderson Sings Free in the Open Air, 1939."

Marian Anderson performing in front of the Lincoln Memorial, April 9, 1939.

Marian Anderson receives the Spingarn Medal from the NAACP; Eleanor Roosevelt awards her the medal.

Washingtonian Bernice Hammond opens the Hammond Dance Studios on U Street, offering classes in ballet and other forms of dance. Hammond remains a pioneering presence on the dance scene for over sixty years, establishing many successful dance and cultural programs and organizations.

Popular physical education instructor E. B. Henderson publishes *The Negro in Athletics*. For over thirty years Henderson has organized athletic groups, events, and competitions. He is also active on the board of the local branch of the NAACP.

E. B. Henderson, author.

The *Pittsburgh Courier* organizes the Committee on Participation of Negroes in the National Defense Program under the direction of Rayford Logan, professor at Howard University. The committee seeks the complete integration of blacks into the military and also demands that the black population receive a fair share of wartime employment and educational opportunities.

The Lincoln Colonnade remains a popular ballroom for Washington's black elite events.

The Langston Golf Course opens on Benning Road NE.

September 1. Germany invades Poland, propelling Europe into World War II.

December 29. Kelly Miller, writer, lecturer, and former Howard University dean, dies in Washington, D.C.

1940

Mary Church Terrell publishes *A Colored Woman in a White World*. In her autobiography Terrell discusses her wealthy family upbringing in Atlanta, her studies in Europe, her arrival in Washington, and her political activities in the clubwomen's movement.

Howard University establishes a school of music under the direction of Lulu Vere Childers. In 1942 the university awards her an

During this period the annual President's Birthday Balls were presented at the Lincoln Colonnade Ballroom. First Lady Eleanor Roosevelt attended, accompanied by several carloads of prominent Hollywood personalities, including Cesar Romero, Lucille Ball, John Garfield, Jinx Falkenberg, Red Skelton, Jose Iturbi, and many others. During the Truman administration the Colonnade was attended by First Lady Bess Truman and her daughter, Margaret.

—Henry Whitehead, unpublished manuscript, Anacostia Museum

The opening of the T Street Post Office, the first post office in D.C. with an all-black staff, 1940.

honorary doctorate for her achievements in music instruction. The following year Childers returns to her home in Howell, Michigan, where she dies in 1946.

Elizabeth Cotten moves to Washington, D.C., to live with her daughter. She takes a job at Lansburgh's department store. Cotten taught herself to play banjo and guitar as a child. She played songs by ear and by age twelve wrote a blues song, "Freight Train." But by the time she moves to Washington, she has given up music. At Lansburgh's she retrieves a lost little girl and returns the child to her mother. The girl, Peggy, is the daughter of Mike Seeger, folksinger and folklorist. Within a year, Cotten leaves Lansburgh's to work for the Seeger family. There she begins playing the guitar again and eventually records "Freight Train" and other songs in 1958. Cotten becomes an acclaimed blues musician in the 1960s.

Owen Dodson becomes a professor in the drama department at Howard University. Dodson, an influential writer and theatrical director, authors plays, novels, and poetry, along with maintaining a successful teaching career.

October 25. Benjamin O. Davis Sr. (born in Washington, D.C., in 1877) is appointed brigadier general in the U.S. Army by President Roosevelt. Davis becomes the highest-ranking black person in the armed services. He is assigned to Fort Riley, Kansas, and his son Lieutenant Benjamin O. Davis Jr. is assigned to serve as his aide.

1941

January 20. Franklin D. Roosevelt is inaugurated as president.

January 26. The NAACP designates today as "National Defense Day." Demonstrations are held in cities nationwide. William Hastie

Socialites enjoy the "Guardsmen Dance" at the Lincoln Colonnade, 1940s.

and other blacks lead a campaign to protest racial segregation in the military. Their concerns focus on segregated military units; soldiers being segregated on public transportation; black soldiers being assigned to noncombat duties; and a lack of promotion opportunities for black officers.

January. A. Philip Randolph and the March on Washington Committee put out a call for people to protest against racially discriminatory hiring practices in defense-related industries. Nationwide, branches of the committee begin organizing to bring tens of thousands of black marchers to Washington in July.

January. The U.S. War Department announces the formation of an all-black unit stationed at Tuskegee Institute—the 99th Pursuit Squadron. Mechanics and other support personnel are trained at Chanute Field, Rantoul, Illinois. A separate military flight training school and an airfield are designed by black architect Hilyard Robinson and constructed at Tuskegee. The facilities are completely segregated, including separate drinking fountains and rest rooms.

Black nurses are admitted to the U.S. Army Nurse Corps due to the efforts of Mabel Staupers and her supporters. However, a quota system prevents the complete integration of black nurses into the corps.

Black military men are especially hard hit by the need to travel from post to post. An example of the growing tension occurs on July 8, when four black soldiers are arrested for refusing to move to the segregated black section of a train going from Washington, D.C., to Richmond, Virginia.

June 25. After intense negotiations with representatives of African American civil rights organizations—including A. Philip Randolph; Eugene Davidson, assistant director of the March on Washington Committee; Thurman Dodson, D.C. chair of the March on Washington Committee; and Rayford Logan—President Franklin D. Roosevelt issues Executive Order 8802, which bans discrimination in hiring by defense industries and establishes the Federal Employment Practices Commission to hear complaints and to monitor discrimination against blacks. On June 28 A. Philip Randolph cancels the March on Washington.

July. The U.S. War Department launches its training facility for black pilots at Tuskegee Air Field at Tuskegee Institute in Alabama. Initially, it was called the "Tuskegee Experiment," because many in the War Department doubted that black pilots could perform well. Lieutenant Benjamin O. Davis Jr. is among those selected for flight training.

The Supreme Court, in a case brought by U.S. Congressman Arthur Mitchell, rules that separate facilities in railroad travel must be substantially equal.

Frederick Gregory is born in the Anacostia neighborhood of Washington, D.C. He becomes the first African American astronaut.

After being elected president of his fraternity, Alpha Phi Alpha, in his senior year, Edward Brooke graduates from Howard University. When Pearl Harbor is attacked, Brooke joins the 366th Combat Infantry Regiment.

The Negro Caravan is published. Edited by Sterling Brown, Ulysses Lee, and Arthur Paul Davis, it becomes one of the most influential anthologies of black literature. Brown is also awarded a Guggenheim Fellowship for Creative Writing.

December 7. Pearl Harbor is bombed by the Japanese military. The United States enters World War II.

1942

Kansas native Gordon Parks arrives in Washington, D.C., to work as a photographer in the Farm Security Administration. It is the first time he has ever been to the city. He later recounts his experience in *A Choice of Weapons*.

March. Captain Benjamin O. Davis Jr. is among the first black pilots graduating from the Tuskegee training program. Among

I came to Washington, excited and eager, on a clear cold day in January.

[I] walked toward the business section and stopped at a drugstore for breakfast. When I sat down at the counter the white waiter looked at me as though I were crazy. "Get off of that stool," he said angrily. "Don't you know colored people can't eat in here? Go round to the back door if you want something." Everyone in the place was staring at me now. I retreated, too stunned to answer him as I walked out the door.

I found an open hot dog stand. Maybe this place would serve me. I approached the counter warily. "Two hot dogs, please."

"To take out?" the boy in the white uniform snapped.

"Yes, to take out," I snapped back. And I walked down the street, gulping down the sandwiches.

I went to a theater.

"What do you want?"

"A ticket."

"Colored people can't go in here. You should know that."

I remained silent, observing the ticket seller with more surprise than anything else. She looked at me as though I were insane. What is this, I wondered? Was Stryker playing some sort of joke on me? Was all this planned to exasperate me? Such discrimination here in Washington, D.C., the nation's capital? It was hard to believe.

—Gordon Parks,
A Choice of Weapons, 1967

those graduating with him are First Lieutenant George S. Roberts, First Lieutenant Mac Ross, Second Lieutenant Lemuel R. Curtis, and Second Lieutenant Charles DeBow. Shortly thereafter, Davis is promoted to lieutenant colonel and is named commander of the all-black 99th Pursuit Squadron.

The *Pittsburgh Courier* and other newspapers promote the idea of the "Double V" war campaign among blacks. The two Vs stand for two victories: in the wars against fascism and against racism.

May 17. Elmer W. Henderson, field representative for the Committee on Fair Employment Practices, which was created to encourage hiring blacks in war industries, travels south from Washington,

D.C., on the Southern Railway line on official business. He is denied service in the dining car and complains to the Interstate Commerce Commission. The commission orders the railway company to make provisions for black travelers, and in response, two tables for blacks are reserved in each dining car. These tables are screened off from other diners by a curtain. With the support of the NAACP, Henderson appeals all the way to the Supreme Court. In 1950 the Supreme Court rules that such segregated dining cars violate the Interstate Commerce Act.

July 20.   The first Women's Army Auxiliary Corps (WAAC) trainees arrive at Fort Des Moines to learn skills required of officers. There are 440 women, 40 of whom are black. Congress had mandated that 10.6 percent of WAACs were to be black, in proportion to the percentage of population that was black. Evelyn F. Greene and Harriet M. West (later Harriet M. Waddy) are two of the first graduates. In the next few classes, four other Washington residents are commissioned as officers: Ethel E. Haywood, Blanche L. Scott, Evelyn F. Overton, and Gladys E. Pace.

Madame Evanti and Mary Dawson establish the National Negro Opera Company.

John Edwin Washington publishes *They Knew Lincoln,* the culmination of his lifelong interest in President Lincoln and in the black people who were in contact with the president. Aside from his contribution to Lincolniana, Washington was a key figure in District public schools. He taught and served as principal in several elementary schools and also taught in high schools. He was an outstanding coach and sponsor of athletic activities and had a dental practice until ten years before his death in 1964.

Architect Albert Cassell enters into a deal with evangelist Elder Lightfoot Solomon Michaux to purchase land in northeast Washington, D.C., and erect the Mayfair Mansions housing complex. Cassell dreamed of developing a project for "African American tenants" and since 1936 had been searching for a suitable parcel of land in the District. Cassell overcame several obstacles: When the Federal Housing Authority (FHA) and other lending institutions denied him support, he conducted a house-to-house survey of black tenants to show that they were already paying an average of $15 a month. When he took his survey results to the FHA, he was informed that he needed a political constituency. As a result, Cassell joins with Michaux and three other men to form a company to develop Mayfair Mansions. After experiencing some financial difficulties and being refinanced a number of times, the project is finally completed. By 1949 only Cassell, Michaux, and Michaux's Gospel Spreading Association hold interest in the property. But by 1954, when he appears before the Senate Banking Committee, Cassell—whose dream started it all—is complaining that he has been squeezed out completely by Michaux.

November. Alain Locke edits an issue of the Survey Graphic entitled "Color: Unfinished Business of Democracy"; the articles look back on the past twenty years. The issue follows up on the earlier Survey Graphic that he edited in 1925.

November. Duke Ellington performs at Fort Dix, New Jersey, in a nationally broadcast event over the ABC Blue Network. The event is part of the Coca-Cola Spotlight Bands series. Ellington is busy in November breaking attendance records during a performing stint at Chicago's Regal Theater, where he receives a citation for his wartime fundraising efforts.

1943

January 1. D.C.'s Negro National League baseball star Josh Gibson is rushed to the hospital, suffering from a nervous breakdown. For much of the year, he is confined to St. Elizabeths Hospital when not playing ball.

January. Led by Pauli Murray, Howard University students begin demonstrating against racial segregation at local restaurants and theaters. The only major restaurants that serve blacks are in Union Station, the YMCA, and some government agencies.

January 31. William Hastie resigns from the War Department. Despite all his efforts at combating racial discrimination, he is disappointed that he was unable to dilute racial segregation in the

Program book, La Traviata, *August 28, 1943.*

armed forces. In recognition of his efforts, the NAACP awards him the Spingarn Medal later this year. Hastie returns to Howard University Law School.

Dr. Charles Drew, professor of pathology at Howard University Medical School, is called upon to organize blood supplies for civilian and military casualties. Heading the Blood for Britain campaign, Dr. Drew modifies the technology for producing blood plasma so that it can be mass-produced for shipment to British soldiers and air raid victims. Drew also serves as director of the American Red Cross Blood Bank, where he protests against the policy of segregating blood supplies according to the race of the donors. (Before January 1942 blacks were completely disqualified as blood donors.) He returns to teach surgery at the medical school and to oversee the Department of Surgery at Freedmen's Hospital.

June 2. The first day of combat for the 99th Pursuit Squadron. Its target is the island of Pantelleria, off the southern coast of Italy. By June 11 the enemy-held garrison there surrenders under the impact of aerial bombing.

August. Lillian Evanti, internationally renowned opera singer, wins critical acclaim for her performance in *La Traviata* with the National Negro Opera Company, Washington, D.C.

Alonzo Aden, author and curator.

Dr. Hildrus A. Poindexter, a professor at Howard University Medical School since 1931, wins acclaim for his wartime contributions. He serves in the Pacific as an epidemiologist, a malariologist, and a tropical disease specialist and is awarded many citations and battle stars for courage beyond the call of duty. After the war he returns to Howard University and enters the U.S. Public Health Service, where he is an international consultant in public health and tropical medicine for embassies and government agencies.

September. Recalled to the United States to take command of the 332nd Fighter Group—created by combining the 99th, 100th, 301st, and 302nd squadrons—Benjamin Davis Jr. holds a press conference to defend the 99th against charges by Colonel William Momyer, Major Gen. Edwin J. House, and other white officers that it performed poorly under battle conditions. As a result of Colonel

Ella Watson, a cleaning woman for U.S. government offices.

I found her in a notary public's office and introduced myself. She was a tall spindly woman with sharp features. Her hair was swept back from graying temples; a sharp intelligence shone in the eyes behind the steel-rimmed glasses. We started off awkwardly, neither of us knowing my reason for starting the conversation. At first it was a meaningless exchange of words. Then, as if a dam had broken within her, she began to spill out her life story. It was a pitiful one. She had struggled alone after her mother had died and her father had been killed by a lynch mob. She had gone through high school, married and become pregnant. Her husband was accidentally shot to death two days before the daughter was born. By the time the daughter was eighteen she had given birth to two illegitimate children, dying two weeks after the second child's birth. What's more, the first child had been stricken with paralysis a year before its mother died. Now this woman was bringing up these grandchildren on a salary hardly suitable for one person.

"Who takes care of them while you are at work?" I asked after a long silence.

"Different neighbors," she said, her heavily veined hands tightening about the mop handle.

"Can I photograph you?" The question had come out of an elaboration of thoughts. I was escaping the humiliation of not being able to help.

"I don't mind," she said.

–Gordon Parks,
A Choice of Weapons, 1967

Momyer's report, General George C. Marshall orders a G-3 operations office study of the performance of the 99th. The report finds "no significant general difference" between the 99th and the rest of the squadrons.

October. Art professor James Herring and curator Alonzo Aden establish the Barnett-Aden Gallery, the first private black gallery in America, on 127 Randolph Street NW. The Barnett-Aden provides a venue for the country's emerging black and white artists and also features exhibitions by some of the most well-known black artists. The gallery closes in 1969 after the death of Professor Herring.

1944

The Inter-Racial Section of the Defense Savings Program forms a music committee to "choose the best patriotic song composed by Negroes and to devise adaptations of Negro spirituals." The committee consists of Cab Calloway, Langston Hughes, W. C. Handy, Duke Ellington, and Andy Razaf. Duke Ellington purchases $3,000 worth of war bonds the first year of the drive. He also continues to work with ABC's Blue Network, committing to performances every Saturday from 5:00 to 6:00 P.M. during the weeks before and during the Seventh War Loan drive. Included in Ellington's performances are personal appeals to listeners to purchase bonds in support of the war effort. He is also fabled in jazz circles for his performances at the Swing Shift Dances, a series of concerts held for 140,000 Los Angeles defense workers, as well as for his remarkable appearance at Carnegie Hall in January 1943. In addition to his rigorous fundraising schedule, Ellington appears in a few Hollywood films.

Rayford Logan publishes *What the Negro Wants,* a compilation of fourteen essays by black political leaders. The book makes an impact due to its blunt demand for an immediate end to racial segregation.

Baptist minister Adam Clayton Powell Jr. becomes the first African American elected to Congress from the state of New York.

The Capital Press Club, an organization of black journalists, is established in Washington, D.C.

The Capitol Press Club, 1944.

When [Powell] walked into his House office for the first time . . . a memo from the Speaker greeted him. It was a list of "Do's and Don'ts for Negro Congressmen." Close to the top was, Don't eat in the House Dining Room. When [Congressman Kenneth] Keating came to Congress in 1947, two years later, Powell still couldn't get seated in either the House or the Senate Dining Room. Outraged, Keating decided to attack the Jim Crow law on the Senate side, where the ripples would be greater. . . . Keating asked a liberal senator to invite him to lunch. Keating, in turn, invited Adam and his wife, Hazel Scott, a jazz pianist and singer. . . . The lunch caused some screaming and kicking but Keating had made his point. Once Powell got a little power, he crashed the color barrier in the House Dining Room on his own. He also became the first black to use the congressional shower and to get a haircut. . . . He fought racial prejudice in the Capitol Police and in other places on the Hill as well. Black policemen had always worked the parking lots in the heat and the cold while whites grabbed the cushy inside jobs. Powell changed that.

—Robert Parker,
Capitol Hill in Black and White, 1986

1945

January 20. Franklin D. Roosevelt is inaugurated as president.

April 12. Franklin D. Roosevelt dies in office in Warm Springs, Georgia. Harry S. Truman assumes the presidency.

May 7. Germany surrenders in World War II.

May. The second all-black firehouse, Engine No. 27, opens on the 4200 block of Deane Avenue NE.

Patricia Roberts, born in Matoon, Illinois, in 1924 and later moves to Washington, D.C., graduates from Howard University. Ten years later she marries William B. Harris, a member of Howard University Law School faculty. In 1960 she graduates first in her class

The Hiawatha Theatre, located on 11th and U Streets, 1945.

from George Washington University Law School. She returns to
Howard's law school as an instructor and is made dean of the law
school in 1969.

The District of Columbia Redevelopment Act targets slum areas in
the District and authorizes the National Capital Park and Planning
Commission (NCPPC) to tear them down and develop new housing. Congress also creates the Redevelopment Land Agency and
gives it the authority to purchase land in the District of Columbia
for urban renewal projects. Unfortunately, when low-income blacks
are moved out of such areas during slum clearance projects, they
are often forced out for good.

DESEGREGATION AND
URBAN DISPLACEMENT

1946–1970

Overleaf:

Leaders of the civil rights movement, including Whitney Young, A. Philip Randolph, and Walter Reuther, at a rally, 1963.

Marion Barry, wearing a "Free D.C." pin, makes a statement to reporters on the steps of the District Building, 1966.

THE CIVIL RIGHTS ACTIVITIES OF BLACK POLITICAL AND RELIGIOUS leaders in the 1940s laid the legal groundwork for the achievements of the 1950s and 1960s. Although the 1941 March on Washington, with its implied impact of tens of thousands of people demonstrating in the nation's capital, was never carried out, it shaped the thinking and tactics of the movement for decades to come. In 1957, in the first of many massive civil rights demonstrations in Washington, supporters of racial desegregation gathered from around the country for a prayer vigil for freedom. Led by A. Philip Randolph, the Reverend Martin Luther King Jr., and religious leaders such as the Reverend Stephen Gill Spottswood, over 25,000 people gathered in prayer on the steps of the Lincoln Memorial. Washington, D.C., was the destination and the site of national black protest demonstrations against racial discrimination and in support of the right to vote for years to come, culminating in the Poor People's Campaign in 1968. Black Washingtonians and their institutions, by and large, formed the host community for these events, organizing food, lodging, and medical care for gatherings of demonstrators that sometimes numbered in the hundreds of thousands.

Building on Our Gains

In the local civil rights arena, blacks and civil rights supporters built upon the gains made by the New Negro Alliance in the 1930s. Many of the people in that organization provided the leadership for local antisegregation actions in the 1940s and 1950s. In 1947 Gardner Bishop, a local barber, and concerned parents formed the Consolidated Parents Group, Inc., to fight against racial inequality in the D.C. public school system. They were incensed over the school board's plan to transfer dilapidated school buildings to black students; the board had declared that several new school buildings were to be reserved exclusively for white students.

Other civil rights activists targeted different aspects of racial discrimination in the city. In the early 1950s Margaret Just Butcher (the daughter of the marine biologist Ernest E. Just) waged a public battle from her position on the D.C. Board of Education against segregated schools. When the Lisner Auditorium opened, blacks picketed and protested until the segregated seating policy was changed. The Committee for Racial Democracy also picketed the National Theatre for its racially exclusionary policies. The campaign to integrate the National Theatre was particularly bitter; the managers of the theater refused to admit blacks even when black stage shows and performances were being featured. It took an actors' guild strike lasting two and a half years to bring blacks into the audience. The Police Brutality Committee of the National Negro Congress monitored allegations of brutality on the part of the police force, and picket lines and demonstrations of Howard University students were a common sight in the 1950s and 1960s.

Quietly Desegregating

Located on 19th and C Streets SE, D.C. General Hospital quietly began desegregating its staff and wards in the early 1950s. "Our first integration was in the children's ward," hospital superintendant Dr. Philip Stebbing told a reporter. "The children integrated themselves by playing together in the daytime, although their rooms were separated." Dr. William Montague Cobb and other black doctors and medical professionals waged an ongoing battle to integrate Gallinger Hospital. The struggle over the desegregation of recreational facilities also engaged many parents. The lack of safe places for blacks to swim caused a considerable amount of friction between black community representatives and the D.C. Recreation Department. Black newspapers often reported the drowning deaths of black children, especially in the hot summer months when the Potomac River offered a tempting respite from the heat and humidity. When public recreational facilities were segregated, blacks kept pressure on the city to build more swimming pools; later, civil rights activists targeted segregated recreational facilities—particularly those with swimming pools. Many teachers, social workers, and settlement house workers argued that a lack of such facilities also encouraged juvenile delinquency among inner city and alley youths.

Attacking the "Lost Laws"

At age eighty-six, the indomitable Mary Church Terrell and the Coordinating Committee for the Enforcement of the D.C. Anti-Discrimination Laws launched an attack on segregation in public restaurants, in an effort to force city officials to enforce the civil rights laws passed in 1872 and 1873. These were the so-called lost laws, thus named because they were not included when the city codes were revised in 1901. In 1950 Terrell and three companions entered Thompson's Restaurant on 14th Street NW; when they were refused service, they filed suit against the restaurant. In *District of Columbia v. Thompson Co.*, the Municipal Court ruled against Terrell and the Coordinating Committee in July 1950; the following year the Appeals Court also ruled against them. On June 8, 1953, the Supreme Court ruled in their favor. Justice Douglas delivered the opinion, holding that "we find no other intervening act which would effect a repeal of [the lost laws]." City authorities would have to enforce 1872 and 1873 civil rights laws. Four months later the Coordinating Committee for the Enforcement of the D.C. Anti-Discrimination Laws decided to test the city's enforcement of these laws again when its members successfully attempted to attend a segregated movie house. Shortly thereafter, segregated movie theaters in the city announced that they were suspending their policy of excluding black patrons. In December the committee announced that it was going to test enforcement of the civil rights laws in respect to segregated hotels. Business by business, public facilities were forcibly integrated in the nation's capital.

Bolling v. Sharpe

In 1950 Gardner Bishop and the Consolidated Parents Group, Inc., led eleven black youths into a new school reserved for white students, the John Philip Sousa Junior High School, where they were refused admittance. Among the students in attendance was Spottswood T. Bolling, whose parents, along with the Consolidated Parents Group, filed suit against the D.C. School Board. James M. Nabrit Jr., a Howard University Law School professor, and George E. C. Hayes, a longtime civil rights activist, served as lead attorneys. Gardner Bishop and Burma Whitted launched a fundraising campaign that generated thousands of dollars for legal costs. Two years later *Bolling v. Sharpe* made its way into the annals of civil rights history when the Supreme Court agreed to hear it at the same time as the historic *Brown v. Board of Education of Topeka, Kansas*. In the majority opinion, Chief Justice Warren wrote that "Although the Court has not assumed to define 'liberty' with any precision, that term is not confined to mere freedom from bodily restraint. Liberty under law extends to the full range of conduct which the individual is free to pursue, and it cannot be restricted except for a proper governmental objective. Segregation in public education is not reasonably related to any proper governmental objective, and thus it imposes on Negro children of the District of Columbia a burden that constitutes an arbitrary deprivation of their liberty in violation of the Due Process Clause."

Gains and Losses in Housing

Black Washingtonians also made gains in the struggle against racial discrimination in housing. Since the influx of ex-slaves after the Civil War, many low-income black families found homes in the courtyard communities and the alley dwellings behind more affluent homes and in ghettos of substandard dwellings in Southwest and other parts of the city. These neighborhoods were often the subject of exposés by various government agencies and newspaper reporters. They were also increasingly the targets of "slum clearance" projects, especially in the 1950s. Their colorful histories and rich folklore attracted journalists and anthropological investigators; the awful conditions under which some families lived attracted social workers and health professionals; and the incidence of crime made police arrests a common sight. But hard-working one- and two-parent families were also found there—many of them recent arrivals from Virginia, North Carolina, and South Carolina, who had come to the city seeking employment opportunities and educational advancement for themselves and their children.

In 1934 Congress created the Alley Dwelling Authority, the precursor of the National Capital Housing Authority, to clear out the alleys with the worst housing conditions. In 1945 the District of Columbia Redevelopment Act targeted slum areas, and the Redevelopment Land Agency spurred urban renewal.

The Supreme Court decisions in *Shelley v. Kraemer, Hurd v. Hodge,* and *Barrows v. Jackson,* which made racially restrictive housing covenants legally unenforceable in 1948, eased somewhat the severe housing shortage facing middle-class black families. The *Hurd v. Hodge* case concerned black families who had purchased houses on the 100 block of Bryant Street NW that had a restrictive covenant barring blacks from owning homes in that neighborhood. When white homeowners in the block sued and sought an injunction to remove the black families from their homes, the legal case went all the way to the Supreme Court.

The end of racial covenants opened new neighborhoods to middle-class blacks and greatly expanded their housing opportunities. Brookland, for example, became one of the most popular areas for black professionals, particularly those employed at Howard University. Other areas, such as Shepherd Park, Brightwood, and the homes along 16th Street NW, were also home to black families. As told by David L. Lewis in *District of Columbia: A Bicentennial History:* "Along upper Sixteenth Street and separated from the white [section] west of the park lie two affluent black communities sometimes designated as the 'Gold' and the 'Platinum' coasts, separated by . . . Walter Reed Hospital. Immediately below the hospital is the Gold Coast, an area of large, regal homes with scant space between. Here, most of Washington's oldest and richest black families reside. Above the [hospital] are the rest, in homes generally smaller but more modern." The Gold Coast was populated by blacks in the 1950s, soon after the city's residential segregation laws were rescinded; the Platinum Coast in the 1960s and 1970s.

Urban Renewal

Between 1954 and 1958, approximately 20,000 people were moved out of Southwest Washington. Many black religious and community leaders in Southwest expressed concern over the fate of families being forced to move without adequate plans existing for their resettlement; other leaders focused on resisting these families' displacement. But some blacks defended the RLA and its plans, believing that the urban renewal being carried out in Southwest D.C. would improve living conditions in that part of the city. The historian Keith Melder writes that "While arguments raged, urban renewal moved forward. In addition to the residential renewal, highway engineers evolved plans for a dramatic new six-lane highway, the Southwest Freeway, which would displace blacks from existing rowhouses. . . . And so, between 1954 and 1960 most of the old Southwest disappeared."

During the 1950s and 1960s changes occurred in the racial composition of other neighborhoods that once had hosted large communities of black families. Georgetown, one of the oldest black communities in the city, lost many black families that had long resided there, partly due to the rising cost of living and an increase in property taxes. The exodus of black families accelerated after the passage of the Old Georgetown Act, which created the area's historic district and required that all renovation meet standards that would maintain the neighborhood's historic look. Capitol Hill also lost much of its black population when whites purchased and renovated low-cost townhouses there.

The end of the 1960s saw fundamental changes in local black politics. In 1967 Walter Washington was appointed as the city's first black mayor. One year later residents of Washington were permitted to elect members to the board of education, an important municipal body that launched many long-standing political careers.

The assassination of Martin Luther King Jr. in April 1968 set off several days of rioting in Washington. Many analysts traced the causes of the violence to the simmering resentment of blacks—many of them poor and low-income families—over inadequate housing, police brutality, and limited employment opportunities. By the end of the riot over 7,500 people had been arrested—most for curfew violation. Two months later, when the buses, mule trains, and caravans of the Poor People's Campaign arrived in the city, black Washingtonians were ready to play host.

1946

January. Duke Ellington receives the *Esquire* award for the top jazz band for the second consecutive year.

April. After arriving at the church in 1940 as a student assistant, Reverend Jerry Moore is appointed pastor of Nineteenth Street Baptist Church.

The Dunbar Hotel opens on 15th and U Streets NW. It soon becomes the city's most elegant hotel for blacks.

June 8. The Supreme Court rules that segregation on interstate buses is unconstitutional. The *Washington Afro American* front-page headlines read: "JC Bus Travel Outlawed," "Supreme Court Votes 6–1 in Morgan Case. Jurists Rule State Laws Place Undue Burden

Halloween Party, 1940s.

Outside the Dunbar Hotel.

on Interstate Travel. Jim Crow on Southern buses is dead." Though reporters note that interstate passengers coming from the North are not being segregated on either the Greyhound or the Trailways bus lines running into Richmond, those coming from the South are still being seated in the rear.

June. The Lincoln Heights Dwellings, a housing development occupying the old neighborhood formerly called Lincolnville, opens in the Deanwood area in northeast Washington, D.C. The project is initially made up of 440 housing units, covering 30 acres of land; monthly rents range from $11 for a one-bedroom unit to $51 for four bedrooms. The first residential manager is George W. Miner, a Dunbar High School graduate.

October 29. Members of the Washington Committee of the Southern Conference on Human Welfare picket George Washington University, protesting the exclusion of African Americans from Lisner Auditorium. The picket line intensifies a struggle between university president C. H. Marvin and the campus chapter of the American Veterans' Committee, led by Don Rothenberg, which criticizes Lisner's policy.

December 5. President Harry S. Truman issues Executive Order 9808, which establishes the Presidential Committee on Civil Rights.

December. An interracial group of scholars and labor and political leaders form the National Committee on Segregation in the Nation's

Picketing in front of the Lisner Auditorium, 1946.

Backers of the Fair Employment Practice Commission (FEPC) demonstrate outside the Capitol, 1946.

Capital. Members of the committee include sociologist E. Franklin Frazier, attorney Charles H. Houston, Hubert Humphrey (then mayor of Minneapolis, Minnesota), Howard University president Mordecai Johnson, Peter Odegard (president of Reed College in Oregon), Walter Reuther (head of the United Auto Workers Union), and former first lady Eleanor Roosevelt.

December 21. Dr. Charles Drew is named medical director of Freedmen's Hospital.

1947

February. The Police Brutality Committee of the National Negro Congress, led by Julius Cohen and William Tymous, begins to investigate allegations of brutality on the part of police in Washington, D.C. Complaints of abuse have long been aired by church and civic leaders in the black press.

Michael Uline, owner of Uline Arena, finally gives in to pressure from individuals and organizations involved in professional sports and announces an end to his long-standing policy of excluding blacks from all sports except boxing and wrestling.

February. The Committee for Racial Democracy advertises in local black newspapers for volunteers to picket the National Theatre and the Lisner Auditorium at George Washington University. The two institutions are targeted due to their policy of excluding black patrons.

March. Research conducted by the cultural committee of the National Negro Congress reveals that segregation is pervasive within the country's entertainment industry, including in the District of Columbia. Its report cites the National Theatre, which "has a lily white policy even when shows with mixed casts are playing. . . . Constitution Hall is open on 'special occasions' or when pressure is brought effectively." Actors championing the report include Paul Robeson, Fredric March, and Cheryl Crawford.

March. White women employees in the Bureau of Internal Revenue walk out when an African American woman, Mildred Lindsay, of 1616 Rosedale Street NE, is brought in to work with them. Of the 100 employees in the Statistical Clearing Section office, 52 are black. White women work together at one table, punching statistical cards; black women work together at another table; and one table is worked by both black and white women. The white employees stage the walkout because they are angry that the percentage of black employees is increasing.

April. The National Theatre is served a notice by the Actor's Equity Association, stating, "that unless all races are admitted to audiences on or before May 31, 1948, Equity members will be forbidden to

Launching of a picket line at the National Theatre, 1947.

appear on stage." The thirteen-month grace period was granted to allow for a gradual integration of audiences.

September 12. Following up on his success as a radio evangelist, Elder Lightfoot Michaux has his first televised broadcast on station WTTG. His religious TV programs are broadcast every Thursday evening.

October. The Presidential Committee on Civil Rights publishes its report "To Secure These Rights," which establishes the four basic rights a government must protect: the right to safety; the right to citizenship, such as service in the armed forces and the exercise of voting; the right to freedom of expression; and the right to equality of opportunity. The report calls for numerous measures to combat racism: legislation eliminating discrimination in employment, housing, health facilities, interstate transportation, and public accommodations; the creation of an anti-lynching law; a permanent FEPC; and the necessity of issuing executive orders barring discrimination in the armed forces and the civil service.

December. Gardner Bishop and the Consolidated Parents Group, Inc., lead a school strike in which black parents keep their children

Picketing in front of the school board headquarters, 1947.

out of schools to protest the transfer of dilapidated, distant schools for black students' use. The transfer was approved by a 7–2 vote by the Board of Education and primarily involved the Blow, Webb, S. J. Bowen, Hayes, Brown, and Lennox schools. The schools are reportedly safe to attend, but black parents resent that their children are restricted to hand-me-down school buildings. In addition, the *Washington Afro American* reports, noxious odors are emitted from the coal heating plants of the Blow and the Webb schools. The protesters fight the transfer, as they wish the transfer of newly built schools, rather than older buildings, to colored use.

1948

January. After only six months of marriage, singer Pearl Bailey and Ralph Harlan, local bon vivant and playboy, are amicably divorced.

February. Howard University students lead a demonstration protesting the Central YMCA's policy of refusing to serve blacks in the cafeteria.

The management of the National Theatre decides to show motion pictures exclusively, rather than give in to the demands of the Actor's Equity Association to desegregate its audience.

Gallinger Hospital ends its policy of excluding black doctors and nurses from practicing there. Under an agreement signed with Howard University, black interns and residents will also be allowed to serve in the hospital. The decision is marked as a victory for Dr. William Montague Cobb, who fought for years to integrate Gallinger Hospital.

May 13. The Supreme Court rules in the landmark case of *Hurd v. Hodge* that restrictive housing covenants are not legally enforceable. Racially restrictive housing covenants—agreements preventing the sale of property to individuals based on race and ethnicity—are widespread in Washington, D.C., and make it difficult for many blacks to find suitable housing. The Supreme Court decision overturns previous decisions rendered by the District Court and the U.S. Court of Appeals. Charles H. Houston made the argument against the covenants before the court.

In eight years the city's African American population has grown from 215,398 to 285,988, creating pressure on the residential housing available to blacks. Because of restrictive covenants, blacks—though comprising 24 percent of the city's population—are limited to 20 percent of the District's housing units. City leaders continue to call on the National Capital Housing Authority to construct more public housing. Twenty-six housing projects are run by NCHA, including Langston Terrace Apartments, James Creek Dwellings, Parkside Dwellings, and Barry Farms. Rents typically range from $11 to $40 per month.

Charles H. Houston, one of the lawyers in Hurd v. Hodge.

The *Washington Afro American* notes that black Washingtonians were directly involved in *Hurd v. Hodge:* "The cases covered in the high court's decision involve 20 colored families in the unit block of Bryant Street. Paul R. Stewart, 150 Bryant Street, 87 year-old, partially deaf man, one of the litigants, gave vent to his pent up feeling on hearing of the decision with a loud 'Thank God.' "

May 14. Accomplished soprano and opera singer Carmen Balthrop is born in the District of Columbia.

July. President Truman issues Executive Order 9981, which calls for the desegregation of the armed forces. The order states that "there shall be equality of treatment and opportunity for all persons in the armed services without regard to race, color, religion, or national origin." It also creates a presidential Committee on Equality of Treatment and Opportunity in the Armed Services.

Rear Admiral P. S. Rossiter, retired chief of staff in the U.S. Navy, admits that he banned the use of Red Cross blood at Gallinger Hospital because it was not labeled "colored" or "white." Dr. Jacob Weinstein, chief of the Gallinger blood bank, states that "in actuality, there is no difference between 'colored' and 'white' blood."

August. Robert C. Weaver (on the staff of the American Council on Race Relations) informs an audience at Teachers College, Columbia University, in New York City, that "We have educated our minority groups for opportunities that we have not educated our majority groups to make available." Weaver also commented on the president's order concerning the armed forces, remarking that the legislation "opened up debate where silence once existed."

Brigadier General Albert Cox, commanding officer of the District National Guard, decides not to integrate the D.C. National Guard. The decision is in direct conflict with President Truman's nondiscrimination order.

September. An Olympic boxing star from Covington, Virginia, is jailed after refusing to leave his seat and move to another section of a train. The boxer, Norvell Lee, an electrical engineering student at Howard University and a veteran of the Pacific Theater in World War II, was arrested on a train bound for Washington, as he sat in a colored car that was later changed to a white car after several white passengers entered it. Lee resisted leaving, arguing that he was the first person in the car and that if anyone should move, it should be the white passengers. The police were called in to remove Lee. Lee posts a $250 bond and is released.

September. Ras H. S. Imru, Ethiopian dignitary and cousin of Emperor Haile Selassie of Ethiopia, is asked to sit in a segregated section reserved for blacks when attending an event for the American Association for the Advancement of Science at DAR Constitution Hall. As soon as President Truman enters the hall, Imru is approached by an usher who attempts to escort him from the diplomat section to the colored section. The AAAS chief administrative officer, Dr. Forrest Moulton, later apologizes to Ras Imru in person and blames the staff of the hall.

October. Four months after the passage of the Women's Armed Services Integration Act, making women permanent members of the U.S. military and allowing for their enlistment in the ROTC, a base for the WACs is established at Fort Lee, Virginia. Charles Houston and Walter White object to the bill because it lacks any measures to prevent segregation; they criticize Mary McLeod Bethune's support for the bill.

October. Georgetown University drops its racial bar, admitting four black students to Georgetown University Law School.

November 15. The first black WAC company begins training at Fort Lee. The commanding officers are Bernice G. Henderson, Doris M. Norrel, and Ann G. Hall.

November 27. Segregated restroom facilities are erected during the preparations for the inauguration of President Truman. No individual claims responsibility for labeling the toilets "For Colored" and "For White," and the designations are removed soon after an article complaining about them appears in the *Washington Afro American*.

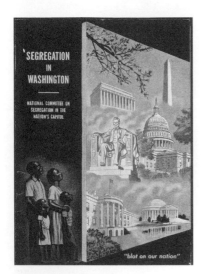

The cover of Segregation in Washington, *1948.*

In 1950 the only places in Washington where blacks could be seated to eat were the cafeterias at Federal office buildings, the 17th and K Streets YWCA, Union Station, National Airport, the Methodist Building Cafeteria, Hains Point Tea House, and the American Veterans' Committee Club on New Hampshire Avenue.

—Sandra Fitzpatrick and Maria Goodwin, *The Guide to Black Washington: Places and Events of Historical and Cultural Significance in the Nation's Capital,* 1990

The Truman inauguration becomes the first integrated one since that of William Howard Taft in 1909.

December. *Segregation in Washington* is published by the National Committee on Segregation in the nation's capital.

December 21. Actor Samuel L. Jackson is born in Washington, D.C. Although he is raised in Chattanooga, Tennessee, he often returns to spend his summers in the Parklands neighborhood in Southeast D.C.

1949

January 20. Harry S. Truman is inaugurated as president.

Congressman William L. Dawson becomes the first black to head a congressional committee, when he is named chairman of the House Committee on Government Operations.

Clarence C. White, violinist and former teacher at the Washington Conservatory of Music and School of Expression, presents his play, *Ouanga,* a musical based on the life of the Haitian Emperor Desalines.

Mary Church Terrell and other civil rights activists establish the Coordinating Committee for the Enforcement of the D.C. Anti-Discrimination Laws, to pressure city officials to enforce the 1872 and 1873 civil rights laws that forbade discrimination in public places.

The Catholic Archdiocese of Washington orders parochial schools to be integrated.

1950

Mary Church Terrell, Reverend W. H. Jernagin, and two other members of the Coordinating Committee for the Enforcement of the D.C. Anti-Discrimination Laws are refused service at Thompson's Restaurant at 725 14th Street NW. They sue the restaurant and other segregated eating establishments. They argue that such segregation violates the 1872 civil rights laws, but their case is dismissed in July 1950 by the municipal court.

The manager told us we could not be served in the restaurant because we were colored. I said to him, "Do you mean to tell me that you are not going to serve me?" The manager replied that he could not. He apologized for his action, stating that it was not his fault but it was a policy of the John K. Thompson Co. not to serve Negroes. I asked him if Washington was in the United States and if the United States Constitution applied here. The manager replied, "We don't vote here."

—From Mary Church Terrell's deposition,
after trying to eat at a segregated restaurant

April 1. Dr. Charles Drew has a fatal car accident while driving to a medical conference at Tuskegee, Alabama. Despite some accounts to the contrary, he is not denied emergency entry to medical facilities after the accident. He receives emergency medical attention but succumbs to the injuries that he received in the accident.

Charles Drew, physician and surgeon.

April 3. Educator and historian Carter G. Woodson, founder of the Association for the Study of Negro Life and History, dies. Woodson authored or coauthored nineteen books on African American history. He was responsible for Negro History Week, which he founded on February 19, 1926. Woodson developed and distributed the *Journal of Negro History,* the *Bulletin of Negro History,* and many African American history kits. A determined man, Woodson sought to end racist depictions of African Americans in history books and once said, "If a race has no history, if it has no worthwhile tradition, it becomes a negligible factor in the thought of the world, and it stands in danger of being exterminated."

April 22. Dr. Charles Hamilton Houston dies in Bethesda, Maryland, and is interred at Lincoln Memorial Cemetery. Houston, an accomplished lawyer, is remembered for his achievements in the legal field, as well as for his inspirational speeches and writing. Houston once wrote to a student that "The most important thing . . . is that no Negro tolerate any ceiling on his ambitions or imagination." Later this year he is awarded the Spingarn Medal posthumously.

Carter G. Woodson in his study, 1948.

May 25. Joanne M. Braxton is born in Freedmen's Hospital. Braxton becomes an accomplished poet in the 1970s.

July 11. An all-black infantry unit, the 24th Infantry Regiment, arrives in Korea after leaving Japan. The 24th achieved the first U.S. victory in Korea after recapturing Yech'on.

July 19. Judge William Henry Hastie is confirmed by the Senate to the Third U.S. District Court of Appeals, the highest judicial post ever held by an African American at that time.

September 11. Gardner Bishop leads eleven black youths into a new school for whites, the John Philip Sousa Junior High School, where the students are refused admittance on the grounds of race. Among the students in attendance are Spottswood T. Bolling. James Nabrit, a Howard professor, files suit against Melvin Sharpe, president of the D.C. Board of Education, in *Bolling v. Sharpe*.

October 31. Earl Lloyd is the first black man to play in an NBA game, when he signs on with the Washington Capitols. After seven games he leaves to serve in the Korean War, returning to basketball in 1952. He is later named assistant coach with the Detroit Pistons, the first black coach in the NBA.

November 20. E. Ethelbert Miller is born in New York City. Miller becomes an acclaimed poet and an influential figure in the African American literary community.

1951

January. Thurgood Marshall is sent to Japan to investigate the court-martial proceedings of thirty-two blacks convicted of violating the 75th Article of War. Marshall finds that racial preconceptions about blacks contributed to the convictions and that the tribunals were too quick in their deliberations.

President Harry S. Truman's Executive Order 10308 creates an eleven-member President's Committee on Government Contract Compliance to enforce nondiscrimination within the federal contracting process.

Judge William H. Hastie.

Mabel Staupers, founder of the National Association of Colored Graduate Nurses, receives the Spingarn Medal from the NAACP.

Elbert Peets, landscape architect, proposes a rebuilding plan for Southwest Washington. Peets's plan calls for gradual changes to the neighborhood that will prevent large-scale displacement of area residents. Instead, the Redevelopment Land Agency develops a plan to raze most of the buildings in the community bounded by South Capitol and 4th Streets SW, and between E and I Streets SW. Most black families removed from the area cannot afford to live there after the high-income structures are built. The Waterside Mall replaces the old buildings on the waterfront.

November 7. New management at the National Theatre finally rescinds the theater's policy of excluding blacks, ending an Actor's Equity boycott of two and a half years. Plays and other stage performances are once again featured there.

1952

February 17. Dorothy Maynor becomes the first African American to sing in Constitution Hall. In 1939 Marian Anderson was banned from singing there by the Daughters of the American Revolution.

Fabled pianist Henry Grant dies. Grant taught music at Dunbar High School, in addition to composing, directing choirs, and leading the L'Allegro Glee Club. He also performed piano recitals, was director of the Washington Conservatory of Music, and helped to found the National Association of Negro Musicians in 1919, serving as editor of its journal.

The U.S. Supreme Court allows James Nabrit to submit his case directly to the high court, thus joining *Bolling v. Sharpe* with *Brown v. Board of Education of Topeka, Kansas.*

1953

January 20. Dwight D. Eisenhower is inaugurated as president.

In *Barrows v. Jackson,* the Supreme Court rules that the award of damages for the violation of a restrictive covenant contravenes the equal protection and due process clauses of the Fourteenth Amendment.

James M. Nabrit, civil rights attorney.

William Leo Hansberry is awarded a Fulbright Research Scholarship to study in Africa. With the help of the fellowship, he travels and conducts research in fourteen different countries. Hansberry also establishes the Institute of African-American Relations in Washington, D.C., this same year.

James Amos Porter is appointed head of the Department of Art and director of the art gallery at Howard University.

March 13. Marian Anderson performs in Constitution Hall, giving the first of six concerts.

The Washington National Housewives League, Inc., is formed, with Mrs. Arna J. Bugg as president. The league is an affiliate of the National Negro Business League; its mission is to "reveal to Negro womanhood the possibilities of self-help" by patronizing those businesses owned by Negroes or that "employ Negroes in varied capacities according to their fitness and abilities," and "by instilling in our children that business and commerce are noble pursuits."

Community activist Julius Hobson becomes president of the Slowe Elementary School PTA. Hobson, born in Birmingham, Alabama, in 1922, was a graduate of Tuskegee Institute and Howard University. He later becomes active in the desegregation of Woodbridge Elementary School and a leading member of the Federation of Civic Associations and of the NAACP.

June 8. The Supreme Court decides the Thompson Restaurant case in favor of the plaintiffs. The Supreme Court decision passes by a rule of 8–0 and states that in the District of Columbia, restaurants may not refuse service to "well-behaved and respectable" Negroes. The decision reinforces the District civil rights acts of 1872 and 1873, referred to as the lost laws because they were omitted from the D.C. law code in 1901.

Chicago Defender reporter Ethel L. Payne establishes the newspaper's bureau in Washington, D.C.

The Lend-A-Hand Club purchases a building at 2501 20th Street NE for the Ionia R. Whipper Home for Unwed Mothers, continuing a tradition of twenty years of helping young black women.

Lyndon B. Johnson and Ethel Payne, c. 1968.

September 15. William L. Houston, Charles Houston's father, is buried in Lincoln Cemetery, following a memorial service at Rankin Chapel on the Howard University campus. Houston was considered the dean of black attorneys in the city and upon his death at age eighty-three was the oldest practicing attorney in the city. Born in Mound City, Illinois, Houston came to the District to study at Howard University Law School, graduating in 1882. From 1921 to 1936, he taught law at Howard University; in 1924 he formed a law firm with his son, Charles. Houston was an active member of the Democratic Party and served in many functions. He was also a member of the Board of Education of the District of Columbia from 1921 to 1924.

September 23. The Coordinating Committee for the Enforcement of the D.C. Anti-Discrimination Laws, led by Mary Church Terrell and Reverend W. H. Jernagin, begins a new campaign, this time focusing on movie houses that refuse to admit black patrons. On the occasion of her ninetieth birthday, Mrs. Terrell and Reverend Jernagin successfully demand admittance at a segregated theater. Shortly after that, the Stanley, Warner, and Loews theater chains announce that they are ending their whites-only policy. Almost

1,000 friends and supporters gather at the Statler Hotel to honor Mary Church Terrell on her birthday.

The Consolidated Parents Group, Inc., led by Burma Whitted and Gardner Bishop, launches a series of fundraisers to build financial support for a legal challenge to the segregated school system in the District. James M. Nabrit, professor of law at Howard University, and George E. C. Haynes are the attorneys arguing the case before the Supreme Court. Sarah and Spottswood Bolling are among the plaintiffs. They are seeking to have their son attend a segregated school.

A study by the Washington Housing Association reveals that over 15,000 outhouses are still being used in the District of Columbia. At a Senate Judiciary subcommittee hearing, the poor living conditions of Dixon Court, an alley community off 3rd and H Streets SW, are reviewed in some detail. Investigators found outdoor water faucets, outhouses, a lack of heating facilities in the middle of winter, and multiple family members sharing a single bed.

1954

January. Before a crowded room of black and white parents, Dr. Margaret Butcher, an outspoken African American on the Board of Education, unsuccessfully attempts to force the board to address the issue of school integration. When Colonel West A. Hamilton and Wesley A. Williams, the other two black board members, refuse to second Dr. Butcher's motion, the local branch of the NAACP calls for their resignation. Supporters of school integration hold a civic assembly at Turner Memorial Church in support of Dr. Butcher. The daughter of professor Ernest Everett Just, Dr. Butcher is also a professor at Howard University. Poet Georgia Douglas Johnson writes a poem dedicated to her in the midst of all the furor.

Dr. William Montague Cobb resigns from the local branch of the NAACP to protest its call for the resignation of Hamilton and Williams. As a result, Cobb and branch president Eugene Davidson engage in a public dispute carried out within the organization itself and in the pages of the *Washington Afro American*.

Benjamin O. Davis Jr., born in Washington, D.C., in 1912, is appointed to the rank of general in the U.S. Air Force. Davis becomes the first black general in the United States armed forces.

February. The 13th Street photography studio of Robert S. Scurlock, the son of Addison Scurlock, is destroyed in a fire. Robert Scurlock taught photography at the Capital School of Photography and also at Howard University. He later opens the Customcraft Studio at 1813 18th Street NW.

February 24. At a hearing before the Senate Permanent Investigating Committee, Annie Lee Moss, a black clerk employed by the Army Signal Corps, is accused by Senator Joseph R. McCarthy of being a communist and of handing over top-secret codes to the communists. At her appearance before the committee on March 11, Moss professes ignorance of communism and denies ever being a communist or attending any meetings. When she testifies in her own defense, Senator McCarthy leaves the room, but Senators John L. McClellan of Arkansas and Stuart Symington of Missouri denounce the hearsay evidence used against her, amid applause from the public galleries.

April 26. Dixon Court, a notorious alley dwelling, is the first location to be demolished in preparation for urban renewal plans.

May. The D.C. Recreation Board ends segregated playgrounds in the District of Columbia. Immediately integrated are the Edgewood playground at 3rd and Evarts Streets NE and the Turkey Thicket playground near Catholic University. Blacks had fought for four years to use these two playgrounds.

May 17. The Supreme Court rules in the case of *Brown v. Board of Education of Topeka, Kansas*, that "separate but equal" educational facilities are "inherently unequal," mandating an end to segregation in public schools. Chief Justice Warren also rules segregation in D.C. public schools unconstitutional in the case of *Bolling v. Sharpe*. Sarah Bolling was one of the plaintiffs in the D.C. case. When her son was not allowed to attend Sousa Junior High School

An alley dwelling in Logan Court, 1940. This is representative of most alley dwellings that were eventually demolished to make way for urban renewal.

near their home, she and the Consolidated Parents Group initiated a legal suit. "When I go to work," Bolling said, "I look and think it's terrible for my boy passing by schools he ought to be going to, and yet must go all the way across town to school."

June. When the head of the D.C. school board, Dr. Hobart Corning, attempts to implement a gradual plan for school integration, supporters of integration erupt at a school board meeting and vow to replace him. The Corning plan, which would have delayed full integration for one school year, is finally rejected by a vote of the school board.

June 9. African American philosopher and educator Alain LeRoy Locke dies of complications from heart disease in New York City. Locke was working on his ninth book, *The Negro in American Culture,* at the time of his death. A commemorative article in the *Washington Afro American* noted that the diminutive Locke was known

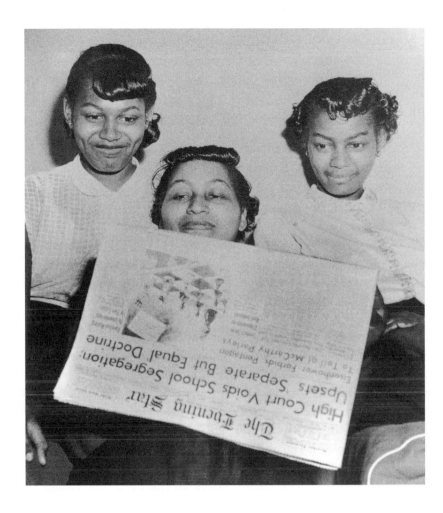

Local plaintiffs in the school integration case, Mrs. James C. Jennings and her daughters, pose for a photograph displaying newspaper headlines announcing the Supreme Court's decision.

on the Howard University campus as the "Little Professor." Locke was a mentor to many of the students, as well as to some of the professors. He formed friendships with many notable blacks of the period, including Langston Hughes, Duke Ellington, and Ralph Bunche.

July 28. Mary Church Terrell, who died on July 24, is laid to rest after hundreds of blacks pay homage at the national headquarters of the National Association of Colored Women at 1601 R Street NW, where her body lies in state. The next day mourners arrive as much as three hours early at Lincoln Memorial Temple Congregational

Ella Rice, the only African American teacher at the all-white Henry Draper Elementary School, 1954.

Church to attend the funeral, and loudspeakers have to be added to accommodate the large crowd outside the church. Telegrams and letters of condolence pour in from around the country, including one from Paul Robeson, which reads in part: "America loses one of its great daughters, a worthy sister of Frederick Douglass, Harriet Tubman and Sojourner Truth in her unceasing militant struggle for full citizenship of her people." Terrell leaves her spacious home at 1615 S Street NW to her daughter during her daughter's lifetime; after her daughter's death the house will go to Howard University.

After attorney Thurgood Marshall announces a need for funds to support the legal assault on public school segregation, the *Washington Afro American* and other black newspapers announce a "Dollar or More to Open the Door" campaign, raising $17,300.

August. The U.S. Army Signal Corps suspends Annie Lee Moss from her job, leveling a number of charges against her. Army officials charge that she joined the Communist Party in 1943 and was assigned to the Northeast Club, Frederick Douglass branch; that she had been given a Communist Party membership book; that she subscribed to the *Daily Worker;* and that her family had roomed for two weeks with Hattie Griffin, an active member of the Communist Party. Moss denies all the charges, contending that she had never heard of the Northeast Club or of the Frederick Douglass branch; that she had never subscribed to the newspaper or attended any meetings. Renowned attorney George E. C. Haynes is her counsel.

August. In an article headlined "Ghost Town, D.C.," the *Washington Afro American* notes that large sections of housing in southwest D.C. are being razed. Describing the red light districts that used to flourish in certain parts of the area, the reporter recalls, "Those were the days when red light districts abounded, when Four-and-a-Half Street was the great half-white way of the Southwest when you entered a café with one hand on your pocketbook." The article states that the old Southwest community is being replaced with a "new look." "The transition for Southwest is meeting with mixed reactions. There are those who say 'it's the finest thing that ever happened to the Southwest.' Opponents of the project say 'it's a Trojan Horse.' "

Black architect Hilyard Robinson, member of the National Capital Planning Commission, defends the plans for the Southwest redevelopment program, while Southwest community activist Leon S. Calhoun takes the opposite view. The article concludes with the following passage: "It is the 'Master Plan,' and in days to come it will move into Northwest and Southeast Washington. They, too, will have their 'Ghost Town'—and later, 'the new look.' "

September. The all-white Federation of Citizens' Associations files suit in U.S. District Court to stop the integration of the public schools system in the District of Columbia. Led by Dr. C. Herbert Marshall, the Federation of Civic Associations, consisting mostly of black residents, closely monitors the case.

September 22. Inspired by the Supreme Court civil rights decision, eighty-four-year-old Reverend William H. Jernagin organizes a ceremony at the Lincoln Memorial celebrating the ninety-first anniversary of the signing of the Emancipation Proclamation. Jernagin, a long-time political activist who served as pastor of the Mt. Carmel Baptist Church, brings together black religious and business leaders from around the country to support his idea of a "Lincoln Thanksgiving Pilgrimage" to Washington, D.C. As many as 1,000 gather at the memorial to pray, preceded by a 250-car cavalcade. Speakers at the event include Reverend Smallwood E. Williams.

The Capital Transit Company agrees to hire black streetcar and bus operators in the District of Columbia.

October 4. Anti-Negro student demonstrations spread across the District of Columbia. Eastern, McKinley, and Anacostia High School students are the most active in protesting the integration of black students into their schools.

October 9. Anti-integration demonstrations end at public schools in the District of Columbia. The last holdouts are seventy-five student picketers at Anacostia High School. These students disperse

Eastern High School students march to Anacostia High School in a protest over integration, 1954.

Recently a white patient at Casualty Hospital, Mrs. [Smith] of Brandywine, Maryland was moved from the white ward after a colored minister had visited and prayed with her. Despite her protests that she was white, Mrs. Smith was taken to the colored ward, and told by a nurse: "You have disgraced the entire white ward."

It was only after a long-distance telephone call verified Mrs. Smith's statement about her race that she was removed to a private room.

—The *Washington Afro American*, September 25, 1954

after school superintendent Hobart Corning threatens disciplinary action.

December. Anacostia neighborhood resident Charles Qualls heads the Coordinating Committee of Anacostia and Vicinity, a group of local black civic activists. One of the first actions of the group is to contact the board of the Frederick Douglass Memorial and Historical Association to offer assistance in stopping the deterioration of the Frederick Douglass home. Despite the home being managed by the memorial association, conditions at the Douglass home are poor and the grounds and buildings are in disrepair. To finance some repairs, the memorial association sells five acres of Douglass's land for the development of the Cedar Hill Gardens apartment complex and the Glen Gardens housing project, but the Anacostia coordinating committee charges that not enough is being done and demands an accounting of the money being spent. Part of the problem is the lack of clear responsibility; the Frederick Douglass Memorial and Historical Association owns the land, but the National Association of Colored Women's Clubs holds the mortgage for the house.

1955

January. Representative William Dawson is selected to sit on the House District Committee. He is the first African American to be appointed to the congressional body that oversees the District of Columbia.

The U.S. Supreme Court denies the motion of the Federation of Citizens' Associations in Washington, D.C., to file a friend of the court brief asking for a delay in the onset of school integration. The federation is made up of fifty-seven all-white neighborhood-based citizen associations. Black residents had formed their own neighborhood organizations, which they called civic associations. The all-black Federation of Civic Associations supports the immediate integration of D.C. public schools.

February. *Washington Afro American* reporter Louis Lautier becomes the first African American reporter to be admitted to the National Press Club. Sponsored by Drew Pearson and Marquis Childs, he is admitted by a vote of 377 to 281.

February. Actress Tallulah Bankhead gives an interview to *Washington Afro American* reporter Samuel Hoskins, supporting school integration, integration of theaters, and home rule for Washingtonians. "It's a shame people living here have no vote. They pay taxes and can't say how their money is to be spent. Every person should be permitted to vote, particularly in Washington, the nation's capital," Bankhead says from backstage in the National Theatre.

The Capitol Hill Restoration Society is formed. The organization supports the efforts of families and other people purchasing inexpensive homes on Capitol Hill. Typically, the new buyers would restore the town houses, thereby greatly improving their property values. As a result of low-income families selling their homes, some of the old black residential areas on Capitol Hill begin to lose population.

May 18. Celebrated activist Mary McLeod Bethune dies in Daytona Beach, Florida. Bethune was famous for her educational initiatives and her work establishing the National Council of Negro Women, an organization that she served as president until 1949.

The Federation of Civic Associations warns its members that many black neighborhoods may be adversely affected by the city's

Reporter Louis Lautier at the Capitol.

redevelopment plan. "If we don't find out what is going on here, we may wake up one morning and find all of us relocated to the far southeast and the far northeast. If we do, it will be our fault," says Harvey Brown, the chairman of the federation.

Reporter Al Sweeney's popular column "The Rambling Reporter" in the *Washington Afro American* covers local political news and black politics in the District. Other popular features are "What's Cooking," by Trezzvant Anderson; sports column "A to Z," by Sam Lacy; and society column "Pearlie's Prattle," by Pearlie Cox.

Because of the large numbers of black Washingtonians who are first- or second-generation migrants from North Carolina, the *Washington Afro American* also features regular columns such as "News from the Twin-City" (Winston-Salem, North Carolina), "Rambling about Goldsboro," "Notes about Lumberton," "Spotlight on Charlotte," and "Keeping Up in Salisbury."

May 31. The U.S. Supreme Court orders that the integration of public schools proceed at once and "with all deliberate speed."

June. *Washington Afro American* publisher Carl Murphy receives the Spingarn Medal.

July. Blacks protest a white policeman's shooting of unarmed black Safeway truck driver Nelson Martin during an argument at a traffic jam on 1st Street and Florida Avenue NW.

August 25. Emmett Till, a fourteen-year-old boy from Chicago, Illinois, is murdered in Leflore County, Mississippi, because he was believed by some white residents to have whistled at a white woman.

December 1. Rosa Parks refuses to move to the "colored" section of a Montgomery, Alabama, bus.

December 5. Reverend Martin Luther King Jr. leads a boycott of the Montgomery, Alabama, bus system by the city's African American community.

1956

January. In one of the most talked-about events in decades, described in the local press as the uniting of two kingdoms, Pearl Verna Williams, daughter of Reverend and Mrs. Smallwood Williams, marries Dr. William V. Jones, son of Bishop and Mrs. O. T. Jones of Philadelphia, in an elaborate affair, in which every member of the wedding party wears mink.

Washington celebrates Brotherhood Week, a seven-day celebration of local integration efforts.

Dr. Margaret Butcher is not reappointed to the D.C. school board, despite petitions bearing 12,000 signatures that call for her reappointment being presented to District Court judges. Instead, Mrs. Ruth B. Spencer is appointed.

Southern members of the House District Subcommittee, led by Representative James C. Davis, launch an investigation of juvenile delinquency and school standards in the D.C. public schools. The subcommittee's hearings are discredited in the press and by most other congressmen, due to their efforts to influence witness testimony and to blatantly use the hearings as a tool against integration.

March 12. The "Southern Manifesto" is signed by 101 southern congressional members. The manifesto attacks the Supreme Court decision desegregating public schools and encourages state and local officials to resist federal efforts to integrate their schools.

August 20. Duke Ellington appears on the cover of *Time* magazine.

November. Sterling Tucker becomes executive secretary of the D.C. Urban League.

The board of the D.C. branch of the YMCA votes to reject the integration of facilities and programs. Led by Dr. Edward C. Mazique, members of the 12th Street YMCA unsuccessfully challenge the branch to desegregate.

December 8. Jackie Robinson is awarded the Spingarn Medal by the NAACP for the highest achievement by a Negro.

1957

January 20. Dwight D. Eisenhower is inaugurated as president for a second term.

February. The D.C. NAACP, the Pigskin Club (a men's organization of black and white sports fans who sponsor youth programs), members of United Auto Workers locals 585 and 813, and other union members picket the National Football League Owners, specifically targeting George Marshall, owner of the Washington Redskins football team, for his refusal to hire black team players.

February. Dr. Emmett Scott, former assistant to Booker T. Washington and later special assistant to the secretary of war during World War I, lies gravely ill in the public ward of Freedmen's Hospital. Members of the Mu-So-Lit club and the Howard University faculty take turns visiting at his bedside. Ralph Matthews, reporter for the *Washington Afro American,* pays tribute to Scott and notes that he was well attended during his illness: "Fully capable of paying his own way, due to both his own property holdings and two pensions, he preferred to remain in a public ward where he could enjoy the companionship of other men."

The D.C. branch of the NAACP, along with many other black Washingtonians, renews its efforts to organize a campaign against police brutality when a popular minister's son, Walter L. Scott Jr., is mistakenly arrested and beaten—for the second time in six years.

March. Liberian Ambassador George Padmore is a guest speaker at the Mu-So-Lit Club's annual Lincoln-Douglass celebration.

The Southern Christian Leadership Conference is formed in 1957 as an outgrowth of the Montgomery bus boycott. Reverend Martin Luther King Jr. heads the SCLC until his death.

E. Franklin Frazier, professor of sociology at Howard University, publishes *Black Bourgeoisie,* his analysis of the black middle class. The book wins international acclaim but draws harsh responses from many members of the local middle class, who think it paints too negative a portrait of black strivers.

May. Led by A. Philip Randolph and Reverend Martin Luther King Jr., over 25,000 people from around the country gather on the steps of the Lincoln Memorial to support civil rights struggles. The "Prayer Pilgrimage for Freedom" also seeks to emphasize the need for federal support for local civil rights efforts.

A. Philip Randolph, civil rights and union activist, 1942.

Prayer vigil for freedom, 1957. Among those seated in the front row are Martin Luther King Jr. and Ralph Abernathy.

June. President Eisenhower signs the Civil Rights Act of 1957, the first civil rights act since 1875. The 1957 Civil Rights Act creates a new division within the Justice Department: a presidential Commission on Civil Rights and an assistant attorney general in charge of the commission's activities. The act also reinforces the right of all citizens to vote, stating that "No person . . . shall intimidate, threaten, coerce or attempt to intimidate, threaten or coerce any person for the purpose of interfering with the right of such other person to vote."

Social clubs, offering a network of friends, recreational activities such as cards and bridge, and other diversions, are all the rage among black Washingtonians. Some of the better known include the Girl

Lieutenant Dan Pittman, the first African American officer of the 13th precinct, Metropolitan Police Department.

Friends, the Dukes, the All States, Arbutus, the Charmettes, Club Philitus, the Continentals, the Helping Hand, Club 29, La Comrades, the Mannequins, Mystic Hypnotism, the New Deal, the Queenettes, Les Amies, the Tall Girls, Midnight, El Diez, Club Dejour, and the Toppers.

June 28. Martin Luther King Jr. is awarded the Spingarn Medal by the NAACP.

September 4. President Dwight D. Eisenhower sends 1,000 para-troopers from the 101st Airborne Division to Little Rock, Arkansas, to enforce the *Brown* public school desegregation decision.

1958

January. Before a crowd of more than 1,200 people, Elder Lightfoot Solomon Michaux dedicates his new Temple of Freedom Under God at 2030 Georgia Avenue NW. The minister, famous for his "Happy Am I" radio sermons, arrived in the District of Columbia in 1930 from Newport News, Virginia. He first held services in a

U.S. government statistics show a rate of 12.2 percent unemployed, with African Americans experiencing 19 percent unemployment. Almost 17,500 people are without jobs in the District.

Typical of growing unemployment is the daily gathering of men at the Georgia-Alaska Ave, NW District line looking for any kind of work. They huddle about and rush construction trucks from outer Maryland sites.

"You got some work, Mister? I'll work for you," is the familiar hopeful proposition. . . . Police seem to be the biggest trouble for the work-seekers, they say. . . . The men are kept on the move from one side of the Line (across the street) to the other by Maryland and District police to keep the sidewalks clear.

—The *Washington Afro American,* 1958

rented room on Georgia Avenue; the new temple, with a main auditorium and two side balconies, was constructed at a cost of $335,000. President Eisenhower, among others, sends congratulatory greetings to the congregation.

Howard University renames its main law school building after Dr. Charles Hamilton Houston.

March. The National Association of Colored Women celebrates burning the mortgage of its national headquarters at 16th and R Streets NW. It is the heyday of the black women's clubs. The association supports homes for unwed mothers, senior citizen homes, settlement houses, schools, and other programs in almost every state in the country. The association sponsored the Janie Porter Barrett School in Virginia until 1948, when the state took it over.

March 14. William Sidney Pittman, born on April 21, 1875, in Alabama, dies in Texas. Pittman, a graduate of the Tuskegee Institute and the Drexel Institute, moved to Washington in 1905 to start an architectural firm. He designed numerous public facilities, college buildings, and hotels, including the 12th Street YMCA. He became the first African American to win a federal contract to design a building, accomplishing this feat in 1907. He later moved to Texas, where he was the first African American architect to practice in the state.

March 27. Reverend E. Franklin Jackson, pastor of the John Wesley A.M.E. Zion Church, later president of the Washington NAACP, leads a protest against the failure of stores to hire black clerks and salespeople. Blacks boycott white-owned businesses during the "Day of Prayer for Merit Hiring and Abstinence from Shopping." City Commissioner Robert McLaughlin meets with Jackson in an unsuccessful effort to head off the demonstration.

April. The Council on Human Relations is established by D.C. city commissioners to promote equal opportunity employment in the District of Columbia. Sterling Tucker, president of the D.C. Urban League, is instrumental in its development.

Reverend E. Franklin Jackson in a protest.

April. At age eighty-seven, historian and collector Henry Slaughter dies, leaving behind an important collection of historical documents and first-edition books on African American history. A retired Government Printing Office employee, Slaughter lived at 1264 Columbia Road NW until his death.

Representatives Adam Clayton Powell Jr. and Charles Diggs, along with historian Rayford Logan, help establish the D.C. chapter of the

Even those who favored the move will accept with regret and a feeling of nostalgia the final decision to close Armstrong High School.

Both Armstrong and Dunbar are relics of an era which has past [sic] and their long history of rivalry in athletics and the competitive drills were steeped in tradition from which the whole city extracted a great deal of pleasure.

Although we took pardonable pride in these exchanges, we were not blinded to the fact that these demonstrations were inherently evil because they represented a mythical community within a community and were repugnant to the democratic ideal.

The spectacle of two segregated schools competing for the "City Championship" from which the major part of the school system was excluded was a farce and a delusion. . . .

To all of those who found the hallowed halls of Armstrong High School a place of comfort and youthful joy, we extend our sympathy and share their grief at its passing into the limbo of cherished institutions.

But now that death has been decreed let us quickly dry our tears and move on to a brighter day.

—The *Washington Afro American*,
May 31, 1958

Friends of the West Indies Federation, an organization supporting efforts of the governments of several West Indian nations to join together in a pan-Caribbean federation.

May. The Redevelopment Land Agency announces plans for its first major project in northwest D.C., the "slum clearance and rehabilitation" of eighty acres of housing in an area "from Florida to Massachusetts Ave. and North Capitol St. to the railroad yards to the east." As a result, 923 families will be forced to relocate.

June 21. Band leader and songwriter Ford Thompson Dabney, born in Washington, D.C., in 1883, dies in New York City. Dabney toured the vaudeville circuit, managed a theater, and early in his career was the staff pianist for President N. Alexis of Haiti.

Summer. Marvin Caplan, a white resident in the Manor Park neighborhood, forms Neighbors, Inc., an organization composed of black and white residents in far northwest Washington, D.C. The goal of the organization is to fight real estate speculation and block-

Students from Armstrong High School making model airplanes, c. 1942.

busting by forming strong block clubs. The block clubs try to keep neighborhood values up by maintaining physical standards in each neighborhood and sponsoring activities for neighborhood residents. Neighbors, Inc., fights against blockbusting in Manor Park, Brightwood, Takoma Park, and Shephard Park.

August 22. Ben's Chili Bowl opens at 1223 U Street NW. It soon becomes famous among neighborhood residents and Howard University students for its chili dogs. Ben's Chili Bowl, a favorite of comedian Bill Cosby and a neighborhood landmark, is open to this day and continues to serve breakfast, lunch, and late-night customers returning from the thriving U Street club scene.

October. Ten thousand young people from around the country arrive in Washington to demonstrate at the Lincoln Memorial for civil rights for African Americans. A delegation of students seeks unsuccessfully to meet with President Eisenhower. Speakers and organizers at the "Youth March for Freedom" include Harry Belafonte, Coretta Scott King, A. Philip Randolph, and Jackie Robinson.

November 19. John Randolph Pinkett Sr. dies at age seventy. Pinkett was a popular and active businessman, opening a real estate and insurance firm, John R. Pinkett, Inc., out of offices in a two-story building that his brother Roscoe built. Later, Pinkett took over the entire building at New Jersey Avenue and N Street NW. Pinkett supported and was a member of the greater U Street community, the 12th Street YMCA, the Pigskin Club, the Boule, and the Kappa Alpha Psi fraternity. He also taught business courses part-time at Howard University and was a planner of the Georgetown Day School, the first fully integrated school in the D.C. metropolitan area.

1959

January. Reverend E. Franklin Jackson, minister at the John Wesley A.M.E. Zion Church, is elected head of the D.C. NAACP; he replaces the retiring Eugene Davidson.

In an editorial about the U.S. census in the *Washington Afro American*, editors note that the census shows that the "non-white" population of the District is 53 percent: "The nation at large offers bigger and better opportunities for whites than it does for colored persons of the same educational level. This makes it possible for the former to obtain better jobs at higher pay than those offered by the Federal government locally. Thus the conditions which drive young white people out of Washington lure young colored people to the city. No other city in America offers the same chance for employment on the white-collar level to colored youth as Washington. Colored persons are forced to seek employment in Federal agencies while whites may find better jobs in private industry."

March. Daisy Bates, president of the Arkansas NAACP, speaks at Shiloh Baptist Church on the civil rights struggle in her state.

Flaxie Pinkett, the daughter of John Pinkett, takes over the Pinkett real estate business, becoming one of the most influential business-women in the city.

April. African students from Howard University and other schools picket in front of the British Embassy to protest British actions in Nyasaland.

April. Walter Edward Fauntroy is installed as pastor of the Greater New Bethel Baptist Church. Fauntroy was born on February 6, 1933, in the District of Columbia, and was a graduate of Dunbar High School in 1952. After graduation Fauntroy attended Virginia Union College and Yale University Divinity School, where he earned a Bachelor of Divinity degree in 1958.

Melvin Deal establishes a school to teach West African drumming and dance and also starts a performing troupe, the African Heritage Dancers and Drummers.

May. The local Nation of Islam Temple No. 4, at 1325 Vermont Avenue NW, sponsors Elijah Muhammad to speak before an audience of nearly 6,000 people at the Uline Arena. Minister Lucius, head of the local temple, hosts a Spiritual Feast after the event.

May 22. President Eisenhower appoints Benjamin O. Davis Jr. to the rank of major general.

July 4. Funeral services are held for Bob Harrison, owner of the landmark Harrison's Café. Most of the café's employees have worked there for over thirty years and are longtime community residents.

July 15. Hundreds of black mourners fill the Jarvis Funeral Home and spill onto the street during funeral services for Alfred E. (Puddin' Head) Jones, a well-known gambler and philanthropist. Jones, called "The Mayor of 14th Street," was beloved by many for his generosity. He paid for food baskets to be distributed to poor families and sponsored huge Christmas parties each year for needy children. A native of Rocky Mount, North Carolina, Jones was also known for his on-the-spot loans to those in need.

July 17. Billie Holiday, born Elenora Fagan on April 7, 1915, in Baltimore, Maryland, dies of a drug overdose after a two-month hospital stay. Holiday frequented the club scene in the U Street area and performed at the Crystal Caverns, now the Bohemian Caverns, on U Street.

Howard University establishes an African studies program with the support of the Ford Foundation. E. Franklin Frazier is appointed as chairman. William Leo Hansberry, who had long championed African studies at the university, is excluded from consideration because his views on African civilizations are considered too radical by some university officials and professors.

September. When attorney William Harris and his wife, Patricia Roberts Harris, try to see one of the new apartments at 800 4th Street SW, the manager calls the police to eject them from the building. The incident is widely reported in the local black press, which charges that it confirms rumors that the new housing constructed on land recently cleared of poor blacks by the Southwest Redevelopment program would exclude them in the future. Other blacks complained of the same treatment, but William Harris is a prominent local attorney and tells his story to the black press. Patricia Roberts Harris tells a *Washington Afro American* reporter that "My husband asked him why he was so upset and he replied that the apartment building was not integrated and that everybody knew that it was not." Patricia Roberts Harris is former director of the

Puddin' Head Jones—Saint or Villain?

As it must to all men, death came Friday to Alfred E. (Puddin' Head) Jones, a familiar figure in the Washington gambling fraternity.

Usually editorial obituaries in newspapers are reserved for those individuals whose contributions to society are made on the less seamy side of community life. However, Puddin' Head, as he was affectionately known, was a paradox in the fact that although he was associated with what is commonly known as the underworld he possessed a heart and a social consciousness which placed him far above many of those who looked down their noses at him.

Born in the backwoods of North Carolina, he migrated to Washington, where early in his career he became embroiled with the law. Seeking to rehabilitate himself during the depression, he found every door of legitimate opportunity shut against him and he was driven by desperation back among the people who lived on the fringe of the law who made full use of his talents.

. . . But unlike many of his fraternity who wasted their substance in conspicuous consumption and self indulgence, Puddin' Head lived modestly, conducted a business and used his wealth compassionately to help the less fortunate.

He saw to it that no ex-con was ever subjected to the fate which he received. He provided soup kitchens for the down-and-out and permitted no victim of puritanical society to go hungry. . . . Not only did he help those who, like himself, had run afoul of the law, but he tried to prevent juvenile delinquency by providing Christmas dinners for thousands of youth and indigent families throughout the city.

His Yule parties given at the YMCA and the Police Boys Club were the biggest of their kind ever given in Washington over many years. . . .

Puddin' Head Jones was not a heroic figure. Nor one whom we could hold up as a model for youth. . . .

Whatever else may be said of Puddin' Head Jones, it cannot be denied that he possessed a love of humanity and gave unselfishly of what he had for those less fortunate than himself.

—The *Washington Afro American*, July 15, 1959

Delta Sigma Theta sorority and also has served as a professional lobbyist for the American Council for Human Rights.

November. George Marshall, owner of the Washington Redskins football team, requests to be excluded from a nondiscriminatory clause in a contractual agreement signed with the D.C. government. In its agreement for the promised use of the Municipal Stadium then under construction near the National Armory, the

Redskins management agreed not to discriminate in their employment practices. Marshall worries, however, that because the Redskins team has not yet hired a black player, it will be subject to legal challenges around that issue. As he feared, two months later the Association of the Oldest Inhabitants of the District of Columbia begins pressing the D.C. Council of Human Relations to investigate whether the Redskins management has violated its contract with the city.

1960

January 12. Charles Manuel Grace, founder of the United House of Prayer for All People, a religious denomination based in Washington, D.C., with more than 1.5 million followers, dies in Los Angeles, California. Callers—many in disbelief and shock—flood the switchboards at the two local District of Columbia churches that belong to the United House of Prayer for All People. After lying in state in Los Angeles, Grace's body is viewed in Charlotte, North Carolina; Newport News, Virginia; Washington, D.C.; Philadelphia; Newark; and finally, New Bedford, Massachusetts.

At the wake in Washington, more than 38,000 people pay their respects. A funeral cortege of 1,000 people follows the coffin as it is brought from 6th Street and Pennsylvania Avenue to the main church at 601 M Street NW.

Grace's mansion at 11 Logan Circle NW is one of the most imposing homes in the area, though it has been unoccupied for the last few years except for occasional visits by Bishop Grace. His annual evangelical revivals at Griffith Stadium were elaborate events, with biblical plays and historical epics acted out onstage and mass baptisms for scores of worshipers.

February 1. The Greensboro sit-in takes place in Greensboro, North Carolina, as four black teenagers sit at the whites-only lunch counter at the Woolworth store. The four teenagers—Franklin McCain, Joseph McNeil, Ezell Blair Jr., and David Richmond—are all freshmen at N.C. A&T State. Franklin McCain spent most of his youth in the District of Columbia.

William Waring Cuney publishes *Puzzles*, his first collection of poetry. Cuney was born on May 6, 1930, in the District of Columbia;

his mother taught in the public schools and his father was a federal worker. He graduated from Armstrong High School and attended Howard University. His most famous poetry was published during the 1960s.

Willie L. Miles is appointed chairperson of the Carter G. Woodson Building Fund by the Association for the Study of Negro Life and History. She has served as Woodson's secretary and worked at the association for over seventeen years. Miles (known to everyone as Miss Miles) will continue to work faithfully for the association for the next thirty years, becoming a popular and authoritative figure in the association's headquarters.

May 6. President Eisenhower signs the Civil Rights Act of 1960, which spells out penalties for obstructing citizens' right to vote.

Dr. Edward W. Hawthorne's work on hypertension and the heart and his efforts to develop a top-quality cardiovascular research laboratory in the early 1960s result in one of the largest grants from the National Institutes of Health that Howard University has ever received. (The cardiovascular research laboratory at the university still bears his name.) He later helps reorganize the curriculum of the medical school and is also instrumental in designing the university computer center.

June 30. For the rest of the summer, black and white community leaders and the Non-Violent Action Group—a local organization headed by Reverend Laurence Henry, Esther Delaplaine, and Hyman Bookbinder—picket in protest of Glen Echo Park's policy of excluding blacks. Thirteen picketers are arrested and convicted of trespassing.

Former NAACP attorney Frank Reeves is elected the first black Democratic national committeeman from the District of Columbia. The following year, black political leaders put a great deal of pressure on President Kennedy to appoint Reeves as the city's first black commissioner, but Kennedy appoints Walter N. Tobriner, head of the D.C. Board of Education, to the post. Reeves becomes a close adviser to President Kennedy.

Reverend Walter Fauntroy campaigns to protest against housing redevelopment programs that have removed substandard and low-income housing from black residential areas and replaced them with moderate and high-income housing. Instead of urban renewal, he insists it should be called "urban removal."

October 2. The original Washington Senators team plays its last game in Washington, D.C. The expansion of the American League allows owner Calvin Griffith to move the Washington Senators to Minneapolis, Minnesota, where they become the Minnesota Twins.

1961

January 20. John F. Kennedy is inaugurated as president.

January. During one of the inaugural parties, as Frank Sinatra and Mr. and Mrs. Nat King Cole are entering the host's residence, a white reporter covering the event asks Sinatra sarcastically if Mrs. Cole is his date for the night. The *Washington Afro American* notes the incident in its coverage of inaugural events and ridicules the reporter and her comment. A month later, Sinatra writes a letter to the *Afro American*'s Chuck Stone:

> Dear Mr. Stone:
>
> I just received the tear sheet from your January 28th edition from Guy McIlwaine. Let me begin by saying I am grateful for the comments in your editorial. The fact that the woman reporter tried to bait me . . . shows more than ever what vicious determination there is constantly [to] undermine the good work in racial relationships that we are all trying to achieve. It happens constantly, I suppose, and it will continue to happen until proper education is administered not only by teachers to children, but by parents to children everywhere in the world. . . . Keep the faith and keep up the good work.
>
> Very Truly Yours,
> Frank Sinatra

Julius Hobson is appointed to head the Washington, D.C., chapter of the Congress of Racial Equality (CORE). Hobson, a Birmingham, Alabama, native, attended the Tuskegee Institute for two years, served as a second lieutenant in the U.S. Air Force, and later studied economics at Howard University. He begins a years-long campaign of picket lines and demonstrations against local businesses that refuse to hire black clerks and salespeople, which is ultimately successful.

President Kennedy appoints Robert C. Weaver as head of the Federal Housing and Home Finance Agency. Weaver, a Washingtonian, was a former member of the New Negro Alliance and a leading member of President Roosevelt's "Black Cabinet." During confirmation hearings, southern congressmen try to prevent his appointment by suggesting that Weaver was or still is a communist supporter.

President Kennedy approves the creation of the Special Protocol Service Section. Part of the SPSS's responsibilities will be to help prevent incidents of racial discrimination against visiting African diplomats. Pedro Sanjuan, the head of the new SPSS, creates lists of friendly locales for the diplomats to frequent, as well as a list of special schools for the diplomats' children to attend. The SPSS will serve as a defensive measure to ensure that African diplomats are not offended by racial discriminatory incidents. However, the difficulty of implementing the protocol becomes apparent soon after the plans are devised.

March 8. Dr. William H. Fitzjohn, chargé d'affaires of Sierra Leone, stops to eat at a Howard Johnson restaurant in Hagerstown, Maryland, and is denied service by the restaurant staff. President Kennedy invites Dr. Fitzjohn to the White House, and the State Department apologizes to Sierra Leone, but the incident is used by the Soviet Union in articles and news accounts to argue that racism is still pervasive in the United States.

March 29. Kansas becomes the thirty-eighth state to ratify the Twenty-third Amendment to the Constitution, which gives residents of Washington, D.C., the right to vote in presidential elections for the first time.

March 31. After a summer of picket lines and demonstrators, Glen Echo Park opens this season as an integrated facility. For the first time, blacks will be allowed to enter the amusement park.

April 10. The new Washington Senators baseball team returns to major league play under owner Pete Quesada. Some Washingtonians welcome the change, pointing out that Calvin Griffith refused to hire African Americans from the United States. Only dark-skinned Cubans were allowed to play on the Senators while he was owner. The new Senators team includes three African Americans: Bennie Daniels, Willie Tasby, and R. C. Stevens.

April 15. The Washington chapter of the All-African Students, with the assistance of the United Auto Workers and the American Committee on Africa, sponsor an African Freedom Day at the Metropolitan Baptist Church. This event is the precursor to the later celebration of "African Liberation Day." Press releases for the event note that " 'African Freedom Day' was so designated by the first All-African Peoples Congress in Accra, Ghana, December 8–15, 1958. It called for April 15 of each year to be set aside in observance of Africa's freedom struggle." Keynote speakers include Kenyan Tom Mboya; Kenneth Kaunda, later president of Zambia; and Supreme Court justice William O. Douglas.

April. Law school professor and civil rights attorney James M. Nabrit Jr. is inaugurated as president of Howard University.

Newspaper reporter Carl Rowan moves to Washington, D.C., from Minneapolis to take on the position of deputy assistant secretary of state for public affairs.

May 4. Bayard Rustin and members of CORE test the new Supreme Court rulings against segregation in interstate travel by conducting freedom rides across the Upper South. They leave Washington, D.C., on May 4 with several Howard University students and local residents. In response to the brutal attacks on the freedom riders by supporters of segregation, Attorney General Robert Kennedy sends U.S. marshals to Montgomery, Alabama, to quell the violence. Many of the freedom riders are arrested and beaten. Julius Hobson, director of CORE in the Washington area, holds rallies and organizes support for the detainees; he also trains freedom riders in nonviolent techniques.

May. Nannie Helen Burroughs lies in state at the National Trade and Professional School for Women and Girls in Deanwood. Over 800 mourners attend her funeral at Nineteenth Street Baptist Church, where Reverend Jerry A. Moore Jr. presides over the memorial service. She was a member there since 1892.

June. Walter Washington, a Howard University graduate born in Georgia and raised in Jamestown, New York, is appointed executive director of the National Capital Housing Authority. In an interview with the *Washington Afro American*, Washington notes that one of his biggest problems will be finding sites for additional public housing: "Most of our housing concentration has been in the Northeast and Southeast because land is both cheaper and vacant. Land in those areas sells for approximately $1 a foot. In the center of the city, it costs about $4 a foot. We've been criticized for building in those two sections because it tends to concentrate people there with large families—who have the greatest need. But the problem is simple: where do they go?"

John B. Duncan testifying before the Senate District Committee after being nominated by President John F. Kennedy, 1961.

President Kennedy appoints D.C. recorder of deeds John B. Duncan as the city's first black city commissioner after Frank Reeves withdraws his name from consideration.

August. Channing Phillips is appointed pastor at Lincoln Memorial Temple Congregational Church.

September 10. During one of Elder Lightfoot Solomon Michaux's annual ballpark meetings, he debates Minister Elijah Muhammad in front of a huge crowd at Griffith Stadium. The event is headlined "Christianity vs. Islam," and over 4,000 people gather to hear the two religious leaders discuss the merits of the two religions.

Under the leadership of Julius Hobson, local CORE members continue to pressure department stores, retail shops, and other private employers to hire African Americans. Hobson joins with local ministers to organize boycotts of places that refuse to stop discriminating against blacks.

September 21. The last baseball game is played at Griffith Stadium. The stadium is razed and a new Freedmen's Hospital building is erected in its place. Major League games, sports, and other events will take place in the new District of Columbia Stadium (renamed the Robert F. Kennedy Stadium in 1969).

The Twist, a black dance popularized by Chubby Checker, sweeps Washington, D.C.'s house parties and night spots.

Artist Claire Haywood and dance instructor Doris Jones establish the Capitol Ballet Company in the District.

November. Political activist Malcolm X (El-Hajj Malik El-Shabazz) debates Bayard Rustin at Howard University. The topic is "Integration or Separation." Each speaker makes a thirty-minute presentation and then has a ten-minute rebuttal. During the debate, Malcolm X calls for a separate nation for black people, which Rustin calls utopian. The audience, mainly students, shows its support for the debaters with applause and shouts of approval. Several times Malcolm X brings down the house with his examples, but Rustin also scores points with the audience.

Walter Fauntroy is appointed director of the Washington branch of the SCLC.

1962

Bobby Mitchell is traded from the Cleveland Browns to the Washington Redskins. Mitchell becomes the first black player in Redskins history.

Freedmen's Hospital is renamed Howard University Hospital.

Marjorie Lawson becomes the first black female judge in Washington, D.C.

Radio station WOOK reigns supreme among young black Washingtonians, who enjoy its top-ten soul music programming. Critics point out the lack of public affairs programming on serious issues like civil rights and community and local political activities.

Washingtonian Billy Stewart gets his first important singing gig—at the Howard Theatre. Like Duke Ellington, Stewart is a graduate

U.S. Census results reveal that African Americans own 47 percent of the homes in Washington, D.C.

of Armstrong High School. Stewart is known throughout Washington for his performances in school concerts and local talent shows. His first hit is "Fat Boy," which comes out shortly after his debut at the Howard Theatre.

1963

Congressman Charles Diggs is appointed to the House District Committee. He joins Congressman William Dawson on the committee.

A committee of concerned citizens organizes the Temporary Committee for the Negro in Mass Communications. The organization protests the founding of a new Negro television station, WOOK-TV, as its members believe that an all-black station serves only to further the cause of segregation in the media in the District. They also criticize District radio and television stations for their lack of initiative in hiring colored personnel in the areas of technical support and high-level management, as well as the failure to incorporate colored citizens in their programming agendas. The committee consists of Jesse O. Dedman Jr., president of the D.C. Chamber of Commerce; Henry L. Dixon Jr., president of the D.C. Federation of Civic Associations; the Reverend Walter E. Fauntroy, regional representative to the Southern Christian Leadership Conference; George G. Fleming, president of the Negro Community Council of the National Capital Area; Julius Hobson, chairman of CORE D.C.; and Sterling Tucker, executive director of the Washington Urban League.

August 27. W. E. B. DuBois, famed scholar and founder of the Niagara Movement, publisher of *The Crisis* and one of the early leaders in the NAACP, dies on the eve of the March on Washington for Jobs and Freedom.

August 28. More than 200,000 people gather at the Lincoln Memorial for the March on Washington for Jobs and Freedom, in what was the largest protest march in the nation's history until the 1990s. Marchers demand legislation to end discrimination in education, housing, employment, and the courts. Walter Fauntroy serves as local coordinator for the march.

Inspired by the March on Washington for Jobs and Freedom, Baltimore native Roland Freeman, born in 1936, launches his

As Appeal to You from
JAMES FARMER
Congress of Racial Equality

MARTIN LUTHER KING, JR.
Southern Christian Leadership Conference

JOHN LEWIS
Student Non-violent
Coordinating Committee

A. PHILIP RANDOLPH
Negro American Labor Council

ROY WILKINS
National Association for the
Advancement of Colored People

WHITNEY YOUNG
National Urban League

to MARCH on
WASHINGTON
WEDNESDAY AUGUST 28, 1963

America faces a crisis . . .
Millions of Negroes are denied freedom . . .
Millions of citizens, black and white, are unemployed . . .

We demand: — Meaningful Civil Rights Laws
— Massive Federal Works Program
— Full and Fair Employment
— Decent Housing
— The Right to Vote
— Adequate Integrated Education

In our community, groups and individuals are mobilizing for
the August 28th demonstration. For information regarding
your participation, call the local Coordinating Committee
for the

MARCH ON WASHINGTON
FOR JOBS AND FREEDOM

1417 You Street, N.W.   ADams 2-2320

CO-CHAIRMEN
Rev. Walter E. Fauntroy, Coordinator   Edward A. Hailes
Joseph A. Beavers   Julius W. Hobson
E. Charles Brown   Sterling Tucker

Flyer for the "March on Washington."

*Civil rights leaders in front of the
Lincoln statue at the Lincoln
Memorial, 1963.*

Demonstrators march down North Capitol within sight of the Capitol, 1963.

A young protester at the March on Washington, 1963.

Civil rights marchers dining, 1963.

photographic career. Freeman begins documenting the civil rights movement. He later documents the SCLC-sponsored Poor People's March from Marks, Mississippi, to Washington, D.C.

November 1. Robert Weaver, at a speech in Philadelphia before the Friends Housing Cooperative, states that the public housing program has in the past "established a pattern of clearing away integrated neighborhoods where low income families had lived, and replacing them usually with new—and segregated—housing." Weaver notes that the pattern of segregation "infected the early days of the urban renewal program. The FHA, which was primarily concerned with encouraging private investment in home building, adopted the prevalent real estate doctrine that the introduction of non-whites into a white neighborhood would result in a decline in property values."

November 22. In Dallas, Texas, President Kennedy is assassinated as he rides in an open limousine during a motorcade through the city. Governor John Connally is also wounded. Kennedy's successor, Vice President Lyndon B. Johnson, is sworn into office on the presidential plane at Dallas Airport, less than two hours after the shooting. Kennedy's body lies in state at the Capitol Rotunda, where over 250,000 people come to pay the late president a last tribute.

1964

January. The White House is picketed by fifth- and sixth-grade students carrying signs that read: "Jobs and Freedom," "No More Georgias," and "Before I'll Be a Slave, I'll Be Buried in My Grave." According to their spokesperson, Lawrence Dunbar Twyman III, a ten-year-old student, the group is trying to raise awareness on the subjects of jobs and freedom for African Americans. The students organized the demonstration with the help of the Student Non-Violent Coordinating Committee. The SNCC adviser says, "All we did was to help them block out their signs. They even knew freedom songs before they came, exactly what they wanted to tell the president, and what they wanted on their signs." The group sings songs associated with the civil rights movement, such as "We Shall Overcome" and "Ain't Gonna Let Nobody Turn Me 'Round."

February 27. African American educator, writer, and women's rights activist Anna Julia Hayward Cooper dies. Born into slavery in

Over 51 percent of all blacks in college are enrolled in historically black colleges and universities.

Raleigh, North Carolina, on August 10, 1858, Cooper was widowed by age twenty-one. She then taught at the M Street High School in Washington, D.C., for forty years and received her Ph.D. from the Sorbonne in 1925. At the time of her graduation, Anna Cooper was sixty-six; she was one of the earliest African American women to receive her doctorate.

March. Malcolm X breaks from the Nation of Islam, whose spiritual leader is Elijah Muhammad. He forms a new organization called the Organization of Afro-American Unity.

Michael R. Winston begins teaching at Howard University in the history department. He later serves in many teaching and research positions, eventually becoming dean of liberal arts.

Cortez Peters Sr. dies. Peters held the title of world's fastest typist, as he typed at a remarkable 100-plus words per minute. He established the Cortez Peters Business College in 1934 at 920 U Street NW, located in the Murray Brothers Printing Company building. The school closed in the 1970s, but before closing, it taught more than 40,000 students and provided formally trained African American secretaries to the U.S. government.

James Hampton dies. Hampton, a janitor turned sculptor, was famous for his ecclesiastical works of art. His *Throne of the Third Heaven of the Nations Millennium General Assembly,* discovered after his death, is a mysterious collection of 180 handmade objects. Among the ornately crafted works is the engraving *Where There Is No Vision the People Perish.*

Julius Hobson stages protests outside the Washington Hospital Center, calling for its integration. This same year Hobson leaves CORE to start his own organization, Associated Community Teams (ACT).

Calvin Rolark launches the *Washington Informer,* an African American newspaper that focuses on local and community events.

Eleanor Holmes graduates from Yale University Law School. She marries Edward Worthington Norton in 1965. Active politically, she helps to establish several black and feminist organizations, such as the National Black Feminist Organization and the National Political Congress of Black Women, after serving as assistant legal director of the ACLU (American Civil Liberties Union). In 1982 Eleanor Holmes Norton begins teaching law at Georgetown University.

July 2. Lyndon B. Johnson signs the Civil Rights Act of 1964, which prohibits segregation in public places and forbids the federal government from conducting business with firms practicing racial discrimination. He also creates the Equal Employment Commission.

November 3. For the first time District residents participate in the presidential election. The three presidential electors cast their vote for Lyndon Baines Johnson.

December 8. The *Washington Afro American* reports on the educational practice known as the track system, which places students within different learning tracks. The tracks are basic, general, and honors for elementary and junior high schools, with senior high schools having an added college preparatory and regular track. The basic track was designed for children diagnosed as "mentally retarded but educable." The news article cites stories about the improper placement of students into the basic track, who in actuality belong in far more academically stringent classes. A female student with a 130 IQ was placed in the basic track, forcing her to learn at a slow pace. Another student, a young boy, was deemed "mentally retarded," causing his parents to remove him from the D.C. public school system. Upon removal, the boy was placed in a Catholic school, where he became an honor student. The vast majority of the students in basic track classrooms consists of impoverished African Americans. Dr. Euphemia L. Haynes, a school board member, observes, "The picture it [the track system] presents seems to be very like one which might have resulted from division on the basis of socio-economic level or on the basis of race."

December 16. Photographer Addison Scurlock dies. Aside from working in his studio at 9th and U Streets NW, close to his home on

Addison Scurlock documented the legends of the black community and became a legend himself. He stands in front of portraits of, from left to right, Booker T. Washington, W. E. B. DuBois, and Sterling Brown.

12th and U Streets NW, Scurlock was employed as the official photographer of Howard University. For nearly half a century Scurlock was considered the premier photographer in Washington, and it was often said that if Scurlock didn't photograph your wedding, you weren't really married. Scurlock documented virtually every aspect of middle-class African American life in the District of Columbia. The Scurlock Collection has been acquired by the Smithsonian Institution and is now at the National Museum of American History.

1965

January 20. Lyndon Baines Johnson is inaugurated as president.

January 26. The demolition of Griffith Stadium begins. By August 14 it has been completely razed. Today 999 of the original seats from Griffith Stadium are still in use at Tinker Field in Orlando, Florida.

February 21. Malcolm X is assassinated in the Audubon Ballroom in New York City.

March. James Amos Porter is awarded the National Gallery of Art Medal and Honorarium for Distinguished Achievement in Art Education.

March 2. In a speech at Howard University, Dr. Martin Luther King Jr. condemns U.S. policy in Vietnam.

April. At age fifty-two, Major General Benjamin O. Davis Jr., the highest-ranking African American officer in the U.S. armed forces, is appointed chief of staff of U.S. forces in South Korea and second in command to all UN forces in Korea by President Johnson. President Johnson also recommends to the Senate Davis's promotion to the rank of lieutenant general. Upon hearing the news, Davis calls his father, the illustrious retired military officer Benjamin O. Davis Sr., and says, "Dad, I've won my third star."

June 16–20. More than 235,000 Methodists gather at the Baltimore Annual Conference at the Metropolitan Memorial Church in Washington. The meeting, convened by Bishop John Wesley Lord, unites the approximately 200,000 white Methodists with the approximately 35,000 colored members of the Methodist Church. Lord previously announced that two of Baltimore's eight merged and enlarged districts will be headed by African American superintendents.

August 6. President Johnson signs the Voting Rights Act of 1965, which outlaws obstacles to voting, such as a literacy test and poll taxes, and empowers the Justice Department and the attorney general to intervene in voting registration and the voting process on the local, state, and federal levels.

September. Julius Hobson resigns from his police advisory post because "nothing has been done to deal with acts of police brutality and discourtesy continually being perpetrated against poor colored people of this community." Furthermore, Hobson notes, "Of the mounting number of charges against the police resulting from their actions against the poor, not one in the last five years has resulted in disciplinary action against a single policeman so charged."

September 24. Lyndon Johnson announces Executive Order 11246, which prohibits contractors doing more than $100,000 in business with the federal government from discriminating in their employment practices.

November 3. William Leo Hansberry dies in a Chicago hospital at age seventy-one. He received numerous honors and awards in recognition of his path-breaking scholarship in African studies, including a college of African studies named after him in Nigeria.

Poet Dudley Randall (born in 1914 in Washington, D.C.) establishes an African American publishing company, Broadside Press, in Detroit, Michigan. The establishment of the publishing house grants up-and-coming black poets an outlet for expression. Randall opens the press "so black people could speak to and for their people." In the 1960s and 1970s Broadside Press gives early exposure to poets such as Etheridge Knight, Haki R. Madhubuti (formerly Don L. Lee), Nikki Giovanni, and Sonia Sanchez.

President Lyndon B. Johnson appoints Patricia Roberts Harris as ambassador to Luxembourg, making Harris the first female African American ambassador. She serves in the position from 1965 until 1967.

Civil rights organizer Marion Barry, born in Itta Bena, Mississippi, and raised in Memphis, Tennessee, arrives in Washington to head the Washington, D.C., chapter of the Student Non-Violent Coordinating Committee.

President Johnson creates the Department of Housing and Urban Development and one year later appoints Robert Weaver to head the bureau.

Neighborhood and community groups establish the Emergency Committee on the Transportation Crisis, an organization to coordinate efforts to prevent the construction of freeways threatening several neighborhoods. Julius Hobson and other leaders in the organization argue that the planned freeway construction primarily targets areas with black residents. Although the organization has both black and white members, a popular slogan is "No White Men's Road Through Black Men's Homes." The Takoma Park–based activist Sammie Abbott coined that slogan and others and also served as graphic artist for movement literature and posters.

At the onset of the National Football League (NFL) season, a record 140 black players are on team rosters. The Washington Redskins start the 1965–1966 season with eleven black players, placing them behind Baltimore and Cleveland, each with thirteen black players.

1966

Pearl Williams Jones, born on June 28, 1931, in the District of Columbia, debuts as a singer-pianist at Town Hall in New York. She becomes a renowned gospel singer and lectures widely across the United States and Europe.

President Johnson awards Duke Ellington a Presidential Gold Medal of Honor.

The Shaw neighborhood is designated by the Redevelopment Land Agency as an inner-city area in need of urban renewal.

February. Marion Barry announces the formation of the Free D.C. Movement. With the support of a number of influential local religious and political leaders, Barry begins organizing boycotts of

A "Free D.C." poster.

277

businesses that do not support home rule. Establishments are asked to post a sign with the emblem of the Free D.C. Movement. Those that refuse are subject to picket lines and boycotts.

Congress establishes Federal City College in the District of Columbia as a public college of liberal arts and sciences. The school maintains an open admissions policy from the beginning. Frank Farner, associate dean at the University of Oregon, is appointed as the first president.

May 14. Poet Georgia Douglas Johnson dies of a stroke in Washington, D.C. After her death, cleaners dispose of twenty years' worth of her unpublished works.

Robert Clifton Weaver, born in 1907 in Washington, D.C., is appointed secretary of the newly formed Department of Housing and Urban Development, becoming the first black cabinet official in U.S. history.

Huey Newton, Bobby Seale, and other young blacks form the Black Panther Party for Self-Defense in Oakland, California. The radical black organization advocates armed defense of black communities against police brutality and assumes a pro-socialist political stance.

1967

January 3. Edward William Brooke III (representing Massachusetts) becomes the first African American to serve in the U.S. Senate since 1881.

March 1. Congress censures congressman Adam Clayton Powell Jr. for misuse of public funds and removes his twenty-two years of seniority. The following year Congress refuses to seat him.

March 30. Washington, D.C., native Jean Toomer dies. Toomer is recognized as a literary genius, largely on the basis of his three-part work *Cane*. The first section of *Cane* is comprised of prose portraits of African American women. The second part of the book is set in Chicago and Washington, D.C. The third part, "Kabnis," is modeled around an African American intellectual much like Toomer himself.

May 22. Literary legend Langston Hughes dies in New York City. Hughes, born in Joplin, Missouri, on February 1, 1902, is famous for his short stories, poems, and plays. During the 1920s, Hughes lived first with relatives in Washington and later at the 12th Street YMCA. He was a key figure in the Washington literary scene.

June 5. The Supreme Court bars a law in Virginia banning interracial marriages, in the case of *Loving v. Virginia*. The decision effectively voids antimiscegenation laws, many of which remain in the constitutions and the legal codes of southern states. Richard and Mildred Loving, a white man and a black woman, were married in 1958 in Washington, D.C. When they moved to Virginia, they were prosecuted.

June 13. Thurgood Marshall is appointed associate justice of the Supreme Court, becoming the first African American Supreme Court justice.

June 19. The Supreme Court rules in favor of activist Julius Hobson, who filed suit alleging racial discrimination in the way that the D.C. school system distributes school resources. U.S. District Judge J. Skelly Wright rules in the *Hobson v. Hansen* case that there is de facto segregation of blacks in the District of Columbia and orders the public school system to abolish the "track system," which delegates students to different "tracks," or levels of instruction. Black students were usually assigned to lower tracks, which received unequal funding and attention and provided for fewer educational, employment, and career options. Wright orders black students to be bused from crowded schools to less-crowded schools in northwest neighborhoods.

The first black Supreme Court justice, Thurgood Marshall.

August 1. Rioting breaks out in the Shaw area; firemen and policemen are stoned by groups of young blacks.

September 15. The Smithsonian Institution establishes the Anacostia Museum under the direction of Reverend John R. Kinard. The Anacostia Museum begins as a neighborhood museum and initially features various objects from exhibitions in other Smithsonian museums, but it quickly becomes a museum of African American history and culture. Early staff members include Louise Hutchinson, James Mayo, Zora M. Felton, Carolyn Margolis, Michael Fischer, and Larry Erskine Thomas.

With funds from a federal grant, Marion Barry and Mary Treadwell establish Pride, Inc., an organization that provides inner city residents with educational and skills programs, including reading clinics, high school diploma programs, and job training.

Walter Fauntroy and other concerned citizens create the Model Inner City Community Organization (MICCO), a coalition of 150 organizations, churches, and community groups, in order to ensure that community residents are involved in urban renewal projects being planned for the Shaw area of Washington, D.C.

Congress approves a government structure for D.C. that provides for an appointed mayor and a city council and the removal of the three-person board of commissioners.

October. The Reverend Jesse L. Jackson, national director of "Operation Breadbasket," the economic and labor program of the SCLC, speaks at the Church of the Redeemer, 15th and Girard Streets NW, in support of home rule. Jackson pushes an agenda of consumer power, in which blacks will seek compliance with their demands by supporting black-owned establishments and boycotting other businesses and organizations.

At Howard University, Stephen Abel, a twenty-year-old junior majoring in sociology, leads a free speech and Black Power demonstration. Among other requests, Abel, a graduate of Cardozo High School, argues that the university administration should change the freshman requirement of humanities to African American history. Abel, a strong proponent of community involvement in student protest, states that "Howard only trains students to go into white society. We need courses to bring students to their own people."

November. President Lyndon B. Johnson appoints Walter E. Washington as the mayor of Washington, D.C.; Washington is the city's first black mayor. Johnson also appoints a majority of African Americans to the city council, including Joseph Yeldell.

December 4. Martin Luther King Jr. announces the Poor People's Campaign and calls for a "Poor People's March on Washington" for next spring.

December 7. Lillian Evans Tibbs (Madame Evanti) dies. Evanti was born in the District on August 12, 1890. Over the course of her illustrious opera career, Evanti performed in Europe, the United States, the Caribbean, and South America.

President Johnson appoints Walter Fauntroy as vice chairman of the D.C. City Council. He serves in that position until 1969, despite the fact that conservative congressmen demand his resignation because of Fauntroy's membership in the local Black United Front.

Allegations of police brutality are again raised by local blacks. John Hechinger, City Council chairman, notes that nineteen years after the creation of the Complaint Review Board, only one complaint has been sustained. Recruitment campaigns to enlist African Americans into the MPD are launched, and the racial composition of the MPD begins to change.

1968

Dorothy Rudd Moore, a Howard University–trained musician and composer, helps to found the Society of Black Composers.

Students take over the administration building at Howard University, demanding the resignations of university officials.

> America is at a crossroads of history, and it is critically important for us, as a nation and a society, to choose a new path and move upon it with resolution and courage. It is impossible to underestimate the crisis we face in America. The stability of civilization, the potential of free government, and the simple honor of men are at stake.
>
> —Martin Luther King Jr., press conference announcing the Poor People's Campaign

March 31. Martin Luther King Jr. is the guest speaker at the Washington National Cathedral. He shares his fears about the growing desperation of poor people in America.

April 4. At 6:01 P.M. the Reverend Martin Luther King Jr. is assassinated while standing on the second-story balcony of his room at the Lorraine Motel in Memphis, Tennessee.

April 4. Around eight o'clock that night, in response to news of Martin Luther King's murder, riots begin at the intersection of 14th and U Streets NW. One of the first places targeted is the Peoples Drug Store at 14th and U Streets, where some people throw bricks through the windows. Looting and arson begin to spread along the U Street corridor and along 14th Street. Police, greatly outnumbered by the crowds, make some arrests.

April 5. Stokely Carmichael holds a press conference in the morning; he speaks at a rally that afternoon on the quadrangle in front of Douglass Hall at Howard University. That afternoon Mayor Washington and President Johnson attend a memorial service at Washington National Cathedral.

Shortly after noon, the National Guard is called in to protect government buildings and restore order. Army troops are also put on alert at Fort Myer and Fort Belvoir in Virginia, Fort Meade in Maryland, and Fort Bragg in North Carolina.

Many black public school students walk out of school this morning. Some go immediately home because of apprehension over further violence; some march to Howard University, where students are organizing memorial programs and protest rallies; others join the growing crowds of blacks gathering along 14th and U Streets, 7th Street, H Street between 2nd and 15th Streets NE, and in Anacostia. Looting and fires begin to spread among the shops and businesses. Over 500 fires will be set during the next three days, and a state of emergency is declared by the mayor's office.

Cyrus Vance is brought in to serve as coordinator of the National Guard, federal troops, and police force. He served in the same capacity during the 1967 riots in Detroit. Vance emphasizes the use of large numbers of troops to secure riot-torn areas and the use of tear gas, as opposed to bullets. Soon a haze of tear gas hangs over parts of the city.

Troops begin arriving in the city around 5 P.M. They are the first federal troops to be deployed in D.C. since those against the Bonus Marchers in 1932. The plan to use troops to protect the capital, called Operation Cabin Guard, was devised after the Detroit riots a year earlier. At 5:20 P.M. Mayor Washington declares a curfew to take effect in ten minutes—at 5:30.

April 6. Mayor Washington declares a curfew for 4 P.M. By this time more than 13,600 troops and guardsmen are stationed around the city. More than 1,500 people are arrested that day—most of them not for looting or arson but for curfew violation. By the end of the disturbances, 12 fatalities are recorded; 7 people have perished in fires. Over 7,500 people have been arrested, mostly for curfew violation. The police sweep up large numbers of men, women, and children, including onlookers, bystanders, and those running errands.

April 13. Troops begin leaving the city.

April 15. Mayor Washington lifts the state of emergency.

April. Dr. Martin Luther King Jr.'s final article is published in *Look* magazine.

April. Trials of those arrested during the riots begin almost immediately. Most people are released on $1,000 bond, but the bonds for the accused varied wildly, depending on the presiding judge. Defense attorneys for the accused are recruited from the mostly white District Bar Association; many black attorneys are angered because the all-black Washington Bar Association is not included in the call for attorneys. They also complain that blacks are allowed to participate in the process only as defendants. In "Ten Blocks from the White House," an examination of the riot conducted by the staff of the *Washington Post,* Ben W. Gilbert points out: "Although the chief prosecutor at the court, Joel D. Blackwell, was a Negro, almost all his staff members were white, as were fifteen of the eighteen-judge panel. It turned out that most proceedings during the hectic

We intend, before the summer comes, to initiate a "last chance" project to arouse the American conscience toward constructive democratic change. The nation has been warned by the President's Commission (on Civil Disorders) that our society faces catastrophic division in an approaching doomsday if the country does not act. We have, through this non-violent action, an opportunity to avoid a national disaster and to create a new spirit of harmony.

—Dr. Martin Luther King Jr., final article in *Look* magazine, April 1968

The Southern Christian Leadership Conference's Statements of Demands for Rights of the Poor, dated April 29–30 and May 1, 1968, stipulates the campaign's demands in broad terms:

1. A meaningful job at a living wage for every employable citizen.

2. A secure and adequate income for all who cannot find jobs or for whom employment is inappropriate.

3. Access to land as a means to income and livelihood.

4. Access to capital as a means of full participation in the economic life of America.

5. Recognition by law of the right of people affected by government programs to play a truly significant role in determining how they are designed and carried out.

riot period involved black defendants, prosecuted by white men and defended by white men who were appointed by white judges."

Because of significant delays in processing people through the legal system, some of the arrested are held for more than forty-eight hours without seeing a judge. The American Civil Liberties Union files a complaint, demanding that all arrested persons who have been held for more than twenty-four hours without seeing a judge be freed; it also complains about the excessive bail. Although the Washington Bar Association supports the ACLU, its suit is unsuccessful.

May. The Poor People's March, led by Reverend Ralph D. Abernathy, begins as caravans from all over the country head toward Washington, D.C.

Participants travel to Washington, D.C., in buses, cars, and trains. Most spectacularly, some arrive by mule train. The Poor People's Campaign uses nine caravans: the "Eastern Caravan," the "Appalachian Trail," the "Southern Caravan," the "Midwest Caravan," the "Indian Trail," the "San Francisco Caravan," the "Western Caravan," and the "Mule" and "Freedom" Trains.

The Eastern Caravan enters Washington, D.C., in mid-May with approximately 800 people, including many Puerto Ricans from New York City. The Appalachian Trail caravan consists of whites and African Americans from Tennessee, Kentucky, southwest Virginia, and West Virginia. The Southern Caravan winds through the deep South and includes Mexican Americans and whites. The Western Caravan includes Mexican Americans, as well as Native Americans from New Mexico and Oklahoma. The Indian Trail begins in Seattle, Washington, and goes east through Montana, North Dakota, and Minnesota.

Resurrection City, the name of the ad hoc living arrangements, becomes a muddy shantytown. A professor of architecture designed Resurrection City, complete with a city hall, a dispensary, a dining tent, a "Poor People's University," and a "Soul Center." A psychiatrist is on call, and the city even has its own zip code! Resurrection City is built on fifteen acres of West Potomac Park, across the Reflecting Pool to the Lincoln Memorial. The parkland permit for the city is roughly six pages long and prohibits the U.S. Park Police from entering the grounds, as Resurrection City will maintain its own police force. The Soul Center tent and the Poor People's University provide locations for teaching multiracial education courses. In addition to the educational courses, the Poor People's Campaign sponsors seminars held at the Highlander Center and throughout Washington, D.C., at Catholic University, Howard University, American University, George Washington University, and Georgetown University.

May 25. Ralph Abernathy appoints Bayard Rustin to organize and prepare the poor for "Solidarity Day." Rustin issues an "Economic Bill of Rights."

June 6. Presidential candidate Robert Kennedy is assassinated in California.

June 7. Bayard Rustin resigns over issues central to the Poor People's Campaign. Ralph Abernathy appoints Sterling Tucker, director of the Washington Urban League, as Rustin's replacement.

A poster from the Poor People's Campaign, June 19, 1968.

June 13. New legislative goals for the Poor People's Campaign are developed, and Tucker issues a list of forty-nine demands. Administrative demands focus on federal food programs, job programs, education, health services, and welfare benefits to the poor. Legislative demands include the passage of a bill to create 2.4 million jobs over a four-year period, the provision of $5.5 billion toward new housing, and the repeal of the new welfare amendments that would freeze federal welfare contributions at the January 1, 1968, level.

June 24. The permit expires for the temporary shelters (Resurrection City) built near the Lincoln Memorial. At the intersection of 14th and U Streets, a protest of about 200 people ensues—the same location where the Washington riots began two months earlier. Violence erupts again. Park rangers slow the tide of the protest until Assistant Chief Jerry Wilson calls in the newly formed Civil Disturbance Unit. The CDU manages to disperse the crowd by using over 1,000 tear gas canisters. Mayor Washington is praised by businessmen and whites but criticized by many civic leaders for allowing the CDU to disperse the crowd with aggressive tactics, police dogs, and an overwhelming use of force. The police arrest 175 people, including Ralph Abernathy.

The Poor People's Campaign, Solidarity Day, 1968.

285

Resurrection City, 1968.

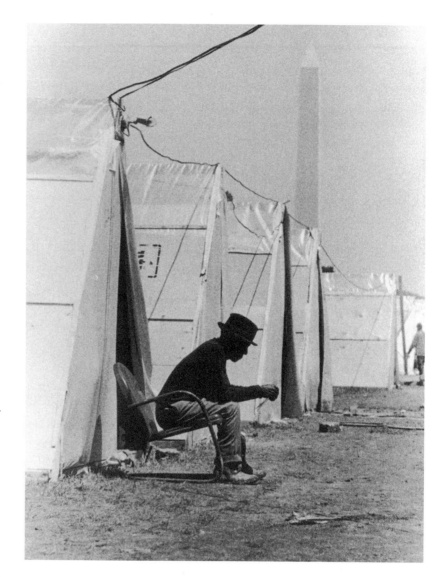

Economic Bill of Rights

1. Recommit the Federal Government to the Full Employment Act of 1946 and legislate the immediate creation of at least one million socially useful career jobs in public service;

2. Adopt the pending housing and urban development act of 1968;

3. Repeal the 90th Congress's punitive welfare restrictions in the 1967 Social Security Act;

4. Extend to all farm workers the right—guaranteed under the National Labor Relations Act—to organize agricultural labor unions;

5. Restore budget cuts for bilingual education, Head Start, summer jobs, Economic Opportunity Act, Elementary and Secondary Education Acts.

—Bayard Rustin, 1968

Dr. William Montague Cobb and doctors, nurses, and other medical personnel from Howard University organize health-care services for the people camped in Resurrection City. After the marchers leave the city, many of these same medical professionals continue to work together and establish the Howard University Mississippi Project, an organization dedicated to bringing medical care to Quitman County, Mississippi.

Military occupation at 6th and K Streets NW, 1968.

October. Reverend Elder Lightfoot Solomon Michaux, head of the Gospel Spreading Church, dies. Michaux was known for his religious pageantry, including massive baptisms in Griffith Stadium, complete with a 150-member flag corps, the "Cross Choir," that performed during the baptismal services. Michaux began preaching on the Virginia coast in 1907 and established the first of his nine churches in Newport News, Virginia, in 1930. In 1930 Michaux started a religious radio show called the *Happiness Hour,* which was later nationally broadcast.

Louis Michaux, son of Elder Michaux, is named executor of the multimillion-dollar estate, which included controlling stock in the Mayfair Mansions and Paradise Manor apartment complexes.

Swearing in of the first elected D.C. Board of Education, by Supreme Court Justice Thurgood Marshall, January 27, 1969.

October 16. At the summer Olympics in Mexico City, Tommie Smith and John Carlos, the gold and bronze medal winners of the 200-meter run, give the "Black Power" salute of a single black-gloved fist held high in the air, with heads bowed, during the medal ceremony. The United States Olympic Committee suspends them and bans them from the Olympic Village.

November 21. District citizens elect members to the D.C. Board of Education for the first time.

The Drum and Spear bookstore opens in the 2700 block of 14th Street NW. The bookstore, which sells black nationalist and Pan-Africanist literature, becomes a gathering place for black activists.

Football star Bobby Mitchell retires. Mitchell played in four Pro Bowls, three as a member of the Washington Redskins.

1969

January 20. Richard M. Nixon is inaugurated as president.

Dr. Billy Taylor, pianist and composer, becomes the first black band director for a network television series when *The David Frost Show* signs him to a contract. Taylor was born in Greenville, North

Carolina, in 1921 but grew up in Washington. He attended Dunbar High School and took piano lessons from Henry Grant, the same teacher who taught Duke Ellington.

Patricia Roberts Harris is appointed dean of Howard University Law School. The first woman to be appointed dean, she serves in that position until 1972.

Political activist Ralph Featherstone returns to Washington, D.C., from Atlanta, where he worked in SNCC offices. He becomes manager of the Drum and Spear bookstore. Featherstone, a graduate of D.C. Teachers College, taught speech therapy in public schools in the District but quit to do political organizing for SNCC in the South.

April. Of 500 cafeteria workers employed in restaurants around the U.S. Capitol, 100 organize a trade union. The employees, 90 percent of whom are black, form the Capitol Hill Employees Association.

June 16. In *Powell v. McCormack,* Adam Clayton Powell Jr. wins the right to resume his position as a congressman from the state of New York. The Supreme Court rules that Powell's constitutional rights were violated and Powell resumes his seat.

October. One hundred elementary school pupils stage a protest at Van Ness School, at 5th and M Streets SW. The students march around the plastic-sheeted windows of the building, chanting, "We want windows at the Van Ness School, quick!" as two students beat out a rhythm for the marchers. The students and their teachers are upset at the school administration's Buildings and Grounds Department, which promised glass windows for the new school year. The windows were not installed within the time promised, and children and students were forced to deal with the elements, as rain, wind, and cold weather entered their classrooms. One teacher threatened to bus 150 students to the Presidential Building of the school administration and hold classes there if the demands were not met.

At Howard University, students hold a mass protest against the Vietnam conflict. One thousand students and activists meet to listen to American University Student Union president Moose Osato Foster speak. Foster says that "As black people, we have to begin to think collectively. Once we thought success was to get your slice of the pie, but now we know different. Also, before we consider ourselves part of any community, we must be able to work together with people."

1970

January 17. Washington singer Billy Stewart is killed in an automobile accident in North Carolina. Stewart and three other band members were in a car that plunged into the Neuse River. He is buried at Harmony Cemetery in Washington, D.C.

February. Almost 4,000 concertgoers riot after waiting five hours for the band Sly and the Family Stone to perform at Constitution Hall. Black radio stations, including local WOOK, call for a boycott of Sly Stone's records.

March. An explosion kills Ralph Featherstone and a companion who are traveling in a car near Bel Air, Maryland. Many think that the bomb was meant for H. Rap Brown, who is currently on trial for inciting a 1967 riot in Cambridge, Maryland.

A secret will of Elder Michaux is uncovered in a New York City law firm, granting Rabbi Abraham Abraham, a confidant of Michaux, control of the Michaux estate.

Stokely Carmichael returns from a year-long stay in Africa. Soon after arriving in the United States, Carmichael is issued a subpoena at his mother's home, requesting his presence at a "Star Chamber Proceeding," a closed-door Senate conference that excludes the public and the press. Senator James O. Eastland of Mississippi, who wants to question Carmichael about black revolutionary activities, enacts the summons. Due to the short notice given, only Strom Thurmond of South Carolina and Birch Bayh of Indiana, who protest the manner in which the hearing was called, attend the hearing. Carmichael responds to most questions by invoking the Fifth Amendment at the advice of his lawyer, Howard Moore.

July. Local blues singer and popular emcee George Craft, "The President of the Blues," collapses while hosting at Rocky's Club on Benning Road NE. His rendition of "Down on the Farm" and "Up in Yale" were popular with local audiences.

The Howard Theatre closes its doors.

Rayford Logan begins to campaign in earnest against the use of the word *black* to refer to African Americans. He insists on using *Negro* and attacks in letters and writings those who abandon the old term. Logan refuses to attend any event that includes the term in its literature; he leaves meetings and often ends conversations abruptly if anyone uses the word *black* in his presence.

Robert Hooks forms the D.C. Black Repertory Company.

August. The FBI places black radical Angela Davis on the FBI's list of ten most wanted fugitives.

The Joint Center for Political Studies, a black think tank, is established by Howard University. Frank Reeves is appointed as its first director. The mission of the center is to assist black elected officials around the country and to groom future elected and political leaders.

November 26. The highly decorated career military man Benjamin O. Davis Sr. dies in Chicago, Illinois.

General Benjamin O. Davis Sr.

BLACK POWER AND THE STRUGGLE FOR HOME RULE

1970–2000

Overleaf:

"Pan African Day" at Malcolm X Park.
Stokely Carmichael (Kwame Ture), the
All-African People's Revolutionary Party
leader, speaks to the crowd, 1976.

Million Man March participants,
October 16, 1995.

IN MANY WAYS THE PASSAGE OF THE 1965 VOTING RIGHTS ACT SET THE scene for African American political achievements in Washington during the 1970s and afterward. When previously disenfranchised blacks in the South began to vote, some southerners in Congress who had been hostile to the interests of Washington, D.C., and who had led the congressional opposition to local self-government were voted out of office. In an event marking the tenth anniversary of home rule in the District, Walter Fauntroy recalled how he went to the South Carolina hometown of Congressman John McMillan and urged black and white voters to defeat McMillan in the upcoming election. He also mailed 10,000 letters to black voters throughout the South and asked them to demand that their congressman support home rule in the District of Columbia. Fauntroy knew that voters in the South (particularly, black voters who had been given the franchise less than a decade earlier) were an essential part of the strategy to achieve home rule for the city.

Aftershock

In 1968 Congress voted to allow District residents to elect members to the Board of Education for the first time since 1871. The year 1968 was pivotal for black Washingtonians, by any measure. After the trauma of Martin Luther King Jr. being assassinated, there was the shock of the riots, which left the city unsettled and anxious about the intensity of the anger revealed by residents in many of the city's poorest neighborhoods. The riots also served as a wake-up call to Congress and political officials that some kind of change in how the city was run was not only overdue but politically expedient. Five years later President Nixon signed the Home Rule Act, which allowed residents to elect a mayor and a thirteen-member city council.

Those first elections to the D.C. Board of Education served as a launching pad into public office for local activists and political aspirants. The elections to the school board ushered in a new era of black electoral politics in the city. They provided a base for black participation in political processes and governance for the first time since Frederick Douglass and two other blacks, John Gray, a successful caterer, and Adolphus Hall, a local miller, were appointed members of the governor's council by President Ulysses Grant; and Solomon G. Brown, a black Smithsonian Institution employee, and James A. Handy, a black A.M.E. bishop, were elected to the House of Delegates.

In 1971 Julius Hobson, Sam Smith, Hilda Mason, and others founded the D.C. Statehood Party, a local political party with a mission of making the District of Columbia the country's fifty-first state. After Hobson's election to the City Council in 1974, the D.C. Statehood Party held a seat in the city council continuously until 1998, when council member Hilda Mason was defeated.

Stretching Out: Alternatives Emerge

There was also an active group of black radicals who articulated alternative political ideologies and agendas. For the most part, their organizing efforts were focused on younger blacks. Howard University and the University of the District of Columbia were strongholds of black radical political activity, but it most often focused on national and international issues, as opposed to local politics. In the early 1970s Stokely Carmichael (who later changed his name to Kwame Ture), Bob Brown, and other activists founded the Washington, D.C., branch of the All-African People's Revolutionary Party, a pan-Africanist organization inspired by the teachings of African leader Kwame Nkrumah. These and other local organizations were the driving force behind the observation of the annual African Liberation Day and Malcolm X Day celebrations—

many of which were held in Meridian Park (informally renamed Malcolm X Park by area residents) well into the 1980s.

Despite the closing of the Howard Theatre in 1970 and the slow decline of U Street, Washington still had an active local arts and entertainment scene. Long-standing and popular restaurants like Florida Avenue Grill and Ben's Chili Bowl remained in the area, but U Street was no longer the center of black entertainment and business. Instead, nightclubs, restaurants, and businesses stretched out along Georgia Avenue, H Street, Florida Avenue, and other major streets where black populations were concentrated.

Thriving Arts and Popular Culture in "Chocolate City"

Dance and visual arts studios also thrived. Painters like Alma Thomas, Sam Gilliam, and Jeff Donaldson and some of the artists associated with the Howard University School of Art were widely influential. The actor Robert Hooks and other Howard University students formed the D.C. Black Repertory Theater, a seminal theater company, in the early 1970s. Renowned dance instructor Doris Jones, who had opened her studio in 1945, continued her work with budding ballet and modern dance performers throughout the 1990s. The dancer and choreographer Melvin Deal, who began teaching West African dance in 1959, established a popular dance instruction studio in southeast Washington, which remains open today and has become a landmark institution within the community.

Amateur and professional black photographers established two important photography organizations, the Exposure Group (formerly Positive Image) and Photoplay, which are still active today. In the field of literature, poet Gaston Neal launched a series of community-based arts and literature programs in the early 1970s. Many of them were developed in collaboration with Pride, Inc., an organization established by Marion Barry to create job opportunities for inner-city residents. In the mid-1970s the author and arts activist Ethelbert Miller began the Ascension series of poetry readings, which introduced African American poetry to a community-based audience. Washingtonian Marita Golden emerged as a major author with a number of successful novels, nonfiction work, and a widely acclaimed memoir in the 1980s. And in 1992 Washingtonian Edward P. Jones published his collection of short stories about blacks in the nation's capital, *Lost in the City,* which was nominated for the National Book Award.

Black Washington also made its mark within the field of popular music. Since the mid-1970s, a unique blend of percussion, instruments, and voice known as go-go has dominated the local music scene. Though ideally suited to live performance, with its format of call-and-response between audience and performer, go-go music has received wide play on commercial radio stations across the country.

It was also in the 1970s that black people in the know named the nation's capital "Chocolate City." The name underlined the fact that Washington was a majority black city, and that in many ways it still served as the cultural and political (and certainly social) capital of black America. It also not so subtly reinforced the idea that there was a Washington distinct from the Federal City, as represented by the "marble city" on Pennsylvania Avenue and Capitol Hill. Part of the optimism and enthusiasm came from the mid-decade victory of limited home rule—home rule and even statehood being closely linked in many people's minds to the realization of local black political power. (The converse is considered by some local blacks an even more evident truth—that the denial of home rule and even statehood reflects an effort to deny black political power in the nation's capital.)

The Barry Era: Rise and Fall

The election of Marion Barry to the D.C. school board in 1971 marked the beginning of the public career of a personality whose life, when examined closely, reads more like high opera than mere biography. After an adventurous and courageous stint as a civil rights organizer in the deep South, Barry came to the city in 1965 to establish the Washington office of the SNCC. He brought with him the organizing skills learned in the South, which enabled him to lead demonstrations against police brutality and a bus fare increase in Washington. Along with Mary Treadwell, Barry started the community-based organization Pride, Inc., which provided job skills and education for inner-city young people. He led a Free D.C. protest movement in the late 1960s that targeted local businesses with protest marches and boycotts if they did not support home rule for the District of Columbia. In 1977 he was shot in the chest and nearly killed when an extremist group seized the District Building. Despite his early history and reputation as a political radical and a black militant, Barry did not come to the mayor's office as an antiestablishment candidate. After completing his apprenticeship on the school board and serving for several years on the City Council, he received the endorsement of the *Washington Post* the first time he ran for mayor in 1978.

At the very beginning of Barry's mayoral tenure, he brought people from SNCC and the civil rights movement into city government, to fill positions as aides and assistants. The Barry administration provided an economic and political base for many in the growing black middle class by facilitating local blacks' access to city jobs and official positions and greatly expanding their opportunities to obtain municipal contracts. Barry also established landmark programs for seniors and young people. But the mismanagement of several city agencies, the corruption of some individuals within the Barry administration, a growing fiscal crisis in the city budget, and the personal behavior of the mayor himself began to generate increasing criticism among city residents and within the national media. Congress appointed a Financial Control Board to oversee the city government. Even after an embarrassing arrest and conviction on charges of drug possession, however, Barry was still able to attract enough votes—primarily from black voters—to win election to the City Council and later to regain the mayor's office. The Barry political engine finally ground to a halt when he withdrew from the mayoral race in 1998. Barry had been mayor of Washington, D.C., for sixteen years.

Though the prohibition against racially restrictive covenants allowed black Washingtonians to live in areas of the city that had previously been restricted, black and white residents remained largely separated, with Rock Creek Park serving as the unofficial dividing line between the concentration of white families and black families in the District of Columbia. Income had a great deal to do with the segregated housing patterns in the city, as there was a significant disparity in income between black and white residents.

After World War II, the expansion of public transportation, improved roads in the suburbs, and the establishment of new federal and military jobs in areas just outside the District of Columbia resulted in a large-scale movement of white residents from the

District of Columbia into the suburbs. White emigration from the city was also spurred by the desegregation of the public schools and the banning of racially restrictive covenants. By 1971 approximately 95 percent of Washington, D.C., students were African American.

After 1980 the increasingly expensive cost of living in Washington, D.C., also encouraged many black residents to relocate to suburban areas in Maryland. Many black and white families leaving the city complained of high crime rates and poor public schools. The population in the District of Columbia declined from around 625,000 in 1985 to 554,000 in 1996. By the 1980s the trend of white flight had reversed, and more whites began coming into Washington than were leaving. The *Washingtonian* magazine quotes demographer George Grier of the Greater Washington Research Center as finding that "in the late 1980s, almost as many African-American families as whites left D.C. But because two-thirds of those who moved into D.C. were white—mostly singles and young couples—the net loss of blacks was three times as great."

He further observed that most of those blacks who were leaving had middle-income households—"thus confirming the impression that D.C. is fast becoming home to the poor and the rich." (Many of these blacks were also attracted to the idea of living in Prince George's County, which had long been touted as an emerging center of the black middle class.) This out-migration, however, represents only one period within a long and dynamic history of movement of black population to and from Washington and the surrounding areas of Maryland, Virginia, and even North Carolina.

Preserving a Historic Legacy

Washington residents elected Anthony Williams mayor of the city in 1998. Before he came to Washington, Williams had served as an alderman in New Haven, Connecticut. Williams was working as the chief auditor at PEPCO when he went after the position of chief financial officer for the city. Marion Barry nominated Williams, and the City Council confirmed his appointment in 1995. In the 1998 mayoral election campaign, Williams won the Democratic primary and easily achieved victory over Republican candidate Carol Schwartz.

1971

January. The D.C. Statehood Party is founded by Julius Hobson, Sam Smith, Hilda Mason, Chuck Stone, Doug Moore, Jesse Anderson, and other political activists.

January. D.C. native Colonel Hassan Jeru-Ahmed (formerly Albert R. Osborne) and the Blackman's Volunteer Army of Liberation establish the Blackman's Development Center, offering methadone drug treatment.

January. Artist Gaston Neal helps to organize an arts show benefit at the Corcoran Gallery of Art for Pride, Inc., a community-based self-help organization.

January 15. More than 1,000 people march to the U.S. Capitol Building with over 3 million signatures for a national legal holiday celebrating the birthday of Martin Luther King Jr. Reverend Dr. Ralph David Abernathy, SCLC president, addresses the crowd: "We

To those who have been trying so hard and long to bring some semblance of unity in the approach of Black citizens in their political fights for freedom and equality, let it be remembered that it was in the 1920s that Kelly Miller, famed sociologist, tried to form a union of all Black organizations to be called The Negro Sanhedrin, but failed.

—The *Washington Afro American*, January 9, 1971

The DC statehood movement started in the fall of 1970 in a barren church hall on East Capitol Street. A few of us, our chairs pulled in a small circle, had gathered to organize the campaign of civil rights activist Julius Hobson for non-voting congressional delegate— one of the city's few elected offices at the time.

—Sam Smith, *The Statehood Papers*

The last major march in the District to support a national holiday celebrating the birthday of Martin Luther King Jr., 1971.

Congressman Walter E. Fauntroy,
c. 1971; congressional portrait.

are not begging, but we are demanding that the 'people's holiday,' January 15, be made a legal holiday."

Walter E. Fauntroy wins the Democratic primary for the nonvoting delegate to the House of Representatives. He beats out several other contenders, including Reverend Channing E. Phillips; Julius Hobson, candidate for the D.C. Statehood Party; and independent candidate Dr. Thomas W. Moore Jr.

M. Carl Holman is appointed director of the Urban Coalition, an organization formed to stimulate capital investment in U.S. inner cities. Holman had arrived in Washington in 1962 to work for the U.S. Civil Rights Commission.

April 19. D.C. citizens elect New Bethel Baptist Church pastor and longtime political activist Walter E. Fauntroy as the nonvoting delegate to the House of Representatives. (Fauntroy is the District's first elected representative since Norton P. Chipman, who was elected in 1871.) He defeats Republican candidate John A. Nevius and D.C. Statehood Party candidate Julius W. Hobson, receiving almost 60 percent of the vote. Reverend Douglas E. Moore, head of the Black United Front, also runs as an independent candidate. Moore runs on a black nationalist platform and advocates statehood for D.C.; he receives 1.1 percent of the vote. Fauntroy remains in office until 1990.

Political activist Marion Barry is elected to the District of Columbia Board of Education and becomes its president.

May. Delegate Walter E. Fauntroy holds week-long meetings in each District voting ward to discuss home rule legislation with Washington residents.

The Black Congressional Caucus is founded by Congressman Charles Diggs of Detroit and representatives Shirley Chisholm, William Clay, George Collins, John Conyers, Ronald Dellums, Augustus Hawkins, Ralph Metcalf, Parren Mitchell, Robert Nix, Charles Rangel, Louis Stokes, and Walter E. Fauntroy.

Over 50 percent of the public housing units are located in southeast D.C., across the Anacostia River. Housing conditions in many

Members of Pride, Inc., including Marion Barry (striped shirt), Walter Washington (center), Carroll Harey (black suit), and Secretary of Labor Willard Wirtz (right), 1968.

projects are so poor that a group of nine residents sues the National Capital Housing Authority for failing to provide adequate maintenance services.

The Association for the Study of Negro Life and History moves from the home of its founder, Dr. Carter G. Woodson, to 1407 14th Street NW.

Howard University's soccer team wins the NCAA Division I Championship. It is the first time that a historically black college has won in this division.

December 9. Civil rights activist and Nobel Peace Prize–winner Ralph Bunche (born in 1904) dies.

1972

August. The Martin Luther King Jr. Public Library opens in downtown D.C.; the building is designed by architect Mies van der Rohe.

Julius Hobson runs for U.S. vice president, along with presidential candidate Benjamin Spock. The two candidates are fielded by the

People's Party, an antiwar party with a pro-civil rights, pro-environment platform.

Charles Diggs is elected chairman of the House of Representatives Committee on the District of Columbia, replacing Congressman John L. McMillan (D-SC), a longtime opponent of home rule. He holds a set of hearings that raises the issue of home rule in the nation's capital.

Washington native Pearl Williams-Jones (born in 1931) receives an honorary doctorate from Lycoming College for her achievements in teaching and in performing gospel music with her Pearl Williams-Jones Soul Trio. Two years later she receives a National Endowment for the Arts grant for research in gospel music.

Native Washingtonian and jazz lyricist Andy Razaf (born Andrea-mentania Paul Razafinkeriefo, 1895–1973) is inducted into the Song-writers Hall of Fame. Some of his best-known songs include "Ain't Misbehavin'," written with Thomas "Fats" Waller, and "Stompin' at the Savoy." He dies one year later in Los Angeles.

The Washington chapter of the All-African People's Revolutionary Party is founded by black activists and college students in the area. Influenced by the philosophy of Ghanian leader Kwame Nkrumah, they advocate pan-Africanism. The organization begins to host African Liberation Day marches each May in the District, drawing crowds of several thousand.

The 12th Street Branch YMCA is renamed the Anthony Bowen Branch of the Metropolitan Washington YMCA.

Dr. Roland Scott establishes the Howard University Center for Sickle Cell Disease, on the basis of new research on sickle cell disease and its particular impact on African American populations. It is the first major medical research center at the university.

1973
January 20. Richard M. Nixon is inaugurated as president.

January. Seven men break into a home at 7700 16th Street NW, murdering seven residents, four of whom are children. The residence, purchased by Los Angeles Lakers star basketball player Kareem Abdul-Jabbar, belongs to a group of several Hanafi Muslims. Seven Nation of Islam members from Philadelphia are charged; five are sentenced to prison.

May 27. Marion Barry marries Mary Treadwell. They met while both were students at Fisk University. They worked with the Free D.C. Movement in the 1960s and founded Pride, Inc., together. Their marriage lasts four years.

Dr. Luther A. Gibson founds the All Souls House of Prayer at 1830 9th Street NW.

Michael R. Winston is appointed head of the Moorland-Spingarn Research Center at Howard University. He remains there until 1983, when he becomes vice president for academic affairs at the university. Winston is recognized as one of the outstanding scholars of his generation, serving as consultant and board member in many academic institutions. He leaves the university in 1990.

Catherine "Cathy" Hughes becomes general manager for Howard University radio station WHUR. Hughes, a native of Omaha, Nebraska, came to Washington in 1971 to teach in Howard University's Communications Department.

November. Bernice Johnson Reagon, civil rights activist and vocal director of the D.C. Black Repertory Theater, holds a voice workshop that launches Sweet Honey in the Rock, an a cappella performance group that combines political activism with song. Sweet Honey becomes one of the most popular singing groups in the country, touring nationally and internationally. The group also composes and performs much of the music for the movie *Beloved*. Previously, Reagon was a member of the SNCC Freedom Singers; later she works as curator and historian at the Smithsonian Institution.

December. President Nixon signs the District of Columbia Self-Government and Reorganization Act of 1973, popularly known

Cathy Hughes, one of the founders of Radio One, in the 1970s.

as the "Home Rule Act." The proposal grants D.C. the right to an elected mayor and a thirteen-member city council, consisting of a representative from each of D.C.'s eight wards and four members and a council chair chosen at large. The measure eradicates the three presidentially appointed commissioner positions created by Congress in 1874. The act is limited, however—D.C. residents still have no voting representative in Congress. Congress maintains control over the District's court system and budget, as well as the right to override legislation passed by the D.C. city council.

1974

May. Human Kindness Day is celebrated in the District. Over 50,000 people gather at the Washington Monument, but violence breaks out.

Early in Mayor Walter Washington's campaign of 1974, young people's energy and votes were recognized as being important elements for victory.

May. "Pan African Day" is held at Malcolm X Park. All-African People's Revolutionary Party leader Stokely Carmichael addresses a crowd of 12,000 to 15,000 African Americans.

May 7. The new home rule charter is approved by D.C. citizens. The referendum allows for the creation of Advisory Neighborhood Commissions (ANCs) to advise the city council on neighborhood issues.

May 24. Edward Kennedy "Duke" Ellington (born on April 29, 1899, in Washington, D.C.) dies. Over 10,000 attend his funeral in New York. His son, jazz trumpeter Mercer Ellington (born on March 11, 1919, in Washington, D.C.), leads the Duke Ellington Orchestra after his father's death. He will also begin to archive and preserve his father's musical legacy. A large Duke Ellington collection is housed at the Smithsonian Institution.

July. A memorial statue of Mary McLeod Bethune in Lincoln Park in Southeast Washington is unveiled by the National Park Service. The statue was created by African American artist Robert Berks of New York. It is the first statue of an African American or a woman to be erected in a public park space in the nation's capital.

Musician Duke Ellington.

August 9. *President Richard Nixon resigns, due to his impending impeachment.*

August 9. *Gerald L. Ford is sworn in as president.*

September 12. After a long campaign by local Catholics to appoint an African American, Father Eugene A. Marino is chosen as auxiliary bishop for the Archdiocese of Washington. In 1988 he leaves Washington for Atlanta, where he is installed as archbishop.

November. The first National Annual Conference of Afro-American Writers is held at Howard University. Conference attendees spark a debate about the black arts movement of the previous decade.

November 5. For the first time in a century, elections are held for local D.C. officials. Incumbent Walter E. Washington, who served as appointed mayor for seven years, is elected mayor of Washington, D.C. Supreme Court Justice Thurgood Marshall swears in the new mayor at the D.C. District Building in January 1975. Mayor Washington serves for only one term.

Lois Mailou Jones, an important painter in the Harlem Renaissance and an art professor at Howard University for many years.

November. Elected to the city council are Sterling Tucker, chairman; D.C. Statehood Party activist Julius Hobson Sr.; Marion Barry; Reverend Douglas E. Moore; Reverend Jerry A. Moore, at large; John A. Wilson; James E. Coates; Polly Shackleton; Arrington Dixon; William R. Spaulding; Nadine P. Winter; Willie Hardy; and Wilhelmina Rolark. The city council establishes thirty-six Advisory Neighborhood Commissions in 1976.

Poet and literary critic E. Ethelbert Miller (born in 1950, New York) begins the Ascension series, designed for young and new poets to give public readings in the D.C. area.

Poet, playwright, and D.C. native May Miller (1899–1995) reads her poem "Not That Far," in honor of Walter Washington's mayoral inauguration. She also reads at the inauguration of President Jimmy Carter.

E. B. Henderson, a graduate of Howard University and the first African American man certified to teach physical education in U.S. schools, is inducted into the Black Sports Hall of Fame. Henderson, who became well known in the city for his letters to local newspapers protesting racial discrimination, was also director of the Department of Health, Physical Education, and Safety from 1925 to 1954 and a NAACP member.

The former home of General Oliver Otis Howard, founder and first president of Howard University, becomes a National Historic Landmark. The building is located at 607 Howard Place NW, on Howard University's campus.

The Duke Ellington School of the Arts opens on the site of the former Western High School, with the backing of local arts activists Peggy Cooper Cafritz and Mike Malone. Funded by both D.C. public funds and the Ellington Fund, the school opens its doors to talented youths committed to dance, music, visual arts, theater, literary arts, media arts, and museum studies.

1975

City Council Chairman Sterling Tucker appoints Marion Barry to oversee the finance and review board. Barry argues for a commuter tax to bring revenue into the District from suburban commuters, especially those on the majority white police force. The City Council rules that city employees must reside in the city.

Chicago educator Barbara Sizemore, the first black woman to head a major school system, is dismissed as superintendent of D.C. schools. After Sizemore's two years on the job, Vincent E. Reed is appointed to succeed her. Reed oversees a steady increase in test scores for D.C. students during his tenure. In 1981 Floretta McKenzie is appointed superintendent of schools.

The Howard Theatre reopens briefly after a five-year hiatus.

The Nineteenth Street Baptist Church moves to the former B'nai Israel Jewish Congregation synagogue at 16th and Allison Streets NW.

Today the Howard is remembered as a vaudeville house comparable to Harlem's Apollo Theatre and the Lincoln is remembered as a movie theatre. Yet, the Apollo did not open its doors to Blacks until a full quarter century after the Howard Theatre. In addition, it is the Howard Theatre, not the Apollo, that is the nation's oldest existing legitimate theatre originally constructed to serve the cultural interests of Black Americans. Furthermore, the Lincoln Theatre was more than just a movie house. It was a gathering place for Washington's Black society where first-run movies and stage presentations appeared in the theatre and debutante balls and grand events were held in the Lincoln Colonnade Ballroom. With its opulent interior and proscenium stage, the Lincoln Theatre epitomizes the golden age of the grand movie/vaudeville palace.

—Henry Preston Whitehead,
The Howard Theatre Foundation

Singer Lena Horne was a headliner at the Howard Theatre during the 1940s and 1950s.

The construction of new hospital facilities in 1975 allows the medical staff at Freedmen's Hospital to expand beyond its original purpose of providing health care and medical education. A new emphasis on research is added to its mission. At this time its name is changed to Howard University Hospital, to reflect the new and enlarged vision.

The former home of Mary Church Terrell and her husband, Robert H. Terrell, is designated a National Historic Landmark.

Elgin Baylor (born in 1936, in Washington, D.C.), former member of the Los Angeles Lakers and basketball coach, is inducted into the Black Athletes Hall of Fame. Once an All-American basketball player at Spingarn High School, Baylor became one of the top-ranked basketball players in the country. He was also elected to the NBA Hall of Fame in Springfield, Massachusetts.

Black government employees at the Department of Health, Education, and Welfare form Blacks in Government (BIG) to fight against racial discrimination and to foster job training and promotion opportunities for black workers in federal, state, county, and municipal government.

Sterling Brown publishes his second volume of poetry, *The Last Ride of Wild Bill and Eleven Narrative Poems,* over forty years after *Southern Road.*

1976

A city law requiring the District to reserve 25 percent of city contract money for minorities is passed by the D.C. City Council.

Marion Barry is reelected to the city council. He builds a powerful and loyal constituency with a campaign that includes gay rights and poverty issues.

March 27. The Washington Metropolitan Area Transit Authority (WMATA) officially launches a rapid-transit rail system to operate in D.C. and the nearby Virginia and Maryland suburbs. Black neighborhoods in Washington and the surrounding suburbs lobby

The first elected District of Columbia City Council, 1976.

Metro officials in order to hasten the development of Metro stations in their areas.

Three D.C.-area natives take home gold medals in the Montreal Olympic Games: Sugar Ray Leonard, 139-lb.-class, boxing; and Kenny Carr and Adrian Dantley, basketball. Sugar Ray Leonard goes on to become world boxing champion.

Radio station deejay Melvin Lindsay begins hosting *The Quiet Storm* on WHUR. With its smooth adult format of jazz and ballads, *The Quiet Storm* becomes one of the most popular shows in the area.

Four former residences of prominent African Americans in D.C.'s history are declared National Historic Landmarks: the home of Mary Ann Shadd Cary, abolitionist and journalist, 1421 W Street NW (later demolished); the home of Charlotte Forten Grimké, abolitionist, 1608 R Street NW; the home of Blanche K. Bruce, 909 M Street NW; and the home of Dr. Carter G. Woodson, historian and creator of Black History Week. St. Luke's Episcopal Church at 15th and Church Streets NW—one of the oldest African American Episcopal churches in Washington—also receives this designation.

We assume that my great grandmother, Rosa Ann, decided to settle in the Anacostia area because of her former association with hills as a child in North Carolina. . . . This house is built on one of the highest peaks in Washington. From up here she could look out and see anyone coming up the hill. . . . My great-grandfather, James William Howard, was a blacksmith and an itinerant minister. He founded Macedonia Baptist Church in May, 1866. It was the first Baptist church for black people in Anacostia.

—Ella Pearis,
autobiographical manuscript,
Anacostia Museum

Vernard Gray opens the Miya Gallery at 11th and G Streets NW. The gallery features African art, clothing, and crafts. Gray also establishes a hair-braiding salon on the first floor, one of the first such establishments in the city.

The first World Black and African Festival of Arts and Culture (FESTAC) is held, bringing together people of African descent and other ethnicities from countries around the world.

November 14. Washington resident Ella Pearis gives an interview to the *Washington Post* from her great-grandmother's house, discussing her family's roots in Anacostia.

1977

January 20. James Earl "Jimmy" Carter Jr. is inaugurated as president.

February. Carolyn Smith, Howard University graduate and the first black woman to pass the D.C. CPA exam in 1969, becomes the District's new treasurer after the resignation of Charles L. Walker.

February 14. Adams-Morgan neighbors on Ontario Road NW protest the transformation of their rented low-cost residences into expensive one-family houses. Many tenants receive eviction notices, forcing them to vacate their homes in just thirty days. One tenant tells *Washington Post* staff writer LaBarbara Brown: "They [the developers] want the blacks out so the high class blacks and whites can come in. . . . They don't want people who have nothing."

February 17. Joanna Willis, wife of D.C. cab driver Calvin Willis, gives birth to quadruplets—three girls and one boy. They are the first quadruplets born at the George Washington University Medical Center and the first born in the District for almost forty years.

March. Plans are announced for the first major chain supermarket to be constructed in D.C.'s inner city in almost ten years. The building, part of the redevelopment plan for the former O Street Market, which has been closed since the riots, will be jointly owned by Giant Food, Inc.; the Shaw Project Area Committee (a community group); and the D.C. Development Corporation.

March. The U.S. District Court in Washington, D.C., gets its first black chief justice, William Benson Bryant. Bryant, who graduated from Howard University Law School in 1936, was appointed to the United States District Court in August 1965. He serves as chief judge from March 1977 to September 1981.

March 9. Approximately ten Hanafi Muslims seize the national headquarters of the Jewish service organization B'nai B'rith, threatening to behead the 134 hostages. They take over the District Building, shooting and killing WHUR-FM reporter Maurice Williams and giving City Councilman Marion Barry a near-fatal shot to the chest. The Hanafis have been training with weapons at their 7700 16th Street NW residence—the same home where seven of their members were murdered in 1973. Among the demands of apparent leader Hamaas Abdul Khaalis are to remove from theaters the newly released movie on the prophet Mohammed; to deliver to Khaalis the seven Nation of Islam members suspected of killing his family, as well as the person responsible for the death of Malcolm X; and to repay Khaalis's $750 contempt-of-court charge for disrupting the murder trial in 1973. After negotiating for three hours with the Washington chief of police and ambassadors from Iran, Egypt, and Pakistan, the kidnappers surrendered and released the hostages. A plaque honoring Maurice Williams is later placed outside the District Building pressroom.

March. In response to the Hanafi Muslim seizure of the B'nai B'rith headquarters, the militant Jewish Defense League (JDL) marches in front of the Hanafi residence in Northwest D.C. Rabbi Meir Kahane, a founder of the JDL, leads the marchers.

March 23. At-large City Council member, D.C. Statehood Party member, and longtime political activist Julius Hobson dies of cancer while still in office. During his term on the City Council, he was responsible for the Referendum Act, which gave citizens the right to draft legislation and place it on voting ballots, and the Non-Criminal Police Surveillance Act, which limited police surveillance of politically active individuals and groups. Hilda Mason, also a member of the D.C. Statehood Party, replaces him on the city council.

Hilda Mason of the Statehood Party in her District Building office, 1983.

August 1. Federal City College, Washington Technical Institution, and Miner Teachers College are joined to form the University of the District of Columbia.

November. The third National Annual Conference of Afro-American Writers is held at Howard University. Organized by Stephen Henderson, John Oliver Killens, and Haki Madhubuti, the conference provides African American writers with the chance to interact and to discuss the state of black literature. Howard hosts four more conferences between 1977 and 1983.

Patricia Roberts Harris is appointed secretary of Housing and Urban Development by President Jimmy Carter, becoming the first African American woman to serve in the cabinet.

The old Dunbar High School building is torn down.

1978

January. Native Washingtonian Burtell M. Jefferson becomes Washington, D.C.'s first African American chief of police. He serves as chief until 1981, when Maurice T. Turner Jr. is appointed to replace him.

January. After serving as a test pilot for NASA, native Washingtonian Frederick D. Gregory is chosen to be an astronaut. He graduated from Anacostia High School in 1958, the U.S. Air Force Academy in 1964, and the George Washington University in 1977.

May. Howard University awards an honorary Doctor of Humane Letters degree to musician and composer Stevie Wonder.

May 21. Malcolm X Day is celebrated by almost 4,000 in Anacostia Park. In attendance are former Black Panther Bobby Seale and D.C. councilwoman Wilhelmina Rolark, who encourage participants to exercise their voting power.

June. Bullets team member Wes Unseld is named Most Valuable Player in the NBA finals for the 1977–1978 season.

June. In the basement of a Hyattsville police station, fifteen-year-old Terrence Johnson shoots and kills two Prince George's County police officers with one of their own guns. The incident sets off a massive political defense campaign on behalf of Johnson, a student at Bladensburg Junior High School. The Terrence Johnson Legal Defense Fund Committee, made up of supporters of Johnson's defense campaign, claims that he shot the two policemen—Albert Claggett IV and James Swart—in self-defense while he was being beaten.

August. Congress passes the D.C. Voting Rights Amendment, which will enable D.C. residents to have voting representation in both the House of Representatives and the Senate. The amendment will have to be approved by thirty-eight states within seven years.

August 30. The *Washington Post* endorses Marion Barry for the 1978 mayoral election.

September. Marion Barry, Sterling Tucker, and incumbent Walter Washington face one another in the Democratic primary for the mayoral election. Tucker, having secured the endorsement of Walter Fauntroy, is considered the best bet to unseat Washington, but in a surprise upset, Barry wins the primary election.

November. Marion Barry becomes mayor of the District of Columbia by a landslide in the general election after having gained only a

You will know by now, if you have been reading our editorials on the Democratic primary for mayor, that we think someone should replace Walter Washington, and that the choice comes down, as a practical matter, to one between City Council Chairman Sterling Tucker and Council Member Marion Barry. Which should it be? Our strong belief is that it should be Marion Barry.

—Editorial,
The *Washington Post,* 1978

small majority vote in the primary election. John Ray, who entered the mayoral race, withdrew, and threw his support to Barry, is awarded Barry's old seat on the City Council.

December 13. Ella Baker, civil rights activist and SCLC and SNCC organizer, celebrates her seventy-fifth birthday at Howard University Law School. In attendance are several D.C. officials: Eleanor Holmes Norton, Mayor-Elect Marion Barry, Howard University Law School dean Wiley Branton, and Councilman John Wilson.

Marion Barry marries Effi Cowell. It is his third marriage.

Reverend Willie F. Wilson becomes pastor of the Union Temple Baptist Church. The church, founded in 1967 by Reverend Chester R. Smallwood, is one of the most popular churches east of the Anacostia River. Reverend Wilson becomes an important political player in local electoral and community politics.

A group of photographers forms Positive Image, a photography organization for amateur and professional photographers. In 1986 the group is reorganized as "the Exposure Group." In 1997 Jason Miccolo Johnson, Jim Johnson, and Marvin Jones incorporate the group under the official name, the Exposure Group African American Photographers Association, Inc. It remains an active and well-known arts organization, hosting meetings of photographers from around the metro area and organizing photo exhibitions and workshops.

Native Washingtonian Edward W. Brooke III (born in 1919), the first African American senator since Reconstruction, loses his seat after having served two terms.

The Charles Sumner School, which was originally established in 1872 as the headquarters of the District's colored school system before desegregation, is designated a historic site. After the collapse of its roof two years later, the school is transformed into a museum and an archive of D.C. public schools.

Painter Alma Thomas (born in 1891) dies. A member of the Washington colorist school, she was famous for the shimmering fields of color in her paintings. Thomas was the first student to graduate from Howard University's Department of Art and was a longtime art teacher at Shaw Junior High School.

John Turner Layton Jr. (born in 1894, Washington, D.C.), Howard University Dental School graduate and vaudeville entertainer, dies in London. Late in life, he worked with England's BBC Television, gaining fame as a variety artist.

The D.C. Corrections Department and the University of the District of Columbia host the first annual graduation day at the Lorton Reformatory, giving inmates a chance to take college courses and receive college degrees.

1979

January 2. On Inauguration Day, newly elected mayor Marion Barry and his wife, Effi, lead a march from Malcolm X Park to the District Building, where Barry is sworn in by Supreme Court Justice Thurgood Marshall. His core administration includes several former SNCC activists.

February. A severe snowstorm shuts down the District for one day. Mayor Barry is criticized in the local media for his lack of preparedness and his unwillingness to accept responsibility for the foul-up.

June. We Love Anacostia Day is held in Anacostia. The festive parade and celebration contradict media images of violence and crime in the Southeast D.C. neighborhood. The parade's grand marshal is TV news reporter Bruce Johnson.

Jerry Washington, also known as "The Bama," begins broadcasting a blues program from 11 to 2 in the afternoon on WPFW. *The Bama Hour* quickly becomes one of the most popular blues programs in the country.

Congress establishes the Pennsylvania Avenue Development Corporation to redevelop downtown Washington, D.C., between the White House and the U.S. Capitol Building.

Button worn by many people during the We Love Anacostia Day festivities.

Sam Smith ends his assistantship to Mayor Barry during Barry's first term, when, he says, "black power cut a deal with white power. The middle class and poor of either race weren't part of the deal although they were mightily affected by it."

D.C. superintendent of schools Vincent Reed experiences conflicts with the Barry administration over rising costs in school expenditures. Reed discovers that the rising costs are due to a change from white to African American suppliers, who happen to charge more. During the winter, the African American–owned oil company Tri-Continental Industries not only charges 25 percent more than the previous white-owned supplier, Steuart Petroleum, but also refuses to deliver oil during two cold days. Reed threatens to shut down the schools but is given money for Steuart Petroleum to make deliveries in the meantime. Reed resigns the next year.

Marion Barry moves from Capitol Hill to the Hillcrest section of Southeast D.C.

Patricia Roberts Harris is appointed secretary of the Department of Health, Education, and Welfare by President Jimmy Carter.

Political activist Eugene Kinlow Sr. is elected to fill the seat of departing Board of Education member Betty Ann Kane. Kinlow has long been active in the parent-based organizations in Ward 8 public schools.

The Marshall Heights Community Development Organization (MHCDO) is developed in Ward 7 by Loretta Tate and other community leaders. Over the next few years the MHCDO makes many improvements in the community, including refurbishing the East River Park Shopping Center and the Kenilworth Industrial Park, renovating and building new housing, and providing social services to residents. In 1991 MHCDO's committed efforts to advocating self-help prompt a visit from Queen Elizabeth II of England.

1980

January. Entrepreneur Robert L. Johnson establishes Black Entertainment Television in D.C. Johnson, a cable TV lobbyist, borrowed

Robert Johnson in his Georgetown office in the early days of BET, 1981.

from businessmen to establish the company. The first programs air on cable TV that month.

Cathy Hughes purchases WOL radio from her ex-husband, Dewey Hughes, and becomes its sole owner. WOL-AM becomes the flagship station of her media company, Radio One, Inc.; later, she purchases several other successful stations, including WMMJ, WYCB, and in 1994 WKYS. In 1999 the company goes public, making Hughes the first African American woman with a company on the NASDAQ stock exchange.

The Redevelopment Land Agency begins a controversial program of selling land parcels to minority-white partnerships. Several major development projects are launched with minority partners. At Metro Center, white developer Nathan Landow joins with black D.C. Democratic chairman Robert Washington, white developer Oliver Carr, and Ted Hagans, another African American partner. The project partners vow to create office space, stores, a hotel, and low-income housing, though ten years later, nothing had been built. The project is eventually sold to Oliver Carr, the city's largest developer.

August. Prime Minister Robert Mugabe of Zimbabwe speaks at Howard University's Cramton Auditorium to a house full of cheering university students and other supporters. Mugabe thanks the crowd for its support during the war in the former Rhodesia.

A group of young musicians at the Barry Farm housing project begin to make music with an assortment of instruments—from milk crates to synthesizers. Calling themselves the Junkyard Band, they play "junk funk" go-go music. In 1984 they are featured in a cameo appearance in the movie *DC Cab*. Go-go band Experience Unlimited becomes widely known while still in high school for its performances at the Panorama Room at Our Lady of Perpetual Help in Anacostia. Musician Chuck Brown gains popularity performing with the Soul Searchers; Brown puts go-go on the national map with his 1979 hit "Bustin' Loose."

November. D.C. citizens approve Initiative 3, establishing the D.C. Statehood Commission to lobby residents in D.C. and the other states for local statehood. It also calls for a constitutional convention to draft a state constitution.

1981

January 20. Ronald Reagan is inaugurated as president.

January. The Cardozo High School marching band is the first in the D.C. metropolitan area to march in the Tournament of Roses Parade in Pasadena, California.

February. Mayor Barry's former wife, Mary Treadwell, is convicted of improper use of funds from Pride, Inc.

April 25. Bishop Smallwood E. Williams leads his family members and congregation to the site of the new multimillion-dollar Bible Way Temple, located at the corner of New Jersey and New York Avenues NW.

July. Maurice T. Turner Jr. is appointed chief of the Washington, D.C., police force. He serves until July 1989, when Isaac Fulwood replaces him.

On January 15, 1981, "Happy Birthday to you, Dr. Martin Luther King Jr.," is sung by Stevie Wonder (with microphone) to about 100,000 people on the Washington Monument grounds.

September. The District opens Benjamin Banneker High School, a magnet school for the academic study of literature, math, science, and foreign languages.

Tom Mack, general manager of Tourmobile, a local enterprise providing guided tours around the nation's capital, buys the business

Bishop Smallwood E. Williams, leading his congregation in a celebratory parade to the newly constructed Bible Way Temple.

from Universal Studios, becoming owner of the area's largest tour services company.

1982

February 12. The Frederick Douglass Home in the Cedar Hill section of Anacostia is designated a National Historic Site. After Douglass's death in 1895 and until 1982, the house was maintained by Douglass's widow, Helen Pitts Douglass, and later by the Frederick Douglass Memorial and Historical Association and the National Association of Colored Women's Clubs. The house becomes a commemorative house museum, run by the National Park Service.

Mayor Marion Barry declares June 12 as Ethel Payne Day in the District of Columbia. Payne, an award-winning journalist, lived and worked in the District for many years.

Congress declares 1318 Vermont Avenue NW—the last residence of Mary McLeod Bethune and the former headquarters for the National Council of Negro Women—a National Historic Site. In 1991 the National Park Service opens the house as a commemorative museum. Also located on the site is the National Archives for Black Women's History.

September. The Washington, D.C., Reggae Festival, Inc., features its first Reggae Festival in Malcolm X (Meridian Hill) Park.

October. Forty-five delegates elected by D.C. voters for a constitutional convention meet to draw up a state constitution for the District of Columbia.

November 2. After polls show that a slight majority of D.C. voters has endorsed the charter for D.C. statehood, the City Council approves a bill to amend the new state constitution.

November 4. Rayford Logan dies.

November. Anti-Klan protesters organize demonstrations against the Ku Klux Klan when that organization announces a rally and a march in the nation's capital. Thousands of anti-Klan demonstrators show up, but only a handful of Klan members attempt to march. Later, police and demonstrators clash, and windows of downtown businesses are smashed.

November. Marion Barry is reelected mayor of Washington, D.C., defeating Republican candidate E. Brooke Lee, Jr.

November. Frank Smith, a longtime Student Nonviolent Coordinating Committee activist, is elected to the City Council, to represent Ward 1.

The Anthony Bowen 12th Street YWCA is closed due to the building's deteriorating condition.

Historians Rayford Logan and Michael Winston publish the *Dictionary of American Negro Biography*.

1983

Dance instructor Doris Jones is forced to close the Capitol Ballet, due to lack of funds.

April. Fifteen-year-old Louis Morton breaks into the Reptile House at the National Zoo and makes away with two poisonous Gaboon vipers. During Morton's bus ride home, the snakes bite through the garbage bag Morton has placed them in and inflict him with a painful and deadly wound, alarming other passengers and the bus driver, Jane White. He is rushed to the hospital, and anti-venom serum is flown to the city to save his life. Morton has been an amateur animal keeper and a self-taught snake fancier since before the age of seven. He later tells *Washington Post* reporter Courtland Milloy that as a child he was known to all his neighbors as "Snakeboy."

May. In celebration of the opening of McCollough's Plaza, a complex of church-owned apartment buildings, the congregation of the United House of Prayer for All People marches through the Shaw neighborhood. The apartment complex is named in honor of Bishop Walter McCollough.

June 21. Playwright Owen Dodson (born in 1914) dies.

Button worn by supporters of Jesse Jackson's campaign.

Jesse Jackson declares his candidacy for president of the United States. He runs on a pro–civil rights, pro-environment, and pro-labor platform under the umbrella of the National Rainbow Coalition.

1984

March. Singer and Washington native Marvin Gaye is shot and killed by his father in Los Angeles, California.

U Street's historic Lincoln Theatre closes.

Jesse Jackson runs for president, winning almost 400 delegates and finishing behind Walter Mondale and Gary Hart. Five years later he relocates to Washington, D.C..

The Lincoln Theatre hosted many jazz greats, including Duke Ellington, Cab Calloway, and Ella Fitzgerald (pictured), back to camera.

Karen Johnson is sentenced to serve time for contempt of court; she refuses to testify in support of claims by the U.S. Attorney's office that she sold drugs to Mayor Barry.

Anti-apartheid activists in the Free South Africa Movement attract hundreds of supporters to demonstrate in front of the South African embassy. A number of celebrities, religious leaders, and political officials participate in the demonstrations, including law professor Eleanor Holmes Norton, city councilman John Ray, journalist Ethel Payne, and Jewish community spokesman Hyman Bookbinder. The educational and lobbying organization Trans-Africa, led by Randall Robinson, helps by providing leadership and logistical support.

Initiative 7, which calls for the city to provide overnight shelter for all homeless people in the District, is passed by the D.C. City Council. The Pitts Motor Hotel in the neighborhood of Columbia Heights becomes a homeless shelter.

Over 700 people gather in Meridian Hill Park (locally known as Malcolm X Park) to celebrate African Liberation Day.

Sterling Brown is appointed the first poet laureate of the District of Columbia. After his wife, Daisy Turnbull Brown, dies in 1979, he is cared for by his sisters who live next door to his house in Brookland. Brown dies in 1989, beloved by a great many former students, fellow writers, and friends.

Randall Robinson, founder and president of TransAfrica.

1985

Frederick D. Gregory is selected as a pilot for the *Challenger* space shuttle.

August 22. Since what would have been the Twenty-seventh Amendment has not been approved by three-quarters of the states, as required by Congress, Washington residents lose the opportunity to have voting representatives in Congress.

Director of Employment Services Ivanhoe Donaldson is convicted of embezzling funds, bringing an end to a long and varied career in politics. Donaldson served as a close adviser to Jesse Jackson and Marion Barry.

Guyana native Kojo Nnamdi begins hosting the *Evening Exchange,* a local news commentary and talk show on Howard University's television station.

November. Anti-apartheid activists in Washington launch a new wave of demonstrations against the South African government. Demonstrations at the South African embassy attract increasingly larger crowds of supporters.

1986

November. Marion Barry is reelected to a third term as mayor of Washington, D.C., defeating white Republican candidate Carol Schwartz.

November. Harry Thomas Sr. is elected to the D.C. City Council, representing Ward 5. He serves three terms on the council, until he loses his seat to Vincent Orange in 1998.

The Black Family Reunion, an event sponsored by the National Council of Negro Women that celebrates the strength of the black family, is held on the National Mall.

Dr. Thomas Battle is appointed director of the Moorland-Spingarn Research Center at Howard University. Battle, an alumnus of Howard University and a graduate of George Washington University, previously served as curator of manuscripts. Under his direction, Moorland-Spingarn remains one of the outstanding repositories of African American historical manuscripts and photographs in the country.

The Frank Reeves Center for Municipal Affairs at 14th and U Streets NW is completed. The building is named after Frank D. Reeves, the first black Democratic committeeman in the District of Columbia.

1987

Former city councilman Arrington Dixon is appointed chairman of the D.C. Taxicab Commission by Mayor Barry. Two years later the

Washington Lawyers' Committee for Civil Rights Under Law files a discrimination suit against local cab companies, charging that blacks hailing cabs in the District were almost seven times more likely than whites to be passed up by empty cabs.

1988

April. Charles Ramsey is appointed as chief of police in Washington, D.C.

August 9. M. Carl Holman, poet, editor, scholar, and civil rights leader, who was president of the National Urban Coalition for the last seventeen years, dies at age sixty-nine of cancer at Howard University Hospital.

Political activist and long-standing electoral campaigner Absalom Jordan enters the City Council race against Wilhelmina Rolark for Ward 8.

Washington band EU (Experience Unlimited) has an international hit with "Da Butt." The song is featured in director Spike Lee's movie *School Daze*.

1989

January 20. George Bush H. W. is inaugurated as president.

May. City Council chairman David A. Clarke announces that he will enter the mayoral campaign. Former police chief Maurice Turner and city councilpersons Charlene Drew Jarvis and John Ray also enter the race. Jesse Jackson remains undecided as to whether he will run for mayor.

May. The eighteenth annual Malcolm X Day celebration draws almost 25,000 people to Anacostia Park, where speakers include Mayor Marion Barry and Jesse Jackson. Melvin Deal's troupe, the West African Heritage Dance Company, and the go-go band Experience Unlimited perform.

May 31. C. L. R. James, Caribbean-born political historian, Marxist philosopher, novelist, political activist, and cricket writer who was a professor of history at Federal City College and the University of the District of Columbia in the 1970s, dies at age eighty-eight at his home in London.

August. Jesse Jackson relocates from Chicago, Illinois, to Washington, D.C. Many residents and political commentators believe that he is planning to run for public office in the District.

September. Marion Barry makes a vulgar gesture at a crowd after he is booed at the annual Adams-Morgan Day street fair, prompting calls from some of his opponents in the mayoral campaign to withdraw from the race.

October. Members of the D.C. City Council approve a resolution praising Nation of Islam leader Louis Farrakhan for his antidrug activities in Northeast Washington neighborhoods. As a result, council members come under criticism from residents for their endorsement of the controversial political leader. When City Council members David A. Clarke, John Ray, and Charlene Drew Jarvis point out that they did not support the resolution, Reverend Willie Wilson, pastor of Union Temple Church and co-chairman of Sharon Pratt Dixon's mayoral campaign, threatens them with a recall petition. D.C. City Council members later meet with local Jewish leaders to discuss the resolution and try to alleviate tensions that result from the incident.

November. Mayoral candidates John Ray and Charlene Drew Jarvis accuse Mayor Marion Barry of using racial rhetoric to divide the city and gain the support of black voters.

November 22. Frederick D. Gregory (born in 1941, Washington, D.C.) makes history as the first African American astronaut to command a flight into space, on the spacecraft *Discovery*. Gregory was a graduate of Anacostia High School, the U.S. Air Force Academy, and George Washington University. In 1991 he serves as commander of the *Atlantis*.

Reverend George Augustus Stallings Jr. breaks from the Roman Catholic Church to establish the African-American Catholic Congregations. His church varies from the Roman Catholic tradition in several

Reverend George Stallings, founder of the African-American Catholic Congregations.

significant ways: gays and lesbians are admitted, women can be ordained priests, and priests are not required to be celibate. Stallings celebrates what he calls an African American Catholic service.

City Lights, an educational program that focuses on residents of public housing in Washington, D.C., is established. The program offers mentoring, reading and writing programs, and other skill enhancement programs to children in public housing. It also launches an oral history project that works with seniors.

1990

January. The FBI and the D.C. Metropolitan Police snare Mayor Marion Barry in a drug sting. The mayor is caught on videotape smoking crack cocaine with Hazel Rasheeda Moore, a local model. After his arrest, he begins an addiction treatment program and a substance abuse program. Barry is convicted of misdemeanor possession of cocaine and is sentenced to six months in a federal prison.

Abandoning his mayoral campaign after his arrest, Marion Barry runs for City Council member at large, the position he won in 1974. He loses the election to Linda Cropp and Hilda Mason. It is his first political defeat since arriving in D.C. in the 1960s.

July. Edward Franklin Fletcher, one of the founders of the FotoCraft Camera Club, dies. A freelance photographer, Fletcher worked with the *Pittsburgh Courier,* the *Washington Afro American,* and the Naval Ordinance Laboratory, and served as photographer general. In his honor the FotoCraft Camera Club establishes the Edward Fletcher Award for first prize in color print photography.

August 17. Longtime D.C. resident and performer Pearl Bailey (born in 1918) dies. She gained early fame performing in two of historic U Street's famous night spots—Jungle Inn and Republic Gardens.

September. Novelist Marita Golden establishes the Zora Neale Hurston/Richard Wright Foundation. The foundation's mission is to "develop, nurture and sustain the world community of writers of African descent." The foundation also establishes the Hurston/Wright Award for college student writers of African descent and the Hurston/Wright Writers' Week, a summer workshop for African American writers.

November. Sharon Pratt Dixon (born in 1944), former vice president for community relations at PEPCO and a Democrat involved in national party activities, is elected mayor of Washington, D.C. She is a native Washingtonian and a graduate of Howard University and Howard Law School. Dixon's platform promises to cut the city's payroll and to fight youth crime by stiffening criminal penalties.

November. Eleanor Holmes Norton becomes Washington, D.C.'s new House of Representatives delegate, following Delegate Walter Fauntroy's term. A graduate of Dunbar High School, Antioch College, and Yale Law School, Norton served in New York as a civil rights lawyer and a public official before becoming Equal Employment Opportunity Commission chair in 1977. Delegate Norton and Mayor Kelly (formerly Dixon) work together to increase federal support to the city in 1991–1992.

November. After serving sixteen years on the City Council, representing Ward 2, John A. Wilson (born in 1943) wins the chair of the D.C. City Council. Yet his struggles with depression lead

D.C. delegate Eleanor Holmes Norton.

Councilman Wilson to take his own life in 1993. In 1996 the District Building, headquarters for the city government, is renamed the John A. Wilson Building.

1991

Spring. Rioting breaks out in the Mt. Pleasant neighborhood; participants are primarily impoverished and unemployed young men from Central America, as well as black and white youths.

May. Mt. Zion United Methodist Church, the oldest black church in old Georgetown, celebrates its 175th anniversary.

October. Newly elected Mayor Sharon Pratt Dixon makes good on her promise to trim the city's payrolls by laying off more than 300 city workers. There are immediate protests, and laid-off workers seek legal help in their campaign to be reinstated. A number of them eventually do regain their jobs.

December. After years of protesting its delay, Anacostia area residents finally see the opening of the Metro's green line Anacostia

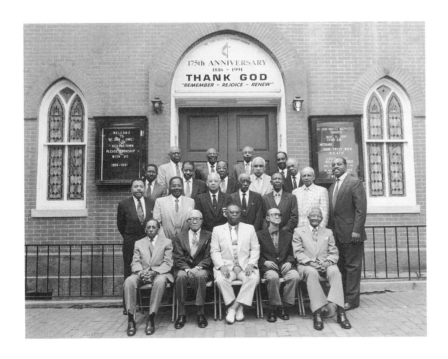

The United Methodist Men's Club of Mt. Zion United Methodist Church of Georgetown, celebrating the church's 175th anniversary, 1991.

station. Councilmember Wilhelmina Rolark and 200 supporters and community activists celebrate on a cruise down the Potomac on the *Spirit of Washington*.

December 7. Mayor Sharon Pratt Dixon marries businessman James R. Kelly III, in her sister's home in Brookline, Massachusetts. There is a small gathering of friends and family, and the couple takes a short honeymoon in Hawaii. To the surprise of many, the mayor changes her name to Sharon Pratt Kelly.

The D.C. courthouse is renamed the H. Carl Moultrie Court House in honor of the former D.C. Superior Court chief justice H. Carl Moultrie Sr. Chief Justice Moultrie held this position from 1978 until his death. Moultrie did not finish law school until he was forty-one years old. President Nixon appointed him as a Superior Court judge in 1972. He became the first black chief justice in 1978.

Jesse Jackson is elected as a Shadow Senator to lobby Congress for statehood for the District of Columbia. It is a nonvoting office in the Senate.

The D.C. government restores and reopens U Street's Lincoln Theatre, a $9 million project.

Langston Golf Course is named to the National Register of Historic Places and is administered by the National Park Service. The golf course, located north of Benning Road, was one of the earliest opened for African American golfers.

R. David Hall is elected president of the D.C. School Board, a position that he holds for five terms. Hall was first elected to serve on the board in 1982 and has been the incumbent since that time.

Radio talk show host Derek McGinty debuts in his new location on WAMU, where he hosts *The Derek McGinty Show* and co-hosts the popular local radio program *D.C. Politics Hour* with commentator Mark Plotkin. McGinty stays with WAMU until 1998.

When federal and city officials take Britain's Queen Elizabeth to visit families in Marshall Heights, neighborhood resident Alice Frazier greets the queen with a big hug, spurring headlines in newspapers around the world.

The U Street/Cardozo Metro station opens, stimulating the development of new businesses and restaurants along U Street.

Restoration of the abandoned and derelict Whitelaw Hotel begins. The renovated building houses low-cost apartments for moderate-income families.

1992

Delegate Eleanor Holmes Norton wins the right to vote in the House of Representatives and is appointed to serve on the Committee on the Reorganization of the Congress. Two years later the House votes to repeal the voting rights of the delegate representing the District of Columbia.

Maxine Waters—like Eleanor Holmes Norton—is one of a handful of black women in Congress. She is pictured here with former senator Paul Simon and actor Danny Glover.

July. 8 Rock, a community-based African American cultural center established by local artists and entrepreneurs, opens in Anacostia. The center features readings, poetry slams, and other cultural programs and literary events.

November. Senator Richard Shelby of Alabama proposes that the Senate legalize the death penalty in the nation's capital. Washington, D.C., residents vote down his initiative.

After completing his prison term, Marion Barry returns to Washington, D.C., and successfully runs for City Council against council member Wilhelmina Rolark for representation of Ward 8.

1993

January 20. William Jefferson Clinton is inaugurated as president.

January 24. Thurgood Marshall dies; he was the first African American to become a Supreme Court justice.

August 28. The thirtieth anniversary of the 1963 March on Washington is observed.

Statehood supporters establish Citizens for New Columbia, an organization established to educate people about the D.C. statehood movement. The leadership includes Congressman Walter Fauntroy, City Councilman John Ray, and longtime political activist Josephine Butler.

1994

January. Marion Barry marries Cora Masters, a political science professor at the University of the District of Columbia. Masters previously served as D.C.'s boxing commissioner until she was forced to step down in 1988 after being accused of double billing for travel expenses.

May 14. D.C. native Dolores Kendrick is appointed poet laureate of the District of Columbia. Kendrick, a former educator at the School Without Walls, is author of the award-winning *The Women of Plums: Poems in the Voices of Slave Women* (1989).

July 1. D.C. native Hugh Price (born in 1941) becomes CEO of the National Urban League.

October 23. Calvin Rolark dies. Rolark was a long-standing Washington political figure, publisher of the *Washington Informer,* and founder of the United Black Fund. He was well known for his folksy sayings, like "If it is to be, it is up to me" and "The only people who can save us, for us, is us."

November. Eleanor Holmes Norton is elected to her third term as D.C. delegate to the House of Representatives.

November. Marion Barry is elected mayor of D.C. after having defeated Mayor Sharon Pratt Kelly and at-large council member John Ray in the primary election. In the general election he defeats Republican Carol Schwartz for a second time. After the election, Barry urges those residents who express disappointment with his reelection to "just get over it."

To help alleviate the District's public housing crisis, D.C. Superior Court judge Steffen Graae decides that the housing authority be administered by a court-appointed receiver.

The first "Remembering U Street" festival is held, celebrating "Black Broadway's" historic vibrant nightlife from 1910 to 1960. Over 200 photographs documenting the heyday of U Street are displayed in an outdoor street exhibit.

Local literary and cultural group WritersCorps is founded. The organization places writers in public housing facilities to conduct writing programs and workshops. Five years later it receives the Presidential Committee on the Arts and Humanities "Coming Up Taller" Award.

Imani Temple, the home base for the African-American Catholic Congregations, opens on Capitol Hill at 609 Maryland Avenue NE. The congregation previously met in school auditoriums before finding its present location. Reverend George Augustus Stallings Jr., bishop of the church, considers it divine providence to find a site on Capitol Hill.

Renowned pianist and longtime D.C. resident Dr. Billy Taylor (born in 1921) becomes an artistic adviser for the Kennedy Center. His "Billy Taylor's Jazz at the Kennedy Center" becomes an annual event.

1995

April. Congress appoints the District of Columbia Financial Responsibility and Management Assistance Authority to oversee financial matters in the District government. The five-member control board will have authority to manage the District's budget. Stephen Harlan, Joyce A. Ladner, Constance B. Newman, and Edward A. Singletary are appointed as board members, and Andrew F. Brimmer serves as chairperson. Some city councilmembers complain that Brimmer and the control board make decisions without consulting them or other city officials.

September. Washington native Denyce Graves debuts at the Metropolitan Opera in what soon becomes a signature role of *Carmen*. A graduate of the Duke Ellington School of the Arts, the mezzo-soprano becomes an international star, performing in operas and concerts around the world.

October. Anthony Williams is appointed chief financial officer of the District of Columbia. Williams later holds a series of community meetings in each ward of the city to explain his plans for restoring the city's financial health. Williams's objectives include trimming the city budget and reducing the number of city employees.

October 16. The Million Man March, organized by Louis Farrakhan and the Nation of Islam, is held in Washington, D.C. The event is purported to have peaceably drawn 1 million African American men, to demonstrate inspiration concerning family, community, and unity. There is much debate about the number of men who actually gather; estimated counts range from 400,000 by the National Park Service to over 1 million by the event's organizers.

December 17. Dorothy Porter Wesley, pioneer librarian and bibliophile, dies.

Million Man March button.

Opera singer Denyce Graves.

The historic Anthony Bowen 12th Street YMCA building at 1816 12th Street NW, the first YMCA built for African Americans in the nation, is designated a National Historic Landmark. In 1972 the building was named the Anthony Bowen Branch of the Metropolitan Washington YMCA, in honor of its founder. It closed in 1982 and reopens in 2000 at 1325 W Street NW. The original building will become the Thurgood Marshall Center for Service and Heritage and home to the Shaw Heritage Center.

1996

The Armstrong Adult Education Center closes. This is the end of the old Armstrong Technical High School that opened in 1902.

Composer George Theophilus Walker receives the Pulitzer Prize in Music for his composition *Lilacs for Voice and Orchestra*. The following year Mayor Marion Barry declares June 17 to be George Walker Day in Washington, D.C.

Ron Brown, the first African American secretary of commerce, was killed in a plane crash in 1996.

November. Longtime political activist Sandy Allen is elected to the D.C. City Council for Ward 8, after defeating Eydie Whittington. Allen, born and raised in Ward 8, defeated Whittington on her second attempt at the office.

1997

January 20. William Jefferson Clinton is inaugurated as president for his second term.

WritersCorps creates the Youth Poetry Slam League in four D.C. middle schools. The group uses poetry slams and writing workshops to expose youths to creative writing. The group will soon expand to include teams based in the Bronx and San Francisco. Its first Bring in Da Slam rent party and spoken word poetry slam is held in the Borders Bookstore at 18th and L Streets NW.

1998

January. In what he regards as the crowning public achievement of his professional career, Chief Financial Officer Anthony Williams holds a press conference in which he releases an audit of the city budget that shows—instead of a deficit—a projected surplus of over $160 million.

April. Charles Ramsay is appointed chief of police in Washington, D.C.

May 21. Mayor Marion Barry announces that he will not seek office or run for reelection to the Mayor's office. He claims to have left a strong legacy to the city, including rebuilding the downtown area, providing Washington youths with more than 100,000 summer jobs, and increasing access to city jobs and city contracts to African Americans.

> Some people wrestle for dominance or authority, and they immediately attack and assert. . . . My approach, psychologically, from the time I was little, is to just let it ride, let it ride, and then—at the right moment—move in. You are going to get a lot more, coming in below the radar, and moving up, than if you just came in and got shot down from the beginning.
>
> —Anthony Williams

> I've had a lot of homers, a lot of triples, doubles and singles. More homers, more doubles, more triples than I've had strikeouts. More ups than downs.
> —Marion Barry, at his last mayoral press conference, December 30, 1998

July 18. The African American Civil War Memorial opens to the public. Located on historic U Street, the monument serves as memorial to black soldiers who volunteered to fight in the Civil War. The sculpture was designed by artist Ed Hamilton and includes on a *Wall of Honor* the names of the soldiers of the U.S. Colored Troops who served in the war.

November. Anthony Williams, a Harvard Law School graduate and chief financial officer of the District of Columbia, is elected mayor. His symbol is the bow tie, which he usually wears in his public appearances.

> I interviewed Tony Williams [for chief financial officer of the District of Columbia], . . . but I didn't spend enough time talking to him about the job.
> —Former D.C. mayor Marion Barry,
> The *Washington Post* magazine, June 4, 2000

Mayor Anthony Williams.

November. In an election-day upset, Adrian Fenty defeats longtime council member Charlene Drew Jarvis in the race for representing Ward 4 in the City Council.

Former U.S. Army General Colin Powell at the 1998 African American Civil War Memorial dedication.

If you buy books on the history of theater, the history of black theater is not there. White theater has been researched from the advertisements posted in the newspaper. But in black theater, groups would get together and perform, and would print up tickets and tack up posters on trees—and that's all that there was. So when those posters got destroyed, there was no written history of what happened. . . . Black people always had theater, [but] commercial theater for black people didn't get started until the 1900s. Instead, shows were performed in churches or community centers, in whatever space was available. These tickets provide insight into the kind of performances being organized, and into who might have been attending.

—Henry Whitehead,
The *Washington Post,* February 1, 1998

The True Reformer's Hall is purchased by the Public Welfare Foundation, and plans are made for its preservation and renovation.

2000

July. A demolition crew working to transform the former J. R. Giddings School building at 315 G Street SE, which housed one of the District's earliest schools for free African Americans, discovers approximately thirty theater tickets dating to 1889, announcing African American actors. The tickets advertise actress Louise A. Smith, "Introduced by the Honorable Frederick Douglass as the Only Colored Lady Dramatist." According to former Howard Theatre president Henry Preston Whitehead, the tickets are an unusual find.

Louisiana native and longtime political activist Donna Brazile serves as campaign manager during the final months of former vice president Al Gore's 2000 presidential campaign. In 1984 she served as deputy campaign manager for Jesse Jackson.

AFTERWORD

Washington, D.C., wears its history well. The future hangs in an open closet, waiting to be worn. As I write these words, our country is at war against Iraq. Security is once again a major concern for Washington residents. Life is different from previous years. We have become more cautious. Our nation is vulnerable to acts of terrorism. Still this city wakes, stretches, and goes about its business. No longer is Washington, D.C., a community of primarily African Americans. This city, this place I call my home, reflects the many colors of the world. It's a civic rainbow of new challenges. Enter the city by way of Reagan National Airport or Union Station and you'll encounter a "rosary" of cabdrivers speaking diverse languages. New immigrants are changing old black neighborhoods. The children of Frederick Douglass now go to school with people from Asia, Central America, Africa, and the Middle East.

Meanwhile, there are power shifts taking place and new political and economic partnerships forming. A growing gay community is helping to provide new meaning to our understanding of civil rights. This will require African Americans to be more tolerant and fight homophobia. We must embrace everyone who calls this city home. Washington is a symbol of democracy not only for the world but also for its own residents.

I came to Washington in 1968. I was a skinny kid from the South Bronx who enrolled at Howard University. Rumor has it that I came to the educational mecca to find a wife. My story is just one of many. New York at times seems to be a distant memory. I've raised two children since being in D.C. Like many ex-New Yorkers, I've discovered that there is a world beyond New Jersey. My interest and love for black history and literature has its beginnings in Washington. I can still remember the first time I heard Sterling A. Brown read his poems and tell his "lies" on Howard University's campus.

Washington, D.C., has been blessed with genius. Great men and women have walked our streets. We have the responsibility to remember and study the past. Here, where slaves once lived and segregation's chains held our hands, is also the place where Martin Luther King Jr. described his dream. Our city enters a new century where African Americans must renew their hope in a changing world. Our circles must remain unbroken. Our future is glorious and filled with light. Washington D.C., continues to be a bright morning star.

—E. Ethelbert Miller,
Howard University

BIOGRAPHIES

Numa Pompilius Garfield Adams (February 26, 1885–August 29, 1940). Numa P. G. Adams, born in Delaplane, Virginia, became Howard University Medical School's first black dean in 1929, under the administration of Howard's first black president, Mordecai Johnson. He also established the first residencies—including the surgical residency program in 1936—for doctors wishing to pursue specialties in medicine. As dean, Adams transformed the medical school by challenging instructors to pursue higher degrees, instituting stricter admissions standards, and seeking funding for advanced medical education.

Alexander Thomas Augusta (March 8, 1825–December 21, 1890). The physician Alexander Augusta experienced many firsts during his lifetime. In 1863 he was appointed surgeon of the army medical service and received the rank of major in the Union Army—the highest rank held by a black man at that time. From 1863 to 1864, Augusta headed Freedmen's Hospital, becoming the first black person in charge of a hospital in the United States. He later taught anatomy in Howard University's newly established Medical Department, making him the first black offered faculty membership of an American medical school. He served as dean of the medical faculty for ten years, leaving in 1877. Despite his military status and achievements, his application to join the D.C. Medical Society in 1869 was rejected. He is buried at Arlington Cemetery.

Pearl Bailey (March 29, 1918–August 17, 1990). A long-time D.C. resident, Pearl Bailey, born in Newport News, Virginia, was widely recognized as a jazz singer and an actress. Early in her career, she gained fame performing at two famous nightspots on D.C.'s historic U Street: Jungle Inn and Republic Gardens. Bailey's theatrical performances include *Hello, Dolly!* in 1967; she starred in the film *Porgy and Bess* in 1959.

Henry E. Baker (born c. 1859). Henry E. Baker, a Patent Office examiner, researched black inventors who had received patents. Finding over 400 black inventors, Baker compiled four large volumes of their patent drawings and specifications. Baker's research enabled black congressman George Washington Murray to produce the *Congressional Record* of black inventors and to present it before Congress in 1894. Baker was also an organizer of the Freedmen's Savings and Trust Company.

Benjamin Banneker (November 9, 1731–October 9, 1806). Benjamin Banneker, recognized as the first black man of science and the first to publish an almanac, was born in rural Maryland. A self-taught man, his independent study of mathematics and astronomy led him in 1753 to build a working clock without having seen one before, gaining him local fame. In 1791, despite being in his early sixties, he was chosen by Major Andrew Ellicott to help survey the boundaries for the nation's new capital, the District of Columbia, although poor health forced Banneker to leave the project after three months. The next year, using his own astronomical calculations, Banneker published his first almanac, which he continued to issue until

1797. That same year he sent then Secretary of State Thomas Jefferson a letter and astronomical calculations to challenge Jefferson's views of blacks' racial inferiority. Banneker's letter and Jefferson's response were published and distributed in a pamphlet. In 1970 a circle near L'Enfant Plaza in the District was named after Banneker.

George Bell (c. 1761–1843). George Bell, though illiterate and born a slave, dedicated most of his free life to educating blacks in D.C. In 1807 Bell, along with Nicholas Franklin and Moses Liverpool—all illiterate and recently freed slaves—built the Bell School, the first District schoolhouse for black children. Though the school closed shortly after opening, Bell later attempted to start another educational institution. In 1818 he and other District blacks organized the Resolute Beneficial Society to provide health and burial insurance for its members and for indigent blacks. They also established the Beneficial Society School, a free school for black children that operated in the former Bell School building until around 1822. The school's second instructor, John Adams, was the first black man to teach in the District.

Mary McLeod Bethune (July 10, 1875–May 18, 1955). The educator, political activist, and National Council of Negro Women founder Mary McLeod Bethune was born in South Carolina. In Florida the Daytona Educational and Industrial Institute, established by Bethune in 1904 for young black women, merged with Cookman Institute of Jacksonville to become Bethune-Cookman College. Bethune later became the college's president and received a NAACP Spingarn Medal for her achievements in education. In the early 1930s Bethune could be found in Washington, D.C., protesting segregation in store employment, along with other black Washingtonians. In 1935 she established the National Council of Negro Women, headquartered at her home. President Herbert Hoover appointed her to the Conference on Child Health and Protection. When President Franklin D. Roosevelt established the Office of Minority Affairs in 1936, he named Bethune its administrator; she was also appointed to direct the Division of Negro Affairs of the National Youth Administration. It was the highest government rank a black woman had ever held. In 1974 a commemorative statue of Bethune was erected in Lincoln Park; it was the first statue of an African American or a woman in the nation's capital.

Amanda (Mattie) R. Bowen (died February 1914). Amanda Bowen was born in Maryland and came to Washington during the Civil War to be an educator and a mission worker among the poor. She established the Sojourner Truth Home for Working Girls in 1895.

Anthony Bowen (1809–1871?). Born a slave in Maryland, Anthony Bowen actively committed himself to the improvement of black life in the District. Nine years after purchasing his freedom, Bowen and thirteen other black former members of Ebenezer Methodist Church formed the Wesley Zion Church on "the Island" in Southwest Washington. He organized the church's Sunday school and ran it from his house, which doubled as an Underground Railroad stop. In 1853 Bowen established the country's first YMCA for colored men, known as the 12th Street Branch. Also a clerk in the Patent Office, Bowen in 1863 joined Frederick Douglass and other prominent black Washingtonians in a massive effort to recruit black men into the military. Two companies of black troops were formed as a result.

Benjamin Griffith Brawley (April 22, 1882–February 1, 1939). The author and educator Benjamin Brawley, born in Columbia, South Carolina, became one of the most published, renowned scholars of his time. A professor of English at Howard University from 1910 to 1912 and 1931 to 1939, he taught literature with a focus on black writers and artists. Brawley published seventeen books, including *A Social History of the American Negro* (1921) and *Early Negro American Writers* (1935). He penned essays, book reviews, and articles on literature, drama, music, and African American history. He also wrote six poetry chapbooks. In 1927 Brawley refused a prestigious Harmon Foundation award for excellence in education. On the day of Brawley's funeral, Howard University stopped classes and activities in his honor.

Arthur Brooks (November 25, 1861–September 7, 1926). Arthur Brooks spent an active career in the military and served as confidant to several presidents. From 1888 to 1918 Captain Brooks commanded the Colored High School Cadet Corps, succeeding the group's founder, Major Christian Fleetwood. In 1897 he was appointed commander of the 1st Separate Battalion of the D.C. National Guard, where he served until 1912. Major Brooks's many positions at the White House—particularly, custodian of the Executive Mansion—made him a witness to many important events at the White House.

Ron Brown (August 1, 1941–April 3, 1996). Ronald Harmon Brown was born in Washington, D.C. His father,

William Brown, was the manager of the Hotel Theresa in Harlem. Because of his father's position, Brown was exposed to many important black celebrities while growing up. After graduating from college and serving in the military, Brown attended law school at St. John's University. He began working at the Urban League in 1968 and was named director of the National Urban League's Washington office in 1973. He became a lobbyist on Capitol Hill in 1981 and was elected chairman of the Democratic National Committee in 1989. In 1993 Brown was appointed as the secretary of the U.S. Department of Commerce. He died in a plane crash on April 3, 1996.

Solomon G. Brown (February 14, 1829?–1906). Solomon G. Brown served in several assistantships at the city post office; he was also an assistant to the Morse code developer, Samuel F. B. Morse. During the installment of the first magnetic telegraph linking Washington and Baltimore, Brown reportedly carried the first telegraphed message to the White House. From 1852 to 1906, Brown worked in the foreign exchange and transportation divisions of the newly created Smithsonian Institution. A self-taught man, Brown produced Smithsonian illustrations and diagrams, which he used as he lectured widely on natural history. Brown became the president of the National Union League in 1866. He served three one-year terms in the House of Delegates, Territorial Government of D.C., representing Hillsdale (Anacostia) residents. Brown also wrote and published poetry.

Sterling Allen Brown (May 1, 1901–January 13, 1989). The poet and literary critic Sterling Brown was born to Reverend Sterling Nelson Brown, a Lincoln Memorial Temple Congregational Church pastor and a former Howard University faculty member. An English professor at Howard from 1929 to 1969, Brown published his first book of poetry, *Southern Road,* in 1932. Over forty years later, his second, *The Last Ride of Wild Bill and Eleven Narrative Poems* (1975), was published. From 1936 to 1939, Brown served as the editor of Negro Affairs at the WPA Federal Writers Project, where he was instrumental in refocusing WPA slave interviews to concentrate on the former slaves' day-to-day lives. In 1941 Brown edited *The Negro Caravan.* Brown received several honors: a 1975 Guggenheim Fellowship for Creative Writing, honorary degrees from several colleges, and the first poet laureate of the District of Columbia in 1984. Though *The Collected Poems of Sterling A. Brown* (1980) was published late in Brown's career, it won him excellent reviews and much recognition.

Blanche Kelso Bruce (March 1, 1841–March 17, 1898). Blanche K. Bruce, a Virginia-born politician, became the second black person elected to the U.S. Senate and the first to serve a full term, representing Mississippi from 1875 to 1881. Though born a slave, Bruce had the rare opportunity to gain a formal education. During the Civil War, he taught and founded a school for blacks in Kansas. Known for his political savvy, Senator Bruce quickly became a dominant figure in Washington, especially among the black political and social elite. During his term, he conducted an investigation into the bankruptcy of the National Freedmen's Savings and Trust Company. After his Senate term, Bruce served in two of the highest presidential-appointed positions reserved for blacks at the time: register of the Treasury (1881–1885; 1897) and recorder of deeds for the District of Columbia (1889). These positions put Bruce in an advantageous economic and political position from which to launch his real estate and insurance ventures. He became one of the District's wealthiest residents.

Ralph Johnson Bunche (August 7, 1903–December 9, 1971). The civil rights activist and diplomat Ralph Bunche, born in Detroit, was the first African American to win a Nobel Prize. In 1945 he also became the first African American to become a State Department division head. Bunche created and chaired Howard University's Political Science Department. He participated in the Dumbarton Oaks Conference in 1944 in Washington and helped organize the United Nations. Bunche's more than twenty years of peacekeeping efforts with the UN earned him many distinctions, including the 1950 Nobel Peace Prize. Bunche also rallied for civil rights, organizing protests, working with the NAACP, and participating in the 1963 March on Washington and the 1965 Selma-to-Montgomery Voting Rights March.

Nannie Helen Burroughs (May 2, 1879–May 20, 1961). An educator and a feminist, Nannie Helen Burroughs helped to found the National Association of Colored Women in 1896. In the early 1900s Burroughs worked with the National Baptist Convention (NBC) in Pennsylvania and Kentucky. Her speech "How the Sisters Are Hindered from Helping," delivered at the NBC in 1900, made way for the development of the Woman's Convention, which allowed black women to discuss social, religious, and political issues. In 1909 Burroughs established the National Training School for Women and Girls (renamed the Nannie Helen Burroughs School in 1964) in the Lincoln Heights section of Washington. Her goal was to educate students in industrial skills and in the "three Bs": bible, bath, and broom. Burroughs managed the school until her death. In addition to her organizational duties, she authored two church plays in the 1920s: *The Slabtown District Convention,* a satirical comedy focusing on the early black Baptist church conventions; and *Where Is My Wandering Boy Tonight?* used for Mother's Day programming in the churches.

Francis Louis Cardozo (February 1, 1837–July 22, 1903). Francis Louis Cardozo, educator, minister, and former South Carolina secretary of state, helped shape Preparatory (later M Street) High School into the country's top educational institution for blacks. After briefly teaching Latin at Howard University, from 1871 to 1872, Cardozo worked with the Treasury Department in 1877. He became Preparatory High School's principal in 1884. Despite his accomplishments there, Cardozo departed the school in 1896 after a campaign by *Washington Bee* editor William Calvin Chase to oust him. In 1928 Cardozo Business High School, a business/vocational school named in his honor, opened in Washington.

William Warrick Cardozo (April 6, 1905–August 11, 1962). William Warrick Cardozo, the grandson of the educator Francis L. Cardozo, was a pioneer in the research of sickle cell anemia. In 1937 Cardozo practiced medicine in D.C. and was an instructor at the Howard University College of Medicine and at Freedmen's Hospital. For twenty-four years he was a school medical inspector for the D.C. Board of Health. His sickle cell research showed the disease's high probability of being inherited and its prevalence in African descendants.

Mary Ann Shadd Cary (October 9, 1823–June 5, 1893). Mary Ann Shadd Cary, the Delaware-born abolitionist journalist and educator, became the first woman to earn a law degree from Howard University's Law School in 1870 and the first African American woman to become an attorney in the United States. In 1870 Cary's attendance at the Woman Suffrage Convention in Washington, D.C., led to her petitioning the Judiciary Committee of the House of Representatives for the right to vote. She was one of the few women to register to vote in 1871. Cary founded the Colored Women's Progressive Franchise Association in 1880, which rallied black women to address their specific political and economic concerns.

Albert Irvin Cassell (1895–November 30, 1969). The Maryland-native Albert I. Cassell became one of the most prominent African American architects and engineers during his lifetime. In the 1920s he launched a successful career as an instructor and later the head of Howard University's Department of Architecture. He designed many of Howard's buildings: the gymnasium, the armory, and the athletic field (1924); the College of Medicine building (1926); three women's dormitories (1931); the chemistry building (1933); Founders Library (1938); and with architect William A. Hazel, the home economics building (1921) and the Frederick Douglass Memorial Hall (1935). He also designed the Masonic Temple (1930), the Odd Fellows Temple (1932), and the James Creek Alley Housing Development (1940–1941). In 1934 Cassell helped to create the College of Applied Science (later, College of Engineering and Architecture). From 1942 to 1946, Cassell designed the Mayfair Mansions housing development, buying the land with his own money. The design won him an award from the D.C. Board of Trade's Committee on Municipal Art.

William Calvin Chase (February 2, 1854–January 3, 1921). A Washingtonian, William Calvin Chase, known to be an opinionated and outspoken advocate for black rights, also had a successful newspaper career. In his early writings Chase spoke out about what he believed to be the corruption of black schools by school officials, resulting in the departure of the M Street High School principal Francis L. Cardozo. Starting in 1882, Chase published and edited the *Washington Bee,* a weekly newspaper that he continued to bring out for thirty-nine years. His abrasive words caused him to be indicted for libel several times (he labeled W. E. B. DuBois a "water-brained theorist" and Booker T. Washington an "accommodating apologist"). However, the *Bee* quickly became one of the country's most important black newspapers, reporting on key issues such as racism, politics concerning blacks, race riots, and lynchings.

William Montague Cobb (October 12, 1904–November 20, 1990). A graduate of Howard University Medical School, the D.C. native William Montague Cobb became well known for his physical anthropology research and writings, which challenged theories of racial inferiority. He was a popular professor of anatomy at Freedmen's Hospital for over forty years. Also an eminent historian and author, he published several articles on black history.

Dr. Cobb was at heart an educator and an activist, serving vigorous presidencies in such organizations as the Anthropological Society of Washington, the Medico-Chirurgical Society of D.C., and the NAACP. Dr. Cobb led efforts to integrate the medical profession in the District and to convince the American Medical Association to prohibit racial discrimination in its local affiliates. He also organized the medical services for the 1965 March on Selma, led by Dr. Martin Luther King Jr. Dr. Cobb published over 600 articles in professional journals. Even after he retired in the early 1970s, he continued to be an active educator, serving as a visiting professor and a consultant at several universities, until his death.

George F. T. Cook (June 18, 1835–August 7, 1912). George F. T. Cook, a former slave and the son of Reverend John Francis Cook, was appointed as superintendent of District Colored Schools in D.C. from 1868 to 1900. During Cook's term as superintendent, education for black students greatly improved. In addition to being offered a wide range of instruction, they were taken on field trips to the Library of Congress, Congress, and other places of interest.

Helen Appo Cook (1837–November 20, 1913). Helen Appo Cook, along with other socially and politically active Washington women like Charlotte Forten Grimké and Anna Julia Cooper, founded and presided over the Colored Women's League of Washington, D.C., in 1892. The league organized relief efforts for destitute black families, led the struggle for improved sanitation in alley dwellings, and fought for better public schools for black children. The organization introduced kindergartens into the colored public school system as well. Cook also helped to establish the National Association of Colored Women. The wife of John F. Cook Jr., she was instrumental in building the Sumner School in 1871.

John Francis Cook (1810?–March 21, 1855). In 1843 the educator John F. Cook was ordained as the first black Presbyterian minister in the District. Cook, an ex-slave born in the District, studied at the Columbian Institute and secured a clerk job. Around age twenty-four, he became the director of the institute and renamed it Union Seminary. He developed a rigorous course of classical and practical studies, making the seminary equivalent to a high school. Some of the District's white citizens, threatened by Cook's efforts to educate blacks, destroyed his school dur-

ing the 1835 Snow Riot. Cook sought protection in Pennsylvania, where he built another school. Upon his return to the District in 1836, Cook became the secretary of the Convention of the Free People of Color in Washington, D.C. In 1841 members of Israel Bethel A.M.E. Church, led by Reverend Cook and Charles Stewart, formally organized the Fifteenth Street Presbyterian Church, the first such denomination in the District. In 1843 Cook was elected the church's first pastor and created a school there, serving both until his death. Reverend Cook was survived by his three sons: John Jr.; George, who ran the church school until its closing in 1867; and Samuel, a District physician.

John Francis Cook Jr. (September 21, 1833–January 20, 1910). John F. Cook Jr., a son of Reverend John F. Cook, was among the first blacks to be elected to citywide District positions in 1868. After serving as a clerk in the city tax collector's office, the D.C. Office of the Justice of Peace, and other government offices, Cook became the District tax collector from 1874 to 1888 and was also elected to the Board of Aldermen. During his day, Cook became one of the wealthiest and most prominent black men in the city.

Will Marion Cook (January 27, 1869–July 19, 1944). The son of the Howard University Law School dean John Hartwell Cook, Will Marion Cook was a musical prodigy. After attending the Oberlin Conservatory of Music and studying in Berlin, he made his debut as a concert violinist in 1889 in Washington. The next year Cook became the director of the American Orchestra Club, a musical club and performing group organized by the black military leader Major Christian Fleetwood. In collaboration with the poet Paul Laurence Dunbar in 1898, Cook wrote the musical score for *Clorindy, the Origin of the Cake Walk*, which became a Broadway hit. Under the name Will Marion, he composed for the vaudeville team of Bert Williams and George Walker; *In Dahomey* (1902) was a popular favorite. In the early 1900s he held several "Home Concerts" in Washington, showcasing black performers who had gotten their start in the city. Cook also published *A Collection of Negro Songs* in 1912. Mercer, the son of Cook and his singer and actress wife, Abbie Mitchell, was a well-known Howard University professor.

Anna Julia Haywood Cooper (August 10, 1858–February 29, 1964). The educator Anna Julia Cooper was born a slave in Raleigh, North Carolina. In the early 1880s she was one of the black Washingtonians who met weekly to discuss politics, literature, and the arts in the "Saturday Circle" or the "Saturday Nighters." In 1892 Cooper and Helen Appo Cook founded the Colored Women's League of Washington, D.C., an organization responsible for organizing relief efforts for destitute black families. In 1893 she co-hosted with the abolitionist Frederick Douglass and the educator Lucy Ellen Moten a lecture by the anti-lynching activist Ida B. Wells at the Metropolitan A.M.E. Church. Cooper was the only woman elected a member of the American Negro Academy. Following Robert H. Terrell's resignation as the principal of M Street High School in 1900, where she taught, Cooper became the school's second black female principal, serving in this position from 1901 until 1906. In 1929 she also became the second president of Frelinghuysen University in Washington, D.C. Sadly, the university—founded in 1907 for the education of the black working population—operated for only a short time.

Alexander Crummell (March 3, 1819–September 10, 1898). Alexander Crummell, a clergyman, was an early black nationalist who believed that Christianization and education could empower and civilize blacks in the United States and Africa. From 1853 until 1861, he and his family lived in Liberia, performing missionary work. Crummell took over St. Mary's Episcopal Church in D.C. in 1873, increasing its membership. In 1880 Reverend Crummell founded St. Luke's Episcopal Church and served as the church's rector until 1894. In protest of the lack of African American bishops in the Episcopal Church in 1883, he organized the Conference of Church Workers Among Colored People. In 1897 he established in D.C. the American Negro Academy, an organization to promote African American scholarship, create archives for black research, and encourage the publishing of scholarly work. Reverend Crummell also founded the Minister's Union in the District and the Commission on Work Among Colored People, an interracial Episcopalian organization.

Joseph O. Curtis (died 199?). The photographer Joseph O. Curtis spent thirty years photographing his beloved neighborhood of Southwest Washington. He received his first camera at a young age and began photographing city life in the 1920s. When Southwest was demolished between 1954 and 1960 for urban renewal, Curtis's many images became a nostalgic reminder of a vanished community.

Benjamin Oliver Davis (July 1, 1877–1970). A native Washingtonian, Benjamin O. Davis was appointed as brigadier general in the U.S. Army in 1940, making him the first African American awarded the rank of general. He served in Cuba and in the Philippines.

Benjamin Oliver "Chappie" Davis Jr. (December 18, 1912–July 4, 2002). The D.C.-born Benjamin O. "Chappie" Davis Jr., like his father, was one of the nation's top-ranking African American military leaders. Davis was the second African American to become a U.S. military general and was the first black in the U.S. Air Force to become a lieutenant general. He became a four-star general in 1998.

Shelby James Davidson (May 10, 1868–1931). The Kentucky-born scientist Shelby J. Davidson arrived in the District in 1887 and began working in the auditing department of the U.S. Post Office Department. His fascination with machinery led him to patent a rewind device for adding machines in 1908, after spending two years designing it. The device was used in Davidson's line of work.

Owen Vincent Dodson (November 28, 1914–June 21, 1983). In 1947 Owen Dodson began teaching at Howard University and chaired the Drama Department from 1957 to 1967. In 1949 Dodson led the Howard Players to tour fourteen European cities. During his life, Dodson acted, wrote, produced, and directed over 100 plays. He also published poetry compilations and novels, and one of his short stories received a Paris Review Award. *Owen's Song,* a production featuring a compilation of Dodson's plays, poems, and stories, was performed at D.C.'s Colony Theatre in 1972 and at the Kennedy Center in 1974.

Frederick Douglass (February 1817? 1818?–February 20, 1895). Frederick Douglass escaped from bondage in Maryland to become a world-renowned abolitionist, orator, newspaper editor, and community and political leader. He published the *North Star* (1847) and the *Douglass Monthly* (1859) and edited the *New National Era* (1870). His autobiographical publications include *My Bondage and My Freedom.* He was twice invited to the White House to discuss war matters with President Lincoln, including the disparity in pay and rank of black and white soldiers. Douglass became the first black person to be assigned to a presidential-appointed position and served in several other important posts: secretary of the commission to investigate the feasibility of a U.S. annexation of Santo Domingo (1870); marshal of the District of Columbia (1877–1881); recorder of deeds for the District of Columbia (1881); and minister and consul general to Haiti (1889–1891). In 1874 Douglass became the president of Freedmen's Savings and Trust Company, but the bank's financial instability proved to be an embarrassment to him. The bank closed shortly after his term. In 1877 Douglass purchased land on Cedar Hill, a farm in Uniontown (now Anacostia), becoming one of the area's first black landowners and residents. His funeral at the Metropolitan A.M.E. Church was attended by thousands.

Joseph Henry Douglass (July 3, 1871–December 16, 1935). Joseph Henry Douglass, a grandson of the abolitionist Frederick Douglass, became the first black violinist to perform transcontinentally. At an early age he taught himself to play the violin, which both his father and grandfather had played. Douglass performed with Major Christian Fleetwood's American Orchestral Club around 1891, becoming its director in 1892. He also directed the New Republic Theater orchestra, in 1921. His wife, Fannie Howard Douglass, a pianist and a D.C. public school teacher, sometimes performed with him. During his career, Douglass, who was the first to head the violin department at Howard University's School of Music, gave performances at every institution for the education of blacks.

Charles Richard Drew (June 3, 1904–April 1, 1950). Charles Drew, one of the District's most celebrated figures, was known for his groundbreaking research in blood plasma. Dr. Drew was one of five Howard University Medical School faculty members selected to participate in a Rockefeller Foundation–funded fellowship, which enabled him to pursue postgraduate studies at Columbia University, 1938–1940. There, he wrote a dissertation that established him as the nation's leading expert on blood preservation. Dr. Drew returned to Howard as a professor of surgery and later as the head of the Medical School's Department of Surgery. He also served in several top appointments at Freedmen's Hospital. In 1944 he was appointed an examiner by the American Board of Surgery, becoming the first black to hold this position. During World War II, Dr. Drew modified the technology for producing blood plasma so that it could be mass-produced for shipment to British soldiers and air-raid victims. He also served as the director of the American Red Cross Blood

Bank before returning to Freedmen's Hospital. In 1950 Dr. Drew had a fatal car accident while en route to an Alabama medical conference. Despite stories to the contrary, he was not denied emergency entry to medical facilities; he received emergency medical attention but died due to injuries from the accident.

Robert Todd Duncan (February 12, 1903–February 28, 1998). The actor and classical singer Robert Todd Duncan was born in Danville, Kentucky. He taught at Howard University from 1931 to 1945 and operated a voice studio in D.C. late in his career. Duncan made his opera debut as a baritone in New York, performing in Mascagni's *Cavalleria Rusticana*. He starred in the role of Porgy in 1932 in the Gershwin musical *Porgy and Bess*. In 1972 Duncan performed the title role in *Job* at the Kennedy Center. His talents were recognized with many honors, including an NAACP award, the 1945 President of Haiti's Medal of Honor and Merit, and a celebratory concert held by the Washington Performing Arts Society in 1978.

William Clarence "Billy" Eckstine (July 8, 1914–March 8, 1993). The singer Billy Eckstine, born in Pennsylvania, attended Armstrong High School in Washington, D.C. He began his professional singing career in D.C. nightclubs and in the early 1930s performed in many other cities with jazz great Earl Hines. He formed his own band, which featured such notables as "Dizzy" Gillespie, Charlie Parker, and Sarah Vaughan. Eckstine's band was significant in exploring bebop music during the transition from swing to bop. Some of his most famous recordings include "Jelly, Jelly"; "My Foolish Heart"; and "A Prisoner of Love."

Edward Kennedy "Duke" Ellington (April 29, 1899–May 24, 1974). The Washingtonian Duke Ellington has been called the single most important figure in jazz history. An Armstrong High School graduate, he earned the nickname "Duke" at an early age because of his stylish dress. In 1917 he formed his first band, a trio called Duke's Serenaders. The band performed at the True Reformers Hall in Washington, while Ellington became a band contractor in the city. In 1923 he formed a five-member band called the Washingtonians, which relocated to New York to perform. By 1927 Ellington was directing an eleven-member band at the famous Cotton Club, with performances being broadcast each evening on the radio. His time at the club was productive: he recorded over 160 compositions between 1928 and 1931. Ellington composed five film scores, as well as a ballet for Alvin Ailey and the American Ballet Theater. Ellington's honors and achievements were innumerable: he received sixteen honorary doctorates, honors from two U.S. presidents, a 1959 NAACP Spingarn Medal, and a host of music awards, including three Grammys. In the District, Western High School was renamed the Duke Ellington School of the Arts, and the Calvert Street Bridge was renamed the Duke Ellington Bridge. In 1986 the U.S. Postal Service issued a commemorative stamp in his honor.

James Reese "Jim" Europe (February 22, 1881–May 9, 1919). The conductor and composer James Reese Europe, born in Mobile, Alabama, became one of the most influential figures in early jazz history. Europe learned to play the violin, possibly under the tutelage of concert violinist Joseph Henry Douglass. He spent a large portion of his career in New York, where he performed on the piano and became the music director for several shows. As the director during World War I of the U.S. 15th Infantry Band, Lieutenant Europe introduced brass-band jazz to major European cities under the Allies. Called the "Hellfighters," Europe's band included members from the United States and Puerto Rico. In the 1920s Europe toured with musician, producer, and theater owner Ford T. Dabney. He and Dabney were credited with creating the fox trot, the turkey trot, the castle trot, and other famous dances. While at a concert in Boston, a band member attacked Europe, causing his death. He was given a public funeral in New York City—the first ever for an African American in the city. He was buried in Arlington Cemetery.

Lillian "Madame Evanti" Evans Tibbs (August 12, 1890–December 7, 1967). Born in Washington, D.C., Lillian Evans Tibbs became an internationally acclaimed opera singer. Her parents instructed her in music at an early age, making her locally famous. Upon finishing her education at Miner Teachers College and the Howard University School of Music, she toured under the name Madame Evanti. In 1925 she made her professional debut in Europe, singing with the Paris Opera Company. In addition to her performances in Europe, Madame Evanti performed in the United States and South America. Some memorable performances include her invitation to sing at the White House for Presidents Harry S. Truman and Dwight D. Eisenhower and her 1943 role in *La Traviata* with the National Negro Opera Company.

Rudolph Fisher (May 9, 1897–December 16, 1934). The poet Langston Hughes described the Washington native Rudolph Fisher as the "wittiest" of the Harlem Renaissance writers. He spent much of his adult life in New York, dividing his time between a career in medicine and his pursuits in fiction writing. In 1925 he published four short stories, one of which was reprinted in *Best Short Stories of 1925.* He again received that honor in 1934. One of Fisher's two novels, *The Conjure-Man Dies: A Mystery Tale of Dark Harlem* (1932), was recognized as the first detective novel published by an African American. Fisher's *Conjur' Man Dies,* a play based on his first novel, was produced in New York in 1936. After his death, much of his work was forgotten until 1956, when the poet and Howard University professor Sterling Brown encouraged one of his students to write a prose study of Fisher.

James H. Fleet (?–1861). James H. Fleet was a former slave trained in medicine by the American Colonization Society, which endeavored to send African Americans back to Africa. However, Fleet refused to immigrate to Liberia in 1834. The next year he became involved with the black convention movement, and the year after, in 1836, he established a school for free blacks. Though the school was burned down in 1843, Fleet opened a new one and remained there until his retirement in 1851. A local political leader, he was also a popular performer, playing the flute, the guitar, and the piano with his wife and accompanist, Hermione.

Christian Abraham Fleetwood (July 21, 1840–September 28, 1914). The military hero Christian A. Fleetwood was born in Baltimore, Maryland, to free black parents. Like the educator James H. Fleet, he was educated with support from the American Colonization Society, though, unlike Fleet, he did travel to Liberia in 1856. From 1857 to 1860, Fleetwood was a student at the Ashmun Institute (Lincoln University) and in 1860 founded a short-lived newspaper, the *Lyceum Observer.* For his bravery while serving as a sergeant major in the 4th Regiment, U.S. Colored Volunteer Infantry, Major Fleetwood received a Congressional Medal of Honor. From 1881 to 1914, he served as a clerk in the War Department and in 1887 was commissioned a major in the Washington Cadet Corps of the National Guard. He also organized the American Orchestra Club, a musical club and performing group. Fleetwood and his wife, Sara Iredell, became one of Washington's most influential black couples.

Sara Iredell Fleetwood (April 17, 1841–February 1, 1908). Sara Iredell Fleetwood, a graduate of the Institute for Colored Youth in Philadelphia, trained under Dr. Daniel Hale Williams at Freedmen's Hospital Training School. She was in Freedmen's first graduating class of nurses in 1896. Five years later she became the first black superintendent of the Training School for Nurses. In 1907 Fleetwood was the first and only black woman to be appointed to the Nurses Examining Board of the District of Columbia. An incorporator and member of the Colored Woman's League, she distributed clothes to the needy during the 1893 depression. Married to Major Christian Fleetwood, she hosted weekly literary meetings at their Washington home.

Edward Franklin Frazier (September 24, 1894–May 17, 1962). The sociologist E. Franklin Frazier left a legacy of research and publications on race relations, family life, black youth, and the black middle class that would serve scholars for years to come. The Baltimore-born scholar attended Howard University's College of Arts and Sciences, graduating with honors in 1916. In 1934 he became a professor and the chair of Howard's Sociology Department and directed the Social Work Program from 1935 to 1943. Frazier, who reorganized the department and significantly increased its enrollment, earned the nickname "Forceful Frazier" from his students. He later became a member of Howard's newly created program in African studies. Frazier wrote numerous articles and books, including *Black Bourgeoisie* (1957). In 1942 he was appointed a Library of Congress Resident Fellow and founded and presided over the District of Columbia Sociological Society from 1943 to 1944. He also presided over the American Sociological Society, becoming the first African American president of a majority-white professional organization. From 1951 to 1953, Frazier was the chief of the Division of Applied Sciences of the United Nations Educational, Scientific, and Cultural Organizations (UNESCO).

Daniel Freeman (1868–after 1919?). The Alexandria-born photographer Daniel Freeman, who opened his first studio in Washington, D.C., in 1885, claimed to be the first black photographer in the city. Freeman, who studied under the District photographer E. S. Pullman, captured images in D.C. from 1881 to 1919. He also founded the Washington Amateur Art Society. At the 1895 Cotton States Expositions in Atlanta, he installed the exhibit of the District of Columbia in the Negro Building.

Marvin Gaye (April 2, 1939–April 1, 1984). The singer Marvin Pentz Gay Jr. (later, Marvin Gaye) grew up in Washington, where he sang in his father's church choir and in school was trained in drumming and the piano. He also performed with neighborhood R&B bands. In 1961 Gaye signed a record deal with Motown, where he gained fame as an R&B recording artist. Notable songs include "What's Going On" and "Stubborn Kind of Fellow"; he also recorded "I Heard It Through the Grapevine" and "Ain't No Mountain High Enough" with Tammi Terrell. Gaye's father fatally shot him the day before his forty-fifth birthday, in 1984.

Charles Manuel "Daddy" Grace (1881?–January 12, 1960). Bishop "Daddy" Grace founded the United House of Prayer for All People in 1926. The church was said to have more than 3 million members in more than sixty cities. In the 1920s the national headquarters of the United House of Prayer for All People was established in the nation's capital.

Richard Theodore Greener (January 30, 1844–May 2, 1922). Richard T. Greener, born in Philadelphia, was the first African American to graduate from Harvard University (1870). He also served as the dean of the Howard University Law School for a year before working in the Treasury Department and practicing law in the District. From 1872 to 1873, Greener was the interim principal of Preparatory High School. In 1873 he became the principal of Sumner High School, served as associate editor of the *New National Era*, and worked in the U.S. attorney's office for the District of Columbia.

James M. Gregory (?–January 1916). James M. Gregory, the first graduate of Howard University, began teaching there in 1868. In 1886 he terminated his presidency at the New Jersey Street Manual Training and Industrial School to become a trustee of the D.C. public schools.

Thomas Montgomery Gregory (August 31, 1887–November 21, 1971). Thomas Montgomery Gregory was born in Washington, D.C., in 1887 and founded Howard University's student drama group, the Howard Players. He was its director until 1924. Gregory taught at Howard beginning in 1910 and served as a professor of public speaking and the director of dramatic arts at Howard. With the scholar and black arts advocate Alain Locke, Gregory co-edited *Plays of Negro Life: Source Book of American Negro Drama,* published in 1927.

Angelina Weld Grimké (February 27, 1880–June 10, 1958). Angelina Weld Grimké was an educator, a playwright, and the author of poetry and short stories. Grimké, born in Boston, was the daughter of the prominent attorney Archibald Grimké and the grandniece of the white abolitionists Angelina Grimké Weld and Sarah Grimké. In 1902 she began teaching English at Armstrong Manual Training School and later taught at Dunbar High School. In 1916 her play *Rachel* was produced by the NAACP at Miner School. The play dramatized the life of a woman who refused to have children, fearing to raise them in a racist society—a theme evident in some of Grimké's poetry. Though *Rachel* was criticized by some as race propaganda, the scholar W. E. B. DuBois and the drama educator T. Montgomery Gregory acclaimed it as the country's first successful black drama.

Archibald Henry Grimké (August 17, 1849–February 25, 1930). The lawyer Archibald H. Grimké became active in D.C. community politics—especially relating to public schools—which earned him a prestigious NAACP Spingarn Medal in 1919. The brother of Reverend Francis James Grimké, he was born a slave in South Carolina, his father a white man and his mother a slave. Grimké served as the third president of the American Negro Academy (1903–1919), following the terms of the scholar W. E. B. DuBois and the clergyman Alexander Crummell. He also helped to form the NAACP, serving as the president of its local branch from 1914 to 1923. In 1916 Grimké, along with many black political activists in Washington, protested the increase of segregation in the District in front of the House District Committee. Grimké also openly opposed segregated training for blacks during WWI and supported A. Philip Randolph's socialist and unionist organizing.

Francis James Grimké (November 4, 1850?–October 11, 1937). Francis James Grimké, distinguished clergyman, was born to a slave mother and a white father in South Carolina. The brother of lawyer Archibald H. Grimké, he married Charlotte Forten, the daughter of the Philadelphia abolitionist John Forten. In 1878 Grimké was appointed as pastor of the Fifteenth Street Presbyterian

Church, a hub for Washington's elite colored society. Grimké retired in 1925 but remained active at the church and other institutions until his death. Grimké helped to found the Afro-Presbyterian Council in 1893. Recommended to succeed the former white Howard University president John B. Gordon, Grimké served on the university's board from 1880 to 1925. He helped to establish the American Negro Academy in 1905. In 1917 Grimké publicly refused to purchase Liberty Bonds, on the basis that the country discriminated against its own citizens.

Julia West Hamilton (1866–February 22, 1958). Julia West Hamilton was an avid church and civic activist in the District of Columbia, for which she received a 1948 D.C. Citizen's Award. She was active in Metropolitan A.M.E. Church, served as the president of the Phillis Wheatley YWCA for twenty-eight years, and filled leadership positions in several black women's organizations, including the Vicinity Federation of Women's Clubs and the National Association of Colored Women. In 1938 the Julia West Hamilton League was created, its motto being "The only gift is a portion of thyself." In 1969 Julia West Hamilton Junior High School in Northeast Washington was named in her honor. Colonel West A. Hamilton, the son of Julia Hamilton and her husband, John Alexander Hamilton, was also a well-known figure in the city, serving on the District Board of Education and operating a popular publishing business on U Street.

James Albert Handy (June 1, 1881–?). James A. Handy, born in Maryland, served as a bishop of the African Methodist Episcopal Church. He was a member of the House of Delegates of the D.C. territorial government from 1871 to 1873.

William Leo Hansberry (1894–October 17, 1965). In 1922 William Leo Hansberry, the director of Howard University's Department of History, was the first in the nation to teach a college course on African history. Born in Gloster, Mississippi, and known as the "father of African history," Hansberry pursued a life of intense, dedicated scholarship in ancient African civilizations. At Howard, over 800 students were enrolled in his three courses on African history, and among his students was the future Nigerian president and notable journalist Nnamdi Azikiwe. Despite Hansberry's groundbreaking scholarship, he faced opposition at Howard University because of his unorthodox theories on ancient African history. Though he was a premier Africanist, he was not chosen to teach in Howard's African studies program, established in 1959. He did, however, receive much recognition for his work, such as a 1953 Fulbright Research Scholarship to Africa and in 1960 an honorary degree from the University of Nigeria (the second conferred); in 1963 Hansberry College of African Studies, University of Nigeria, was named in his honor; and in 1964 he was awarded the Haile Selassie Trust Prize for African Research. Upon his death, he left unfinished a comprehensive five-volume work on African history.

Patricia Roberts Harris (May 31, 1924–March 23, 1985). A Howard University graduate and an Illinois native, Patricia Roberts Harris became the first black female cabinet member. She served as the secretary of Housing and Urban Development (HUD) from 1977 until 1979 during the Carter administration. In 1949 she was the assistant director of the American Council on Human Rights. In 1960 she became a lawyer with the U.S. Department of Justice. She also served Howard University as a faculty member and as the dean of the Law School. Though she resigned after only thirty days of tenure, the appointment made Roberts the first black woman to head a U.S. law school. From 1979 to 1981, she was the secretary of the Department of Health, Education, and Welfare. In 1982 she ran for mayor of the District of Columbia but lost to Marion Barry. In 2000 a U.S. postage stamp was issued, commemorating her life.

William Henry Harrison Hart (1857–January 1934). A prominent attorney and a civil rights advocate, William Henry Harrison Hart was born in Eufaula, Alabama. He served as a law professor at Howard University from 1890 to 1922, becoming the chair of criminal law in 1890 and the dean of agriculture in 1897. From 1893 to 1897, he was the assistant librarian of Congress. He founded the Hart Farm School for Colored Boys and the Junior Republic for Dependent Children, located on the Potomac River, in 1897. A man of diverse accomplishments, Hart produced theatrical plays in D.C. in the 1880s. In 1905 Hart won a Supreme Court appeal for the case *Hart v. the State of Maryland,* after being convicted for not giving up his train seat when traveling from an unsegregated state, New York, to a segregated one, Maryland. The Court ruled in his favor, declaring that Congress—not the states—controlled interstate commerce.

William Henry Hastie (November 17, 1904–April 14, 1976). From 1949 to 1971, William H. Hastie served on the U.S. Court of Appeals, becoming the chief justice and the first African American appointed to a federal bench. A Dunbar High School graduate, Hastie joined Charles H. Houston's law firm, Houston & Houston. In 1933 he became a solicitor and a jurist for the U.S. Department of the Interior. Despite opposition, Hastie was appointed a federal district judge in the Virgin Islands, serving a half term, 1937–1939, after which he became the dean of Howard University Law School. In 1940 he was appointed a civilian aide to Secretary of War Henry L. Stimson but resigned three years later on account of the army's refusal to integrate. Under Hastie's influence, the first black fighter squadron was sent to Liberia and the American Red Cross began to accept blood from blacks, though it was labeled by race. A 1943 NAACP Spingarn Medal recipient, Hastie became the first black governor of the Virgin Islands.

Patrick Francis Healy (February 27, 1834–January 1910). A scholar and a professor at Georgetown, Patrick Healy became the university's first African American president from 1874 until his resignation in 1882. Healy transformed the university, increasing its size and modernizing the academic programs offered there. Healy was born in Georgia to an Irish slaveowner and one of his slaves. In 1877 Georgetown University named one of its buildings in honor of Healy.

Edwin Bancroft Henderson (November 1883–February 1977). A political activist and a Howard University graduate, E. B. Henderson became the first African American certified to teach physical education in the United States. A Washington, D.C., native, Henderson served as the director of the Department of Health, Physical Education, and Safety for nearly thirty years. In 1974 Henderson was inducted into the Sports Hall of Fame.

Andrew Franklin Hilyer (August 14, 1858–January 13, 1925). Andrew Hilyer became a prominent D.C. resident with a longtime commitment to the improvement of African Americans politically, culturally, and economically. Born a slave in Georgia, Hilyer invented a humidifier for heated rooms, patented in 1900. In 1892 he helped to found and presided over the Union League in the District, an organization to foster unity and communication among working blacks of all social classes. The league also printed a directory of black businessmen and inventors. In 1901 Hilyer helped to organize the Samuel Coleridge-Taylor Choral Society, becoming its treasurer. He received his law degree from Howard University. Hilyer also pursued a career in government, was employed as a clerk at the U.S. Departments of Treasury and the Interior, and became the director of the General Accounting Office.

Julius Hobson (May 29, 1922–March 23, 1977). The politician Julius Hobson was a staunch advocate of D.C.'s becoming a self-governed, independent state. A D.C. Statehood Party member, Hobson lost the 1971 election for D.C. delegate but was elected in 1974 as at-large member to the District's first City Council. In 1973 Hobson opposed the appointment of the Congressional Black Caucus founder Charles Diggs to House District Committee chair, for fear that Diggs did not want home rule for D.C. citizens. Legislation introduced by Hobson while serving as a D.C. councilman included the Referendum Act, which gave citizens the right to draft legislation and place it on voting ballots, and the Non-Criminal Police Surveillance Act, which limited police surveillance of politically active individuals and groups.

Marion Conover Hope (1902–1974). An Anacostia community organizer, a social worker, and a youth advocate, Marion Conover Hope arrived in D.C. in 1930. She later organized the Southeast Neighborhood House, a settlement house. A Howard University and Catholic University graduate, Hope helped to found the Anacostia Neighborhood Museum in 1966 and helped design the Anacostia Community School Project, the District's first decentralized school.

Charles Hamilton Houston (September 3, 1895–April 22, 1950). The lawyer Charles H. Houston was the first African American to win a Supreme Court case. A Howard University Law School professor, Houston helped to found the Washington Bar Association in 1925. He and his father, William LePre Houston, established the Houston & Houston law firm. He conducted a Rockefeller-funded national survey on the state of black lawyers for a year before becoming the vice dean of Howard University Law School in 1929. There, he was charged with accrediting the school. He not only completed the task within three years but also shaped the school to reflect his personal policy of standards. Houston trained the law students to be "social engineers," using law for social change and to uphold minority rights. He was the first black attorney paid by the NAACP to join its legal defense fund. Houston also served briefly as an attorney with the Fair Employment Practice Committee but resigned in 1945. A staunch antidiscrimination activist, Houston wrote a civil rights column for the *Washington Afro American* and received a 1950 NAACP Spingarn Medal posthumously.

May Howard Jackson (May 12, 1877–July 12, 1931). The sculptor and educator May Howard Jackson was born in Philadelphia. Deciding not to seek formal training in Europe, she kept a studio in Washington, where she lived with her husband. Jackson created busts of notable African Americans, like the Howard University dean Kelly Miller, the poet Paul Laurence Dunbar, and the scholar W. E. B. DuBois. In 1915 her work was shown at the Corcoran Gallery of Art; in 1916 *Mulatto Mother and Her Child* and *Head of a Child* were displayed at D.C.'s Veerhoof Gallery and others. In 1928 Jackson received the Harmon Foundation award for her bronze bust of Kelly Miller. She possibly influenced the art of her husband's nephew the sculptor Sargeant Johnson, who resided at her home as a young boy.

William Henry Jernagin (October 13, 1869–ca. 1942). W. H. Jernagin was appointed as pastor of the Mt. Carmel Baptist Church in 1912. He was politically active in early civil rights struggles, turning his church into a local center for visiting political leaders. During the visit of Liberia's President King to the District, Reverend Jernagin served as his host.

Georgia Douglas Johnson (September 10, 1877?80?–May 14, 1966). The poet, playwright, and composer Georgia Douglas Johnson was born in Atlanta, Georgia. Early in her career, she published poems in journals such as *Voice of the Negro* and *The Crisis*. After attending Oberlin, she relocated to Washington, where she continued writing and held a weekly salon for D.C.'s black literati in her home. Many of them were members of the New Negro Movement or the Harlem Renaissance—Langston Hughes, Jessie Fauset, Alain Locke, Jean Toomer, Marita Bonner, and others. They called themselves the Saturday Nighters. A prolific writer, Johnson wrote and published poems until her death. Her poetry compilations include *The Heart of a Woman* (1918) and *Share My World* (1962). Johnson won second prize in *Opportunity* magazine for her play *Blue Blood* in 1926 and first prize for her play *Plumes* in 1927.

Mordecai Wyatt Johnson (December 12, 1890–September 10, 1976). Though he was the eleventh president of Howard University, Mordecai Johnson was the university's first president of African descent, serving from 1926 to

1960. By his retirement, enrollment had increased from 2,000 to over 10,000.

Lois Mailou Jones (November 3, 1905–June 9, 1998). Born in Boston, Massachusetts, right after the turn of the century, Jones became one of the most prominent African American artists of the twentieth century, with a career spanning from the Harlem Renaissance through the Black Arts Movement of the 1970s. Jones graduated from the School of the Museum of Fine Arts in Boston in 1927 and began a long and successful career as an art instructor. She came to Howard University in 1930 where she taught for almost fifty years. She traveled and lived in Haiti, France, and in several countries in Africa. Her 1938 painting, *Les Fétiches*, was widely acclaimed. In 1980 she was honored by President Jimmy Carter at the White House, and she continued to paint for almost another two decades. Many examples of her work can be found in museums and fine art collections around the country.

Ernest Everett Just (August 14, 1883–October 27, 1941). The scientist Ernest Just was a pioneer in experimental embryology, fertilization, and cellular physiology, for which he won a 1915 NAACP Spingarn Medal. Dr. Just dedicated many years to Howard University as an instructor of physiology at the Medical School (1912–1920), the director of the Department of Zoology (1912–1941), and the founder of the university's first College Dramatic Club. Just's research opportunities were unfortunately limited by his race. Denied admittance by white research institutions and dissatisfied with Howard's inadequate space, its facilities, and the burden of teaching, Just sought to concentrate on his research in Europe. In 1911 he and three Howard students established Omega Psi Phi, the first fraternity to be founded at a historically black college or university. In 1975 a statue of Just and the three student founders was erected near Howard's Thirkield Hall (formerly, Science Hall), the fraternity's birthplace.

Elizabeth Keckley (c. 1818–1907). Elizabeth Keckley, born a slave in Virginia, became a notable seamstress who created a cutting and fitting system that she taught to District dressmakers. After purchasing her own freedom in Missouri, Keckley came to D.C., where she made dresses for congressmen's wives and First Lady Mary Todd Lincoln. Keckley also became a confidante of Mrs. Lincoln. In 1862 she started the Contraband Relief Association by organizing members of her church congregation to collect funds for the assistance of ex-slaves. From 1868 until her death, Keckley's life was steeped in controversy after she published *Behind the Scenes; or, Thirty Years a Slave, and Four Years in the White House*. She was rebuked by Lincoln's son for publishing his mother's private letters and exposing his mother to criticism. What began as an act of friendship ultimately severed Keckley's relationship with the former first lady, though Keckley asserted that her intentions were pure. Ironically, she lived out her last days at the Home for Destitute Women and Children, an institute she helped to found.

John Mercer Langston (December 14, 1829–November 15, 1897). The Virginia-born attorney, educator, and abolitionist John Mercer Langston arrived in Washington, D.C., in 1868. A year later he was appointed the first dean of Howard University Law School. Because of his successful tenure, he was granted the additional responsibility of serving as the vice president and the acting president of the university, from 1873 to 1875. He also held many other prestigious appointments during his life, including United States minister to Haiti and legal adviser to the newly created Board of Health of the District of Columbia in 1871. In 1894 he published his autobiography, *From the Virginia Plantation to the National Capitol*. The home of Langston and his wife, Caroline Wall Langston, was for some years the center of social life for Washington's black elite. Langston spent the remaining years of his life active in Virginia politics, becoming the first black congressman from Virginia elected to the House of Representatives.

John Anderson Lankford (December 4, 1874–July 1946). The architect John A. Lankford opened one of the District's first black-owned architectural offices. He designed the True Reformer Building, erected on U Street in 1902. It was an imposing building that housed the national offices of the United Order of True Reformers fraternal organization until 1911, as well as a variety of business offices. The building became the social and business hub of the neighborhood. Lankford also helped to found the Howard University School of Architecture in the 1930s.

Rosetta E. Coakley Lawson (c. 1854–April 19, 1936). Coakley arrived in Washington, D.C., in 1862. In 1872 she volunteered with George F. T. Cook to examine teachers' records for D.C. black schools; she was soon elevated to clerk and assistant superintendent, where she served until 1885. Coakley organized a teachers group called the Irrepressibles in 1880. She became an organizer and a lecturer for the Woman's Christian Temperance Union, of which the D.C. chapter made her a lifetime member. Coakley was also instrumental in organizing the Phillis Wheatley YWCA in D.C. In 1909 she became the president of the Home for Friendless Girls in the District of Columbia, a residence founded by Caroline Taylor. Frelinghuysen University was originally located in the home of Lawson and her husband; Lawson herself graduated from Frelinghuysen's School of Chiropractic and Allied Sciences.

John Turner Layton (c. 1841–February 1916). John Turner Layton, born in Freeport, New Jersey, moved to D.C. after the Civil War, during which he had served in the U.S. Armed Forces. He taught music in D.C. public schools in 1883 and in 1895 became the director of music for D.C. black schools, a post he kept until his death. In addition to directing the choir of the Metropolitan A.M.E. church, Layton helped to found the Samuel Coleridge-Taylor Choral Society. Also a hymn writer, he penned such notable hymns as "O God, We Lift Our Hearts to Thee" and "Jesus, Lover of My Soul." His son John Turner Layton Jr., a musician and a vaudeville entertainer, performed with the conductor James Reese Europe's band in New York and earned fame in England onstage.

John Whitelaw Lewis (August 31, 1867–1924?25?). In 1913 Virginia-born entrepreneur John Whitelaw Lewis founded the Industrial Savings Bank in the District. The bank later reopened as the Industrial Bank of Washington, serving black patrons until it closed for two years in 1932. Lewis also constructed the Whitelaw Hotel, the first hotel in Washington, D.C., to be owned and operated by an African American for black clientele. For almost twenty years, the Whitelaw, located in the area known as Black Broadway, was the only luxury hotel in the segregated city that hosted the visiting black elite.

William Henry Lewis (November 28, 1868 or 1869–January 1, 1949). William H. Lewis was the first African American to become the assistant attorney general of the United States. President Taft appointed him to this position in 1911. As with other important appointments of African Americans at that time, Lewis's came about due to the influence of the educator and orator Booker T. Washington.

Alain Leroy Locke (September 13, 1886–June 9, 1954). Born in Philadelphia, Alain Leroy Locke became a major proponent of the New Negro Movement, or the Harlem Renaissance. Dr. Locke served as a mentor to many of the young, innovative writers, artists, and scholars of the time. From 1912 to 1925, he taught English and philosophy at Howard University. In 1925 Locke edited and published one of his most significant publications, *New Negro,* chronicling a significant new trend in the arts and the literature of blacks. The book grew out of a March 1925 issue of *Survey Graphic* magazine, which focused on changing black art, culture, and life in Harlem and included Locke's essays "New Negro" and "Youth Speaks." The result was the New Negro Movement, or the Harlem Renaissance. In 1925, despite his achievements, influence, and publication record, Locke was fired from Howard University, ostensibly because of university reorganization. He returned in 1928 under the administration of Howard's first black president, Mordecai W. Johnson, and lobbied for an African studies program (institutionalized in the 1950s). In 1953 he received a Doctor of Humane Letters degree from Howard University.

Rayford Whittingham Logan (January 7, 1897–November 4, 1982). A Washingtonian and an M Street High School graduate, Rayford Logan became one of the region's most well-known historians. In the 1920s he worked with the Pan-African Congress. Logan taught at Howard University's Department of History, chairing it from 1942 to 1964. He authored several important publications, including a history of Howard University, biographical sketches of black leaders, and the *Dictionary of American Negro Biography,* edited with Michael R. Winston. In the 1940s he worked in the State Department's Inter-American Affairs Bureau and from 1940 to 1945 organized and chaired the Committee on Participation of Negroes in the National Defense Program. Afterward, he served as a member of the U.S. National Commission for UNESCO. Among his many distinctions were honorary doctorates and a 1980 NAACP Spingarn Medal.

Harriet (Alethia) Gibbs Marshall (February 18, 1868–February 25, 1941). In 1903 Harriet Marshall established the Washington Conservatory of Music and School of Expression in the District; she had previously founded a conservatory in Kentucky in 1890. The Washington conservatory gave blacks an outlet for music, as they could not attend white professional musical performances. The school was run by her niece Josephine V. Muse, but after it closed, money from the conservatory allowed Howard University to create the Gibbs-Muse Scholarship Fund for students of music. Marshall was the first to finish the complete program at the Oberlin Music Conservatory. Trained on the piano in the United States and Europe, she not only performed but also in 1900 served as the director for music in Washington's colored public schools and in 1937 established the National Negro Music Center.

Thurgood Marshall (July 2, 1908–January 24, 1993). In 1967 Thurgood Marshall was appointed an associate justice of the U.S. Supreme Court, the first African American to receive this distinction. He served in this position until 1991. The Baltimore-born judge, who studied under the Howard University Law School professor Charles Hamilton Houston, dedicated his early career to civil rights legal defense with the NAACP, helping the organization win twenty-seven of thirty-two Supreme Court cases. Justice Marshall received many distinctions, including a 1946 NAACP Spingarn Medal, several honorary degrees, and an award named after him—the Thurgood Marshall Award of the American Bar Association. Two buildings in the District have been named in his honor: the Thurgood Marshall Center for Service and Heritage (the historic 12th Street Anthony Bowen YMCA) and the Thurgood Marshall Federal Judiciary Building.

Whitfield McKinlay (September 15, 1857–December 21, 1941). The real estate dealer Whitfield McKinlay, born in Charleston, South Carolina, became the collector of the Port of Georgetown under President Taft. In 1907 McKinlay was appointed by President Roosevelt to the Housing Commission. In 1916 he was one of several black Washingtonians who protested the increase of segregation in Washington to the House District Committee.

Robert H. McNeill (born in 1917). The freelance photographer Robert H. McNeill captured images of everyday life and photographed important events in 1930s and 1940s D.C., such as protest rallies against Jim Crow segregation. As a student of photography in New York, he took a series of photographs of domestic workers in search of employment, called the *Bronx Slave Market.* The series was published in *Flash!* and later resulted in McNeill securing a position photographing with the Works Progress Administration and the WPA Federal Writers' Project. He sent his pictures to major black newspapers like the *Washington Afro American,* often writing text to accompany them.

Emma Frances Grayson Merritt (January 11, 1860–1933). The Virginia-born educator Emma Merritt greatly changed and modernized education for black children in the District. A 1901 graduate of the Phoebe Hearst Training School in

D.C., Merritt dedicated her life to public school education from 1876 to 1930 and served as the principal of two schools—Banneker in 1887 and Garnet in 1890, where she created the school's first kindergarten. From 1898 to 1933, she organized and directed the D.C. Teachers' Benefit and Annuity Association. Merritt was the president of the D.C. branch of the NAACP from 1930 to 1933. In 1944 the Emma F. Merritt School in the District was named in her honor.

Elder Lightfoot Solomon Michaux (c. 1885–October 20, 1968). The evangelist and religious leader Elder Lightfoot Solomon Michaux came from Virginia to the District, where he established the Church of God in 1928. The Virginia-born native founded the Church of God Movement. His "Happy Am I" evangelist radio broadcasts were so popular that he was able to establish churches in several other cities, including New York and Philadelphia. He also helped architect Albert I. Cassell develop the Mayfair Mansions housing development. A master of showmanship, Elder Michaux staged massive baptisms in Griffith Stadium and the Potomac River and held other spectacular events, including community marches, around the city.

Kelly Miller (July 1863–December 29, 1939). A premier African American scholar and an educator, Kelly Miller, born in South Carolina during the Civil War, served Howard University for over forty years and was a notable member of Washington's black community. His contribution to Howard, including tenures as a math professor (1890), a sociology professor (1895–1934), and the dean of Howard University's College of Arts and Sciences (1907–1919), prompted people to sometimes call Howard "Kelly Miller's University." Miller was a prolific writer and a lecturer on topics concerning race relations, the education of blacks, and politics affecting blacks. He wrote a weekly column printed in over 100 black newspapers nationwide. In 1908 he published the first of his most prominent works, *Race Adjustment,* which challenged racist notions of black inferiority. After retiring from Howard in 1934, Miller became an advocate for the founding of a national Negro museum, an outgrowth of Howard University's library. The idea was met by much enthusiasm from prominent individuals around the country. Miller was politically active in his community, and in 1923 he advocated a Sanhedrin to mobilize blacks to address racial issues by becoming unified.

Lucy Ellen Moten (1851–August 24, 1933). The Howard University graduate Lucy Ellen Moten, born in Virginia, dedicated her life to the education of blacks in D.C. She became the principal of the Colored Normal School (later, Miner Teacher's College), though the Miner board member Frederick Douglass had to come to her aid twice, due to concern over the moral nature of some of her leisure activities—dancing and going to the theater. She headed Miner Normal School from 1883 to 1920, establishing there a two-year teacher training program that included supervised student teaching. In 1895 Moten earned a medical degree from Howard University's College of Medicine. Though she probably did not practice medicine, she did use her medical knowledge to create a health and hygiene course at Miner. In her will Moten bequeathed over $51,000 to be used as travel funds for Howard University students. In 1954 the Lucy Ellen Moten Elementary School in Anacostia was named in her honor.

Anna Evans Murray (1857–May 5, 1955). Murray was an early advocate for free kindergartens and kindergarten teacher training in Washington, D.C. She was also instrumental in setting up kindergarten training courses at Miner Normal School. Murray taught at Howard University and Mott School in the District and in 1895 served as the education chair of the National League of Colored Women. Murray managed a normal school in 1896, training teachers to instruct kindergarten. She was an active member of the NAACP in the early 1900s. Anna Murray was the wife of the archivist Daniel Murray.

Daniel Alexander Payne Murray (March 24, 1852–1925). The archivist, librarian, and bibliophile Daniel Murray, a Baltimore native, was an employee of the Library of Congress for over fifty years, beginning in 1871. He became one of the most recognized authorities on black literature during his lifetime. When the poet Paul Laurence Dunbar arrived in Washington, D.C., in 1898, he worked at the Library of Congress under the direction of Murray. In 1899 Murray was asked to prepare a display on "Negro Literature" for the American Exhibit at the 1900 Paris Exposition. In preparation for the exhibit, Murray sought the title of every book and pamphlet written by African Americans, which eventually made him the leading authority on black bibliography. Like the distinguished thinkers W. E. B. DuBois, Carter G. Woodson, and William Leo Hansberry, Murray at his death left uncompleted and unpublished what could have been a grand compilation of scholarship and history. He had spent twenty years consulting notable scholars in the United States, the Caribbean, and Africa,

doing research for a comprehensive bibliography of writings about African Americans and race.

Gaston T. Neal (died October 21, 1999). Gaston Neal was a Black Power activist and a poet whose work dealt with human rights and the poor. In the mid-1960s, during the Black Arts Movement, Neal co-founded the New School of Afro-American Thought, which offered free math, drama, and creative writing courses. He organized music festivals in black working-class neighborhoods in the District. In 1971 he started a jazz/poetry series at the Corcoran Gallery of Art. He also co-founded "The Listening Group," an informal gathering of men to discuss jazz, which grew into New Year's parties and annual picnics. Neal, who worked with the Drug Abuse Services Administration and with the D.C. Office of AIDS-HIV, produced *Neecey's Dilemma*, a play about safe sex, in the 1980s. A worker for the Black United Fund, Neal served as an artist-in-residence with the D.C. public school system. Just days before his death, he was awarded the D.C. mayor's Award for Excellence in Service to the Arts.

Daniel Alexander Payne (February 24, 1811–November 29, 1893). Daniel Payne—a South Carolina-born pastor of the Israel Bethel A.M.E. Church and a historian of the A.M.E. church—lived and ministered in the District at different times. Bishop Payne traveled the country performing missionary work and researching the history of the A.M.E. church. He wrote many essays on the education of the clergy in D.C.'s *African Methodist Episcopal Church Magazine*, 1843–1884. In 1881 he established the Bethel Literary and Historical Association at the Metropolitan African Methodist Episcopal Church. The same year he laid the cornerstone for a grand new building for the Metropolitan A.M.E. Church, using his carpentry skills to help construct the building. Bishop Payne produced two publications, *History of the African Methodist Church* (1891) and *Recollections of Seventy Years* (1888), an autobiography. Payne was in charge of Wilberforce University, the nation's first black college.

Leila Amos Pendleton (1860–1938). Aleila Pendleton was a community leader and an advocate of black history. She founded and presided over the Alpha Charity Club, an organization for emergency relief, from 1898 to 1911. In 1907 she founded the Social Purity Club (League) of Washington. From 1889 to 1893, Pendleton served as a teacher in D.C., after which she published short stories in

The Crisis and a book, *A Narrative of the Negro* (1912), that recorded black history from ancient Africa to the present, including Afro-Caribbean and Afro-Latin history.

Channing E. Phillips (died November 11, 1987). The civil rights activist, clergyman, and politician Channing Phillips was born in Brooklyn. Reverend Phillips, while serving as the D.C. Democratic national committeeman (1968–1972) became the first black person nominated for president of the United States by a major political party, after the death of favorite son Senator Robert F. Kennedy. Reverend Phillips arrived in D.C. in 1956, teaching New Testament studies at Howard and American Universities. From 1961 to 1970, he was a senior minister at the Lincoln Temple United Church of Christ in the District. Reverend Phillips served as the executive director of the Housing Development Corporation, which opened over 1,000 units for low-income D.C. residents. A home rule advocate, he ran for the office of D.C. nonvoting delegate in 1971 but lost to Walter Fauntroy.

Pinckney Benton Stewart Pinchback (May 14, 1837–December 21, 1921). P. B. S. Pinchback was the first black state governor, serving as the lieutenant governor of Louisiana. In the 1890s he came to Washington, D.C., with his family. Their grand home on Bacon Street near the Chinese embassy became a center of black elite social activities. Pinchback was the grandfather of the D.C. writer and personality Jean Toomer.

John Pinkett (September 27, 1888–?). John Pinkett, born in Virginia, became an insurance and real estate magnate. Educated in D.C. public schools, he served as the agency director of the National Benefit Life Insurance Company in the District. In 1911 he was selected to be a member of the All-American Football Team.

William Sydney Pittman (April 21, 1875–1958). The Alabama native William Sydney Pittman was an architect and a Tuskegee Institute faculty member. In 1905 Pittman relocated to Washington, where he ran an architectural office. In addition to designing the 12th Street YMCA, Pittman designed a host of public buildings and gained recognition in his field. In 1907 Pittman won a national competition to design the Negro Building for the Jamestown Exposition. Constructed entirely by blacks, the building contained exhibits of black achievement. The same year Pittman married Portia, the daughter of Booker T. Washington.

James A. Porter (December 22, 1905–February 28, 1970). The painter and art historian James A. Porter, born in Baltimore, published *Modern Negro Art* in 1943. The book was the first comprehensive examination of African American art. Porter also served as a professor at Howard University.

Charles Burleigh Purvis (April 14, 1842–January 30, 1929). Charles B. Purvis, the son of the abolitionist Robert Purvis, was appointed the surgeon-in-chief of Freedmen's Hospital in 1881, making Purvis the only black person in charge of a hospital at the time. In 1868 Dr. Purvis was a professor of materia medica and medical jurisprudence at Howard University's Medical Department, becoming the department's only black faculty member. He also chaired obstetrics and women's and children's diseases. In 1869 Dr. Purvis applied to join the D.C. Medical Society but was denied membership.

Calvin W. Rolark (1927–October 23, 1994). Texas-born Calvin Rolark was a District advocate for positive media representations of African Americans, an activist, and a newspaper publisher. He established the *Washington Informer* in the mid-1960s, determined to represent positive news about African Americans, as opposed to reports on violence and crime in popular media. Rolark became the president of the United Black Fund, a charitable organization to aid black and Latino communities, which he helped to found in 1969. By the time of his death, the organization was operating in thirty-nine cities nationwide. He was also an editor at the *New Observer* newspaper company. Rolark, married to the former D.C. city councilwoman Wilhelmina Rolark, supported his wife's political career.

Addison Scurlock (1883–1964). The photographer Addison Scurlock arrived in D.C. in 1900. Seven years later he won the Gold Medal for Photography at the Jamestown Exposition. In 1911 he opened Scurlock Studios, which he operated in D.C. with his wife and sons, Robert and George. He captured images of some of D.C.'s notable black residents, as well as of social and cultural activities in the city. Scurlock was also Howard University's official photographer.

Robert S. Scurlock (1916–December 1, 1994). Following in the tradition of his father, Addison, the photographer Robert Scurlock operated Scurlock Studios until his death.

He and his brother George, who apprenticed with their father at an early age, operated the Capitol School of Photography in the District. There, they trained hundreds of students, including World War II veterans, from 1948 to 1952. While Scurlock worked in the genre of studio portraiture, he also concentrated on news photography for black magazines and newspapers nationwide.

Lucy Diggs Slowe (July 4, 1885–October 1937). Lucy Diggs Slowe was an educator and an activist for women's rights. She was one of the eight students who founded the first black sorority, Alpha Kappa Alpha, in 1908 at Howard University. In 1919 Slowe became the principal of Shaw Junior High School, Washington, D.C.'s first black junior high school. From 1922 until her death, she served as the first black woman dean of women students at Howard University. In 1923 she became president of the National Association of Colored Women and was also involved in the National Council of Negro Women and the YWCA.

May Miller Sullivan (January 26, 1899–1995). May Miller Sullivan was a poet, a teacher, a playwright, and an anthologist. Daughter of the scholar and the Howard University dean Kelly Miller and the teacher Annie May (Butler) Miller, she grew up in a house filled with the most creative and influential African American scholars and writers of the period. Active in the New Negro literary movement in Washington, she was a member of Georgia Douglas Johnson's Saturday Nighters club, and she later served as the poetry coordinator for the Friends of Art in the District of Columbia Program for Public Schools. Upon the establishment of the District of Columbia Commission on the Arts and Humanities, she was named a member by the mayor, representing the literary segment. Her poetry publications include *In the Clearing* (1959) and *Poems* (1962). Her stage works include *Pandora's Box* (1914), *Within the Shadow* (1920), and *The Cuss'd Thing* (1926). In 1935 she published *Negro History in Thirteen Plays*, a volume edited with Willis Richardson. Sullivan read one of her poems at the inauguration of D.C.'s first elected mayor, Walter Washington, and also at the inauguration of President Jimmy Carter.

Alethia Browning Tanner (no dates available). Through sheer perseverance and hard work, Alethia Browning Tanner managed to purchase the freedom of over twenty people, including herself—with earnings made from a tiny garden plot she obtained near the Capitol Building around 1800. She became a popular vendor; tradition claims that Thomas Jefferson was one of her customers and that later she served as a housemaid for him during part of his residency in the capital. In 1810 Tanner bought her own freedom for a total of $1,400, paid in installments. Over the next thirty years she purchased her family members and friends, including her nephew, the notable Washingtonian Reverend John F. Cook, and his family. With her hard-earned funds, Tanner also helped to save the First Bethel Church on Capitol Hill.

Mary Church Terrell (September 23, 1863–July 24, 1954). The activist Mary Church Terrell was the first president of the National Association of Colored Women. In 1887 Terrell arrived in Washington to teach at the Preparatory School for Colored Youth. Married to judge Robert Herberton Terrell, she was twice appointed to serve on the District's Board of Education (1895–1901, 1906–1911). When the National League of Colored Women and the National Federation of Afro-American Women merged in 1896 to form the National Association of Colored Women, Terrell was elected as its first president. During the 1913 Woman's Suffrage parade in Washington, D.C., Terrell led members of Howard University's Delta Sigma Theta sorority in a march side by side with white participants. Her long record of community activism includes a 1933 protest against discrimination in store employment. She published her autobiography, *A Colored Woman in a White World,* in 1940. At eighty-six, Terrell, chairing the Coordinating Committee for the Enforcement of the D.C. Anti-Discrimination Laws, helped the Thompson Test—a lawsuit that went before the Supreme Court in 1954—end segregation of Washington's public accommodations.

Robert Herberton Terrell (November 27, 1857–December 1925). Robert Herberton Terrell was the first African American in the District of Columbia to be appointed as justice of the peace. He was appointed in 1901, due to the influence of Booker T. Washington. In 1910 he was also appointed as judge in the Municipal Court of the District of Columbia, a position he held until shortly before his death in 1925. Terrell, the husband of the activist Mary Church Terrell, was also devoted to education. In 1899 he became the principal of the M Street High School. He also taught at Howard University Law School from 1910 until 1925. In 1931 the Robert H. Terrell Law School was established and named in his honor. The school operated until 1950.

Alma Thomas (September 22, 1891–February 25, 1978). The artist Alma Thomas, from Columbus, Georgia, became the first nationally acclaimed black female abstract artist and was the first black woman to have a solo show at New York's Whitney Museum of American Art. An Armstrong High School graduate, Thomas graduated in 1924 from Howard University's newly created Department of Art. She was a longtime art teacher at Shaw Junior High School, from 1924 to 1960. Upon her retirement, her art career flourished with the production of vivid, colorful abstract paintings. She studied at American University and had her first solo exhibit at the DuPont Theatre Art Gallery in D.C. Some of her notable works include *The Eclipse* and *Red Azaleas Singing and Dancing Rock and Roll Music* (1976).

Thurlow Evans Tibbs Jr. (died January 16, 1997). The Washingtonian Thurlow Tibbs Jr., the grandson of the opera singer Lillian "Madame Evanti" Evans Tibbs, became the director of the Evans-Tibbs Collection, an important collection of African American art and related archives. Valued at over $1 million, the collection included more than 600 works by artists such as Henry Ossawa Tanner, Aaron Douglass, James Van Der Zee, and Betye Saar. An art collector and a dealer, Tibbs operated an art gallery from his Logan Circle home in the District. It was the site of many art exhibits, openings, and receptions in the 1970s and 1980s. Much of Tibbs's collection was donated to the Corcoran Gallery of Art in 1996.

Jean Toomer (December 26, 1894–March 10, 1967). The writer and D.C.-native Jean Toomer (born Nathan Pinchback Toomer) was raised at the home of his grandfather, the former Louisiana lieutenant governor P. B. S. Pinchback. Toomer, a 1914 M Street High School graduate, began working as a temporary superintendent of a small school for black children in rural Georgia in 1921. His experiences there inspired his literary masterpiece *Cane*, a prose poem, published in 1923. Before *Cane*, he had published short works and poems in magazines, including in *The Crisis*. He also wrote two plays: *Balo*, performed at the Howard Theatre 1923–1924, and *Natalie Mann*, about D.C. middle-class life. Toomer was a frequent attendee of Georgia Douglas Johnson's Saturday Nighters club. Despite the success of his first novel, Toomer did not pursue a literary career, as expected, and spent the next three decades of his life traveling and pursuing Eastern and other philosophies and religions.

Carmen Pawley Turner (1931–April 9, 1992). Born in New Jersey, Carmen Turner was a Dunbar High School graduate and attended Howard University. In 1983 she became the first black female appointed as a general manager of the Washington Metropolitan Area Transit Authority (WMATA). She served as the undersecretary for the Smithsonian Institution from 1990 until her death.

Henry McNeal Turner (February 1, 1834–May 8, 1915). Henry McNeal Turner, born free in South Carolina, became active in the African Methodist Episcopal church. In Georgetown, Bishop Daniel Payne ordained Turner a deacon in 1860 and an elder of the Israel Bethel A.M.E. Church—where he also served as a pastor—in 1862. In 1863 a recruitment rally was held at the church, and Reverend Turner encouraged 800 black men to volunteer for service. They formed the 1st U.S. Colored Troops, giving the District of Columbia its first black regiment. The same year President Lincoln appointed Reverend Turner as chaplain to the 1st U.S. Colored Troops. During Reconstruction, Reverend Turner moved to Georgia, where he became prominent in state politics.

John Milton Waldron (May 19, 1863 or 1865–?). J. Milton Waldron, born in Lynchburg, Virginia, was one of the African Americans to initially sign the call to create the NAACP. A pastor at Shiloh Baptist Church and Berean Baptist Church in Washington, D.C., Reverend Dr. Waldron created the Washington branch of the NAACP at Shiloh Baptist in 1912. He was also the treasurer of the Niagara Movement.

William A. Warfield (November 17, 1866–?). The Maryland-born William A. Warfield served as the director and the surgeon-in-chief (since 1901) of Freedmen's Hospital. He received his medical degree from Howard University in 1894.

John Edwin Washington (February 2, 1880–December 6, 1964). The historian and Howard University graduate John Washington chronicled black Washington community life in the 1800s and early 1900s and was a collector of Lincoln memorabilia. His book *They Knew Lincoln* was published in 1942. Based on thirty-five years of extensive interviews conducted by Washington, the book won him special recognition from the Library of Congress in 1947. In 1959 he was made an honorary member of the Lincoln Sesquicentennial Commission. Washington was also a dentist and an art instructor in D.C. public schools, as well as a beloved coach of high school athletics.

Robert Clifton Weaver (December 29, 1907–July 17, 1997). A government official and a Washingtonian, Robert C. Weaver was the first African American appointed to the Cabinet, serving as the first secretary of Housing and Urban Development (HUD) in 1966 in the Johnson administration. A Dunbar High School graduate, Weaver served as adviser and assistant in several different federal agencies. As a member of President Franklin Roosevelt's "Black Cabinet," he worked with the National Defense Advisory Commission. While Weaver served as the NAACP chairman, President Kennedy appointed him chief of the government's Housing and Home Finance Agency. Weaver received the prestigious NAACP Spingarn Medal in 1962. He spent the rest of his life working for the Municipal Assistance Corporation and teaching in New York.

James Lesesne Wells (November 2, 1902–January 20, 1993). The visual artist James Lesesne Wells was one of the nation's leading graphic artists. His 1920s engravings of the Harlem Renaissance and of black workers won him a Harmon Foundation Gold Medal, created in recognition of distinguished art by blacks. He was also known for his 1940s etchings of religious and mythological scenes. A painter and a sculptor as well, Wells's work was exhibited widely. He taught art at Howard University beginning in 1929 and founded the Graphic Arts Department. He retired in 1968. Howard's art gallery was named after Wells and the artist Lois Mailou Jones. In 1980 Wells received an honor from President Carter, and D.C. mayor Marion Barry declared February 15, 1984, "James L. Wells Day" in the District.

Charles Harris Wesley (December 2, 1891–August 16, 1987). The historian Charles H. Wesley was born in Louisville, Kentucky. The second husband of Dorothy Porter, Wesley was a recipient of several honorary degrees. He taught history and modern languages at Howard University and published several articles in Carter G. Woodson's *Journal of Negro History*. In 1921 he was ordained a minister and served at Ebenezer A.M.E. Church in Georgetown and Campbell A.M.E. Church. From 1938 to 1942, he was the dean of Howard University's graduate school. His dissertation *Negro Labor in the United States, 1850 to 1925,* published in 1927, became an important book.

Dorothy Porter Wesley (May 25, 1905–December 17, 1995). The librarian Dorothy Porter Wesley established at Howard University what became known as the Moorland-Spingarn Research Collection. In 1930 the Warrenton, Virginia, native was chosen to organize the university's "Negro Collection," consisting mainly of materials donated by Howard University trustee Jesse E. Moorland. Wesley—despite some initial opposition from the university—acquired diaries, letters, photographs, and other artifacts for the collection, including the private library of the NAACP lawyer Arthur B. Spingarn. She became known as the "shopping bag lady" for her eagerness to collect what many saw as junk but what Porter recognized to be important archival materials for the collection. She was first married to the artist James A. Porter, and after his death married the historian Charles Harris Wesley. Her bibliography, *A Selected List of Books By and About the Negro,* was published in 1936, one of the first by Wesley that would influence the field of bibliography and black American scholarship. In 1971 she received a Distinguished Service Award from the students of Howard University's College of Liberal Arts. The extensive bibliographies she created have become invaluable aids to researchers, and the Moorland-Spingarn Research Center has become one of the largest and most comprehensive repositories of documentation on the history and the culture of African descendants in the United States.

Ionia Rollin Whipper (September 8, 1872–April 23, 1953). Ionia Whipper, born in South Carolina, was an obstetrician who took many unwed mothers into her Washington home. Part of an outstandingly gifted and ambitious family of South Carolina activists, Whipper received her medical degree from the Howard University School of Medicine in 1903, becoming one of the first black female physicians in the country. She practiced obstetrics until shortly before her death. Not content with merely practicing medicine, she created organizations to help unwed mothers and delinquent girls, such as the Tuesday Evening Club. In the 1930s she created the Lend-A-Hand Club to construct a building to house unwed mothers. The United Fund would not support the institution; local blacks had to raise funds to maintain it. Through these efforts Whipper established the Ionia R. Whipper Home for Unwed Mothers in 1931. For many years it was the District's only shelter—privately run or otherwise—to house single black mothers. (Her mother, Frances Anne Rollin Whipper, wrote the first biography of a free-born black, *The Life and Public Services of Martin R.*

Delaney, published in 1868, but it carried the name of Frank A. Rollin.)

Daniel "Dr. Dan" Hale Williams (January 18, 1856–August 4, 1931). Before arriving in Washington, the physician Daniel Hale Williams had come to the attention of the public and enjoyed some celebrity. While at Chicago's Provident Hospital in 1893, which he founded, he successfully performed open-heart surgery, making it one of the first such operations in the country. Affectionately known as Dr. Dan, he became the surgeon-in-charge of Freedmen's Hospital in Washington in 1894 and held the position until his resignation in 1898. His achievements there had an immediate impact upon medical education at the university, particularly in the area of surgical instruction. When he organized the hospital's first program for interns, he made Freedmen's and Provident Hospitals two of the few institutions providing such training for black medical graduates. Williams also established the Training School for Nurses in 1894, where unmarried colored women ages twenty-one to thirty-five were educated in patient care, pediatric care, and nutrition. It began as an 18-month course with 46 students; by 1900, 73 nurses had passed through the school, and the course was eventually extended to 3 years, with clinical experience emphasized.

John A. Wilson (September 29, 1943–May 19, 1993). A civil rights activist with the Student Non-Violent Coordinating Committee, John Wilson worked with Walter Fauntroy on his election campaign to become the first nonvoting District congressional delegate. In 1974 Wilson at thirty-four was the youngest of the first members elected to D.C.'s City Council, becoming its chair in 1991. During his last days, Wilson was said to have been conflicted over running for D.C. mayor in 1994 against Mayor Sharon Pratt Kelly. John Wilson lost his life to depression and suicide. In 1994 the D.C. District Building was dedicated the John A. Wilson Building.

Carter Godwin Woodson (December 19, 1875–April 3, 1950). A pioneer, a Virginia-born historian, and an educator, Carter G. Woodson spent a lifetime dedicated to research in black history. He was known as the "father of black history." While completing his doctoral dissertation, he taught at District public schools, including the prestigious M Street High School. In 1915 Woodson established the Association for the Study of Negro Life and History and began publishing the *Journal of Negro History* in 1916. From 1919 to 1920, he served as the dean of liberal arts at Howard University and was a graduate faculty head and a professor of history. Determined to foster public appreciation of the history of black life and culture, Woodson and the Association for the Study of Negro Life and History created Negro History Week in 1926. It became Black History Month fifty years later. In 1933 Woodson published *The Mis-Education of the Negro,* which argued for making education relevant to blacks in order to counter feelings of inferiority. In 1937 he created the *Negro History Bulletin,* an informational magazine for school teachers.

James Wormley (January 16, 1819–October 18, 1884). A successful businessman and a charter member of the D.C. Chamber of Commerce, the Washingtonian James Wormley began his career as a waiter, a caterer, and an innkeeper. After working in Paris, Wormley returned to the District to open what became known as Wormley's Hotel in 1871. It was one of the city's most fashionable hotels and dining rooms and also a popular place for political meetings and bargaining sessions during the 1877 presidential campaign. The final elements of the "Hayes Compromise" between Rutherford B. Hayes and Samuel Tilden, a political arrangement giving Hayes victory in the presidential election, in exchange for the withdrawal of remaining federal troops from the South, were set into place during meetings at the Wormley Hotel. At Wormley's death, his body lay in state and was viewed by hundreds of mourners at the hotel.

Abdy, E. S. *Journal of a Residence and Tour in the United States.* New York: Negro Universities Press, 1969.

Alexander, Adele L. *Homelands and Waterways: The American Journey of the Bond Family, 1846–1926.* New York: Pantheon Books, 1999.

Apidta, Tingba. *The Hidden History of Washington, D.C.: A Guide for Black Folks.* Roxbury, Mass.: Reclamation Project, 1996.

Bancroft, Frederic. *Slave-Trading in the Old South.* Columbia: University of South Carolina Press, 1996. Originally published: J. H. Furst Co., 1931.

Bedini, Sylvio. *The Life of Benjamin Banneker.* New York: Scribners, 1971.

Booker, Christopher B. *African-Americans and the Presidency: A History of Broken Promises.* New York: Franklin Watts, 2000.

Borchert, James. *Alley Life in Washington.* Urbana/Chicago: University of Illinois Press, 1980.

Bremer, Frederika. *The Homes of the New World: Impressions of America.* 2 vols. New York: Harper and Bros., 1853.

Brown, Letitia W. *Free Negroes in the District of Columbia, 1790–1846.* New York: Oxford University Press, 1972.

Brown, Letitia W., and Elsie M. Lewis. *Washington from Banneker to Douglass, 1791–1870.* Washington, D.C.: Education Department, National Portrait Gallery, 1971.

————. *Washington in the New Era, 1870–1970.* Washington, D.C.: Education Department, National Portrait Gallery, 1972.

Carson, Barbara G. *Ambitious Appetites: Dining, Behavior, and Patterns of Consumption in Federal Washington.* Washington, D.C.: American Institute of Architects Press, 1990.

Christopher, Maurine. *America's Black Congressmen.* New York: Thomas Y. Crowell Co., 1971.

Dabney, Lillian G. *The History of Schools for Negroes in the District of Columbia, 1807–1947.* Washington, D.C.: Catholic University of America Press, 1949.

Drayton, Daniel. *Personal Memoir of Daniel Drayton.* Boston: Bela Marsh, 1855.

Federal Writers Project, Works Progress Administration. *Washington: City and Capital*. American Guide Series. Washington, D.C.: Government Printing Office, 1937.

Fitzpatrick, Sandra, and Maria R. Goodwin. *The Guide to Black Washington: Places and Events of Historical and Cultural Significance in the Nation's Capital*. New York: Hippocrene Books, 1990.

Gatewood, Willard B. *Aristocrats of Color: The Black Elite, 1880–1920*. Bloomington: Indiana University Press, 1990.

Goodwin, Moses B. *History of Schools for the Colored Population in the District of Columbia*. New York: Arno Press, 1969. Originally published as section C-D in U.S. Office of Education, *Special Report of the Commissioner of Education on the Condition and Improvement of Public Schools in the District of Columbia*. Washington, D.C.: Government Printing Office, 1871.

Green, Constance McLaughlin. *The Secret City: A History of Race Relations in the Nation's Capital*. Princeton, N.J.: Princeton University Press, 1967.

———. *Washington: Village and Capital, 1800–1878*. Princeton, N.J.: Princeton University Press, 1962.

Hayes, Laurence John Wesley. *The Negro Federal Government Worker, a Study of His Classification Status in the District of Columbia, 1883–1938*. Washington, D.C.: Howard University, 1941.

Hilyer, Andrew F. *The Twentieth Century Union League Directory*. Washington, D.C.: The Union League, 1901.

Hundley, Mary G. *The Dunbar Story, 1870–1955*. New York: Vantage Press, 1965.

Hutchinson, Louise Daniel. *The Anacostia Story, 1608–1930*. Washington, D.C.: Published for the Anacostia Neighborhood Museum of the Smithsonian Institution by the Smithsonian Institution Press, 1977.

———. *Anna J. Cooper: A Voice from the South*. Washington, D.C.: Published for the Anacostia Neighborhood Museum of the Smithsonian Institution by the Smithsonian Institution Press, 1981.

———. "Efforts for Social Betterment in the Nation's Capital by African Americans: 1880–1918." Lecture at the National Portrait Gallery, October 26, 1993.

Hutchinson, Louise Daniel, and Gail Sylvia Lowe. *"Kind regards of S. G. Brown": Selected Poems of Solomon G. Brown*. Washington, D.C.: Published for the Anacostia Neighborhood Museum of the Smithsonian Institution by the Smithsonian Institution Press, 1983.

Ingle, Edward. *The Negro in the District of Columbia*. Freeport, N.Y.: Books for Libraries Press, 1971.

Jennings, Paul. *A Colored Man's Reminiscences of James Madison*. Brooklyn, N.Y.: G. C. Beadle, 1865.

Johnson, Haynes. *Dusk at the Mountain: The Negro, the Nation, and the Capital—a Report on Problems and Progress*. Garden City, N.Y.: Doubleday, 1963.

Keckley, Elizabeth. *Behind the Scenes, or, Thirty Years a Slave, and Four Years in the White House*. New York: G. W. Carleton and Co, 1868.

Kofie, Nelson F. *Race, Class, and the Struggle for Neighborhood in Washington, D.C.* New York: Garland, 1999.

Kusmer, Kenneth, ed. *Black Communities and Urban Development in America, 1720–1990*. 10 vols. New York: Garland, 1991.

Lesko, Kathleen M., general editor and contributing author; Valerie Babb and Caroll R. Gibbs, contributing authors. *Black Georgetown Remembered: A History of Its Black Community from the Founding of "The Town of George" in 1751 to the Present Day.* Washington, D.C.: Georgetown University Press, 1991.

Lewis, David L. *District of Columbia: A Bicentennial History.* New York: W. W. Norton, 1976.

Logan, Rayford W. *The Betrayal of the Negro: From Rutherford B. Hayes to Woodrow Wilson.* New York: Collier Books, 1965.

———. *The Negro in American Life and Thought: The Nadir, 1877–1901.* New York: Dial Press, 1954.

Logan, Rayford W., and Michael Winston. *Dictionary of American Negro Biography.* New York and London: W. W. Norton, 1982.

Lutz, Tom, and Susanna Ashton, eds. *These "Colored" United States: African American Essays from the 1920s.* New Brunswick, N.J.: Rutgers University Press, 1996.

MacGregor, Morris. *The Emergence of a Black Catholic Community: St. Augustine's in Washington.* Washington, D.C.: Catholic University of America Press, 1999.

McFeely, William S. *Frederick Douglass.* New York and London: W. W. Norton, 1991.

Melder, Keith, with Melinda Young Stuart. *City of Magnificent Intentions: A History of Washington, District of Columbia.* Washington, D.C./Silver Spring, Md.: Intac, Inc., 1997.

National Committee on Segregation in the Nation's Capital. *Segregation in Washington, a Report.* Chicago, November 1948.

The Northern Shaw-Strivers Cultural Resources Survey, Phase II, Final Report. Prepared by Traceries for the D.C. Preservation League, the D.C. Historic Preservation Division, and the Historic Northern Shaw-Strivers Coalition, August 1993.

Northup, Solomon. *Twelve Years a Slave: Narrative of Solomon Northrup.* Mineola, N.Y.: Dover Publications, 2000 (originally published in 1859).

Parker, Robert. *Capitol Hill in Black and White.* New York: Dodd, Mead, 1986.

Parks, Lillian Rogers, and Frances S. Leighton. *It Was Fun Working at the White House.* New York, Fleet Press, 1969.

Paynter, John Henry. *Fugitives of the Pearl.* New York: AMS Press, 1971.

Provine, Dorothy S. *District of Columbia Free Negro Registers 1821–1861.* Bowie, Md.: Heritage Books, 1996.

———. "The Economic Position of the Free Blacks in the District of Columbia, 1800–1860." *Journal of Negro History* 58, no. 1 (1973): 61–72.

Quarles, Benjamin. *Lincoln and the Negro.* New York: Oxford University Press, 1962.

Simmons, William J. *Men of Mark: Eminent, Progressive, and Rising.* Chicago: Johnson Publishing Co., 1970 (reprint of 1887 edition).

Smith, Sam. *Captive Capital: Colonial Life in Modern Washington.* Bloomington: Indiana University Press, 1974.

Snethen, Worthington G. *The Black Code of the District of Columbia, in Force September 1st, 1848.* New York: Published for the A. & F. Anti-Slavery Society by William Harned, 1848.

Terrell, Mary Church. *A Colored Woman in a White World.* New York: G. K. Hall, 1996.

Thomas, Neval H. "The District of Columbia—A Paradise of Paradoxes." In Tom

Lutz and Susanna Ashton, eds., *These "Colored" United States: African American Essays from the 1920s.* New Brunswick, N.J.: Rutgers University Press, 1996.

Torrey, Jesse. *American Slave Trade.* Westport, Conn.: Negro Universities Press, 1971 (originally published 1822).

Tremain, Mary. *Slavery in the District of Columbia.* New York: Negro Universities Press, 1969 (originally published 1892).

Truth, Sojourner. *Narrative of Sojourner Truth.* New York: Penguin Books, 1998.

Washington, John E. *They Knew Lincoln.* New York: E. P. Dutton, 1942.

Weiss, Nancy J. *Farewell to the Party of Lincoln: Black Politics in the Age of FDR.* Princeton, N.J.: Princeton University Press, 1983.

Weller, Charles F. *Neglected Neighbors: Stories of Life in the Alleys, Tenements, and Shanties of the Nation's Capital.* Philadelphia: J. C. Winston, 1909.

PHOTO CREDITS

Page 108: Georgetown University Archives

Page 109: United States Senate Historical Office

Page 110: Library of Congress

Page 114: Brown University Library

Page 115: Moorland-Spingarn Research Center, Howard University

Page 116: Library of Congress

Page 119: Moorland-Spingarn Research Center, Howard University

Pages 123, 126: Library of Congress

Page 127: Courtesy Scurlock Studio Records, Archives Center, National Museum of American History, Smithsonian Institution

Page 128: Library of Congress

Page 129: Brown University Library

Pages 130, 131, 132, 133: Library of Congress

Pages 134, 135: Moorland-Spingarn Research Center, Howard University

Pages 137, 141: Courtesy Scurlock Studio Records, Archive Center, National Museum of American History, Smithsonian Institution

Page 142: Library of Congress

Page 144: Howard University Archives Center

Page 151: Library of Congress

Page 152: Archives Center, Anacostia Museum and Center for African American History and Culture, Smithsonian Institution

Page 154: Robert H. McNeill

Page 155: Martin Luther King Library, Washingtoniana Division, D.C. Public Library

Page 164: James K. Hill Collection

Pages 165, 166, 169: Library of Congress

Pages 170, 171: James K. Hill Collection

Page 175: Library of Congress

Page 177: Archives Center, Anacostia Museum and Center for African American History and Culture, Smithsonian Institution

Page 178: Library of Congress

Pages 179, 180: Courtesy Scurlock Studio Records, Archives Center, National Museum of American History, Smithsonian Institution

Page 181 (top): Library of Congress

Page 181 (bottom): James K. Hill Collection

Pages 183, 184 (top): Courtesy Scurlock Studio Records, Archives Center, National Museum of American History, Smithsonian Institution

Page 184 (bottom): Moorland-Spingarn Research Center, Howard University

Page 185: Courtesy Scurlock Studio Records, Archives Center, National Museum of American History, Smithsonian Institution

Page 188: Robert H. McNeill

Page 189: National Archives

Page 190 (top): Moorland-Spingarn Research Center, Howard University

Page 190 (bottom): Courtesy Scurlock Studio Records, Archives Center, National Museum of American History, Smithsonian Institution

Pages 191, 198: National Archives

Page 199 (top): Robert H. McNeill

Page 199 (bottom): Moorland-Spingarn Research Center, Howard University

Page 200: Courtesy Scurlock Studio Records, Archives Center, National Museum of American History, Smithsonian Institution

Page 201: Moorland-Spingarn Research Center, Howard University

Page 202: Robert H. McNeill

Page 203: Courtesy Scurlock Studio Records, Archives Center, National Museum of American History, Smithsonian Institution

Page 209: Archives Center, Anacostia Museum and Center for African American History and Culture, Smithsonian Institution

Page 210: Moorland-Spingarn Research Center, Howard University

Page 211: Gordon Parks, Library of Congress

Pages 213, 214: Robert H. McNeill

Pages 216: National Archives

Page 217: Martin Luther King Library, Washingtoniana Division, D.C. Public Library

Page 225: James K. Hill Collection

Page 226: Courtesy Scurlock Studio Records, Archives Center, National Museum of American History, Smithsonian Institution

Page 227 (top): Martin Luther King Library, Washingtoniana Division, D.C. Public Library

Page 227 (bottom): Robert H. McNeill

Page 229: NAACP DC Collection, Moorland-Spingarn Research Center, Howard University

Page 230: Martin Luther King Library, Washingtoniana Division, D.C. Public Library

Page 232: Library of Congress

Page 234: Private Collection

Page 235: Courtesy Scurlock Studio Records, Archives Center, National Museum of American History, Smithsonian Institution

Page 236: National Archives

Page 237: Moorland-Spingarn Research Center, Howard University

Page 239: Archives Center, Anacostia Museum and Center for African American History and Culture, Smithsonian Institution

Pages 242, 243, 244, 246: Martin Luther King Library, Washingtoniana Division, D.C. Public Library

Page 248: Courtesy Scurlock Studio Records, Archives Center, National Museum of American History, Smithsonian Institution

Page 251: Library of Congress

Page 252: National Archives

Page 253: Courtesy Scurlock Studio Records, Archives Center, National Museum of American History, Smithsonian Institution

Page 255: Martin Luther King Library, Washingtoniana Division, D.C. Public Library

Page 256: National Archives

Page 266: Martin Luther King Library, Washingtoniana Division, D.C. Public Library

Page 269 (top): James K. Hill Collection

Page 269 (bottom): Martin Kuther King Library, Washingtoniana Division, D.C. Public Library

Page 270 (top): © A/P Worldwide Photos; reprinted by permission of the Martin Luther King Library, D.C. Public Library

Page 270 (middle and bottom): National Archives

Page 274: Courtesy Scurlock Studio Records, Archives Center, National Museum of American History, Smithsonian Institution

Page 277: Martin Luther King Library, Washingtoniana Division, D.C. Public Library

Page 279: Moorland-Spingarn Research Center, Howard University

Page 285 (top): James K. Hill Collection

Pages 285 (bottom), 286, 287, 288: Martin Luther King Library, Washingtoniana Division, D.C. Public Library

Page 291: Courtesy Scurlock Studio Records, Archives Center, National Museum of American History, Smithsonian Institution

Page 292: Milton Williams

Page 293: Archives Center, Anacostia Museum and Center for African American History and Culture, Smithsonian Institution

Page 301: Milton Williams

Page 302: Library of Congress

Page 303: Martin Luther King Library, Washingtoniana Division, D.C. Public Library

Pages 306, 307: David Oggi Ogburn

Pages 308, 309: Courtesy Scurlock Studio Records, Archives Center, National Museum of American History, Smithsonian Institution

Page 311: David Oggi Ogburn

Pages 313, 315, 316: Milton Williams

Page 319: Habeebah Muhammad Collection

Pages 321, 323: Milton Williams

Page 326 (top): Archives Center, Anacostia Museum and Center for African American History and Culture, Smithsonian Institution

Page 326 (bottom): Milton Williams

Page 327: David Oggi Ogburn

Page 331: Hayden Blanc

Page 332: Rhoda Bear

Page 333: Milton Williams

Page 335: David Oggi Ogburn

Page 338: Archives Center, Anacostia Museum and Center for African American History and Culture, Smithsonian Institution

Page 339: Niels Bush

Page 340: David Oggi Ogburn

Page 341: Government of the District of Columbia

Page 342: David Oggi Ogburn

INDEX

*Numbers indicate the year under which the subject or name appears. Names in **bold** indicate people who are included in the Biographies section.*